Lecture Notes of the Institute for Computer Sciences, Social Informatics and Telecommunications Engineering 478

The LNICST series publishes ICST's conferences, symposia and workshops. It reports state-of-the-art results in areas related to the scope of the Institute.

LNICST reports state-of-the-art results in areas related to the scope of the Institute. The type of material published includes

- Proceedings (published in time for the respective event)
- Other edited monographs (such as project reports or invited volumes)

LNICST topics span the following areas:

- General Computer Science
- E-Economy
- E-Medicine
- Knowledge Management
- Multimedia
- Operations, Management and Policy
- Social Informatics
- Systems

Zhu Xiao · Ping Zhao · Xingxia Dai · Jinmei Shu
Editors

Edge Computing and IoT: Systems, Management and Security

Third EAI International Conference, ICECI 2022
Virtual Event, December 13–14, 2022
Proceedings

Editors
Zhu Xiao
Hunan University
Changsha, China

Xingxia Dai
Hunan University
Changsha, China

Ping Zhao
Donghua University
Shanghai, China

Jinmei Shu
Hunan University
Changsha, China

ISSN 1867-8211 ISSN 1867-822X (electronic)
Lecture Notes of the Institute for Computer Sciences, Social Informatics and Telecommunications Engineering
ISBN 978-3-031-28989-7 ISBN 978-3-031-28990-3 (eBook)
https://doi.org/10.1007/978-3-031-28990-3

This Springer imprint is published by the registered company Springer Nature Switzerland AG
The registered company address is: Gewerbestrasse 11, 6330 Cham, Switzerland

Preface

We are delighted to introduce the proceedings of EAI ICECI 2022 the 3rd International Conference on Edge Computing and IoT: Systems, Management and Security. This conference brought together researchers, developers and practitioners from around the world who are leveraging and developing systems, management and security on edge computing and IoT. The theme of EAI ICECI 2022 was "Edge Computing and IoT: Systems, Management and Security".

The technical program of EAI ICECI 2022 consisted of 21 full papers. The conference included four technical sessions. Aside from the high-quality technical paper presentations, the technical program also featured two keynote speeches. The two keynote speakers were Arun Iyengar, who is a co-founder and partner of Intelligent Data Management and Analytics, LLC, and Yan Zhang from the University of Oslo, Norway.

Coordination with the Steering Committee Chair Imrich Chlamtac and the Steering Committee Member Hongbo Jiang was essential for the success of the conference. We sincerely appreciate their constant support and guidance. It was also a great pleasure to work with such an excellent organizing committee team for their hard work in organizing and supporting the conference. In particular, the Technical Program Committee, led by Zhu Xiao and Libing Wu, who completed the peer-review process of technical papers and made a high-quality technical program. We are also grateful to the Conference Manager, Veronika Kissova for her support and all the authors who submitted their papers to the EAI ICECI 2022 conference.

We strongly believe that the EAI ICECI conference provides a good forum for all researchers, developers and practitioners to discuss all science and technology aspects that are relevant to smart grids. We also expect that the future EAI ICECI conferences will be as successful and stimulating, as indicated by the contributions presented in this volume.

March 2023

Zhu Xiao
Ping Zhao
Xingxia Dai
Jinmei Shu

Organization

Steering Committee

Imrich Chlamtac — University of Trento, Italy
Hongbo Jiang — Hunan University, China

Organizing Committee

General Chair

Zhu Xiao — Hunan University, China

TPC Chair and Co-Chairs

Libing Wu — Wuhan University, China
Chen Wang — Huazhong University of Science and Technology, China

Sponsorship and Exhibit Chair

Jingyang Hu — Hunan University, China

Local Chair

Daibo Liu — Hunan University, China

Workshops Chair

Xinxia Dai — Hunan University, China

Publicity & Social Media Chair

Jinmei Shu — Hunan University, China

Publications Chairs

Ping Zhao	Donghua University, China
Havyarimana Vincent	Burundi Higher Institute of Education, Burundi

Web Chair

Tong Li	Tsinghua University, China

Posters and PhD Track Chair

Chenxi Liu	Hunan University, China

Technical Program Committee

Hao Miao	University, Aalborg, Denmark
Lei Mu	King's College London, UK
Songsong Mo	Nanyang Technological University, Singapore
Hettige Kethmi Hirushini	Nanyang Technological University, Singapore
Saha Arkaprava	Nanyang Technological University, Singapore
Balsebre Pasquale	Nanyang Technological University, Singapore
Yuan Xie	National University of Singapore
Xingxia Dai	National Hunan University, China
Jingyang Hu	Hunan University, China
Xiangyu Shen	Hunan University, China
Mengyuan Wang	Hunan University, China
Xiang Xiao	Changsha University, China
Jie Li	Central South University of Forestry and Technology (CSUFT), China

Contents

Models and Methods for Data Management in IoT

Forecasting the Temperature of BEV Battery Pack Based on Field Testing Data

Ka Seng Chou[1,2](✉), Kei Long Wong[1], Davide Aguiari[2,3], Rita Tse[1], Su-Kit Tang[1], and Giovanni Pau[2,3,4]

[1] Faculty of Applied Sciences, Macao Polytechnic University, Macao SAR, China
{kaseng.chou,keilong.wong,ritatse,sktang}@mpu.edu.mo

[2] Department of Computer Science and Engineering, Alma Mater Studiorum, University of Bologna, Bologna, Italy
{davide.aguiari2,giovanni.pau}@unibo.it

[3] Autonomous Robotics Research Center, Technology Innovation Institute, Abu Dhabi, UAE

[4] UCLA Samueli Computer Science, University of California, Los Angeles, Los Angeles, USA

Abstract. Monitoring electric vehicles' battery situation and indicating the state of health is still challenging. Temperature is one of the critical factors determining battery degradation over time. We have collected more than 2.3 million discharging samples via a custom Internet of Thing device for more than one year to build a machine-learning model that can forecast the battery pack's average temperature in real-world driving. Our best Bi-LSTM model achieved the mean absolute error of 2.92 °C on test data and 1.7 °C on cross-validation for prediction of 10 min on the battery pack's temperature.

Keywords: Electric Vehicle · Battery Temperature Forecasts · Electric Vehicle Data · Lithium-ion Battery · Driving Behaviour · Machine Learning

1 Introduction

Battery electric vehicles (BEVs) battery pack temperature monitoring and control is vital for the longevity of the Li-ion batteries (LiBs) life. The essential measurement of the battery pack's internal temperature (IT) is to prevent thermal runaway and the batteries burst into flames for the BEV [12] in autonomous driving area [4]. To increase safety and prolong the LiBs' life, the Battery Management System (BMS) keeps measuring the pack temperature constantly [11]. Based on the geometrical layout of the LiBs' pack, multiple thermistors are deployed at different spots inside the LiBs' container to acquire the precise temperature. However, the performance of this temperature sensing method inevitably depends on the thermal conduction of the individual LiB cell and the pack-based cooling medium (i.e., air, liquid, and phase change materials) [19,24,26].

Z. Xiao et al. (Eds.): ICECI 2022, LNICST 478, pp. 3–17, 2023.
https://doi.org/10.1007/978-3-031-28990-3_1

Meanwhile, the LiB's cells wiring structure (i.e., cells parallel and series connection) also affects the temperature of the modules, which causes some cells to have a higher temperature than the others [5,28]. Likewise, measuring the current temperature of the battery pack is not enough because the thermal delay effect exists from LiB's core to the surface, cell to cell, and finally to the temperature sensors [27]. Therefore, forecasting the temperature during the battery becomes the problem solver for the major degradation of LiBs.

For temperature predictions, existing statistical models are already capable of making a single prediction. For example, the statistical Hidden Markov Model (HMM), the Support Vector Regression (SVR) model, the linear model, and the decision tree for temperature prediction [18,25]. However, these models are not able to predict or represent temperature over time when human factors are involved.

In recent years, machine learning has been used to predict the batteries-related temperature for the BEVs at different portions inside the battery pack. In research from Jaliliantabar et al. [15], an artificial neural network (ANN) is equipped with the phase change materials (PCM) based battery thermal management system (BTMS) to predict the LiBs temperature in different operating conditions by the input of charging rate, PCM type, PCM thickness, and time. Fang et al. [10] used the ANN model to predict the nickel-metal hydride battery surface temperature with the input of ambient temperature, charging rate, and charging time. To predict the discharging temperature, Jiang et al. [16] used the long short-term memory-recurrent neural network (LSTM-RNN) and gated recurrent unit-recurrent neural network (GRU-RNN) to effectively estimate the surface temperature within a maximum absolute error of 0.75 °C.

There are many other studies to forecast the battery system's temperate in different ways for the BMS, including physical, electrochemical, or thermodynamics model [3,9,22]. However, the real-world daily use of the BEV is non-linear and dynamic. This involves much more complicated factors such as the differential from manufacturing, drivers driving behavior, and the temperature climate [6,7,14,21]. For this reason, we collected around 168 h of driving data from an EV in Bologna (Italy) via an IoT device attached to its control units.

This study aims to develop an ANN that effectively keeps drivers aware of the battery temperature conditions in the edge. This network best represents the connection between the LiB pack's temperature and all the feasible corrected input from the IoT device. In specific, the contributions of this study are as follows:

1. a systematic analysis and resampling of the updated real-world collected *Nissan Leaf 2018 EV* driving dataset introduced in [1];
2. development of the neural network for evaluating the Nissan Leaf battery discharge heat dissipation against the optimal temperature range for the edge computing;

The paper is organized as follows: Sect. 2 is an overview of the data collection, in which the IoT device and *Nissan Leaf* battery pack's structure are described. Section 3 focuses on the data preprocessing and feature selection of the collected results from real-world driving. Section 4 describes the method to search for the best neural network and the training environment. The Sect. 5 discusses the results and implications from Optuna tuning and the importance of some weights. Finally, some future improvements are provided in the final section.

2 Approach

2.1 The IoT Device

To gather the ECUs data from the *Nissan Leaf* 2018 model, we used the low-cost IoT device described in [1]. In short, it is an On-Board Diagnostic version II (OBD2) LTE-connected reader that queries the Leaf's Vehicle Control Module at 250 ms intervals continuously. Several parameters are collected and clustered according to their category (i.e. HV battery data, such as its current and voltage at pack level up to its 96 cells voltage; HVAC data, such as cabin and ambient temperature, A/C and its energy consumption; driver's behavior, such as pressure on both acceleration pedal and brake pedal, the car's speed, etc.). The optimal temperature window for a single LiB cell is from 15 °C to 35 °C [14]. According to the SOC, this window has a slight variety corresponding to the cell voltage from 2.5 V (empty) to 4.2 V (fully charged) [13,20]. Figure 1 shows the *Nissan Leaf*'s battery pack which is analyzed to obtain the temperature voltage window. There are twenty-four sub-modules in Leaf's battery pack. Each sub-module consists of eight cells arranged in two units with two sets of two parallel cells. The total voltage is 350 V when all the sub-modules are serialized which is equal to two cells in parallel and 96 sets in series. With this battery pack

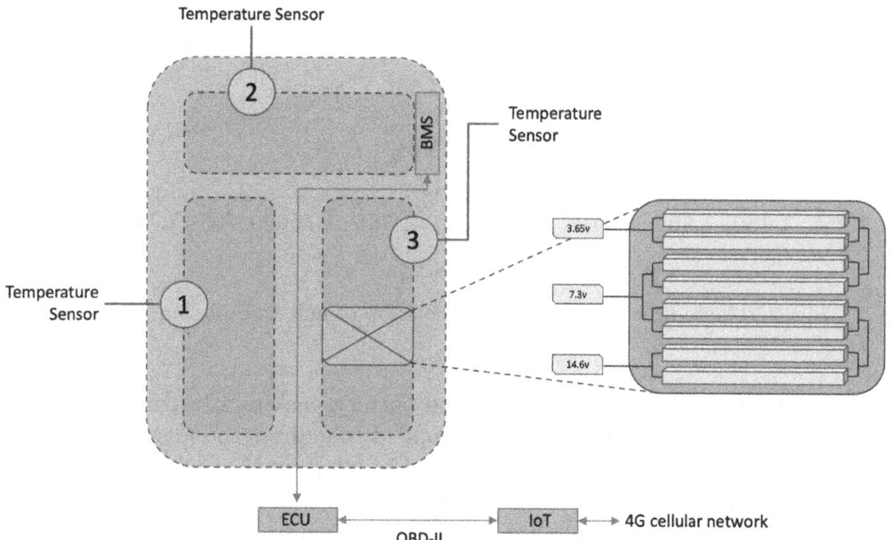

Fig. 1. The structure of the cells in *Nissan Leaf* [17]

structure, the voltage center is shifted to 350 V which is 96 times larger than a single cell. Therefore, the Leaf's temperature voltage window is ranging from 250 V to 450 V.

3 Data Preparation

3.1 Data Cleansing

The full dataset is preprocessed with the following steps for the dataset:

1. selected the test vehicle raw discharge data from 2020-01-09 to 2022-08-03. The total number of rows was 2.4 million (i.e., 168 h);
2. calculation with indirect variables (i.e. instant power, charging power, remaining power, acceleration, and horsepower) for all records;
3. identified and labeled if any, different groups of trips that may exist on a single day with different stopping intervals or different drivers;
4. clustered and labeled different trips: we targeted the power on button, the charging plug state, and the charging mode on the vehicle. We consider a trip which is a set of records that lasts more than 30 min;

All the non-behavior-related features are removed since not all the collected features from the BEV are related to the High-Voltage (HV) battery output. The features (e.g., headlights, fan speed, wipers, etc.) that are powered by the 12 V battery are ignored.

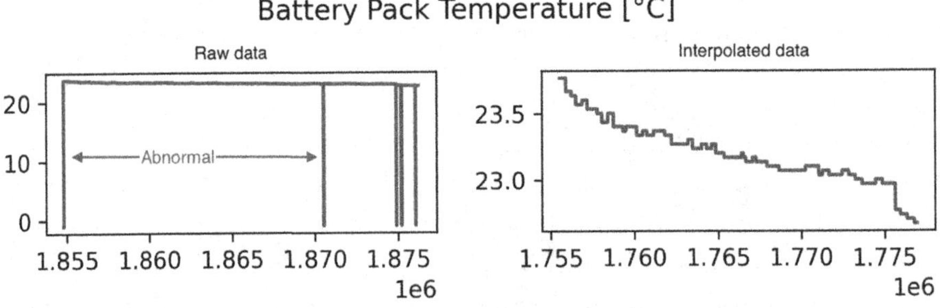

Fig. 2. The bidirectional linear interpolation of null and missing values

Figure 2 shows the interpolation of the battery pack temperature in a trip. The bidirectional linear interpolation is applied to address the missing and null values. Trip-based z-score filtering is adopted to filter out the out-liners. For any values in a feature, the z-score larger than 3 (covered 99% of the data) is set to null and interpolated. Any other abnormal values are interpolated if we identified any. The general summary of the high-quality discharge dataset (~130 h) for the machine learning task is shown in Table 1.

Table 1. The summary of filtered discharging dataset

	Odometer	SOC	SOH	Voltage	Current*	Ambient °C
count	1918299	1918299	1918299	1918299	1918299	1918299
mean	9217.46	74.72	94.41	373.31	-22.47	18.65
std	3213.64	19.16	1.38	19.68	38.49	8.29
min	255	0.32	92.63	0	-370.67	3.5
25%	6673	61.2	93.06	356.13	-39.22	12
50%	9431	78.99	93.91	374.95	-5.59	17
75%	11890	91.39	95.88	391.41	-0.98	24
max	15537	99.11	96.46	655.35	179.66	44.5
Interpolated [%]	3.52	1.31	0.79	0.05	0.05	0
(continued)	Pack 1 °C	Pack 2 °C	Pack 4 °C	All Packs Avg. °C		
count	1918299	1918299	1918299	1918299		
mean	24.95	24.87	23.34	24.39		
std	9.14	8.82	8.11	8.66		
min	5.8	5.6	5.76	5.83		
25%	17.3	17.45	16.4	17.1		
50%	25.2	25.1	23.3	24.7		
75%	32	31.44	29.44	30.97		
max	55	54	48.4	52.47		
Interpolated [%]	0.02	0.02	0.02	0.02		

*The current load is negative when discharging (driving) and positive when regenerative braking.

3.2 Feature Engineering

Data Resampling certain driving-related factors are accumulated due to the long sampling rate on the battery pack's temperature. The fastest temperature sampling rate is about 60 to 90 s after the test on the *Nissan Leaf*. If the 250 ms data is input directly to the machine learning (ML) algorithms, it will cause a non-effective prediction of the results. This means the loss of the ML models would be low, which is repeating the same output values but not effectively predicting the minor changes in the temperature. Figure 3 shows a one-minute resample of the data. Noticing that the simple resample would lose the fine-time granularity meaning of the dataset, we accumulated the driving relational features to compensate for the loss.

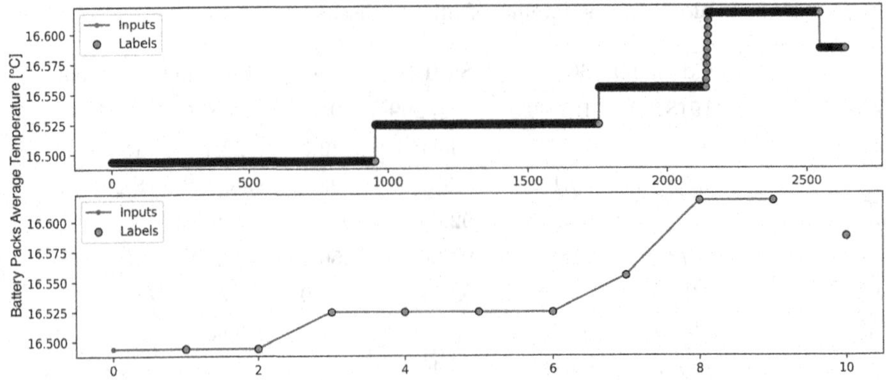

Fig. 3. The temperature sample in 10 min

On every trip, the value of these variables (i.e., accelerator pedal, braking pedal, speed, etc.) grows at the BEV start-up as the extra features. From a training input point of view, a constant accumulation operation is closer to a battery's operating principle, a consequence of a chain reaction from driving manners. Also, Xu et al. [29] revealed that the discrete incremental capacity can improve the estimation accuracy of SOH. Therefore, these features are processed to accumulate at the beginning of every trip.

Cyclical Encoding the timestamp data is encoded into a cyclical representation of a particular day, season, and year with sine (1) and cosine (2) [23]. A total of six new cyclical features (i.e., day sine and cosine, season sine and cosine, year sine and cosine) have been added to emphasize the temperature climate for the ANN.

$$\text{Periodic sine} = \sin\left(timestamp \times \frac{2\pi}{period}\right) \tag{1}$$

$$\text{Periodic cosine} = \cos\left(timestamp \times \frac{2\pi}{period}\right) \tag{2}$$

where:

$$\text{period} = \begin{cases} \text{day} & 24 \times 60 \times 60 \\ \text{season} & 91.31 \times day \\ \text{year} & 365.24 \times day \end{cases}$$

3.3 Data Windowing

The input and output window size is set to 10 (i.e. 10 min). Summarised from the dataset, the average cool-down time for the entire battery pack is approximately 10 to 15 min at 1 °C when driving. The output window size of 10 gives the driver sufficient time to ameliorate the driving behaviors or conditions for the drivers, which is intended to keep the battery pack's temperature in better condition.

To enable the many-to-many predictions of the model, trip data is sliced into the size window for both the input and output for the model training. This consecutive windowing allows the model to predict the next x minutes, based on the current x minutes. The following Fig. 4 demonstrated the construction of ten-time steps of the input and output labels from the dataset. A shuffleable batch of input is generated by sliding the window for the next one-time step. The different NNs (e.g., linear network, LSTM) are processed propinquity to satisfy the network input shape requirements. Finally, the data is split into 70% for training, 20% for validation, and 10% for testing.

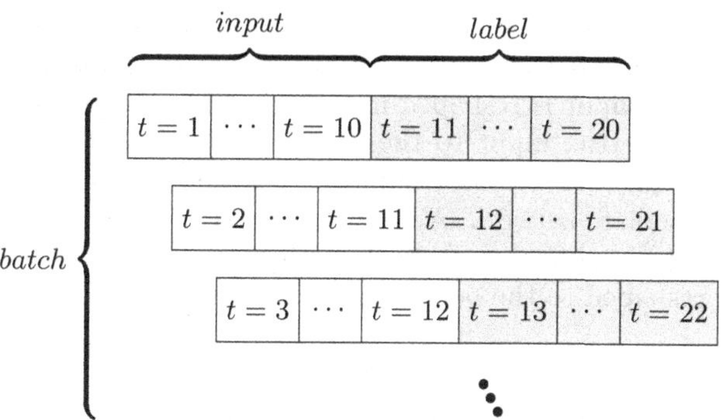

Fig. 4. The consecutive many-to-many window training input for ANN.

4 Models

This section detailed the search method of our best LSTM model for predicting the battery pack's temperature.

4.1 Model Defines

The LSTM model is built in favor of simplicity because of lesser features and reprocessed. Also, the battery temperature prediction tends to perform better in the simple model with less past status by the temperature characteristic [10,15]. In the model evaluation, the Mean Absolute Error (MAE) (4) is adopted. To prevent overfitting of simple machine learning models, L2 regularization (5) is added into the MSE loss function to penalize models.

$$\text{MSE} = \frac{1}{n}\sum_{i=1}^{n}(y_{i,t} - y_{i,p})^2 \tag{3}$$

$$\text{MAE} = \frac{1}{n}\sum_{i=1}^{n}|y_{i,t} - y_{i,p}| \tag{4}$$

$$\text{L2} = \lambda \sum_{i=1}^{n} {w_i}^2 \tag{5}$$

where the $y_{i,t}$, $y_{i,p}$, and n are target value, predicted value, and number of samples in the dataset.

4.2 Hyperparameter Searching

To construct the network and hyperparameter tuning, Optuna is adopted. It is a neural network optimization framework that automates the searching and pruning strategy for different networks [2]. Compared to the grid search and random search, Optuna can reduce the computational resources significantly and better locate the minima. Figure 5 shows the overall structure of the Optuna. Firstly, the three dimension input is reshaped into the batch and the vector of window size times features as the input to the Optuna. The Optuna framework then searches automatically for the best number of layers, neurons, and regularization for the intermediate network. A fully connected (FC) layer is attached after Optuna to convert the different network settings to a constant shape. Finally, the FC layer is reshaped to the output window shape.

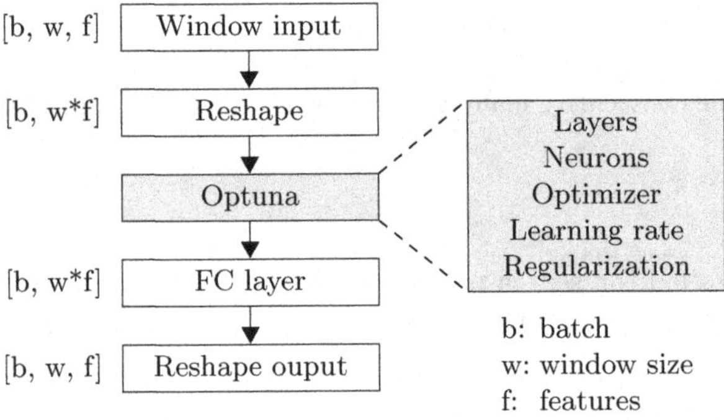

Fig. 5. Optuna framework structure for automatic search and network construction.

Table 2. The Optuna automatic search settings

Optuna	Settings
Max. searches	1,000
Max. layers	10
Neurons	4 to 512
Optimizer	Adam, SGD, RMSProp
Learning rate	1e-5 to 1e-1
Regularization	1e-10 to 1e-3

Table 2 shows the detailed searching parameters setting inside the Optuna layers. The activation and initialization are fixed to Relu and He uniform variance to reduce the searching time. The search of hyperparameter combinations is set to 1,000 for the model. The following Table 3 shows the settings of our best model.

Table 3. The Best Model - Bidirectional LSTM

	Settings
Layers	3
Structure	Bi-LSTM(341) x Bi-LSTM(32) x FC(420)
Optimizer	Adam
Learning rate	6.48E-05
Regularization	1.33E-10
Early stopping	with validation loss
Total parameters	1,257,892

5 Results and Discussion

In this section, the results and implications of our best model are presented. The different datasets and models are compared to identify the most important factors for temperature prediction. The ablation study on the features was also included to verify the importance of feature engineering. The limitations and considerations of our work are also discussed. Finally, the consequences of the capacity loss caused by temperature are explained.

5.1 Justification of the Best Model

The MAE on the prediction of the average temperature of the battery pack is the performance indicator for all models. Table 4 shows the different model comparisons using the test data (10%) and a 10-fold cross-validation. Two output variables are tested that are associated with the constant input of 10 window

Table 4. The MAE benchmarking [°C]

Models	10 Predictions	10-Fold-10	1 Prediction	10-Fold-1
CNN	7.69	7.36	-	-
MLP	7.69	7.35	7.9	7.33
Linear	13.2	12.16	14.74	13.29
LSTM	3.16	2.12	4.14	3.21
Bi-LSTM	2.92	1.7	2.83	2.06

steps: (i) the output of 10 temperature predictions (10 min) which is our main goal; (ii) the output of a single temperature prediction in the last minutes of the 10 min as a reference.

The Bi-LSTM model showed the smallest error of 2.92 °C in the test data and a mean error of 1.7 °C in the cross-validation of the 10 predictions output. When these two errors are averaged, an error of 2.31 °C is the best performance we found for this model. The multi-window linear model showed the worst performance among the models. There is almost no difference in the prediction errors between the CNN and MLP models. For reference, the model with one output shows similar performance. The CNN model is not available for single output due to the restriction to a minimum dimension.

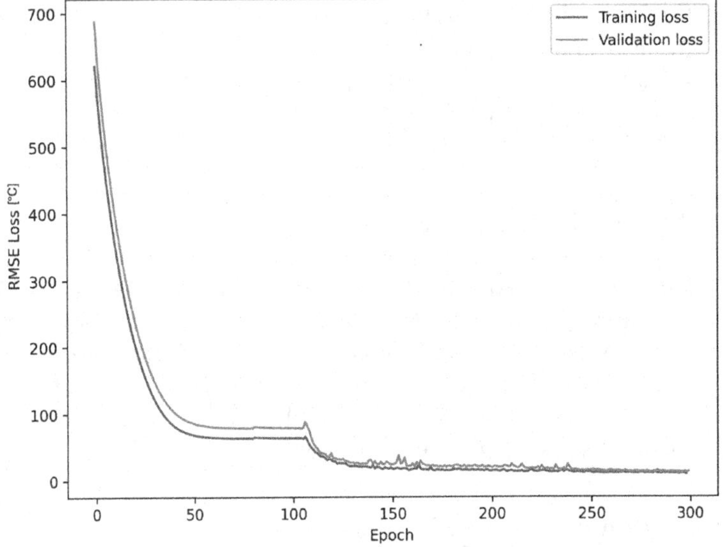

Fig. 6. Training loss on the best model

The training and validation loss is shown in Fig. 6. The training of the model converges smoothly in the first 300 epochs with a time cost of about 2400 s. The validation loss of the model gradually decreases and overlaps with the training loss at epoch 250.

5.2 Ablation Study

The ablation study focuses on the features, as Optuna had sought the optimal structure for the model, which is a standard model without adjustments. Table 5 shows the result of removing accumulated variables, time signals, both accumulated variables and time signals, and trip labels.

Table 5. The MAE on features ablation

Remove	MAE [°C]	10-Fold-10 [°C]
ACC. features	7.69	7.36
Time	3.87	3.87
ACC. and Time	7.69	7.36
Trip label	3.5	3.29

We have found that the accumulated characteristics are of significant importance. When removed, the MAE increases to 7.69 °C. This shows that the Bi-LSTM model is partially based on the linear signal. When the time signal is removed, the MAE of the model increases by about 1 °C. Based on the model results, temporal variations (e.g., seasonal factors or road conditions) also affect the temperature of the battery pack. Finally, the temperature increases by about 0.6 °C when a trip number is removed. In addition, we recorded an MAE increase to 4.41 °C and a 10-fold validation of 2.17 °C when adding the driver ID as a feature.

5.3 Dataset Comparison

To our knowledge, this is the only dataset collected without simulation or modeling on a real *Nissan Leaf's* ECU. Instead of comparing the model to the existing dataset, we compare it to the new dataset assembled from our data. It is because the above feature ablation study shows the importance of features. Also, it may not be comprehensive enough to compare performance with the different battery types, cells, and laboratory-tested datasets [8]. This resampled dataset follows China's mandatory electric vehicle data collection protocol GB/T 32960.3 and our feature engineering steps. The difference between the GB/T 32960 dataset and ours is the sampling rate of 30 s.

Table 6 shows a very small loss of precision in both MAE and 10-fold validation when predicting 10 outputs. Compared to our 250 ms fine-time granularity, the Bi-LSTM model still performs effectively at the 30 s interval for temperature prediction on the battery pack.

Table 6. The MAE difference on the Chinese standard

Dataset	MAE [°C]	10-Fold-10 [°C]
30 s resampled	3.57	1.76
Ours	2.92	1.7
Difference	0.65	0.06

5.4 Statistical Learning Comparison

To understand the performance of our data, statistical learning models are compared. Four one-to-one models, including Support Vector Regression (SVR) with Gaussian kernel, linear, Ada Boost Regressor and Decision Tree Regressor, are implemented to test the prediction errors. The ratio of training and testing is set to 0.67 and 0.33, respectively. Table 7 shows that the linear model achieves the minimum MAE error of 0.41 °C. However, this result cannot be directly compared with our model because it cannot detect the input in the next x minutes.

Table 7. The MAE of the statistical learning approach

Models	MAE [°C]
SVR-Gaussian	6.0258
Linear	0.4058
Ada Boost Regressor	0.612
Decision Tree Regressor	0.8109

5.5 Limitations and Reflection

In this model, we focus on temperature prediction in the edge for the battery packs. Considering the lower computational power in the edge, we did not further address the modeling of driving behavior or user behavior. Infact, other feature extensions can be tried, including higher-order features, factorization machines, or retrieval pools. The performance can potentially be higher than the current model if we apply these behavior modeling techniques instead of simple feature accumulation.

5.6 Capacity Fading

Generally, the optimal temperature range for LiBs is from 15 °C to 35 °C [14]. Jia et al. show the 19.2% capacity fading in Worldwide harmonized Light vehicles Test Cycles at 45 °C after 2,184 cycles [13]. The electrochemistry degradation mechanisms are as followings:

High Temperature when temperature increases at a high voltage and SOC, the electrolyte decomposes and forms gas. Cracks would appear in the cathode, forming an unstable structure that blocks the Li-ion stream and causes capacity fading. Dendrites grow on the anode, which can pierce the separator.

Low Temperature slowing the Li-ion diffusion which causes lithium plating and metalization on the anode and consumes the Li-ion.

By evaluating the performance of these models, it can be concluded that the performance of the EV battery pack's temperature forecasting depends mainly on the model's type. Instead of a complex model and heavy load of training, a simple Bi-LSTM model is the most appropriate depending on our data and possibly the China's GB/T 32960.3 standard EV data. This simple model may also be applied to the EV's ECUs to assist the LiBs' thermal management and the driver.

6 Concluding Remark

In this work, a EV-LiB temperature prediction model was built in a data-driven way including data acquisition, preprocessing, and modeling. From the OBD2 IoT sensor, we processed more than 2.3 million (i.e., 160 h) update to date discharge samples from the *Nissan Leaf* with a sampling rate of 250 ms. The data is filtered and converted into a time series window, with the time signal catering to the machine learning models for many-to-many prediction. For the data with fine temporal granularity, a simple Bi-LSTM model showed the best performance compared to the previous work on the dense model. The model also exhibited similar performance on our reproduced dataset by following the Chinese protocol GB/T 32960.3. Illustrating from the models, the temperature of LiBs is affected by successive driving behaviors, temporal signals, trips, and drivers. In addition, due to the simplicity of this model, it is also possible to act on the EV's control unit to best control the optimal temperature of the battery to extend the battery life.

Acknowledgements. This work was supported in part by the Macao Polytechnic University - Edge Sensing and Computing: Enabling Human-centric (Sustainable) Smart Cities (RP/ESCA-01/2020) and by the H2020 project titled "European Bus Rapid Transit of 2030: Electrified, Automated, Connected" EBRT - Grant Agreement N. 101095882.

References

1. Aguiari, D., Chou, K.S., Tse, R., Pau, G.: Monitoring electric vehicles on the go. In: 2022 IEEE 19th Annual Consumer Communications & Networking Conference (CCNC), pp. 885–888. IEEE (2022)
2. Akiba, T., Sano, S., Yanase, T., Ohta, T., Koyama, M.: Optuna: a next-generation hyperparameter optimization framework. In: Proceedings of the 25rd ACM SIGKDD International Conference on Knowledge Discovery and Data Mining (2019)
3. Buller, S., Thele, M., Karden, E., De Doncker, R.W.: Impedance-based non-linear dynamic battery modeling for automotive applications. J. Power Sources **113**(2), 422–430 (2003)
4. Chen, Y., Tse, R., Bosello, M., Aguiari, D., Tang, S.K., Pau, G.: Enabling deep reinforcement learning autonomous driving by 3D-lidar point clouds. In: ICDIP 2022 (in press)
5. Chiu, K.C., Lin, C.H., Yeh, S.F., Lin, Y.H., Huang, C.S., Chen, K.C.: Cycle life analysis of series connected Lithium-ion batteries with temperature difference. J. Power Sources **263**, 75–84 (2014)

6. Chou, K.S., Aguiari, D., Tse, R., Tang, S.K., Pau, G.: Impact evaluation of driving style on electric vehicle battery based on field testing result. In: CCNC 2023 (in press)
7. Donkers, A., Yang, D., Viktorović, M.: Influence of driving style, infrastructure, weather and traffic on electric vehicle performance. Transp. Res. Part D: Transp. Environ. **88**, 102569 (2020)
8. dos Reis, G., Strange, C., Yadav, M., Li, S.: Lithium-ion battery data and where to find it. Energy AI **5**, 100081 (2021)
9. Doughty, D.H., Butler, P.C., Jungst, R.G., Roth, E.P.: Lithium battery thermal models. J. Power Sources **110**(2), 357–363 (2002)
10. Fang, K., Mu, D., Chen, S., Wu, B., Wu, F.: A prediction model based on artificial neural network for surface temperature simulation of nickel-metal hydride battery during charging. J. Power Sources **208**, 378–382 (2012). https://doi.org/10.1016/j.jpowsour.2012.02.059
11. Garche, J., Jossen, A.: Battery management systems (BMS) for increasing battery life time. In: Third International Telecommunications Energy Special Conference (IEEE Cat. No.00EX424), TELESCON 2000, pp. 81–88 (2000). https://doi.org/10.1109/TELESC.2000.918409
12. Golubkov, A.W., et al.: Thermal-runaway experiments on consumer Li-ion batteries with metal-oxide and olivin-type cathodes. RSC Adv. **4**(7), 3633–3642 (2014)
13. Guo, J., Li, Y., Pedersen, K., Stroe, D.I.: Lithium-ion battery operation, degradation, and aging mechanism in electric vehicles: an overview. Energies **14**(17), 5220 (2021)
14. Han, X., et al.: A review on the key issues of the lithium ion battery degradation among the whole life cycle. ETransportation **1**, 100005 (2019)
15. Jaliliantabar, F., Mamat, R., Kumarasamy, S.: Prediction of Lithium-ion battery temperature in different operating conditions equipped with passive battery thermal management system by artificial neural networks. Mater. Today Proc. **48**, 1796–1804 (2022)
16. Jiang, Y.H., Yu, Y.F., Huang, J.Q., Cai, W.W., Marco, J.: Li-ion battery temperature estimation based on recurrent neural networks. Sci. China Technol. Sci. **64**(6), 1335–1344 (2021). https://doi.org/10.1007/s11431-020-1736-5
17. Kane, M.: See a 2011 Nissan leaf battery dissected professionally: Video (2020). https://insideevs.com/news/390574/2011-nissan-leaf-battery-dissected-professionally/
18. Li, S.T., Cheng, Y.C.: A stochastic hmm-based forecasting model for fuzzy time series. IEEE Trans. Syst. Man Cybern. Part B (Cybern.) **40**(5), 1255–1266 (2009)
19. Liu, C., et al.: Phase change materials application in battery thermal management system: a review. Materials **13**(20), 4622 (2020)
20. Mc Carthy, K., Gullapalli, H., Ryan, K.M., Kennedy, T.: Electrochemical impedance correlation analysis for the estimation of Li-ion battery state of charge, state of health and internal temperature. J. Energy Storage **50**, 104608 (2022). https://doi.org/10.1016/j.est.2022.104608. https://www.sciencedirect.com/science/article/pii/S2352152X22006247
21. Neubauer, J., Wood, E.: Thru-life impacts of driver aggression, climate, cabin thermal management, and battery thermal management on battery electric vehicle utility. J. Power Sources **259**, 262–275 (2014)
22. Pesaran, A.A.: Battery thermal models for hybrid vehicle simulations. J. Power Sources **110**(2), 377–382 (2002)
23. Petneházi, G.: Recurrent neural networks for time series forecasting. arXiv preprint arXiv:1901.00069 (2019)

24. Raijmakers, L., Danilov, D., Eichel, R.A., Notten, P.: A review on various temperature-indication methods for Li-ion batteries. Appl. Energy **240**, 918–945 (2019)
25. Salcedo-Sanz, S., Deo, R., Carro-Calvo, L., Saavedra-Moreno, B.: Monthly prediction of air temperature in Australia and New Zealand with machine learning algorithms. Theor. Appl. Climatol. **125**(1), 13–25 (2016)
26. Smith, J., Singh, R., Hinterberger, M., Mochizuki, M.: Battery thermal management system for electric vehicle using heat pipes. Int. J. Therm. Sci. **134**, 517–529 (2018)
27. Talele, V., Thorat, P., Gokhale, Y.P., VK, M.: Phase change material based passive battery thermal management system to predict delay effect. J. Energy Storage **44**, 103482 (2021). https://doi.org/10.1016/j.est.2021.103482. https://www.sciencedirect.com/science/article/pii/S2352152X21011658
28. Wang, B., et al.: Study of non-uniform temperature and discharging distribution for Lithium-ion battery modules in series and parallel connection. Appl. Therm. Eng. **168**, 114831 (2020)
29. Xu, Z., Wang, J., Lund, P.D., Zhang, Y.: Estimation and prediction of state of health of electric vehicle batteries using discrete incremental capacity analysis based on real driving data. Energy **225**, 120160 (2021)

The Data Exchange Protocol over Multi-chain Blockchain Using Zero-Knowledge Proof

AoXuan Li[1(✉)], Gabriele D'Angelo[2], and Su-Kit Tang[1]

[1] Faculty of Applied Sciences, Macao Polytechnic University, Macao SAR, China
{aoxuan.li,sktang}@mpu.edu.mo

[2] Department of Computer Science and Engineering, University of Bologna, Bologna, Italy
g.dangelo@unibo.it

Abstract. The implementation of blockchain technology is becoming popular among cyber-physical systems. However, the current solutions suffer from scalability and privacy issues. In this position paper, we leverage zero-knowledge proof and multichain technology to propose an efficient system for data transferring across different components. Each component may maintain a private chain storing its data, and the system acts as a relayer between different chains, in which multiple private chains are efficient for appending new data. Only encrypted data is transferred from a source chain to a destination chain. The relayer handles data transferring in two phases: send and receive, and the relayer keeps a Merkle tree of all sent data. In fact, it only transfers the data if the receiver can submit a valid zero-knowledge proof that proves the ownership of the data. The zero-knowledge proof discloses nothing but the statement is true; therefore it protects anonymity for the data owners. This system is secure and satisfies relevant properties such as ledger indistinguishability, transaction non-malleability, and matchability.

Keywords: Zero-knowledge proof · Multichain · Blockchain · Cyber-physical system

1 Introduction

A cyber-physical system combines physical and computational components, and each part is tightly connected [12]. Blockchain is a distributed ledger that may hold any data, which is decentralized and transparent. All records on the blockchain are immutable, and no single party may manipulate the data. Blockchain is widely employed in cyber-physical systems [25], e.g., healthcare

This work is supported in part by the research grant (No.: RP/ESCA-04/2020) offered by Macao Polytechnic University.

Z. Xiao et al. (Eds.): ICECI 2022, LNICST 478, pp. 18–29, 2023.
https://doi.org/10.1007/978-3-031-28990-3_2

[8,10,17], IoT [14,16,22], and smart grid [23]. However, those solutions may suffer from scalability issues on the large scale of data, or they cannot guarantee privacy and anonymity for sensitive data.

Popular blockchain projects, e.g., Bitcoin [20] and Ethereum [29], are limited in throughput due to the computational cost for generating and appending new blocks to the blockchain, in fact, the nodes have to verify all previous blocks are valid. As the blockchain size grows, the cost for adding a new block becomes too expensive. Also, all data on the blockchain is transparent, and all parties may access any data on-chain. Moreover, for sensitive data, e.g., health data and financial data, the blockchain is unable to provide the needed privacy and anonymity.

A multichain approach allows each party to keep a private blockchain, and each blockchain may exchange data via a cross-chain transactions. In a cross-chain or single-chain transaction, the source blockchain network will transfer data to the destination blockchain network. Since each private blockchain is small compared with a single chain containing all data, the multichain approach could accelerate block generations. However, in such a protocol, the sender and receiver addresses are openly available on-chain, and one may track the transaction graph. Many research works show that this setting cannot provide privacy [7,24]. To address this issue, we employ a similar solution as in Zcash [2,15], that is a fork of Bitcoin [20]: the transaction is encrypted with the public key of the receiver, and then this receiver needs to prove the knowledge of the private key. If a sender *Alice* on blockchain A transfers some data to a receiver *Bob* on blockchain B, we want both *Alice* and *Bob* to be anonymous and no other party may know any information about the data.

For example, suppose blockchain A is a private chain of a hospital, and blockchain B belongs to a research institute. *Alice* is a patient in the hospital, and *Bob* is a researcher at the institute. *Bob* wants to retrieve someone's medical records for academic purposes, and *Alice* wants to contribute her data. After the transfer of *Alice*'s data from blockchain A to blockchain B, no one can figure out what the data contains and who the original owner of the data is. To address the first requirement, *Alice* may encrypt her data with *Bob*'s public key. The second requirement commonly refers to transaction unlinkability [4]. When *Alice* sends the data to *Bob*, *Bob* is the new owner of the data. To prove his ownership, *Bob* has to prove that he can correctly decrypt the message. A simple solution is to disclose *Bob*'s private key, and then one may verify the private key by decrypting data sent by *Alice*; however, this solution will also disclose *Alice*'s identity and the data content. To address the issue, we leveraged zero-knowledge proof and Merkle tree to verify the ownership of data. We explained zero-knowledge proof and the Merkle tree in detail in Sects. 2.1 and 3.5.

All data sent from chain A to chain B groups a Merkle tree, and the data sent from *Alice* to *Bob* is one of the leaves. To prove *Bob*'s ownership, he proves the following statements using zero-knowledge proof:

1. he knows a path from the data to the Merkle tree root, and
2. he knows the correct private key.

A zero-knowledge proof reveals nothing but the statements are correct. Since records on a blockchain are public to all nodes, if *Bob* writes the received data to chain B without modification, a malicious user who has access to both chain A and chain B may discover *Alice*'s identity by matching data content. For example, the malicious user may lookup chain A for a sending request where the data content is the same as a record on chain B. Therefore, *Bob* encrypts the data content with a different public key and writes the new ciphertext down on B. The encryption algorithm can guarantee that a malicious user cannot figure out two ciphertexts containing the same plain text if it has been encrypted with different public keys.

We can generalize the two-chain solution to the multichain system. As we mentioned before, a cyber-physical system may combine many components, and each component manages a private chain. To reduce communication complexity across the system, we introduced a middleware of multiple chains, called a relayer, to handle data exchange. Our proposed protocol is a general-purpose protocol so that it can fit in any multichain system supporting smart contracts. For example, financial institutes may employ our protocol to exchange data without a trusted third party. In this case, the institutes increase the data liquidity while protecting user privacy. The protocol also allows different sensors in an IoT system to transfer data efficiently and securely.

Our Contribution. We proposed a data exchange protocol over multi-chain blockchain using zero-knowledge proof. In the protocol, each component maintains a private blockchain, and different components can exchange data through cross-chain transactions. We also designed a relayer to carry data from a source chain to a destination chain, which keeps a Merkle tree of all sent data. This relayer is also responsible for verifying zero-knowledge proofs. This system provides both scalability and privacy for data transfer between different components in a cyber-physical system. It is noteworthy that the sender and the receiver may be on the same chain, i.e., the user sends a single-chain transaction, and there is a single chain that is both the origin and the destination of the transaction. Alternatively, the user can send a cross-chain transaction, and the source chain and the destination chain are on different chains. We illustrate the process in Fig. 1.

2 Background and Related Work

In this section, we describe the background technologies and methodologies that are necessary for understanding this paper.

2.1 Merkle Tree

Merkle tree [19], also called hash tree, is a tree in which every non-leaf node is labeled as the hash value of its child nodes' labels. The top of the tree is the root hash, and each leaf node has an authentication path to the root. It allows efficient verification of membership in a large data set. Figure 2 is an example of a Merkle tree, which contains a root hash rt and labels l_1, l_2, l_3, l_4. Verifying the membership of label l_1 only needs H_2 and H_{34}.

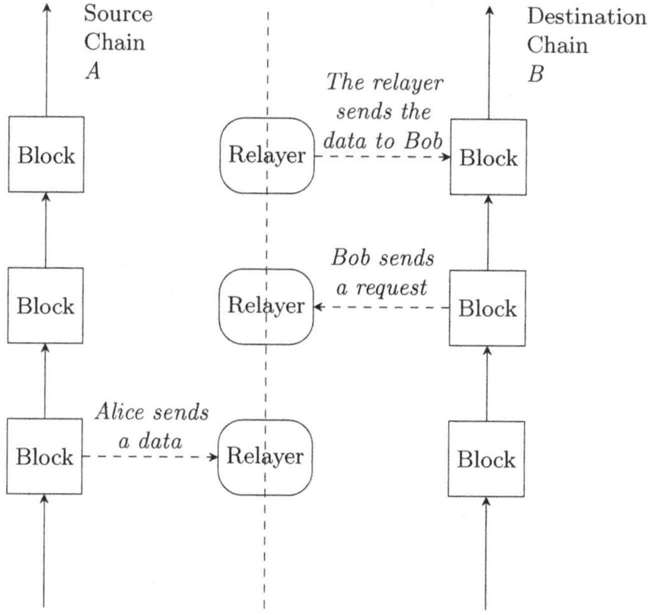

Fig. 1. Protocol Overview.

2.2 Blockchain

A blockchain is a distributed ledger among many network nodes, and records encode as ordered transactions. The transactions compose blocks, and each block links to the previous block with a hash value. The links of hash values make records on-chain immutable. If a malicious user wants to manipulate an intermediate block, the user must modify all the following blocks. Since the blockchain architecture is distributed and decentralized, usually modification is impossible. Bitcoin [20] is the first implementation of a blockchain, which supports asset transactions. Ethereum [29] introduced *smart contracts* into the blockchain, which enabled decentralized applications.

All network nodes have to store the same copy of a blockchain. *Consensus algorithms* allow nodes to agree on the status of the ledger. When a new block joins the chain, the majority of parties need to agree on the validity of the block and the containing transactions. There are different consensus algorithms, and the most popular algorithms are proof-based algorithms and vote-based algorithms [21]. In a proof-based algorithm, the first party who solves a hard puzzle has the right to append a block. In a vote-based algorithm, a block joins the chain if enough parties append the same block. More advanced structures are under investigation now [18,26].

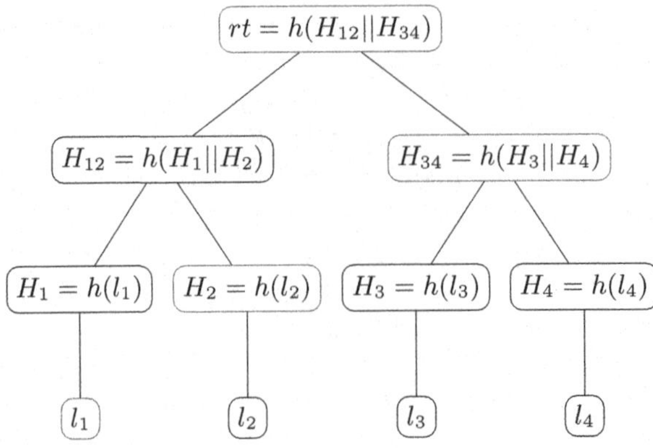

Fig. 2. Merkle Tree.

2.3 Zero-Knowledge Proof

Zero-knowledge proof was introduced by Goldwasser, Micali, and Rackoff [9], which allows a prover to convince the verifier that a statement is true without revealing anything but the truth of the statement. Blum, Feldman and Micali [5] extended the protocol to a non-interactive protocol. Zero-knowledge proof protocols are theoretical advances until recent implementation. The zk-SNARK algorithm [3,13] is the most popular instance of the protocol.

Zk-SNARK stands for Zero-Knowledge Succinct Non-Interactive Argument of Knowledge, in which the proof size is succinct and independent from the complexity of the statement. Zk-SNARK generates proofs in three phases:

1. The setup phase outputs public parameters and the SNARK for a language L in NP.
2. Prover generates a proof π with the instance x and the witness w.
3. Verifier can check the validity of π and x.

2.4 Related Works

Zero-knowledge proof (ZKP) is widely adopted among privacy-preserving blockchains. Zerocash [2] is one of the first projects using zero-knowledge proof on private transactions. However, it only supports intra-chain transactions, and the transaction type is limited to direct payment. Zexe [6] extends the functionality of zerocash and adds supports for conditional smart contracts. It requires users to compute the smart contract on their plain inputs off-line, and then the user generates a ZKP proving the correctness of the off-line computation. Zkay [28] further integrates ZKP with the blockchain by proposing a language for writing private smart contacts, and ZeeStar [27] is a succeeding work of Zkay which introduced a language based on homomorphic encryption. However, those works are very computationally intensive [1], and they are not optimized for data exchange protocols.

3 Preliminaries

In this section, we describe how to construct the protocol with zk-SNARK and other cryptography building blocks.

3.1 Cryptographic Building Blocks

We introduce the formal notation of the cryptography building blocks we use. λ denotes the security parameter. This part is similar to [2] section 4.1.

Collision-Resistant Hashing. We use a collision-resistant hash function $CRH : \{0,1\}^* \to \{0,1\}^{O(\lambda)}$.

Pseudorandom Functions. We use a pseudorandom function family $\mathbb{PRF} = \{PRF_x : \{0,1\}^* \leftarrow \{0,1\}^{O(\lambda)}\}_x$. We then instance three pseudorandom random functions from the same $PRF_x s \xleftarrow{\$} \mathbb{PRF}$ and add different prefix to the input. Namely,

- $PRF_x^{addr}(z) := PRF_x(00||z)$,
- $PRF_x^{sn}(z :) = PRF_x(01||z)$, and
- $PRF_x^{pk}(z) := PRF_x(10||z)$.

Moreover, we require PRF^{sn} to be collision resistant, i.e. one cannot find $(x, z) \neq (x', z')$ s.t. $PRF_x^{sn}(z) = PRF_{x'}^{sn}(z')$.

Statistically-Hiding Commitments. We use a computationally binding and statistically hiding commitment scheme $COMM$. Namely, $\{COMM_x : \{0,1\}^* \to \{0,1\}^{O(\lambda)}\}_x$ where x denotes the trapdoor parameter.

One-Time Strongly-Unforgeable Digital Signatures. We use a digital signature scheme $Sig = (G_{sig}, K_{sig}, S_{sig}, V_{sig})$.

- $G_{sig}(1^\lambda) \to pp_{sig}$. Given a security parameters λ, G_{sig} samples public parameters pp_{sig} for the signature scheme.
- $K_{sig}(pp_{sig}) \to (pk_{sig}, sk_{sig})$. Given public parameters pp_{sig}, K_{sig} samples a public key and a secret key for a single user.
- $S_{sig}(sk_{sig}, m) \to \sigma$. Given a secret key sk_{sig} and a message m, S_{sig} signs m to obtain a signature σ.
- $V_{sig}(pk_{sig}, m, \sigma) \to b$. Given a public key pk_{sig}, message m, and the signature σ, V_{sig} outputs $b = 1$ if validated or otherwise $b = 0$.

We require Sig to be one-time strong unforgeable against chosen-message attacks (SUF-1CMA security).

Key-Private Public-Key Encryption. We use a public-key encryption scheme $PKC = (G_{pkc}, K_{pkc}, PKC.Enc, PKC.Dec)$.

- $G_{pkc}(1^\lambda) \to pp_{pkc}$. Given a security parameter λ, G_{pkc} samples public parameters pp_{pkc} for the encryption scheme.

- $K_{pkc}(pp_{pkc}) \rightarrow (pk_{pkc}, sk_{pkc})$. Given public parameters pp_{pkc}, K_{pkc} samples a public key and a secret key for a single user.
- $PKC.Enc_{pk_{pkc}}(m) \rightarrow Ct$. Given a public key pk_{pkc} and a message m, $PKC.Enc$ encrypts m to obtain a cipher text Ct.
- $PKC.Dec_{sk_{pkc}}(Ct) \rightarrow m$. Given a secret key sk_{pkc} and a cipher text Ct, $PKC.Dec$ decrypts Ct to obtain the plain message m (or $\perp$ if decryption fails).

The encryption scheme PKC is secure against chosen-ciphertext attack and provides both ciphertext indistinguishability IND-CCA and key indistinguishability IK-CCA.

3.2 Concrete Design

In this section, we describe how we instantiate each building block in Table 1.

Table 1. Concrete Design.

CRH PRF $COMM$	Poseidon [11]
Sig	Elliptic Curve Digital Signature Algorithm
PKC	Elliptic-Curve Integrated Encryption Scheme

3.3 Transactions

We introduce two types of transactions.

- Send transactions. A send transaction tx_{send} is a tuple $(cm, con, *)$, where cm is the data commitment, con is the data's encrypted content, and $*$ are other information, e.g., randomness. The transaction tx_{send} records that a user transfer data with commitment cm and encrypted content con.
- Receive transactions. A receive transaction $tx_{receive}$ is a tuple (rt, sn, cm^{new}, con^{new}, $\pi_{\mathsf{RECEIVE}}, *$), where rt, sn is the Merkle root and the serial number for the data on the source chain, cm^{new} is commitment of data on the destination chain, con^{new} is new encrypted content, and $*$ denotes other information. The transaction $tx_{receive}$ records that a user receives some data and writes it down on the destination chain.

3.4 Data

A data is an object d, which contains commitment, encrypted content, serial number, and address.

- commitment, denoted as cm: a string that appears on the ledger once d is sent.
- encrypted content, denoted as con: the encrypted content of d.
- serial number, denoted as sn: a unique string associated with d.
- address, denoted as $addr_{pk}$: an address public key, representing who owns d.

3.5 zk-SNARKs for Receiving Data

We use zk-SNARK to prove a NP statement $RECEIVE$. For the definition of zk-SNARK, we refer to [3] for a detailed explanation. We first provide an informal definition of zk-SNARKs. Given a field $\mathbb{F}$, a **zk-SNARK** for $\mathbb{F}$−arithmetic circuit satisfiability is a triple of polynomial-time algorithm ($\mathsf{KeyGen}, \mathsf{Prove}, \mathsf{Verify}$):

- $\mathsf{KeyGen}(1^\lambda, C) \rightarrow (pk, vk)$. On input: a security parameter λ and an $\mathbb{F}$−arithmetic circuit C, the *key generator* KeyGen probabilistically samples a proving key pk and a verification key vk.
- $\mathsf{Prove}(pk, x, a) \rightarrow \pi$. On input a proving key pk and any $(x, a) \in R_C$, the *prover* **Prove** outputs a non-interactive proof π for the statement $x \in L_C$.
- $\mathsf{Verify}(vk, x, \pi) \rightarrow b$. On input: a verification key vk, an input x, and a proof π, the *verifier* **Verify** outputs $b = 1$ if he/she is convinced that $x \in L_C$.

We recall the corresponding receive transaction $tx_{receive} = (rt,\ sn,\ cm^{new},\ con^{new},\ \pi_{\mathsf{RECEIVE}},\ *)$. To receive a data d, a user u should show that

1. u owns d,
2. commitment of d appears on the ledger,
3. sn is the calculated correctly as the serial number of d,
4. content are matched,

which is formalized as a statement $RECEIVE$ and proved with zk-SNARK. We then define the statement as follows.

- Instances is $x := (rt, sn, h, cm^{new}, h_{sig})$, which specifies a set rt, sn, h for old data, where rt is the root for a CRH-based Merkle tree, sn is the serial number, and h is the signature. It also specifies the public value v^{pub}, commitment of new data cm^{new}, and fields h_{sig} used for non-malleability.
- Witnesses are of the form $a := (path, c, addr_{sk}, d^{new})$ where

$$\begin{aligned} d &= (addr_{pk}, con, \rho, r, s, cm) \\ addr_{pk} &= (a_{pk}, pk_{pkc}) \\ d^{new} &= (addr^{new}_{pk}, v^{new}, \rho^{new}, r^{new}, s^{new}, cm^{new}) \\ addr^{new}_{pk} &= (a^{new}_{pk}, pk^{new}_{pkc}) \end{aligned}$$

Thus, the witness a specifies an authenticated path from root rt to the data's commitment, the entirety information of the data d, the address secret key.

Given a $RECEIVE$ instance x, a witness a is valid for x if:

1. The data's commitment cm appears on the ledger, i.e., $path$ is a valid authentication path for leaf cm in a CRH-based Merkle tree with root rt.
2. The address secret key a_{sk} matches the address public key, i.e., $a_{pk} = PRF^{addr}_{a_{sk}}(0)$.
3. The nullifier key nk matches the address secret key, i.e., $nk = PRF^{addr}_{a_{sk}}(1)$.

4. The serial number sn is computed correctly, i.e., $sn = PRF^{sn}_{nk}(\rho)$.
5. The data d is well formatted, i.e., $cm = COMM_s(COMM_r(a_{pk}||\rho)||con)$.
6. The address secret key a_{sk} ties to h_{sig} to h, i.e., $h = PRF^{pk}_{a_{sk}}(h_{sig})$.
7. New data d^{new} are well formatted, i.e.,
   $cm = COMM_{s^{new}}(COMM_{r^{new}}(a^{new}_{pk}||\rho^{new})||con^{new})$.
8. Content are matched, i.e.,
   $con^{new} = PKC.Enc_{pk^{new}_{pkc}}(PKC.Dec_{sk_{pkc}}(con))$.

3.6 Security

Security of the protocol is characterized by three properties, which we call ledger *indistinguishability*, *transaction non-malleability*, and *matchability*.

Definition 1. *A protocol is secure if it satisfies ledger indistinguishability, transaction non-malleability, and balance.*

We provide the informal definition below.

Ledger Indistinguishability. This property captures the requirement that the ledger reveals no new information to the adversary beyond the publicly-revealed information (e.g. plain text address, coin's public value).

Transaction Non-malleability. This property means no bounded adversary may modify the data stored in a valid receive transaction.

Matchability. This property requires no bounded adversary could receive data other than he/she received from the send transaction.

4 Protocol Overview

Suppose a user *Alice*, denoted as u_A, on Block A want to send data with encrypted content *con* to *Bob*, denoted as u_B, on Block B. Let $PRF^{addr}_x(\cdot)$, $PRF^{sn}_x(\cdot)$ and $PRF^{pk}_x(\cdot)$ denote three pseudorandom functions for a seed x. Each user u_i generates an address key pair $(addr_{pk,i}, addr_{sk,i})$, where $addr_{pk,i} = (a_{pk,i}, pk_{pkc,i})$ and $addr_{sk,i} = (a_{sk,i}, sk_{pkc,i})$, and a nullifier key nk. $a_{pk,i}$ is generated as $PRF^{addr}_{a_{sk}}(0)$. nk is generated as $PRF^{addr}_{a_{sk}}(1)$.$(pk_{pkc,i}, sk_{pkc,i})$ are key-private encryption scheme. Here, we outline the protocol in three steps:

(1) u_A generates randomness r, s, and ρ, where ρ is the data's serial number randomness. Let $COMM$ denote a commit scheme and $PKC.Enc$ denote a public-key encryption scheme. Let $addr_{pk} := (a_{pk}, pk_{enc})$ be u_B's address pair. u_A encrypts data content with pk_{enc} and generates con at first. u_A commits the serial number in two steps:
   1. $k = COMM_r(a_{pk,1}||\rho)$
   2. $cm := COMM_s(con||k)$

   Then, u_A computes the ciphertext $Ct = PKC.Enc_{pk_{pkc}}(con, \rho, r, s)$. The tuple (con, k, s, cm, Ct) is the new transaction tx_{send}. The ledger will keep a CRH(collision-resistant hash)-based Merkle tree $CMList$ of all committed serial numbers (cm). If cm is already in the ledger, the transaction will be rejected. Logically, the data u_A sends to u_B is defined as $d := (addr_{pk}, v, \rho, r, s, cm)$.

(2) u_B can scan over the public ledger and find the transaction tx_{send}. The user then decrypts Ct and gets (con, ρ, r, s).

(3) When u_B wants to receive the data (or more than one received coins), u_B will generate a data d^{new} with newly encrypted content con^{new} and a *zk-SNARK* proof π_{RECEIVE} over the following statements:

For old data d, given the Merkle root rt, serial number sn, u_B knows d and address secret key $a_{sk,1}$ s.t.

- d is well-formatted.
- The address secret key matches the public key, i.e., $a_{pk} = PRF^{addr}_{a_{sk}}(0)$.
- The nullifier key matches the address secret key, i.e., $nk = PRF^{addr}_{a_{sk}}(1)$.
- The serial number is computed correctly, i.e., $sn = PRF^{sn}_{nk}(\rho)$.
- The data commitment cm appears as a leaf of Merkle-tree with root rt.
- New data d^{new} is well formatted.
- $con^{new} = PKC.Enc_{pk^{new}_{pkc}}(PKC.Dec_{sk_{pkc}}(con))$.

The receive transaction $tx_{receive} := (rt, sn, cm^{new}, con^{new}\pi_{\mathsf{RECEIVE}}, *)$ is appended to the ledger, where rt, sn are the Merkle root and the serial number for the old data. The relayer will verify the proof and check if all sn do not appear on the ledger. It will write the new data d^{new} on blockchain B if validated. Furthermore, we employ a message authentication code (MAC) scheme to prevent malleability attacks. A MAC is a code that authenticates a message's source and its integration. When receiving a data, the user samples a key pair (pk_{sig}, sk_{sig}) and use sk_{sig} sign every value associated with the $tx_{receive}$ transaction. The user also computes $h_{sig} := CRH(pk_{sig})$ and $h := PRF^{pk}_{a_{sk}}(h_{sig})$, which acts like a MAC to sign the secret address key. The user then modifies the statement to prove that h is computed correctly. The signature σ along with pk_{sig} are included in the $tx_{receive}$ transaction.

5 Conclusion

In this position paper, we proposed a data exchange protocol over multi-chain blockchain using zero-knowledge proof. The protocol leverages advanced cryptography algorithms and blockchain technologies to provide an efficient and private data transferring algorithm. This protocol preserves the anonymity of the original owner, and the system is secure against malicious users, and provides indistinguishability, transaction non-malleability, and matchability. In future work, we will implement the protocol on the Ethereum Test Network and Hyperledger Fabric and evaluate the performance of the proposed architecture. Moreover, we will simulate the protocol's security against various attack scenarios.

References

1. Almashaqbeh, G., Solomon, R.: SoK: privacy-preserving computing in the blockchain era. In: 2022 IEEE 7th European Symposium on Security and Privacy (EuroS&P), pp. 124–139. IEEE (2022)

2. Ben Sasson, E., et al.: Zerocash: decentralized anonymous payments from bitcoin. In: 2014 IEEE Symposium on Security and Privacy, pp. 459–474 (2014). https://doi.org/10.1109/SP.2014.36
3. Bitansky, N., Chiesa, A., Ishai, Y., Paneth, O., Ostrovsky, R.: Succinct non-interactive arguments via linear interactive proofs. In: Sahai, A. (ed.) TCC 2013. LNCS, vol. 7785, pp. 315–333. Springer, Heidelberg (2013). https://doi.org/10.1007/978-3-642-36594-2_18
4. Bleumer, G.: Unlinkability. In: van Tilborg, H.C.A., Jajodia, S. (eds.) Encyclopedia of Cryptography and Security, p. 1350. Springer, Boston (2011). https://doi.org/10.1007/978-1-4419-5906-5_236
5. Blum, M., Feldman, P., Micali, S.: Non-interactive zero-knowledge and its applications. In: Proceedings of the Twentieth Annual ACM Symposium on Theory of Computing, STOC 1988, pp. 103–112. Association for Computing Machinery, New York (1988). https://doi.org/10.1145/62212.62222
6. Bowe, S., Chiesa, A., Green, M., Miers, I., Mishra, P., Wu, H.: Zexe: enabling decentralized private computation. In: 2020 IEEE Symposium on Security and Privacy (SP), pp. 947–964. IEEE (2020)
7. Bünz, B., Bootle, J., Boneh, D., Poelstra, A., Wuille, P., Maxwell, G.: Bulletproofs: short proofs for confidential transactions and more. In: 2018 IEEE Symposium on Security and Privacy (SP), pp. 315–334 (2018). https://doi.org/10.1109/SP.2018.00020
8. Ekblaw, A., Azaria, A., Halamka, J.D., Lippman, A.: A case study for blockchain in healthcare: "MedRec" prototype for electronic health records and medical research data. In: Proceedings of IEEE Open & Big Data Conference, vol. 13, p. 13 (2016)
9. Goldwasser, S., Micali, S., Rackoff, C.: The knowledge complexity of interactive proof-systems. In: Proceedings of the Seventeenth Annual ACM Symposium on Theory of Computing, STOC 1985, pp. 291–304. Association for Computing Machinery, New York (1985). https://doi.org/10.1145/22145.22178
10. Gordon, W.J., Catalini, C.: Blockchain technology for healthcare: facilitating the transition to patient-driven interoperability. Comput. Struct. Biotechnol. J. **16**, 224–230 (2018)
11. Grassi, L., Khovratovich, D., Rechberger, C., Roy, A., Schofnegger, M.: Poseidon: a new hash function for zero-knowledge proof systems. In: 30th USENIX Security Symposium (USENIX Security 2021), pp. 519–535. USENIX Association (2021). https://www.usenix.org/conference/usenixsecurity21/presentation/grassi
12. Griffor, E., Greer, C., Wollman, D., Burns, M.: Framework for cyber-physical systems: volume 1, overview (2017). https://doi.org/10.6028/NIST.SP.1500-201
13. Groth, J.: Short pairing-based non-interactive zero-knowledge arguments. In: Abe, M. (ed.) ASIACRYPT 2010. LNCS, vol. 6477, pp. 321–340. Springer, Heidelberg (2010). https://doi.org/10.1007/978-3-642-17373-8_19
14. He, Q., Xu, Y., Liu, Z., He, J., Sun, Y., Zhang, R.: A privacy-preserving internet of things device management scheme based on blockchain. Int. J. Distrib. Sens. Netw. **14**(11), 1550147718808750 (2018)
15. Hopwood, D., Bowe, S., Hornby, T., Wilcox, N.: Zcash protocol specification. GitHub: San Francisco, CA, USA, p. 1 (2016)
16. Huh, S., Cho, S., Kim, S.: Managing IoT devices using blockchain platform. In: 2017 19th International Conference on Advanced Communication Technology (ICACT), pp. 464–467. IEEE (2017)
17. Jiang, S., Cao, J., Wu, H., Yang, Y., Ma, M., He, J.: Blochie: a blockchain-based platform for healthcare information exchange. In: 2018 IEEE International Conference on Smart Computing (SmartComp), pp. 49–56. IEEE (2018)

18. Li, A., Serena, L., Zichichi, M., D'Angelo, G., Tang, S.K., Ferretti, S.: Modelling of the internet computer protocol architecture. In: 4th International Congress on Blockchain and Applications, BLOCKCHAIN 2022 (2022, to appear)
19. Merkle, R.C.: A digital signature based on a conventional encryption function. In: Pomerance, C. (ed.) CRYPTO 1987. LNCS, vol. 293, pp. 369–378. Springer, Heidelberg (1988). https://doi.org/10.1007/3-540-48184-2_32
20. Nakamoto, S.: Bitcoin: a peer-to-peer electronic cash system. Decentralized Business Review, p. 21260 (2008)
21. Nguyen, G.T., Kim, K.: A survey about consensus algorithms used in blockchain. J. Inf. Process. Syst. **14**(1), 101–128 (2018)
22. Ouaddah, A., Elkalam, A.A., Ouahman, A.A.: Towards a novel privacy-preserving access control model based on blockchain technology in IoT. In: Rocha, Á., Serrhini, M., Felgueiras, C. (eds.) Europe and MENA Cooperation Advances in Information and Communication Technologies. AISC, vol. 520, pp. 523–533. Springer, Cham (2017). https://doi.org/10.1007/978-3-319-46568-5_53
23. Pieroni, A., Scarpato, N., Di Nunzio, L., Fallucchi, F., Raso, M.: Smarter city: smart energy grid based on blockchain technology. Int. J. Adv. Sci. Eng. Inf. Technol. **8**(1), 298–306 (2018)
24. Poelstra, A., Back, A., Friedenbach, M., Maxwell, G., Wuille, P.: Confidential assets. In: Zohar, A., et al. (eds.) FC 2018. LNCS, vol. 10958, pp. 43–63. Springer, Heidelberg (2019). https://doi.org/10.1007/978-3-662-58820-8_4
25. Rathore, H., Mohamed, A., Guizani, M.: A survey of blockchain enabled cyber-physical systems. Sensors **20**(1), 282 (2020)
26. Serena, L., Li, A., Zichichi, M., D'Angelo, G., Ferretti, S., Tang, S.K.: Simulation of the internet computer protocol: the next generation multi-blockchain architecture. In: 2022 IEEE/ACM 26th International Symposium on Distributed Simulation and Real Time Applications (DS-RT), pp. 119–126. IEEE (2022)
27. Steffen, S., Bichsel, B., Baumgartner, R., Vechev, M.: Zeestar: private smart contracts by homomorphic encryption and zero-knowledge proofs. In: 2022 IEEE Symposium on Security and Privacy (SP), pp. 179–197 (2022). https://doi.org/10.1109/SP46214.2022.9833732
28. Steffen, S., Bichsel, B., Gersbach, M., Melchior, N., Tsankov, P., Vechev, M.: zkay: specifying and enforcing data privacy in smart contracts. In: Proceedings of the 2019 ACM SIGSAC Conference on Computer and Communications Security, pp. 1759–1776 (2019)
29. Wood, G., et al.: Ethereum: a secure decentralised generalised transaction ledger. Ethereum Project Yellow Paper **151**(2014), 1–32 (2014)

A Hybrid Task Offloading and Service Cache Scheme for Vehicular Edge Computing

Linyu Sun[1(✉)], Yancong Deng[2], Xingxia Dai[3], and Zhu Xiao[3]

[1] University of Southern California, Los Angeles, USA
linyusun@usc.edu
[2] University of California, San Diego, San Diego, USA
yad002@eng.ucsd.edu
[3] Shenzhen Research Institute of Hunan University, Changsha, China
zhxiao@hnu.edu.cn

Abstract. The development of 5G, IoT, and other technologies has promoted the emergence of emerging applications, including augmented reality, autonomous driving, and so on. These applications are usually delay-sensitive and energy intensive, which have strict delay constraints and need to consume a lot of computing resources. In order to ensure the quality of service of these applications, this study proposes a framework that combines task offloading and service caching in the local-edge-cloud collaboration system. In order to obtain a satisfactory offloading decision, this study first proposes a distributed task offloading algorithm based on non-cooperative game theory storage which makes the decision of local processing or offloading to the side server with the goal of minimizing system cost over time and energy consumption. Considering the limited storage resources of the edge, this study uses a 0–1 knapsack algorithm to realize dynamic service caching based on task popularity based on the original offloading decision. Based on the results of service caching, if the task initially decides to offload to the edge server and the edge server does not cache the services required by the task, the task will be unloaded locally or to the cloud.

1 Introduction

Due to the highly dynamic requirements of IoV network, a lot of studies focused on task offloading, resource management, Data scheduling, mobility management and application models. Vehicular edge computing (VEC) provides possible solutions to storage and compute resource allocation between vehicles and roadside units (RSU). The continuous growth in mobile applications has also caused an exponential increase in demand for higher computation capacity. Dedicated short-range communication (DSRC) enables vehicles' collaboration with RSU via infrastructure or infrastructure-independent communication. Meanwhile, the fast

Z. Xiao et al. (Eds.): ICECI 2022, LNICST 478, pp. 30–40, 2023.
https://doi.org/10.1007/978-3-031-28990-3_3

implementation of 5G technologies on cellular networks can use cellular vehicle-to-everything (C-V2X) and long-term evolution vehicles (LTE-V) to support low-latency and high-reliable communications for IoV.

Meanwhile, the limited cloud resources with radio access network also allows the resource-constrained mobile terminals (MT) to migrate part or all of the required tasks from the randomly arrived MTs to edge cloud for achieving spatial proximity service characterized by low latency and energy efficiency. Various intelligent transportation systems impose urgent demands on massive data transmission and intensive computing capacity such as self driving, collision warning and high resolution video crowdsourcing.

In this paper, a hybrid offloading scheme of both edge computing and service cache based on cloud computing has been proposed for vehicular network. First a distributed task offloading algorithm based on non cooperative game theory has been driven to make the decision for local processing or offloading to edge server with the goal of minimizing the total system cost over time and energy consumption. Considering the limited storage resources of the edge server, the study uses 0–1 knapsack algorithm to realize the dynamic service caching based on task popularity for the original offloading decision. Based on the result of service caching the offloading decision will be further adjusted to allow the computation mitigation with the cloud resources.

2 Related Work

Many researches have focus on fog computing paradigm for IoV to reach a better performance on time critical task [11–14]. Difference vehicle fog network (VFN) architectures have been proposed to cooperate with edge infrastructures for low-latency and high reliability services in IoV. Liu [1] investigated on adaptive offloading for time-critical tasks in heterogeneous environments and designed a vehicular fog computing based architecture to enable the cooperation among the cloud and fog nodes. Wang [2] proposed a dynamic reinforcement learning scheduling algorithm and deep dynamic scheduling algorithm to solve offloading decisions for fog computing based on Markov decision progress.

However the task assignment and resource allocation proposed for fog computing were designed based on the assumption of static distributed users. The uncertainty of mobility-driven user makes the task schedule more complex in the presence of heterogeneous radio, computing cost and cache resources. Considering the mobility of the vehicles, Saleem [3] designed a Genetic Algorithm-based evolutionary scheme to minimize the total execution latency. Then to obtain an effective task assignment with low complexity, a heuristic named mobility-aware task schedule has been proposed for the evaluation. The cooperative abilities among user terminals also plays a vital rule for the system performance. Peng [4] constructed an online resource coordinating and allocating scheme to minimize the network-wide response latency and energy consumption simultaneously by exploiting Lyapunov optimization theory, which offers partial offloading, cooperative scheduling and computation allocation for practical implementation.

The work in [9,10] studied task scheduling by replication strategy. Sun [5] designed a learning-based task replication algorithm with combinatorial multi-armed bandit theory, which considered the task failure probability as a constraint to guarantee reliability. Mohamed [6] considered multiple sets of users forming service groups due to the participation of each group in the same synchronized activities and formulated the problem as an integer non-linear problem. Then a task offloading and service replication scheme is proposed to minimize the response time while satisfying the group delay requirement.

While researches which are mentioned above are based on cooperation between edge nodes and fog nodes, there are also a number of studies investigated on task offloading and resource allocation based on the vehicular ad-hoc network (VANET). Despite the variety of studies for vehicle to vehicle communication(V2V), the algorithms can be roughly divided into two categories: topology based routing and geographic based routing. In V2V, nodes have high mobility and the topology changes frequently with the time, which means the topology based routing protocols are not suitable in the real situation [7]. Wang [8] investigated geographic based routing protocol and proposed a V2V hybrid model based on the Greedy Perimeter Stateless Routing algorithm, which leads to a better path decision and transmission efficiency.

3 System Model

In this section, first the algorithm structure of hybrid task offloading and service caching scheme is described. Then the computation models of two decision making stage are presented. All the notations used in the system model are listed in (Table 1).

Table 1. Frequently Used Notations

Term	Description
$\mathcal{T}$	total offloading task set
$\mathcal{O}$	task set
d_i	edge execution cost
l_i	local execution cost
s_i	task strategy cost
$\mathcal{G}$	offloading strategy combination set
$\mathcal{H}$	cost compare vector
$\mathcal{Q}$	loss vector
$\mathcal{R}$	potential decision set
C	cache capacity

Figure 1 shows the proposed Hybrid Task Offloading and Service Cache Scheme for Vehicular Edge Computing, which consists of cloud pool, edge server and mobile device set $\mathcal{N} = \{1, 2, ..., N\}$. For the task to be unloaded to the

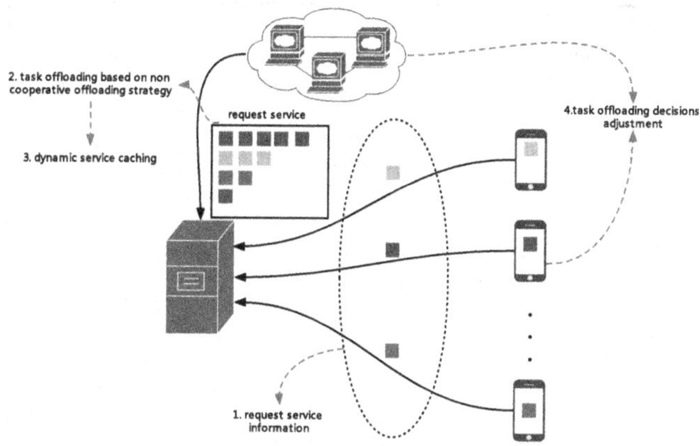

Fig. 1. Illustration of hybrid task offloading and service caching scheme

side server, the IoT device first notifies the side server of the service information requested by the task before the task is transmitted. After receiving the information, the edge server determines the popularity of the service according to the frequency of each service request. The more requests, the higher the popularity, so there are more opportunities to cache in the edge server. Considering the popularity of the service and the limited storage space of the edge server, the edge server downloads the service from the cloud to the cache. If the service requested by the task is cached in the edge server, the task can be processed in the edge; When the requested service is not cached in the edge server, the IoT device needs to adjust the offloading decision of the task, that is, decide whether to unload the task to the cloud or process it locally.

Assuming during one specific time slot every mobile device $n \in \mathcal{N}$ sends one task offloading request to the edge server. The total offloading task set is $\mathcal{T} = \{t_1, t_2 \ldots, t_N\}$. Task set $\mathcal{O} = \{a, b, \ldots\}$ contains all possible task where $a, b, \ldots$ are different task type. $t_i \in \mathcal{O}, \forall i \in \mathcal{N}$.

3.1 Task Offloading Model

Figure 2 shows the algorithm flow for the proposed scheme. The algorithm contains three steps. First, a non-cooperation offloading method is adopted to minimize the total system cost at the edge server. The total system cost is a combination of both local operation cost and geographic-based cost, which is dependent on the offloading strategy chosen for each task.

Each task will be decided whether it will be offloaded to the edge server or reserved for the local process based on its local operation cost l and edge operation cost d, which both are the weighted sum of process time cost and energy cost. Thus the task strategy cost s can be represented as

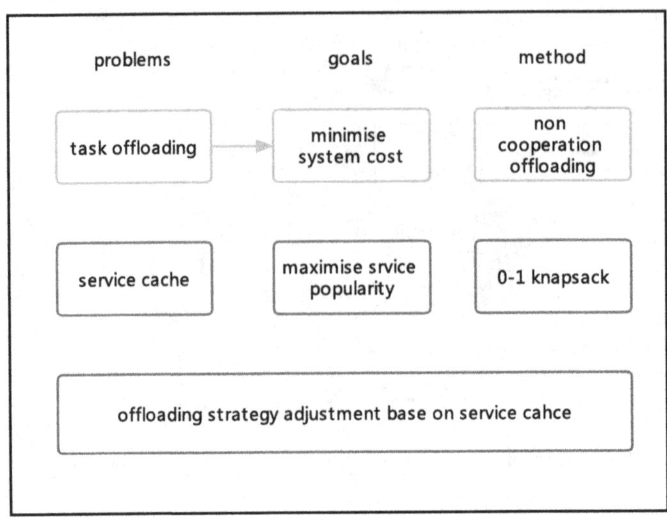

Fig. 2. Illustration of algorithm structure

$$s_i = \begin{cases} l_i & \text{local execution} \\ d_i & \text{edge execution} \end{cases} \quad \forall i \in \mathcal{N} \tag{1}$$

Since the offloading choice of each task can be different in every offloading strategy set. The weighted cost of kth strategy set $g^k \in \mathcal{G}$ can be represented as:

$$g^k = \sum_{i=1}^{N} s_i^k + b \tag{2}$$

where s_i^k stands for the ith task cost for k^{th} strategy set and b is a constant and $\mathcal{G}$ stands for all possible combination of N strategies.

The non-cooperative task offloading strategy is based on the iteration process. During the first iteration process, the task offloading strategy will be chosen randomly for the initialization, assuming the set cost is c^j. The cost compare vector based on j^th strategy choice is $\mathcal{H} = \{h_1, h_2, \dots h_N\}$ where $h_i = g^j - g^i$. If the current offloading choice j has less cost, the value of h would be larger.

Thus, the loss vector $\mathcal{Q}$ for e^{th} iteration process can be represented as:

$$\mathcal{Q}_e = \begin{cases} \mathcal{H}_e & e = 1 \\ \mathcal{Q}_{e-1} + \frac{1}{e*(\mathcal{H}_e - \mathcal{Q}_{e-1})} & e \neq 1 \end{cases} \tag{3}$$

where $q_{i-e} \in \mathcal{Q}_e$ is the loss score of ith offloading strategy compared with current strategy during the eth iteration process. Thus the offloading strategy for e^{th} iteration process can be chosen from the decision set $\mathcal{R}_e \subseteq \mathcal{Q}_e$, where all elements q_i belong to $\mathcal{R}_e$ have positive value.

3.2 Dynamic Service Caching and Task Offloading Decision Adjustment

Algorithm 1 two stages task offloading algorithm

for $t_i \in \mathcal{T}$ **do**
  calculate the local execution cost l_i and edge execution cost e_i
end for
form the weighted strategy cost set $\mathcal{G}$ based on equation (2)
for $e = 1$,$e \leq$iteration time **do**
  update the comparison vector $\mathcal{H}_e$ based on $h_i = g^j - g^i$
  update the loss vector $\mathcal{Q}_e$ based on the equation (3)
  form the decision set $\mathcal{R}_e$, $r_i = q_i$ when q_i is greater or equal than 0, $r_i = 0$ when q_i is less than 0. For each r_i, assign a pickup probability based on $r_i / \sum_{k=1}^{N} r_k$. The next offloading strategy will be generated based on the probability distribution of $\mathcal{R}_e$
end for
based on the required service type for each task, from the storage cost set $\mathcal{W}$ and popularity profit set $\mathcal{P}$, which are corresponded to every task in set $\mathcal{N}$
follows the recursion of equation (5), find the $f(p_i, C)$, which would lead to its corresponding dynamic caching strategy.
based on the offloading strategy and dynamic caching strategy, there will be a further adjustment if a task is offloaded to the edge server and the edge server does not have a cache of it.
the edge server will compare the task strategy cost for both local and cloud execution to decide to final choice for the noncached task.

Assuming the edge server has cache capacity C. The task set $\mathcal{T}$ has been offloaded to the edge server during the specific time slot. Assuming each task $t_i \in \mathcal{T}$ has a storage cost w_i and popularity profit p_i. The relation between the summation of all task weights and the cache capacity can be expressed as $\sum_{i=1}^{N} w_i > C$ where we assume that $w_i < C, i \in \mathcal{N}$.

Based on the task offloading results the 0–1 knapsack is used to maximize the service popularity by caching the popular tasks in the edge server with limited storage space.

Introducing the binary decision variables x_i, with $x_i = 1$ if task is selected, and $x_i = 0$ otherwise. The dynamic service caching problem (DSCP) can be summarised as:

$$\begin{aligned} &\text{maximize } \sum_{i=1}^{N} p_i x_i \\ &\text{subject to } \sum_{i=1}^{N} w_i x_i \leq C, x_i \in \{0,1\}, i \in \mathcal{N} \end{aligned} \tag{4}$$

The optimization problem is solved by a dynamic programming approach. The state $f(p_i, \widetilde{C})$ represents the maximum popularity profits of storage cost $\widetilde{C}$ considering all tasks from 1 to i.

The recursion process for DSCP can be denoted as:

$$f(p_i, \widetilde{C}) = \begin{cases} f(p_{i-1}, \widetilde{C}) & w_i > \widetilde{C} \\ \max(f(p_{i-1}, \widetilde{C}), & \\ f(p_{i-1}, \widetilde{C} - w_i) + p_i) & w_i \leq \widetilde{C} \end{cases} \tag{5}$$

The profit of each task is determined by the number of tasks of the same type in the total offloading task set $\mathcal{T}$. The more tasks of the same kind, the higher the profit of the task, and the greater the chance of being cached by the edge server.

If the task is not cached in edge, the server will compare the cloud processing cost with the local processing cost to determine the further adjustment policy for the offloading strategy.

The complete workflow for both non-cooperative tasks offloading scheme and dynamic service caching along with the final decision adjustment scheme is described in Algorithm 1 as follows:

4 Simulation Results and Analysis

The simulation model is built based on the system architecture proposed in Sect. 3. In the default setting, assume the total number of devices N = 5. Task set $\mathcal{O}$ has 5 different service types. The consumption of CPU computation resources and the storage space of every task type is also different. tasks in set $\mathcal{N}$ will be initialized with a random type from set $\mathcal{O}$.

To compare the performance of the proposed scheme, three solutions have also been implemented, which are described as follows:

1. *TOCS:* This algorithm comprehensively considers task offloading and service caching in the mobile edge computing network, without cloud server assistance.
2. *TO:* This algorithm considers the offloading problem in the mobile edge computing network, without dynamic service caching.
3. *LP:* This algorithm processes all tasks in local IoT devices.

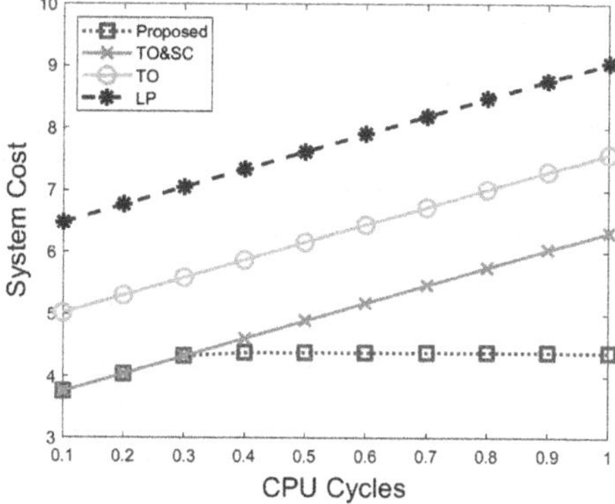

Fig. 3. Comparison of system cost under different CPU cycles

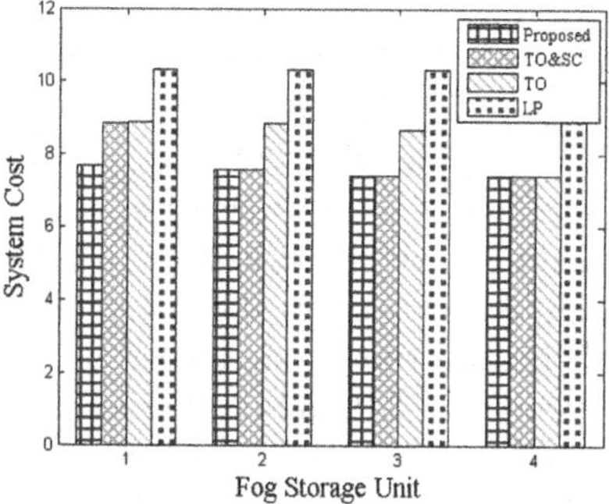

Fig. 4. Comparison of system cost under different storage unit

The experiment changed the number of CPU computing resources required for the fifth task from range (0.1GHz:1GHz). Meanwhile, the local energy consumption and the task size remain the same for tasks. Figure 3 shows the comparison of system cost between the proposed scheme and three different schemes.

With the growth of the CPU cycles, the system cost of *LP* and *TO* grows linearly. The *LP* has the highest cost among all CPU cycles since the scheme does not involve any offloading technique.

Figure 4 compares the system cost for all scheme under assumption of different storage unit. During the first stage all schemes share the same initial condition for task offloading. During the dynamic service caching stage the capacity of storage unit on fog side has been changed in order to compare the system performance.

LP maintains the highest system cost. The proposed scheme has the best performance when the capacity of fog storage unit is small. It has the same performance with other two scheme when the storage capacity is large, generally the proposed scheme has better system cost performance for all fog storage capacities.

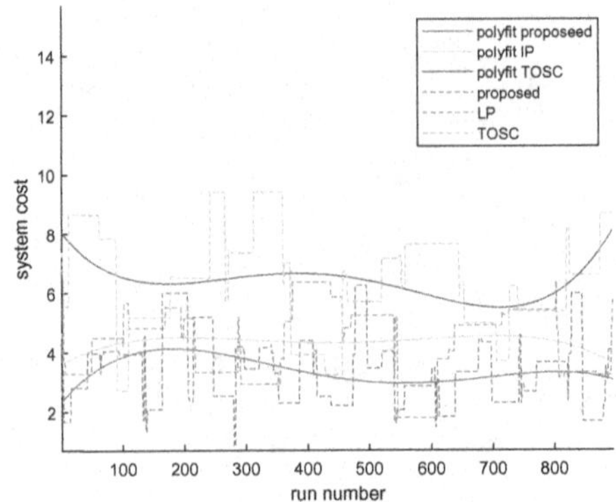

Fig. 5. Comparison of system performance under random task set

Figure 5 shows the difference of system cost under the initialization of random task set. Mobile device set $\mathcal{N} = \{1, 2, ..., 5\}$, number of task type O for task set $\mathcal{O}$ is initialized with random setting where $O \geq N$.

All three schemes share the same initialization condition. The experiment was run 900 times in order to show the statistical performance of all schemes. the dotted line from the figure shows the real time system cost and the solid line are the polynomial fits of the real time system cost.

From the figure it is clear that LP has the highest system cost both in real time and statistical performance. The real time performance of TOSC and proposed scheme are very close but judged by the polynomial fit the proposed scheme has a general better performance on system cost.

5 Conclusion

In this paper, a hybrid offloading scheme of both edge computing and service cache based on cloud computing has been proposed for vehicular network. During each iteration process, the task offloading decisions will be made based on the evaluation of the last decision sets. The complete computation model and the Algorithm process of the two stages task offloading strategy are proposed. Finally, a simulation model is built to compare the performance of the proposed scheme along with three different solutions. The results prove that the proposed scheme has better performance on system cost under different CPU cycles and different storage unit in the edge server. In future directions, Since MEC and D2D offloading are two promising paradigms in the industrial Internet of Things [15]. With the insperation of Heterogeneous Small Cell Networks, heterogeneous tasks with diverse delay requirements, data size, and reliability constraints should be considered [16,17]. Also the task offloading can be improved by incorporating mmWave, massive MIMO. These challenging and interesting extensions are yet left for the future work.

References

1. Liu, C., Liu, K., Guo, S., Xie, R., Lee, V.C.S., Son, S.H.: Adaptive offloading for time-critical tasks in heterogeneous internet of vehicles. IEEE Internet Things J. **7**(9), 7999–8011 (2020). https://doi.org/10.1109/JIOT.2020.2997720
2. Wang, Y., Wang, K., Huang, H., Miyazaki, T., Guo, S.: Traffic and computation co-offloading with reinforcement learning in fog computing for industrial applications. IEEE Trans. Industr. Inf. **15**(2), 976–986 (2019). https://doi.org/10.1109/TII.2018.2883991
3. Saleem, U., Liu, Y., Jangsher, S., Li, Y., Jiang, T.: Mobility-aware joint task scheduling and resource allocation for cooperative mobile edge computing. IEEE Trans. Wireless Commun. **20**(1), 360–374 (2021). https://doi.org/10.1109/TWC.2020.3024538
4. Peng, J., Qiu, H., Cai, J., Xu, W., Wang, J.: D2D-assisted multi-user cooperative partial offloading, transmission scheduling and computation allocating for MEC. IEEE Trans. Wireless Commun. **20**(8), 4858–4873 (2021). https://doi.org/10.1109/TWC.2021.3062616
5. Sun, Y., Zhou, S., Niu, Z.: Distributed task replication for vehicular edge computing: performance analysis and learning-based algorithm. IEEE Trans. Wireless Commun. **20**(2), 1138–1151 (2021). https://doi.org/10.1109/TWC.2020.3030889
6. Mohamed, S.A., Sorour, S., Hassanein, H.S.: Group-delay aware task offloading with service replication for scalable mobile edge computing. In: GLOBECOM 2020–2020 IEEE Global Communications Conference, pp. 1–6 (2020). https://doi.org/10.1109/GLOBECOM42002.2020.9348241
7. Wu, T.-Y., Wang, Y.-B., Lee, W.-T.: Mixing greedy and predictive approaches to improve geographic routing for VANET. Wireless Commun. Mob. Comput. **12**(4), 367–378 (2012)
8. Wang, X., Deng, Y., Wang, T., Zhang, Y., Jiang, H.: A hybrid vehicle-to-vehicle transmission model for vehicular networks. In: 2021 the 11th International Conference on Information Communication and Management (ICICM 2021), pp. 34–40. Association for Computing Machinery, New York (2021). https://doi.org/10.1145/3484399.3484404
9. Saeik, F., et al.: Task offloading in edge and cloud computing: a survey on mathematical, artificial intelligence and control theory solutions. Comput. Netw. **195**, 108177 (2021) ISSN 1389-1286
10. Chen, C.-L., Brinton, C.G., Aggarwal, V.: Latency minimization for mobile edge computing networks. IEEE Trans. Mob. Comput. 1 (2021). https://ieeexplore.ieee.org/document/9557844
11. Siriwardhana, Y., Porambage, P., Liyanage, M., Ylianttila, M.: A survey on mobile augmented reality with 5G mobile edge computing: architectures, applications, and technical aspects. IEEE Commun. Surv. Tutor. **23**(2), 1160–1192 (2021)
12. Liu, L., et al.: Vehicular edge computing and networking: a survey. Mob. Netw. Appl. **26**(3), 1145–1168 (2021)
13. Peng, J., Qiu, H., Cai, J., Xu, W., Wang, J.: D2D-assisted multi-user cooperative partial offloading, transmission scheduling and computation allocating for MEC. IEEE Trans. Wireless Commun. **20**(8), 4858–4873 (2021)
14. Raza, S., Liu, W., Ahmed, M., et al.: An efficient task offloading scheme in vehicular edge computing. J. Cloud Comput. **9**, 28 (2020). https://doi.org/10.1186/s13677-020-00175-w

15. Dai, X., et al.: Task co-offloading for D2D-assisted mobile edge computing in industrial internet of things. IEEE Trans. Industr. Inform. (2022). https://doi.org/10.1109/TII.2022.3158974
16. Jiang, H., Xiao, Z., Li, Z., Xu, J., Zeng, F., Wang, D.: An energy-efficient framework for internet of things underlaying heterogeneous small cell networks. IEEE Trans. Mob. Comput. **21**(1), 31–43 (2022)
17. Jiang, H., Dai, X., Xiao, Z., Iyengar, A.: Joint task offloading and resource allocation for energy-constrained mobile edge computing. IEEE Trans. Mob. Comput. (2022). https://doi.org/10.1109/TMC.2022.3150432

On Enhancing Transmission Performance for IoV Based on Improved Greedy Algorithm

Shuo Deng[1(✉)], Haoyuan Xiong[2], Qixiang Yang[3], Yancong Deng[4], and Xingxia Dai[3]

[1] Tiangong University, Tianjin 300387, China
Sd862@uowmail.edu.au
[2] University of California Los Angeles, Los Angeles, USA
haoyuanxiong@g.ucla.edu
[3] Southwest University, Beibei District, Chongqing, China
lmy1314@email.swu.edu.cn
[4] University of California San Diego, San Diego, USA
Yad002@eng.ucsd.edu

Abstract. With the rapid development of the Internet of Things in human life, Vehicle-to-Vehicle (V2V), Internet of Vehicle (IoV) transmission, a technology is used to make a vehicle can detect the position and movement of other vehicles up to a specified range, which plays a significant role in upcoming cellular networks is expected to reduce the traffic jam and accidents in social life. Based on the idea of Greedy algorithm, a method to find the partial optimal solution to get the global solution, the purpose of improving the system effect can be achieved by using this algorithm into IoV transmission. In this paper, firstly, the development and technical essentials of IoV transmission system as well as the realization principle of greedy algorithm are briefly introduced. Then the rest of paper mainly discusses the performance of four models implementing greedy algorithm in IoV fields based on MATLAB by pairwise comparison of experimental results and analysis.

Keywords: V2V · IoV transmission · Greedy algorithm · Transmission route · MATLAB

1 Introduction

1.1 V2V Transmission

Nowadays, with development of economical society and international technology, more and more things are connected in the form of the network to complete the transmission and communication of data, which greatly facilitates our life. Based on the internet of things, a technology enables data to be stored in a cluster of central computers with super-computing power and applied to all walks of life in human society to achieve intelligent management, D2D (Device-to-device, a new paradigm in cellular network, has been developed in various fields. With advantages of allowing user equipment (UEs) in close proximity to communicate using a direct link rather than having their radio signal

Z. Xiao et al. (Eds.): ICECI 2022, LNICST 478, pp. 41–53, 2023.
https://doi.org/10.1007/978-3-031-28990-3_4

travel all the way through the base station (BS) or the core network, D2D connectivity will make operators more flexible in terms of offloading traffic from the core network, increase spectral efficiency and reduce the energy and the cost per bit [1]. As a detailed research direction of this technology, vehicle-to-vehicle (V2V) communications has been developed to decreases the severe traffic congestion as well as accidents. In United States, more than 5.5 billion hours were dissipated due to traffic jams, which is commensurate with 2.9 billion gallons of fuel costing more than 121 billion dollars [2]. With growth of population of city areas which leads to generation of more cars, the traditional approach to reduce traffic jams by building more road networks is no longer an efficient way as the capacity have reached the limit in many countries [3]. V2V communication and IoV technology is based on single carrier frequency division multiple access (SCFDMA) in the PHY layer of computer networks. The transmitting vehicle can decode and sense the dispatching control information sent by the vehicle within a certain range, in which the design senses the resources that will be occupied or collided by other transmitting vehicles to avoid collision [4]. So V2V communication, as the key technology which enables vehicles to collect previously unobtainable high-fidelity traffic information such as surrounding vehicles' speed, positions, acceleration, destinations, maneuvers and more depending on the protocol design [5]. So based on these advantages, it is possible to apply this technology to our reality life to solve traffic problems.

1.2 Greedy Algorithm

Based on the technical requirements and characteristics of IoV communication, the selection of routes plays an important role in the process of V2V transmission. As a well-known method technique for solving various problems so as to optimize (minimize or maximize) specific objective functions, greedy algorithm is a controlled search strategy that selects the next state to achieve the largest possible improvement in the value of some measure which may or may not be the objective function [6]. When solving the problem, greedy algorithm cannot consider the overall optimal, but decompose the problem into several sub-problems to obtain the step-by-step optimal solution, and then integrate the solution to the problem. Subsequent paragraphs, however, are indented.

Based on the characteristics of the algorithm, in V2V and IoV transmission, considering each vehicle as a sub-problem of the whole problem, it is possible to find the optimal information transmission route of each vehicle and make successive greedy choices in the range from far to near using iterative method, so as to get the optimal transmission route of all vehicles. In real life, the trajectory of traffic is irregular and difficult to predict, so it is unrealistic to analyze the problem from the perspective of considering all vehicles as a whole, in which greedy algorithm is an efficient way to solve this problem. On the other hand, based on the characteristics of fast running speed, simple encoding method and single selection range, the algorithm can effectively reduce the transmission delay and transmission failure rate in IoV transmission, and maintain the information transmission in a controllable hop number, reduce the loss and reduce the cost [7]. The rest of this paper mainly focuses on the performance of greedy algorithm and the advanced methods based on the disadvantages of the original one in Internet of Vehicle transmission.

2 Algorithm System Model Performance

As one of the classical algorithms to solve the problem of point coverage, the core idea of greedy algorithm is to solve the node with the largest degree and iteratively approach the global optimal result with the local optimal result [8]. The rest of this mainly shows four models to demonstrate different aspects of greedy algorithm application in the fields of IoV transmission. The program design and experiment part of this paper is mainly based on MATLAB, the following conditions are set as shown in the table below.

Table 1. The conditions specified in the algorithm

Vehicle position remains unchanged during transmission
The transmission Angle is 90°
The presence of dead-end in the transmission relay assumes transmission through another path
Relay assumes that the target vehicle sends information to the optimal (farthest) vehicle
The congestion delay is 2 ms/per
Vehicles at both ends of the map relay information through other vehicles
Map size: The number of long and wide lanes is 11, and the spacing of lanes is 19

Model1 and model2 illustrate the effect of the traditional algorithm in IoV transmission, and take the transmission range as the variable to further research the transmission effect.

2.1 Model1

According to the idea of finding the partial optimal solution at each step, when realizing greedy algorithm in IoV transmission, it is significant to find the most optimal route to the target vehicle for every starting point. Assume that the location of the vehicle in the map is placed randomly, and the transmission range is determined. The main idea of the program design is as follows.

Firstly, in the main program of building the cellular network, the map is determined, including the length and the width of the image and the number of lanes. Map drawing and random placement of vehicles are performed by two concrete functions and a variable, PLAZA, is used to record the image. In addition, the main program initializes the parameters that reflect the results of the system for subsequent recording of experimental results.

After that, the function named relay is designed to calculate the number of hops, failures and time of delay. In this function, the nested Transmit function plays a major role in the implementation of IoV information transmission using greedy algorithm.

In the transmit function, when the first target vehicle is selected, a function named Numofcars is used to calculate the number of vehicles in specified range with the target as the center. What is more, the positions of these vehicles are sorted by the distance from far to near. The information of the coordinates is stored in an array called POS which is used to find the optimal route and next node transmitted the data. When the number of vehicles in the target range is not zero, according to the POS array obtained by running the above function, the information is transmitted to the farthest vehicle in the range to achieve the optimal path. In the next transmission, the receiving vehicle is taken as the starting point, and the routing table is updated and the optimal path is selected through the above steps. When the last destination vehicle reaches the edge of the map, it is recorded as the end of a V2V transmission. In a transmission, the number of nodes passing through is denoted as hop and the transmission delay is determined randomly by the number of vehicles within the range when the transmission is completed, which is more universal.

Finally, in order to ensure a better fit between the program and the actual situation, 50 iterations of each transmission simulation were carried out to calculate the total data through cellular network, and the data are presented more clearly by drawing charts in MATLAB.

According to the conditions set above, the Fig. 1 shows that the flow of original algorithm based on a single range value.

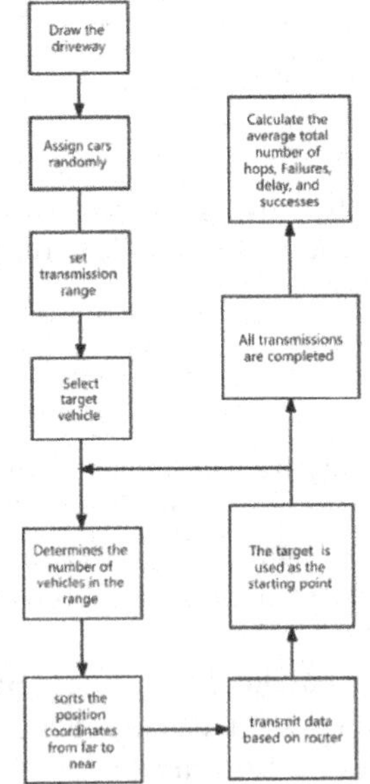

Fig. 1. Original algorithm process

2.2 Model2

Model1 can fulfill the basic purpose of IoV transmission, but it may cause excessive transmission loss or more time of delay in a single range. Based on this consideration, model2 proposes a way to mix two or more ranges into the final transmission range, which solves the above problem well.

Compared to the last one, this model basically retains the structure of the previous algorithm. The difference is that when the range turns to be a hybrid value, the new function called Hybrid-NumofCars is used to calculate each number of vehicles in different ranges and integrates the position sorted from far to near under each range (the range is sorted by small to large). Therefore, when performing the function of transmission named Hybrid-Transmitfun, it is more efficient to select the next transmission node which can achieve the purpose of transmitting by the optimal path in a small range and making it lower time of delay.

In order to improve the transmission efficiency and reduce the cost, the updated greedy algorithm changes the single transmission range (250 m, 350 m, 450 m and 550 m) into a hybrid range. The specific process is shown in the figure below (Fig. 2).

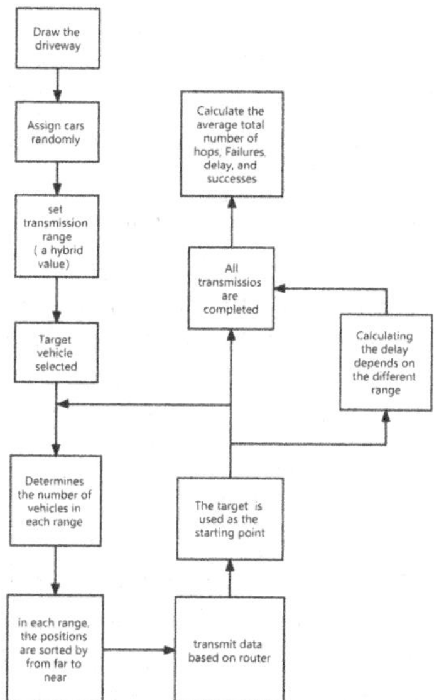

Fig. 2. Greedy algorithm based on hybrid transmission range

Through model 1 and 2, this paper explores the implementation process of general greedy algorithm in IoV transmission and illustrates its application effect in the third part. Based on above two, it is possible to find that the application conditions of the above two models are relatively simple as well as the transmission routes, so they are not completely applicable to the real traffic situation. Therefore, the following model3 and 4 introduces volume which is a variable used to determine the transmission route. The rest of this part mainly shows two models based on above idea update the traditional algorithm to achieve better effect in IoV transmission.

2.3 Mode3

Compared to the previous algorithm, in the algorithm of model3, the same functions are used to draw the map and place the vehicles randomly. In main program called cellular used to form the network, the same arrays storing some data which reflect the performance of the algorithm system are initialized. Then the iteration is ready to run. The difference is that model3 adds a new variation named volume playing an important role in updating the optimal path and selecting the nodes.

In each iteration, as the vehicle density changes continuously, the vehicle position is updated every time a IoV transmission is performed.

In each IoV transmission, the function of relay is used to implement greedy algorithm. Its main idea is as following. Firstly, according to the scale of volume, the vehicle location coordinates on the map are randomly assigned to the source vehicle and the destination vehicle. It is worth noting that for each pair of source and destination vehicles, the vehicle coordinates cannot be the same. Then, the function introduces queue, a four-dimensional array that records the coordinates of the source vehicles, the traffic of the source, and the location of the next node. After that, when transmitting a data from source to destination, a function named NumofCars is also used to calculate the number of vehicles in the specific range between the source and the destination, and the positions of the vehicles are sorted by distance from small to large, which are all stored in an array, POS. If the destination vehicle is the closest vehicle to the source vehicle, the transmission is successful; Otherwise, the nearest vehicle is used as the source, and the coordinates of the destination are loaded into the volume of the vehicle, so as to complete an update of the routing table. In the process of continuously updating the route according to the traffic volume, the information is transmitted in a cycle of optimal route until all the information reaches the destination or the transmission fails. In the communication process of every two vehicles, the information can get the optimal path to be transmitted every time so as to realize the greedy algorithm. Finally, after each transmission, the relay function calculates the delay according to the traffic volume, and calculates the number of hops based on the number of nodes between the source and destination.

After all iterations, the total time of delay, the number of hops and failures are computed by the main program and reflected as figures.

The algorithm flow of Model3 is shown in the Fig. 3 below.

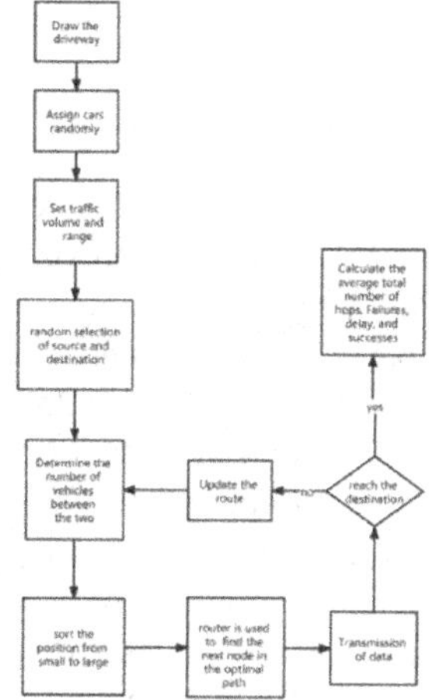

Fig. 3. Greedy algorithm flow based on volume update

2.4 Model4

The algorithm process of Model4 is basically consistent with model3, but the only difference is that after sorting the position distance between the source vehicle and the destination vehicle, this function will further sort the position coordinates according to the traffic volume of each vehicle from small to large, which can be used to get the more better transmission path in order to reduce the delay and transmission loss.

The flow chart of model4 is shown as following (Fig. 4).

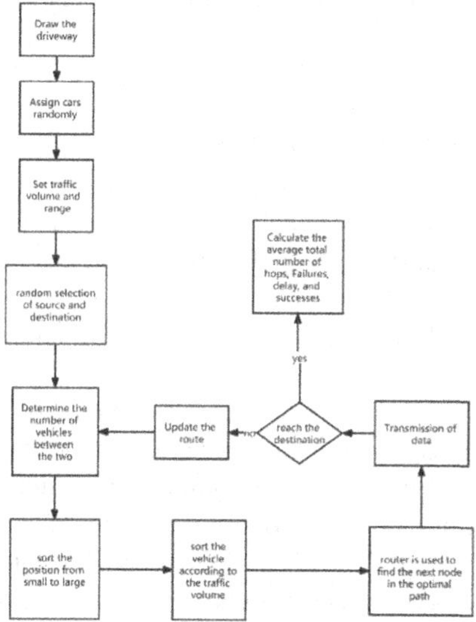

Fig. 4. Greedy algorithm flow based on volume update-new

3 Result and Discussion

3.1 Single Range and Mixed Range

As mentioned above this paper demonstrated the improvement of the transmission range of the original greedy algorithm in IoV, so as to improve the transmission efficiency and reduce the transmission delay and failure rate. In order to fit the actual traffic situation, based on MATLAB codes, this paper tested the single range of transmission range of 250 m, 350 m, 450 m, 550 m, and the mixed range of 250 m & 550 m, 250 m & 450 m, 350 m & 550 m, and 250 m & 350 m & 450 m & 550 m, which are all based on the condition that the number of changes in traffic density is 40, and the change interval is 0.02. The result of the value is clearly shown as following.

In the traditional wireless communication network analysis, the increase of node density, the small transmission distance, and the increase of signal strength will improve the communication quality and connectivity probability, but this will also lead to the enhancement of interference received by the node, which will reduce the communication quality and network connectivity probability [9]. When a vehicle forwards a message to the next vehicle, the wireless channel is affected by a combination of path loss and small-scale fading. When the transmission mode with fewer hops is adopted in the area, the transmission channel condition is poor and the receiving success rate is low. When hops are large, the transmission distance each time decreases, and the average accepted SNR increases, while multi-hop propagation may cause a long delay and higher cost due to more complex network structure [10]. The number of hops in each cycle of transmission is calculated by the function of relay, which completes the computation by counting the number of nodes in each cycle. With the increase of car density, the number of hops obtained from each loop is added to the array, and a common value is obtained after several iterations. The data obtained from the final results are drawn in the form of line graph in the coordinate system with den-change as the X-axis and the number of hops as the Y-axis, and the changes under each range are distinguished by color. When the transmission range of vehicles is small and single, it can be predicted that the number of hops has been maintained in a relatively high range due to the dependence of transmission on each node. However, if the range is large then the number of forwarding nodes required in a specific range is small, the number of hops is small. The result is expected to be seen that the performance of hybrid-range can make the hops of system balance between the two.

As shown in Fig. 5, within a given traffic range, the number of hops in a single transmission range is always maintained at a high (250 m) or low (550) level, which may lead to unstable transmission or excessive transmission energy consumption. However, the number of hops in a mixed range is moderate, which meets above expectation.

In this experiment, when there is no communication vehicle within the set range in the process of cyclic transmission of information, it is marked as a failure. The number of failures in a transmission is also executed by the relay function, and the main program, cellular, calculates the average number of failures and the change of delivery ratio with the increase of vehicle density through cyclic iteration.

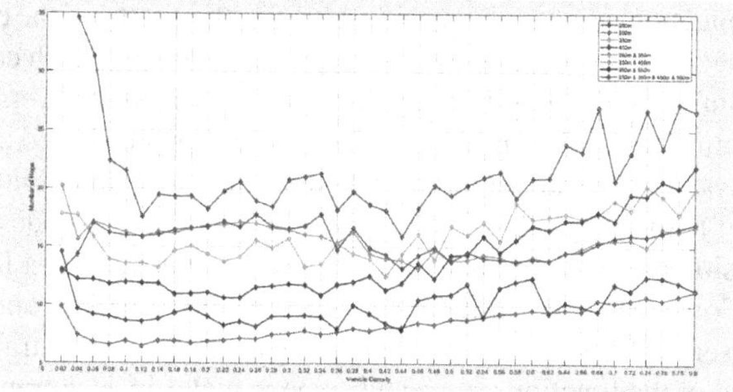

Fig. 5. Number of Hops

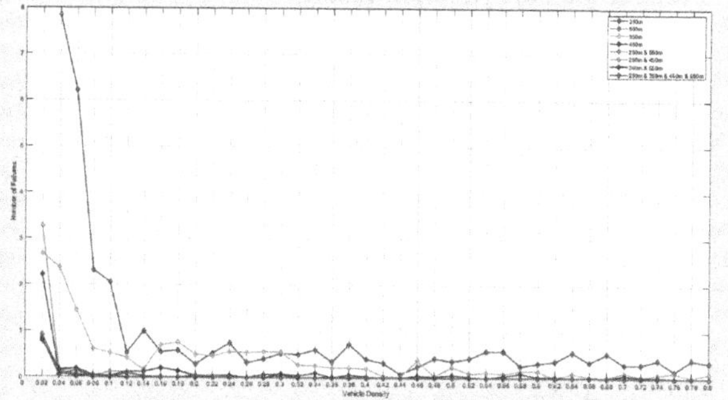

Fig. 6. Number of Failures

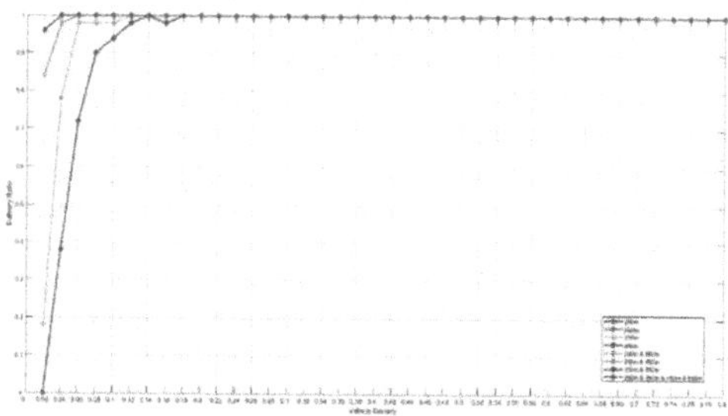

Fig. 7. Delivery Ratio

In Fig. 6, at a low vehicle density, the number of failures is lower and lower as increasement of range, which means a high failure rate in the condition of small transmission range in IoV communication. According to Fig. 7, when the vehicle is maintained at a lower density level, the success rate of information transmission in a single lower range is lower. In the actual traffic conditions, when the car keeps driving at a high speed, such a situation is easy to cause a high accident rate. Therefore, it is very important to increase the transmission success rate by improving the transmission range when the vehicle density is low.

In the communication process of a specific network, the energy of the communication node of wireless network sensor technology is relatively limited, which easily causes the delay of data transmission and thus the loss of data, which affects the overall performance of the communication network application system [11]. As mentioned above, the node efficiency of the system plays an important role in the transmission of information. Due to the limitation of hardware cost, the data storage space of sensor nodes is limited, and the data transmission delay should not be too large [12]. Otherwise, a large amount of data will be lost. Considering the limitation of data transmission delay and the number of hops in the actual sensor network system, the waiting time of each data transmission is set during the running of the function, relay, and some vehicles in each transmission range are randomly selected to cause delay to simulate the actual traffic situation. Finally, the main program iteratively shows the total time of delay and the mean of delay by drawing the line diagram to reflect the experimental results.

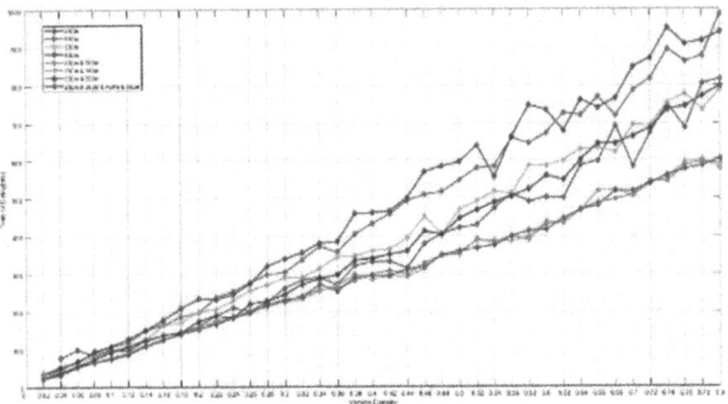

Fig. 8. Time of Delay (ms)

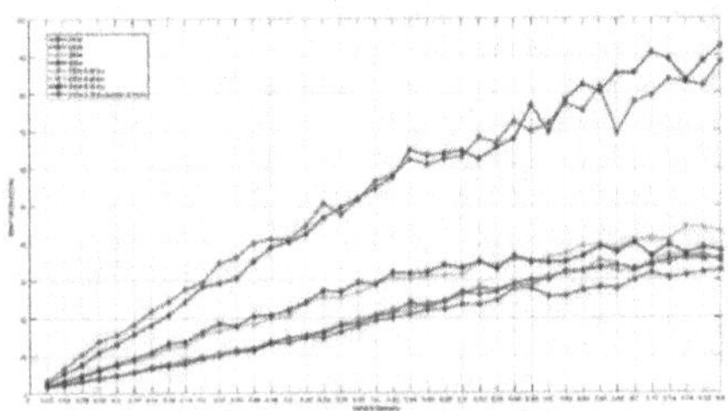

Fig. 9. Mean of Delay (ms)

Figure 8 and Fig. 9 both demonstrate the variation of delay with vehicle density in different ranges. In a single range, when the transmission range is large, with the increase of vehicle density, the number of vehicles involved in relay increases, which directly causes the increase of delay. However, the hybrid range solves this problem well. The updated greedy algorithm optimizes the transmission route and calculates the transmission process separately for different transmission ranges, thus greatly reducing the transmission delay.

By analyzing the above results, it is possible to find that the in the field of IoV transmission, especially in the traffic with low vehicle density, the greedy algorithm in the hybrid transmission range can achieve a good balance between reducing the delay and improving the transmission success rate, and maintain the transmission loss and stability at a moderate level.

3.2 New Algorithm Based on Volume

The data processing and calculation methods of the new algorithm are basically similar to those of model1 and 2. Based on the volume variable, the two algorithms in this experiment also calculate the number of nodes that pass through a cycle through the relay function to get hops and calculate the delay based on the time transmission interval of each message of traffic. Finally, the main program reflects the experimental results by drawing line charts. According to the algorithm structure mentioned above, the result can be expected that because the vehicle location coordinates are sorted according to the traffic volume, the new routing table can make the time of delay of each transmission process lower, which achieves the purpose of optimizing system performance.

According to the conditions in Table 1, in this experiment, the vehicle transmission range is set as 550 m, the traffic volume is set as 100, the vehicle density is changed 40 times with 0.02 interval, and the overall iteration is 10 times to obtain a general result.

The following four figures show the result of performance two model in IoV transmission.

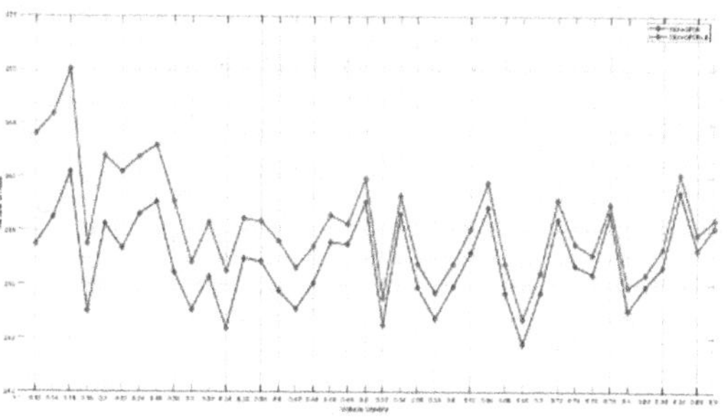

Fig. 10. Number of hops in new algorithm

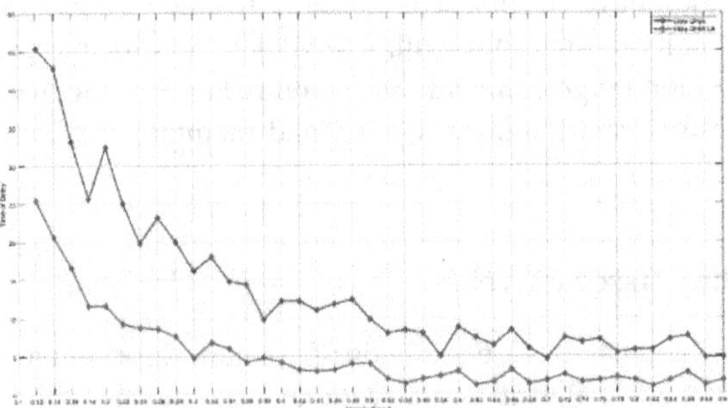

Fig. 11. Time of delay in new algorithm

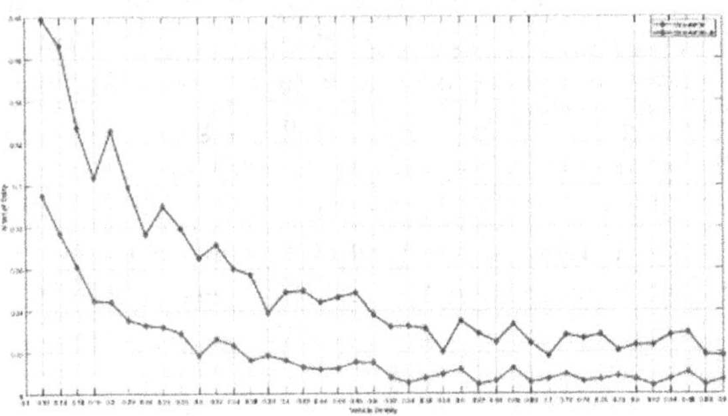

Fig. 12. Mean of delay in new algorithm

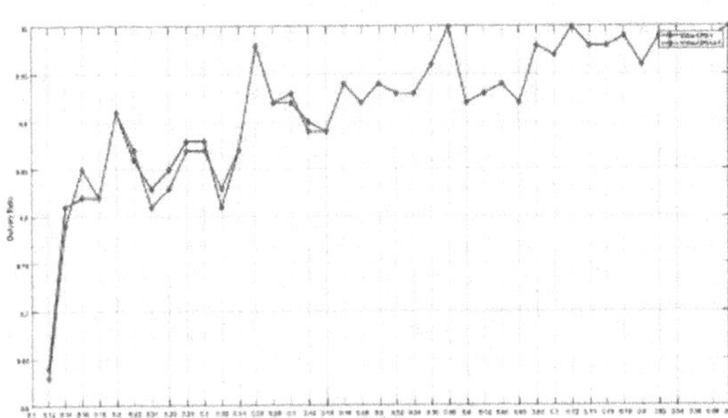

Fig. 13. Delivery Ratio in new algorithm

According to the above results, since sorting vehicle position coordinates using the volume to update the routing table in order to get the optimal path, compared with model3 in Fig. 11 and Fig. 12, the new algorithm greatly reduces the time of delay as well as them mean of delay, in which way it improves the efficiency of system while maintaining similar the number hops and higher success ratio, as shown in Fig. 10 and Fig. 13.

4 Conclusion

As a novel routing protocol for datagram networks, Greedy Perimeter Stateless Routing (GPSR) uses the positions of routers and a packet's destination to make packet forwarding decisions [13]. This paper applies this idea to the field of IoV transmission, and uses MATLAB to establish four kinds of system models based on greedy algorithm to simulate the real traffic situation for experimental testing. The experimental results verify the superiority of greedy algorithm in mixed transmission range and the superiority of the new algorithm which introduces volume to update transmission routes. Both algorithms can reduce system delay and improve system efficiency to a certain extent. In the future development, we also got inspiration on) heterogeneous networks and the social relationship inference model, that gives out new perspective for privacy preservation in mobility data, we can further develop advance greedy algorithm that achieve better performance and provide more positive social impact [14, 15].

References

1. Kar, U.N., Sanyal, D.K.: An overview of device-to-device communication in cellular networks. ICT Express S2405959517301467 (2017)
2. Schrank, D., Eisele, B., Lomax, T.: TTIS 2012 urban mobility report, Texas A&M Transportation (2012)
3. Wu, H.-P., Shen, W.-H., Wei, Y.-L., Tsai, H.-M., Xie, Q.: Traffic shockwave mitigation with human-driven vehicles: is it feasible? In: Proceedings of the First ACM International Workshop on Smart, Autonomous, and Connected Vehicular Systems and Services, 03–07 October 2016, pp. 38–43. ACM, New York City (2016)
4. Thota, J., et al.: V2V for vehicular safety applications. IEEE Trans. Intell. Transp. Syst. **21**(6), 2571–2585 (2020)
5. Hu, F.: Vehicle-to-Vehicle and Vehicle-to-Infrastructure Communications: A Technical Approach. Taylor & Francis, CRC Press, Boca Raton (2018)
6. Greedy Algorithms InTech (2008)
7. Cerrone, C., Cerulli, R., Golden, B.: Carousel greedy: a generalized greedy algorithm with applications in optimization. Comput. Oper. Res. **85**, 97–112 (2017)
8. Wu, S., Sheng, Y., Deng, H.: Optimization method of measurement node selection based on improved greedy algorithm. Comput. Modernization **04**, 79–84 (2021)
9. Jing, T.: Car networking D2D wireless resource allocation algorithms. Southwest Jiaotong University (2019). https://doi.org/10.27414/dcnki.Gxnju.2019.001198
10. Hu, D.: Performance Analysis and Optimization Design of Vehicle Mobile Communication Network in Interference Scenario. Southwest Jiaotong University (2017)
11. Lei, W., Li, S., Chen, J.: A fountain of security information between vehicle transmission scheme and the optimal hop analysis. J. Harbin Univ. Sci. Technol. **17**(5), 70–75+81 (2013). https://doi.org/10.15938/j.jhust.2013.05.023
12. Yang, F., Ma, M.: Delay compensation algorithm for data transmission in wireless multi-hop communication networks. Comput. Simul. **39**(04), 146–149+253 (2022)
13. Karp, B.: GPSR: greedy perimeter stateless routing for wireless networks. ACM Mobicom (2000)
14. Jiang, H., Xiao, Z., Li, Z., Xu, J., Zeng, F., Wang, D.: An energy-efficient framework for internet of things underlaying heterogeneous small cell networks. IEEE Trans. Mob. Comput. **21**(1), 31–43 (2022)
15. Li, J., et al.: Drive2friends: inferring social relationships from individual vehicle mobility data. IEEE Internet Things J. **7**(6), 5116–5127 (2020)

Precise Segmentation on Poly-Yolo, YoloV5 and FCN

Xinyuan Cai[1(✉)], Yangchenchen Jin[2], Yunfei Liao[3], Jiawen Tian[4], and Yancong Deng[5]

[1] Purdue University, West Lafayette, USA
cai282@purdue.edu
[2] Sun Yat-sen University, Guangzhou, China
jinychch@mail2.sysu.edu.cn
[3] University of Electronic Science, and Technology of China, Chengdu, China
pwlykfp@std.uestc.edu.cn
[4] University of New South Wales, Sydney, Australia
[5] University of California, San Diego, San Diego, USA
yad002@eng.ucsd.edu

Abstract. Nowadays, computer vision is becoming more and more popular and is applied to lots of fields. It can be used to detect safe and unsafe behavior happening in construction area [6]. It can also used for auto-vehicle driving, object detection, and so on. Currently, there are several ways to realize this like FCN and YOLO. However, they all exist some limitation. For example, the bounding box of YOLO is always being castigated by the user. There are a lot of versions of YOLO with different solutions to this kind of issues aiming to be used in different circumstances. Poly-YOLO is one of them. It decently solved the bounding box issue by using polygons rather than rectangles. In the paper, we focused on several techniques to achieve object detection. The YOLO approach will be mainly talked about for application, since it can be easily used combined with other algorithms like semantic segmentation, FCN, and etc. to enhance its performance. What's more, the computation speed of Poly-YOLO is the main advantage why people choose YOLO.

1 Introduction

Object detection is one of the most popular topic, since it can be used in wild areas, like self-driving cars, detecting safe and unsafe behavior during the lab, police department, face detection. It is a computer technology involved in computer vision, image processing, machine learning, artificial intelligence, and so on. At the same it is also challenging, especially during the time when there still exists a lot of unsolved problems involving in detecting the subjects overlapping with each other.

Every object has its own features which is useful for us to do the classifications. For instance, all cellphones are rectangular, which is the feature for classification and, at the same time, for computer to learn. Today, we have several techniques that can solve most of the problems when doing the object detection. Basically, it can be divided into two techniques: non-neural approaches and neural network approaches. In most cases, neural network approaches can be more useful, since it can improve itself from

Z. Xiao et al. (Eds.): ICECI 2022, LNICST 478, pp. 54–68, 2023.
https://doi.org/10.1007/978-3-031-28990-3_5

the result of its accuracy. The most six popular tools are: Region Proposals, Single Shot Multi-Box Detector, YOLO, Single-shot Refinement Neural Network, Retina-Net, and Deformable convolutional networks. There is no doubt that YOLO is the most popular one, since it is relatively easy to use and has the smallest size. Therefore, YOLO will also be our main topic in the paper.

Under some circumstances, these existing tools are not enough to satisfy our requirement. For example, the original YOLO algorithm is not precise enough to indicate the bounding objects. Therefore, we can propose a new algorithm from the original version or combine the existing tool to compromise the shortage of each other. Therefore, in the following sections, we will go through the background of some important tools, and then introduce poly-YOLO which is based on existing tools but with huge improvements (Fig. 1).

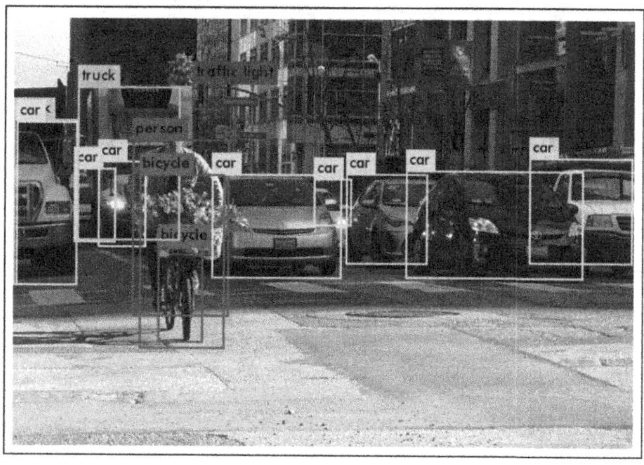

Fig. 1. How YOLO v3 looks like [5].

2 Related Work

2.1 Introduce of FCN

FCN stands for fully convolutional network. It is modified from the original convolutional network. Thus, before moving on to FCN, we focus on the convolutional network first.

The original convolutional network, which is also called ConvNet, is a deep learning algorithm. It can take in some images and then learn the feature among these images. These images need to be pre-processed, and assigned the weight of the feature for ConvNet to learn. The whole structure of convolutional network is analogous to human's brain; each node can be analogous to the neuron inside human's brain. Each neuron stores important information about the features of the images which will be used to detect the category of upcoming images. Although convolutional networks are powerful visual models that yield hierarchies of features, there still exists some limitation. One of the shortages is that it can also take fixed size of images, which is the reason why fully convolutional network shows up.

One step further, for the fully convolutional network, the basic idea is to do the normal convolutional network first and shrink the size of the image. After that, it will do the up sampling which I think is the key point in fully convolutional network. The special difference of this method is that it can take arbitrary size of image instead of fixed size of image [2].

By using the arbitrary size of image as input, we do the normal convolution first, using ReLU, shrink the pool, and repeat these steps. At the end, it uses up sampling to convert the image to specific sizes. Finally we do the classification on the images [2].

In sum, the key point for this FCN will be the upsampling, and with the different combination of up sampling, there are FCN32, FCN16, and FCN8 separately (Fig. 2).

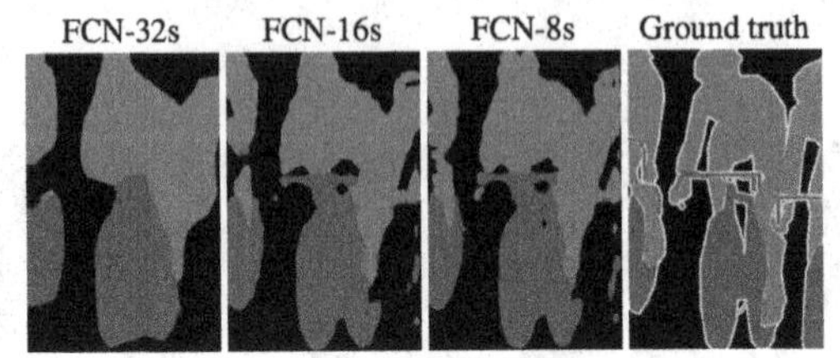

Fig. 2. Difference between FCN32, 16, 8 and Ground truth.

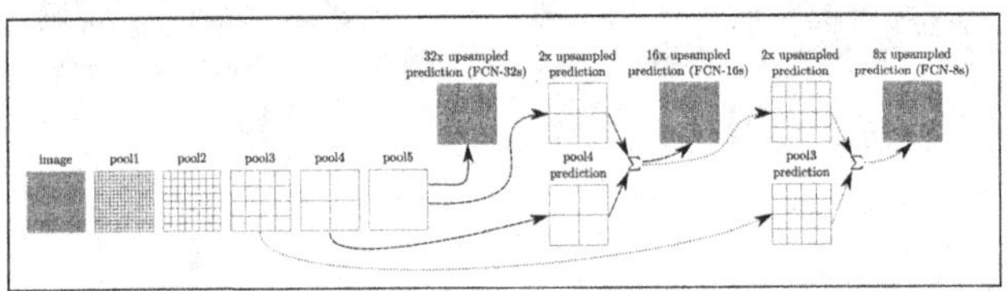

Fig. 3. The architecture of FCN [2]

2.2 Evolution of YOLO

YOLO stands for "You only look once", which is a viral and widely used algorithm. It is famous for its object detection characteristic. The main advantage of YOLO is model's small size and fast calculation speed. The structure of YOLO is straightforward. It can directly output the position and category of the bounding box through the neural network. The speed of YOLO is fast because YOLO only need to put the picture into the network to get the final detection result. YOLO's test results are poor for objects that are very close to each other and in groups. This poor performance is because only two boxes in the grid are predicted and only belong to a new class of objects of the same category.

Except the YOLO v1-5, it also has a few revised-limited versions such as YOLO-LITE and Poly-YOLO, which will be used in the later task. There are five main YOLO versions.

The original YOLO architecture consists of 24 convolution layers, followed by two fully connected layers. However, it has two defects: one is inaccurate positioning, and the other is the lower recall rate.

YOLO V2 improves these two defects from the V1, so it makes YOLO better and faster. The better is in four aspects: batch normalization, high-resolution classier, fine features, and multi-scale training. The faster is in three aspects: Darknet-19, training for clarification, and training for detection [1].

The difference between YOLO V2 and V3 is that YOLO V3 uses multi-scale features for object detection and adjusts the basic network structure. YOLO V3 also adopts feature graphs of three scales. YOLO V3 uses three prior boxes for each position, so K-means is used to get nine prior boxes and divide them into three scale feature maps. Feature maps with larger-scale use smaller prior boxes. What's more, YOLO V3 features extraction network used the residual model. Compared with Darknet- 19 used by YOLO V2, it contained 53 convolution layers, so it was called Darknet-53 [1].

The style of YOLO V4 has huge difference compared to the previous versions, more focus on comparing data, and has a substantial improvement. The integrator characterizes it and finally achieves very high performance. We can summarize it like this: YOLO V4 = CSP Darknet53+SPP+Pan+YOLO V3 [1].

Due to the multiple network architectures used by YOLO V5, it becomes more flexible to be used. At the same time, the model size of YOLO V5 is fairly small without losing the accuracy compared to the YOLO V4. However, people still keep reserved opinion towards YOLO V5 because it is less innovative than YOLO V4, but it has some performance improvements [1].

2.3 Limitations and Improvements

The main target of object detection is to distinguish the objects from the various background. However, sometimes the background contains other distracted objects which are not the objects we are intended to detect but look similar. Here comes the disadvantage of original YOLO algorithm. The original YOLO algorithm uses bounding boxes to indicate the detected objects. Nevertheless, some objects have extremely complex shapes. As a result, the bounding boxes cannot wrap the object tightly so that the distracted items at background will take up most of the areas inside the bounding boxes. To some extents, it reduced the performance of a classifier which will be applied over the bounding box. Shortly, it cannot satisfy the requirement when it comes to precise object detection. Here is the reason why we need poly-YOLO.

As mentioned before, besides these five main versions of YOLO, there also exists modified version of YOLO. One of the most useful one is POLY-YOLO. Poly-YOLO extends from the original architecture of YOLO V3, and, at the same time, it adds the feature of segmentation and improves the performance.

Since using a rectangle to show the boundary of objects is not precise enough, POLY-YOLO appeals to instance segmentation. Instead of rectangle, polygons are used to bound tightly enough around the detected objects. POLY-YOLO can learn itself in size-independent shapes according to the bounding box. Also, to bound tightly, POLY-YOLO can create a dynamic number of vertices per polygon. The number of vertices depends on how complex the shape is. Intuitively, if the number of vertices are large enough, it will be similar as curves by the human-eyes.

What's more, it removes two of its weaknesses: a lot of repeating labels and inefficient distribution of anchors. To solve the label rewriting issue, they adjust the value of scale multiplicator so that the output and input resolutions are equal. To address the inefficient distribution of anchors, POLY-YOLO will create an architecture with a single output to aggregate information from various scales. Such improvements make POLY-YOLO easily to be integrated into various scenarios [3].

3 Comparative Methodology

3.1 Mathematics of FCN

Fully Convolutional Network is used to generate multi-dimension array rather than one-dimension array which is used by CNN. The basic architecture is shown in the Fig. 3. The FCN structure is divided into 5 blocks and 2 convolutions. We can divide 5 blocks into two groups: block 1–2 and block 3–5. For block 1–2, the input data will be convoluted twice, followed by a pooling process. The number of process of convolution is different between two groups. For block 3–5, they have 3 convolutional layers, followed by the same pooling process. Since FCN is based on VGG16, the basic information about each block is the same as the block in VGG16. The basic procedure of VGG16 can be summarized by the Fig. 4.

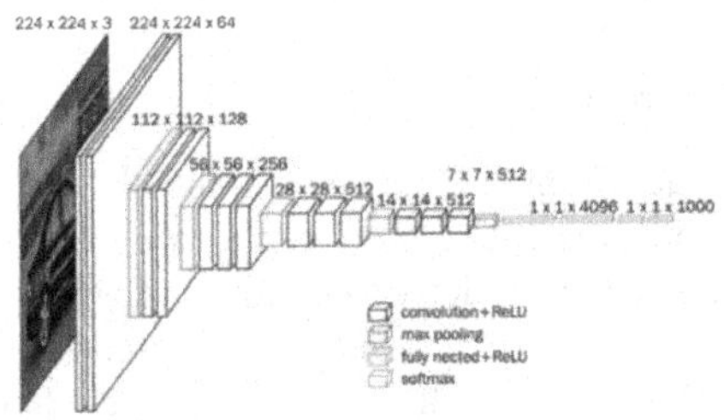

Fig. 4. Structure of VGG16 [4]

From the Fig. 4, it is clear that there are five pools in the model. Therefore, the size of final block five will be 2^5 times smaller than the size of input image. That's the reason why up-sampling is critical in FCN so that the different layers can match with each other. Then they will be added together. In short, up-sampling is to make different layers have same shapes to add with each other. The key point is that up-sampling won't change the dimension, instead it will only change the size - height and width. The following is the steps of up-sampling: [4] (Fig. 5)

- unpooling
- interpolation
- deconvolution
- dilated convolution

There also exists FCN version which is based on ResNet and Vanilla instead of VGG16.

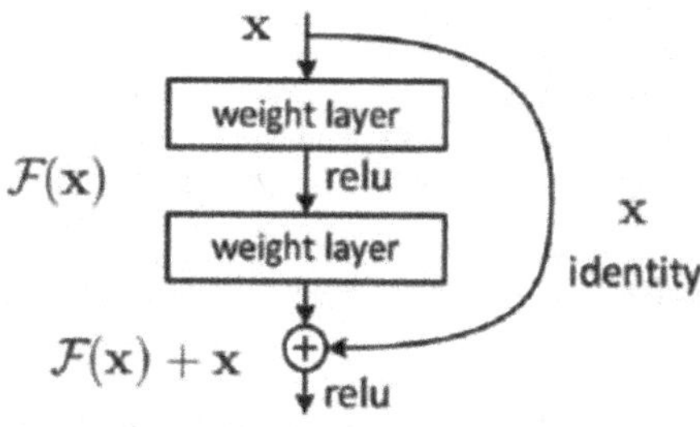

Fig. 5. Principle of residual learning [4]

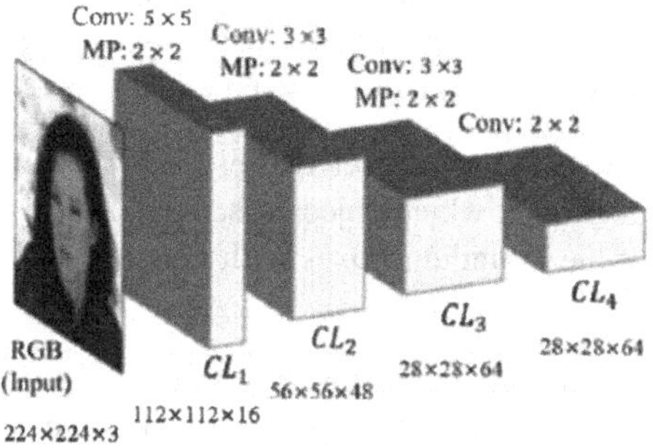

Fig. 6. Structure of Vanilla CNN [4]

For ResNet, instead of 5 blocks with fully connected layer, it uses principle of residual learning to combine different information together, which finally increase the accuracy.

For Vanilla, it replaces 5 blocks in VGG16 with structure in Fig. 6. The Vanilla algorithm won't fuse any layers together. It is just the structure of Fig. 4 and followed by conv6 and conv7.

3.2 Mathematics of YOLO

As mentioned on the related work, there are 5 versions of YOLO: v1 to v5. V1 to V3 were created by Joseph Redmon and Ali Farhadi. Since poly-YOLO is developed upon YOLOv3, we focus on the version 3 of YOLO in this paper which is more accurate compared to the original YOLO.

The general idea of YOLO v3 [7] algorithm is that the input image will be processed by a neural network with a result of bounding boxes and the prediction labels. In detail, one frame will be extracted from a video. Then this frame will be resized to 416×416. The resized frame will be given to the neural network which is similar to CNN, to do the prediction.

There are different neural network can be used by YOLO such as Darknet-19, ResNet-101, ResNet-152, and Darknet-53. The differences between these neural net-

Backbone	Top-1	Top-5	Ops	BFLOP/s	FPS
Darknet-19	74.1	91.8	7.29	1246	**171**
ResNet-101	77.1	93.7	19.7	1039	53
ResNet-152	**77.6**	**93.8**	29.4	1090	37
Darknet-53	77.2	**93.8**	18.7	**1457**	78

Fig. 7. Comparison between different kernels

work are the accuracy and the efficiency. For example, the YOLOv2 uses Darknet-19 and YOLO v3 uses Darknet-53 instead. It is true that Darknet-19 can process more frames per second than Darknet-53, but Darknet-53 has 53 convolutional layers instead of 19, which means that Darknet-53 are more powerful (shows in Fig. 7). The basic architecture of Darknet-53 consists of the following elements [5]: convolutional layers, residual layers, upsampling layers, and skip connections. After processed by Darknet-53, the output vector consisting of the following parameters is return: [5]

- The input image is divided into grid cells. There is a one cell corresponding to an object on the image to predict which object it is.
- The grid will predict the bounding boxes with classification information (Figs. 8 and 9).

There are five components in the bounding boxes (x, y, a, b, c). x, y is the coordinates of the center of the boxes. a, b is the width and the height of the box. c is the confidence value.

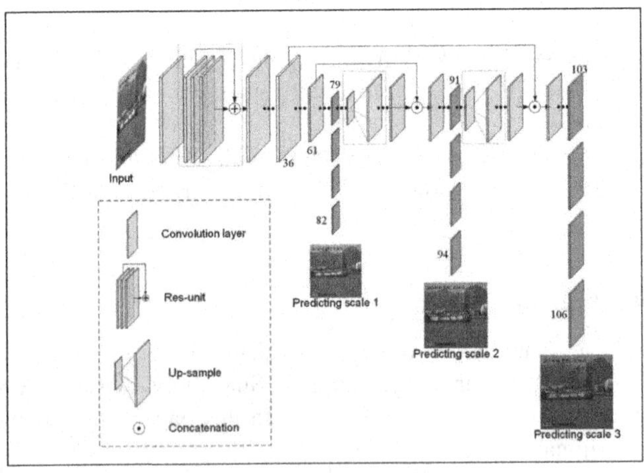

Fig. 8. The architecture of Darknet-53 [5]

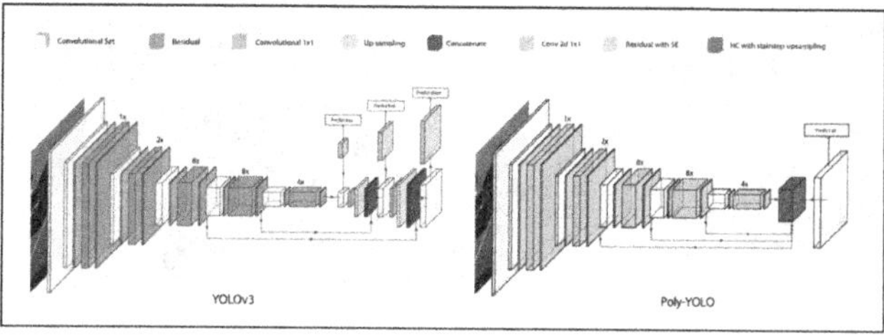

Fig. 9. Comparison between YOLOv3 and Poly-YOLO [3].

It also uses statistical method called "Intersection over Union" to determine whether the object detection algorithm is working or not. The Intersection over Union can be simplified as IOU:

$$IOU = \frac{Area\ of\ Intersection}{Area\ of\ Union}$$

If the result is greater or equal to 0.5, we can label it as "correct".

What's more, to avoid bounding boxes multiple times for each object, it also uses a technique called Non-max Suppression (NMS). The NMS is to guarantee that this algorithm will only detect each subject only once. The basic algorithm about how NMS works is that it first searches for a particular object with largest probabilities, which means it detects the object with the most confidence. Then NMS will also search for the remaining bounding boxes. With the help of IOU mentioned above, the bounding boxes can be suppressed into only one bounding box for each object.

3.3 Mathematics of Poly-YOLO

Poly-YOLO is based on YOLOv3. It solves the label rewriting problem in YOLOv3. There is a scale multiplicator to express the ratio of the output resolution to input resolution r. They donate this ratio as s_k [3]. It is obvious that the ideal goal is to make $r = rs_k$ and we can get that $s_k = 1$. This result means that the output resolutions will be equal to the input resolutions. Under this circumstance, there will be no label rewriting [3]. The U-Net is also using such condition [8]. To provide more accuracy, the Poly-YOLO architecture is using "squeeze-and-excitation (SE) blocks" in the backbone [9], since Darknet-53 has repetitive blocks and each block consist of coupled convolutions with residual connection [3]. Instead, the squeeze-and-excitation blocks uses spatial and channel-wise information to improve the accuracy [3]. However, the limitation of this is that it will slow down the computation speed. The reason why the series of YOLO is popular is that it has high computation speed. Therefore, in the feature extraction phase, Poly-YOLO reduced the number of convolutional filters. It reduces to $3/4$ of the original convolutional filters [3]. At the same time, the precision of Poly-YOLO is still higher than YOLOv3. For the processing speed consideration, they also propose Poly-YOLO lite whose number of parameters is only 16.5M, comparing with YOLOv3 which is 61.5M (Figs. 10 and 11).

Fig. 10. How Poly-YOLO looks like [3].

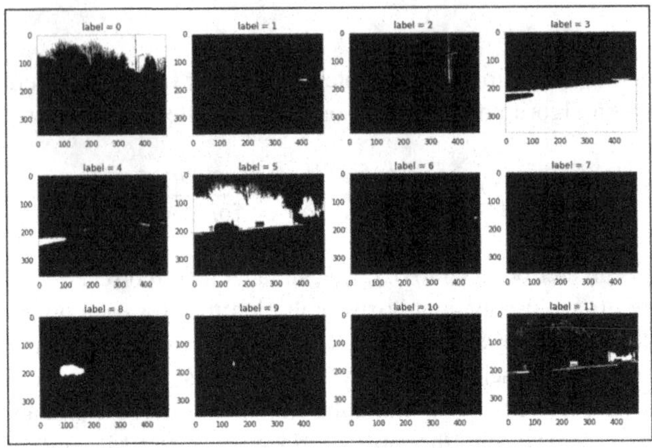

Fig. 11. FCN8 result without color assigned.

There is a sentence at the end of the paper of YOLOv3 saying that "Boxes are stupid anyway though, I'm probably a true believer in masks except I can't get YOLO to learn them" [7]. Thus, Poly-YOLO fixes this issue with bounding polygons instead of rectangle. In YOLOv3, they use Cartesian coordinate system to determine the bounding boxes. In poly-YOLO, they switch to polar coordinate system so that the network can learn more general and size-independent shapes instead of some particular instances with sizes [3]. In more understandable way, for instance, the same objects like cars will have different sizes corresponding to the distance from the cameras, smaller one and bigger one. The polar coordinate system model to train the images by using the angles, relative distance from the center of bounding box, confidence. Clearly, these values will be the same for both objects in the images, no matter the distance from the camera. After getting these values, the distances will be multiplied with these values to get particular values of the cars with different values. Since the values before being multiplied with distance can be shared with the same objects, the learning procedure can be simplified and speed up.

4 Experiments

4.1 FCN8

In an image for the semantic segmentation, each pixel is labeled with the class of its enclosing object. The semantic segmentation problem requires to make a classification at every pixel, which means that the dataset is needed to train the data.

FCN8 first trained the data and did the segmentation with black and white result. We then assigned color to it. In this experiment, we use sns color palette to assign color to the pattern. To simplify the problem, we reshaped all the images to the same size: (224, 224). Since VGG and FCN model both use this image shape. This blog uses a network which takes advantage of VGG structure. As a result, the FCN module becomes much easier to explain when the shape of the image is (224, 224) (Fig. 12).

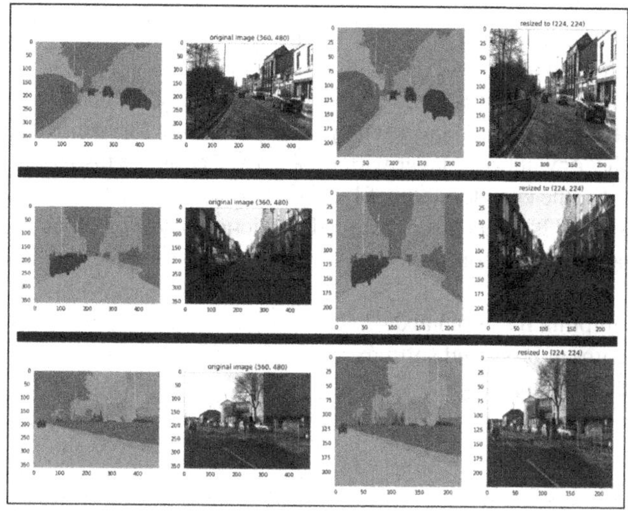

Fig. 12. FCN8 result with sns color palette assigned

VGG and some other successful deep learning models is original designed for performing classification. After combining its convolution layers with max-pooling and then stacking fully connected layers, it becomes able to learn something using global information where the spatial arrangement of the input falls away. For the segmentation task, however, spatial information should be stored to make a pixel-wise classification. FCN allows this by making all the layers of VGG to convolutional layers. Fully convolutional indicates that the neural network is composed of convolutional layers without any fully-connected layers usually found at the end of the network. Fully Convolutional Networks for Semantic Segmentation motivates the use of fully convolutional networks by "convolutionalizing" popular CNN architectures e.g. VGG can also be viewed as FCN. The following method is FCN8 from Fully Convolutional Networks for Semantic Segmentation. It duplicates VGG16 net by discarding the final classifier layer and convert all fully connected layers to convolutions. Output image size is (output-height, output-width) = (224, 224).

The upsampling layer brings low resolution image to high resolution. There are various upsampling methods. This presentation gives a good overview. For example, one may double the image resolution by duplicating each pixel twice. This is so-called nearest neighbor approach and implemented in Keras's UpSampling2D. These upsampling layers do not have weights/parameters so the model is not flexible. Instead, FCN8 uses upsampling procedure called backwards convolution (sometimes called deconvolution) with output stride. This method simply reverses the forward and backward passes of convolution and implemented in Keras's Conv2DTranspose. In FCN8, the upsampling layer is followed by several skip connections. See details at Fully Convolutional Networks for Semantic Segmentation [2]. The following is the general procedure:

- input-height and width must be divisible by 32 because max-pooling with filter size = (2, 2) is operated 5 times
- Block 1 - 1st Convolutional layer with pool
- Block 2 - 2nd Convolutional layer with pool
- Block 3 - 3rd Convolutional layer with pool (save a copy for fusing upsampling)
- Block 4 - 4th Convolutional layer with pool (save a copy for fusing upsampling)
- Block 5 - 5th Convolutional layer with pool (save a copy for fusing upsampling)
- Set up VGG for the encoder parts of FCN8
- Conv6–7: (FCN-32s) and (2x up-sampled prediction based on block 5)
- 4 times upsampling for conv7: (FCN-32s) and (2x up-sampled prediction based on block 5)
- 2 times upsampling for pool3 and 4
- combine the upsampling and softmax
- create model and load weight.

4.2 YOLO

I choose YOLO v5 for this experiment since it is extremely to get and use. I use it through the torch module included in python. It is an amazingly easy module to use. The result image will have several box with the recognized name at the top left corner. The probability will also show up at the top right corner.

PyTorch supports both pre-trained dataset and customized dataset. It is simple to use pre-trained dataset. All you need to do is to set the parameter: pretrain = true. However, there are more steps if you would like to use customized dataset. The following is the procedure to use the customized dataset:

- create annotations
- create the dataset file
- train the dataset
- use the trained model to make predictions.

4.3 Poly-YOLO

I used pre-trained module inside the Poly-YOLO repository. There are two types of pertained module: poly-yolo and poly-yolo-lite. I used poly-yolo for this experiment. The result of the experiment for Poly-yolo is shown in Figureh. Since I used pertained model, the procedure is fairly simple. All I did is to load the model, setting the parameter $iou = 0.8$ and $score = 0.5$. The final thing is to set the color class. This is necessary because the color will be filled inside the bounding polygon, which can make the detected object stand out. From the Fig. 16, you can see that Poly-YOLO indeed fits the issue of bounding boxes, enabling the objects to be distinguished more easily from each other. However, not every object can be detected in this Fig. 16, which means that the accuracy of poly-YOLO are lower comparing to the FCN8 and YOLO.

5 Conclusion

From the experiment, we can see the advantage and disadvantage of FCN8, YOLOv5, and Poly-YOLO (Figs. 13, 14 and 15).

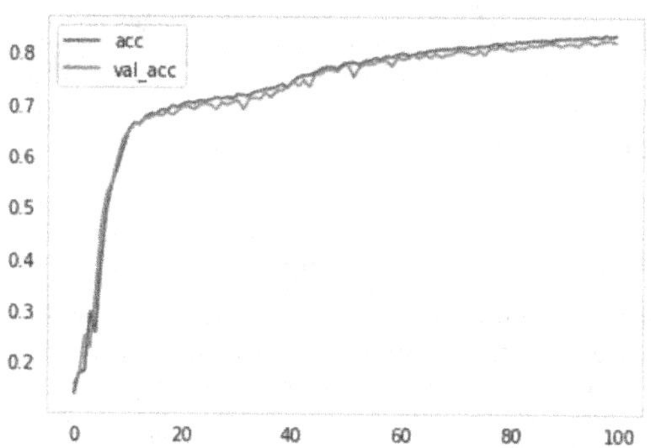

Fig. 13. Plot accuracy and value accuracy vs epoch (epochs = 100)

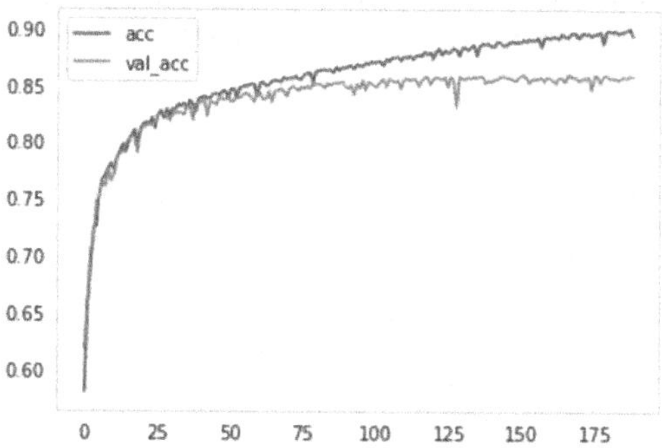

Fig. 14. Plot accuracy and value accuracy vs epoch (epochs = 188)

Fig. 15. The input image and output result from YOLOv5

FCN did a great work in doing the semantic segmentation. It is efficient asymptotically and absolutely. It eliminates a lot of complications needs in other work [2]. The best feature is that it doesn't specify the size of images. It also reduces the quantity of parameters for network because of the multiple convolution and pooling layers. As a result, it can simplify and improve the efficiency of learning. However, the shortcoming is also obvious. It will change the background into the same color, since FCN8 performs the semantic segmentation first, and then uses different color to present each part. Sometimes, it will be hard to recognize the detected object. This method will lose a bunch of information comparing to the original image.

Fig. 16. Experiment result by using Poly-YOLO.

The YOLO method avoids this shortcoming by using a really smart way. It create a bounding box around the detected object. It will show the detected label on the upper-left corner and the probability on the upper-right corner. Therefore, basically it didn't lose any information and that's also the reason why YOLO is extremely appropriate for the real-time detection, since it keeps all the things on the image. Its computation speed is also fast enough for the real-time detection. Therefore, this technique has already been use in a lot of areas, e.g.: using YOLO to detect unsafe behavior happening in the construction area [6]. However, the disadvantage for YOLO is also clear to see. Like the last sentence on the YOLOv3 paper: "Boxes are stupid anyway though, I'm probably a true believer in masks except I can't get YOLO to learn them" [7]. The box will cause a lot of confusions especially when two objects are really close to each other. Sometimes, it will be hard to distinguish which the object the box is bounding to. Poly-YOLO solves the issue of bounding box by using polygon instead of rectangle. By using the mathematical limit thinking, it is understandable that the polygon can be recognized as curved if there are infinite sides. That's how it works. By using multiple sides of polygon, the bounding polygon can be as close as enough to the detected object, which means that it won't bound unnecessary objects to increase the chance of confusion. What's more, in this way, the color can be filled into the bounding polygon to make the detected object stand out and easy to distinguish. Since it won't bound other objects into the bounding polygon, filling in color won't make the image lose any information comparing to the original image. However, due to the excellent the performance of Poly-YOLO, the computation is indeed slower that the other two. But, it is not slow too much. It removes few convolutional layers to increase the efficiency. What's more, the accuracy of Poly-YOLO is also lower than the other two (Fig. 17).

Fig. 17. Difficult to distinguish when objects are too close to each other [7]

In conclusion, each one has its own advantage. From my perspective, I prefer to give Poly-YOLO highest credits among those three. In practical usage, we can choose different tool according to various situations.

References

1. Jiang, P., Ergu, D., Liu, F., Cai, Y., Ma, B.: A review of yolo algorithm developments. Proc. Comput. Sci. **199**, 1066–1073 (2022). https://doi.org/10.1016/j.procs.2022.01.135. ISSN 1877-0509
2. Shelhamer, E., Long, J., Darrell, T.: Fully convolutional networks for semantic segmentation (2016)
3. Hurtík, P., Molek, V., Hula, J., Vajgl, M., Vlasánek, P., Nejezchleba, T.: Poly-YOLO: higher speed, more precise detection and instance segmentation for YOLOv3. CoRR, abs/2005.13243 (2020)
4. Hu, T., Deng, Y., Deng, Y., Ge, A.: Fully convolutional network variations and method on small dataset. In: 2021 IEEE International Conference on Consumer Electronics and Computer Engineering (ICCECE), pp. 40–46 (2021). https://doi.org/10.1109/ICCECE51280.2021.9342059
5. Kumar, S., Yadav, D., Gupta, H., Verma, O.P., Ansari, I.A., Ahn, C.W.: A novel YOLOv3 algorithm-based deep learning approach for waste segregation: towards smart waste management. Electronics **10**(1), 14 (2021). https://doi.org/10.3390/electronics10010014
6. Yu, Y., Guo, H., Ding, Q., Li, H., Skitmore, M.: An experimental study of real-time identification of construction workers' unsafe behaviors. Autom. Constr. **82**, 193–206 (2017). https://doi.org/10.1016/j.autcon.2017.05.002. ISSN 0926-5805
7. Redmon, J., Farhadi, A.: YOLOv3: an incremental improvement. CoRR, abs/1804.02767 (2018)
8. Ronneberger, O., Fischer, P., Brox, T.: U-net: convolutional networks for biomedical image segmentation. In: Navab, N., Hornegger, J., Wells, W.M., Frangi, A.F. (eds.) MICCAI 2015. LNCS, vol. 9351, pp. 234–241. Springer, Cham (2015). https://doi.org/10.1007/978-3-319-24574-4_28
9. Hu, J., Shen, L., Sun, G.: Squeeze-and-excitation networks. In: Proceedings of the IEEE Conference on Computer Vision and Pattern Recognition, pp. 7132–7141 (2018)

Adaptive Approaches to Manage Energy Consumption and Security of Systems

Research on DAG Based Consensus Mechanism for Adjustable Load Metering Data

Zhengwei Jiang[1], Hongtao Xia[1], Li Chang[2(✉)], Ying Yao[3], and Bin Ji[2]

[1] State Grid Zhejiang Electric Power Co., Ltd., Hangzhou 310007, Zhejiang, China
[2] NARI Group Corporation (State Grid Electric Power Research Institute Co., Ltd.), Nanjing 211106, Jiangsu, China
li.chang.narigroup@gmail.com
[3] State Grid Zhejiang Electric Power Co., Ltd., Electric Power Research Institute, Hangzhou 310014, Zhejiang, China

Abstract. The distributed ledger technology of blockchain can provide an efficient solution for the trustworthy problem of adjustable load metering data. However, due to the issues caused by nodal constrained resource of computation and storage, high concurrent transactions, and ledger data expansion with elapsed time, etc., it faces non-trivial challenges to design a consensus mechanism for second-level transaction data. This paper presents a shard-based DAG blockchain architecture for large-scale and distributed internet of things scenarios, where each device is a node of the network. These devices construct a multi-hop network, and by using the shard technology, some neighboring nodes belong to the same shard. The preference relationship between transactions is generated based on the shard-based DAG blockchain, and a scalable high throughput block consensus is designed such that using parallel treatment of transactions the throughput of blockchain can be significantly improved. Finally, to improve the limited computation and storage capability, we use container edge service engine in system design.

Keywords: Container Edge Service · Adjustable Load Metering Data · DAG · Blockchain

1 Introduction

With the deepening of electricity market, it is necessary to enhance mutual trust among power dispatching centers, power trading centers and market members. Block chain technology has the characteristics of decentralization, difficult to tamper with, traceability, openness and transparency, collective maintenance and programmability. It has broad application prospects in digital payment, trusted data management, information security and other aspects, and has attracted wide attention from academia and industry in recent years. It provides a new trust model under the open network, which adopts "autonomous governance and autonomous organization", so that participants can achieve mutual trust under the condition of decentralization. So, with the continuous improvement of load

Z. Xiao et al. (Eds.): ICECI 2022, LNICST 478, pp. 71–81, 2023.
https://doi.org/10.1007/978-3-031-28990-3_6

terminal side device level, the application of block chain technology in source-network load storage market transactions can realize the sharing and mutual trust of transaction data, traceability and tamper-proof, which is an important tool to enhance mutual trust and information security in market transactions, and has an increasingly wide application prospect in power system. Especially, the distributed account book is used to record the adjustable load metering data, and the reliable data storage and electricity fee settlement vouchers are realized in a trustless way, which is helpful to enhance the mutual trust in the source-network load storage transaction behavior.

Decentralization, security and scalability are the "impossible triangle" in blockchain. Traditional blockchain values decentralization and security at the cost of poor scalability, which is mainly manifested in a serious lack of throughput. Take Bitcoin as an example [1]. Because of the strict limitation of the fast time and the need for six block confirmations for each transaction, each Bitcoin transaction takes at least an hour to be confirmed, with more than 150,000 transactions queuing for confirmation at its peak. Therefore, the high latency of confirmation processing makes the processing rate (TPS) of Bitcoin only 5–7 times per second [2], and the TPS of Ethereum is 30–40 times per second, which is far less than the mainstream payment tools such as Visa and Alipay, of which the peak processing capacity of Visa is 60,000 unit per second [3], Alipay's peak processing capacity is as high as 85 thousand and 900 pens per second.

The scalability bottleneck of traditional blockchain is mainly attributed to its consensus mechanism and storage structure. Whether it is the workload proof mechanism or the rights and interests proof mechanism, it essentially requires the whole network nodes to participate in the accounting right competition to reach a consensus on each transaction in the system, which seriously limits the throughput of the block chain system. At the same time, Blockchain uses a chained serial structure to store blocks, only one block can be stored in each round, otherwise there will be a fork, and the capacity of each block is very limited, which makes it difficult to support high-concurrency application scenarios. On-chain expansion technology often cures the symptoms but not the root cause, and is prone to frequent bifurcation and increase the risk of double-flower attacks, thus affecting the security and stability of the system. The off-chain expansion scheme cannot use Bitcoin during the channel survival period, and only collects the data of both sides of the transaction, which may destroy the decentralization and tamper-proof characteristics.

In this context, block chain technology based on Directed Acyclic Graph (DAG) is on the stage. DAG block chain replaces the chain serial structure of traditional block chain with tree or mesh structure, supports multi-node parallel write operation, effectively avoids the serial write limitation of chain structure, and greatly improves the system throughput. It has become a promising research direction to solve the scalability problem of block chain, and has been warmly sought after by academia and industry since it was proposed, and many innovative projects and DApps based on DAG have emerged. Unlike traditional block chains, DAG distributed account books can use blocks or transactions as basic storage units. And the base unit (block or transaction) of each ledger may reference one or more predecessor units, or may be simultaneously referenced by one or more successor units. According to the different ways of data organization in the DAG ledger, two different types of distributed ledger technologies are derived: block-based DAG (BDAG) and transaction-based DAG (TDAG). TDAG allows users of the whole network to operate the ledger. BDAG only opens the operation authority to miners, TDAG can use network resources in real time and support high concurrency, while BDAG only uses network resources after the block is generated.

The distributed ledger of adjustable load metering data with friendly source-network load storage needs to reach a consensus on second-level time particles, and supports high-concurrency data transactions of massive nodes in the Internet of Things environment. At the same time, the distributed ledger of adjustable load metering data is mainly applied to edge devices with weak networking capacity and limited computing resources. Also, from a security standpoint, the number of lightweight clients should not be too large. This requires the use of containerized edge computing service engine to enhance the networking and computing capabilities of edge devices, so that adjustable load metering data can be quickly linked on the device side, while ensuring data security. Therefore, combined with the practical application scenarios of adjustable load metering data, in this paper, we will design an improved TDAG distributed ledger structure, which is suitable for the distributed Internet of Things scenario and can adjust the load metering data, and is able to effectively prevent nodes from doing evil and attacking and quickly reach a consensus among nodes.

2 Related Work

DAG is a new generation of blockchain technology for the future. From the perspective of topology model, it has evolved from single chain to tree and mesh, from block granularity to transaction granularity, and from single point transition to concurrent writing, realizing an innovation of blockchain technology from capacity to speed. In the following, according to the data organization structure of the DAG, BDAG technology based on block and TDAG technology based on transaction are introduced respectively, and then the application of block chain technology in power system is introduced.

2.1 Block-Based BDAG Technology

In 2015, Sompolinsky et al. [4] introduced DAG into blockchain technology for the first time, and proposed the Ghost (Greedy heavier-observed sub-tree) consensus algorithm based on DAG. Ghost evolves the single-chain structure of the traditional block chain into a DAG tree structure, and selects the main chain nodes according to the principle of maximum weight subtree. It allows multiple blocks to be packed in parallel, and can solve the expansion problem of transaction processing capacity within a certain range. However, the blocks on the non-main chain will be discarded, and the throughput will not increase linearly with the increase of the number of nodes. In the Inclusive [5] consensus protocol proposed by Lewenbegr et al., each block can refer to multiple parent blocks, sort the whole network blocks based on the network backbone, and then eliminate illegal transactions. As a result, legitimate transactions in all blocks will be included in the final distributed ledger.

In the Conflux [6] protocol, each block has a unique parent edge and multiple reference edges. The parent edge is used for the consensus backbone, while the reference edge is used to determine the order in which the blocks appear. These three protocols are BDAG technology based on consensus backbone, and the throughput of Inclusive and Conflux has a linear positive correlation with the number of nodes.

There are also BDAG technologies that do not require a consensus backbone, including Spectre [7], Phantom [8], and Meshcash [9]. Spectre protocol introduces a voting mechanism to solve the ranking problem of conflicting transactions, but it is not scalable because it cannot sort all transactions globally. The Phantom protocol [10] requires honest miner to reference all end-blocks and must broadcast that flood immediately after the block is generated. Using the greedy algorithm, the blocks generated by the honest nodes form a tightly connected set k-cluster (called the blue set), and the other blocks form the red set. Prioritize blocks in k-cluster as a reward for honest behavior. In Meshcash [11], an honest node generates a new chunk through the PoW mechanism and needs to reference all the end chunks in the DAG view. It introduces two mechanisms, namely, the consensus of the rabbit strategy and the consensus of the tortoise strategy, which can support high block rate and throughput.

2.2 Transaction-Based TDAG Technology

In 2015, the DAG-Chain technology [15] proposed by Sergio Demian Lerner realized the DAG distributed ledger based on fine-grained transactions for the first time. At this time, DAG has evolved into a solution that completely abandons the block chain, which can theoretically greatly improve throughput.

DAG-Chain allows each transaction of the user to directly enter the ledger and participate in the transaction sorting of the whole network. In order to prevent DDoS attacks and avoid waste of computing power, users need to do lightweight PoW before sending transactions. Its main contribution is to introduce the confirmation score () to filter double-flower transactions, and also provides an important reference for the subsequent TDAG technology. IOTA [12] inherits the basic idea of DAG-Chain. Its consensus mechanism Tangle assigns its own weight and cumulative weight to each transaction, where the former is proportional to the size of PoW, and the latter is the sum of the weights of direct or indirect successor units, and then uses Monte Carlo Markov chain algorithm to provide reference for each transaction to select parent nodes. However, when the number of network nodes and transactions is small, it is vulnerable to double-flower attacks. So IOTA introduced an “arbiter” to issue checkpoints and trade confirmations on a regular basis. Avalanche [13] designed a series of basic schemes, including Slush, Snowflake and Snowball, and reached a trading consensus through random interaction sampling between nodes and leaderless Byzantine agreement.

Byteball [14] introduces witnesses and main chains in the consensus mechanism, and then realizes the whole network transaction ranking. Each user may select 12 users or corporate entities of repute or good standing to form a witness list, but must refer directly or indirectly to all transactions posted at the same address. Starting from each end unit, tracing back to the creation unit along the edge of the optimal parent node, a main chain from each end unit is obtained, the main chain intersected in the backtracking process is regarded as the main chain of the system, and the node at the intersection is called Stability Point. Then we assign a main chain serial number to each node on the main chain of the system, and assign a serial number to the non-main chain nodes according to the reference situation. When a double-flower transaction exists, the transaction with the smaller serial number in the main chain is considered legal.

Hashgraph [15] packages each transaction as an event, realizes information exchange through rumor spreading protocol, and carries out virtual voting with the help of locally stored Hashgraph to achieve leaderless Byzantine consensus. It can greatly reduce the communication overhead and effectively resist DDoS attacks. Nano [16] maintains a chain of all transactions for each user, Asynchronous updating of the ledger between different chains can be achieved, but because each transaction bifurcates the sending transaction and the receiving transaction, the corresponding node must be online to complete the transaction. Dexon [17] also uses a block lattice structure as a distributed ledger, which contains several parallel chains, each of which has an independent consensus, and the chains confirm each other by referencing fields. And it utilizes these reference relations to realize that sort of the whole network.

3 Improved DAG Distributed Ledger Technology for Adjustable Load Metering Data

In this paper, we propose a fragmentation-based DAG blockchain architecture for large-scale distributed Internet of Things scenarios. Massive logistics network equipment together to build a multi-hop network, if the traditional chain structure is used, all electricity records need to be stored in the block of each node. However, considering the scale of power consumption records, the efficiency of single chain is low, and the fragmentation scheme must be designed. Within a certain period, a certain number of available adjacent nodes form a fragment. These nodes work together to verify their transactions, generate and save a block, then update the fragment, regenerate and save the block. The blocks are sorted by generation time to form a single block chain. Because the shard is continuously updated, in order to effectively retrieve the persistent record of a node, consensus between asynchronous blocks needs to be achieved throughout the network by creating a DAG structure associated with the blocks. As shown in Fig. 1, the load adjustable node devices in the scenario are used as network nodes to jointly construct a multi-hop network, and a certain number of adjacent nodes are divided into the same fragment by using the fragmentation technology.

The DAG blockchain records all available power as transactions on the node. The transaction record refers to the residential ladder electricity price, calculates the electricity price of a month's electricity consumption in the adjustable load node equipment, and sends out the electricity consumption and the calculation result as a transaction, so as to realize the intelligent charging method. A new block is generated according to all power consumption conditions of each month in the same fragment, and the blocks stored in the fragment form a chain structure according to the time sequence.

In order to establish the partial order relationship between transactions, the consensus committee is dynamically formed within the fragment, and the practical Byzantine fault-tolerant algorithm (PBFT) mechanism is used to determine the order of transactions within the fragment and form a block. A certain weight coefficient is given to each block of the fragment, and the main chain sequence is determined according to the size of the coefficient. Each block keeps the electricity consumption and the electricity charge for a period of time (one month). Each slice maintains a single chain, and each time the slice is updated, the nodes will be scattered in each slice. In order to effectively retrieve the persistent records of a node, a connection is established between the newly recorded block and the old recorded block, and a DAG structure related to the block is created, as shown in Fig. 2.

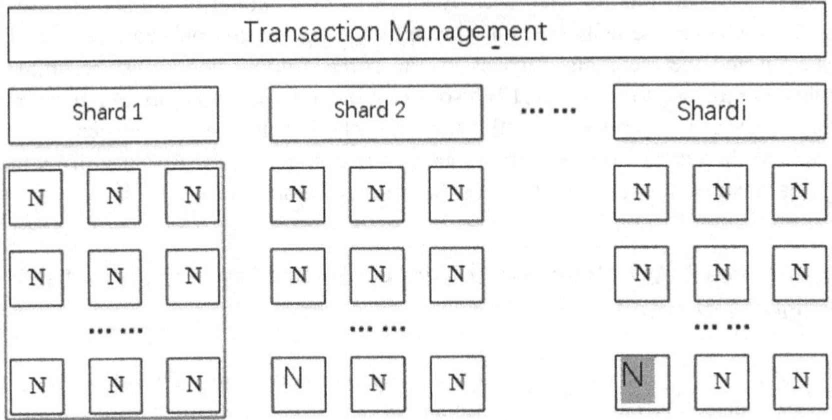

Fig. 1. Blockchain architecture based on fragmentation technology.

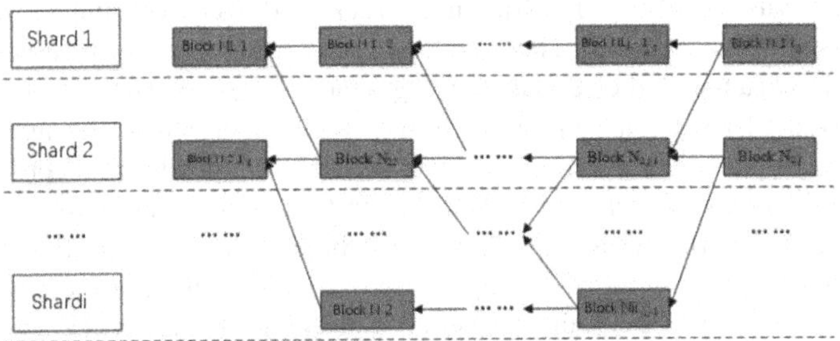

Fig. 2. DAG-based blockchain.

In the block chain based on fragmentation technology, each fragment independently forms a consensus committee and uses the Byzantine Fault Tolerance Algorithm (PBFT) mechanism to generate a block. The details are as follows: The election and update of the members of the consensus committee depend on the random number and the timestamp function. Specifically, suppose there are N nodes, which need to be divided into N pieces. If the number of members of each fragment is K (< N/n), the nodes corresponding to the first n maximum values of the random numbers are respectively allocated to n fragments, the nodes corresponding to the n maximum random numbers from n + 1 to 2 are allocated to n fragments, and so on. The nodes within the shard work together to validate their respective transactions and generate and save a block. Every other cycle, the members of the partition and consensus committee are updated according to the time stamp function and the random number, and the newly generated blocks are saved. Using the Byzantine fault-tolerant algorithm (PBFT) mechanism, the blocks in each fragment are sorted by generation time to form a single block chain.

4 Distribution of Weight Coefficients for Partitioned Blocks

The initialized DAG ledger contains only one creation unit. When a user generates a transaction and broadcasts it to the blockchain system, other users perform transaction verification and consensus according to the DAG graph saved by them.

4.1 Node Punishment and Reward Mechanism

The adjustable load mainly comes from the customer-side load. In the process of load regulation transaction, malicious behaviors such as node evil, malicious competition, attacking the account book and false declaration will lead to invalid transactions. In order to prevent nodes from doing evil as much as possible, the system initializes a credit value CreditVal with 6 points and 10 points for each user. For users who launch attacks such as double-flower trading and DDoS, the system automatically reduces their credit value and deducts 1 point each time. For users with "lazy" behavior, 0.1 points will be deducted each time. As a reward mechanism, the credit value of 0.1 points will be added to the users who discover the double-flower transaction and broadcast it to the whole network in time. A "diligent" node that has not done evil for a period of time (such as a month)., and also increase its credit value appropriately. The higher the user's credit value is, the more reliable the transaction generated or authenticated by the user is, and the transaction generated or authenticated by the user can be preferentially referenced by other transactions.

4.2 Transaction Verification

For each new transaction, certain rules must be followed to verify whether the transaction is valid before forwarding, and the verified transaction will enter the trading pool. For example, to confirm whether the balance of the transaction output party in the predecessor unit after the transaction is negative, it is necessary to query all the transaction records that have been directly or indirectly verified by the transaction output party. And then determine whether the balance is sufficient to pay for the transaction. If the new transaction is not properly validated so that it passes a transaction with a negative balance, it will not be recognized by other transactions.

In order to improve the convergence speed of the DAG ledger, users need to refer to (or verify) n (>1) transactions in the DAG graph as the predecessor unit (or parent node) when sending transactions, and the probability of the "lazy" node being selected as the predecessor unit should be very low, while the "diligent" node should be confirmed as soon as possible. The "lazy" node here means that the node confirms the old transactions that have been verified. Or a lack of careful verification resulting in conflicting transactions (e.g., insufficient balances) being verified. Therefore, this paper requires that these n transactions are all unconfirmed transactions, namely Tip transactions, because there is a possibility of nodes doing evil (such as sending false transaction information), the possibility of Tip transactions in DAG failing to pass verification is greater than that of verified transactions, and false transactions should be identified as soon as possible. The DAG storage space can be simplified, the transaction confirmation efficiency can be improved, and the network communication overhead can be reduced.

4.3 Determination of Transaction Sequence and Main Chain

For each node in the shard u_i the comprehensive weight coefficient is defined as

$$w(u_i) = f(\frac{C(u_i)}{C}, \frac{CreditVal(u_i)}{10}, R)$$

where, $w_1(u_i) \triangleq C(u_i)/C$ represents the ratio of the transaction limit in the unit to the maximum limit of all transactions in the corresponding level set. $w_2(u_i) \triangleq \frac{CreditVal(u_i)}{10}$. To initiate a transaction u_i the user's relative credit value, R is the transaction confirmation ratio, which is the number of Tips that directly or indirectly validate the transaction divided by the total number of Tips, and varies over time. Generally speaking, the larger R is, the more reliable the transaction is. The weighting coefficient is a function of these three, and f can be any normalized function that is positively correlated with these three, such as an average function. So, the weight coefficient is often larger for transactions with high credit value users, large transaction amount or large confirmation ratio. Here we also use the transaction quota as a parameter, because the double-flower transaction is often a large transaction, and the transaction cost is used as a parameter of probability measurement to verify the large transaction as soon as possible. And the weight of each transaction is not based on the cumulative value of the transaction, so that the occurrence of the double-flower transaction can be effectively controlled.

We use the comprehensive weight coefficient to select the parent node, and then dynamically construct the main chain, based on which all transactions are sorted. The main chain construction process starts from the creation unit, and the next node on the main chain (i.e., the parent node) is selected according to the greedy mode based on the weight coefficient. In particular, we first select the transaction with the highest weight coefficient from L (1), the set of all transactions that directly refer to the creation unit, and write it as u_1. If there is a knot (that is, the weight coefficients of multiple transactions are the same), the transaction unit generated by the user with the largest relative credit value is selected. Then, select Direct Reference u_1 as the next node on the main chain, and so on.

After obtaining the main chain, we can assign a main chain sequence number to each transaction on the main chain, and generate a global sorted view to facilitate transaction query. The specific method comprises the following steps of: firstly, setting the serial number of the main chain of the creation unit to be 0, u_1 the sequence number of the main chain is 1, u_1 has a subunit backbone sequence number of 2, and so on. For other transactions in L (H), the serial number is allocated according to the weight coefficient. For example, the transaction with the largest weight coefficient in L (H) except the nodes on the main chain is allocated with the serial number H. 1. The transaction with the minimum weight coefficient is assigned a serial number H. K, where K is the number of elements of L (H). Note that the sequence number here only indicates the order in which the transactions appear in the ledger. For ease of indexing and fast access, the size of the sequence number itself is not important.

5 Containerized Edge Computing Service Enabling TDAG Distributed Ledger

Adjustable load nodes often have weak networking capacity and limited computing resources, so it is difficult to play the role of a full node. The DAG distributed ledger based on transaction is slightly less supportive to lightweight clients than the DAG distributed ledger based on block chain, and there are some security risks. For example, a user's frequent queries of a list of transactions of interest can easily expose relevant address information. Bloom filters can be used to solve some of the problems, but from a security point of view, the number of lightweight clients should not be too large.

Moreover, if the networking ability of the device is weak and the computing resources are limited, it will cause computing and network communication delays such as Hash, which will bring greater security risks. Therefore, we need to enhance the communication and computing capabilities of edge devices through a reasonable device management mechanism with the help of containerized edge computing service engine, so that the adjustable load node can fully meet the needs of the node. To ensure that the adjustable load metering data can be quickly linked on the equipment side, while ensuring the security of the data.

With the help of containerized edge computing service engine, using 4G wireless network and other wired networks to communicate, providing powerful edge computing capabilities, complete security and comprehensive intelligent services, data optimization, real-time response, agile connection and intelligent analysis can be realized on the edge side of the Internet of Things, and the configuration interface is abundant. The acquire data is calculated in real time on that edge side. In addition, with the powerful computing power provided by the edge box, we can build a cloud edge collaboration framework, introduce artificial intelligence technology into DAG distributed ledger, realize the intellectualization of in-chain enhancement and out-of-chain governance, and solve the weaknesses of DAG technology in transaction confirmation and security.

6 Conclusions

In this paper, a transaction-based DAG consensus mechanism for adjustable load metering data is proposed. According to the characteristics of adjustable load measurement data, the partial order relationship between transactions is established by introducing the fragment structure and DAG structure, and the parallel transactions are processed by building a fine-grained transaction sequence relationship, which effectively improves the overall throughput. It can overcome the problem of packaging all transactions into one block in the traditional block chain. In future, we will apply this approach to solve the problems in social networks and mobile computing, etc. [18–31].

Acknowledgements. The authors acknowledge the Project of State Grid Zhejiang Electric Power Co., Ltd. "Research and Application of Key Technologies for Blockchain Supporting Highly Resilient Grid Balance" (Grant: B311DS21000H).

References

1. Nakamoto, S.: Bitcoin: a peer-to-peer electronic cash system. https://bitcoin.org/en/bitcoin-paper
2. Croman, K., et al.: On scaling decentralized blockchains. In: Clark, J., Meiklejohn, S., Ryan, P., Wallach, D., Brenner, M., Rohloff, K. (eds.) FC 2016. LNCS, vol. 9604, pp. 106–125. Springer, Heidelberg (2016). https://doi.org/10.1007/978-3-662-53357-4_8
3. How a Visa transaction works. http://apps.usa.visa.com/merchants/become-amerchant/how-a-visa-transaction-works.jsp
4. Sompolinsky, Y., Zohar, A.: Secure high-rate transaction processing in bitcoin. In: Böhme, R., Okamoto, T. (eds.) FC 2015. LNCS, vol. 8975, pp. 507–527. Springer, Heidelberg (2015). https://doi.org/10.1007/978-3-662-47854-7_32
5. Lewenberg, Y., Sompolinsky, Y., Zohar, A.: Inclusive block chain protocols. In: Böhme, R., Okamoto, T. (eds.) FC 2015. LNCS, vol. 8975, pp. 528–547. Springer, Heidelberg (2015). https://doi.org/10.1007/978-3-662-47854-7_33
6. Li, C., Li, P., Xu, W., Long, F., Yao, A.C.C.: Scaling Nakamoto consensus to thousands of transactions per second. arXiv:1805.03870
7. Sompolinsky, Y., Lewenberg, Y., Zohar, A.: SPECTRE: serialization of proof-of-work events: confirming transactions via recursive elections. https://eprint.iacr.org/2016/1159.pdf
8. Sompolinsky, Y., Zohar, A.: PHANTOM: a scalable BlockDAG protocol. IACR Cryptology ePrint Archive (2018)
9. Bentov, I., Hubácek, P., Moran, T., Nadler, A.: Tortoise and Hares Consensus: the mesh-cash framework for incentive-compatible, scalable cryptocurrencies. IACR Cryptology ePrint Archive (2017)
10. Lerner, S.D.: DagCoin: a cryptocurrency without blocks. https://bitslog.files.wordpress.com/2015/09/dagcoin-v41.pdf
11. Popov, S.: The Tangle. https://assets.ctfassets.net/r1dr6vzfxhev/2t4uxvsIqk0EUau6g2sw0g/45eae33637ca92f85dd9f4a3a218e1ec/iota1_4_3.pdf
12. Rocket, T.: Snowflake to avalanche: a novel metastable consensus protocol family for cryptocurrencies. In: IPFS, pp. 1–21 (2018)
13. Churyumov, A.: Byteball: a decentralized system for storage and transfer of value. https://byteball.org/Byteball.pdf
14. Baird, L.: The swirlds hashgraph consensus algorithm: fair, fast, Byzantine fault tolerance. Technical report, Swirlds Tech Reports SWIRLDS-TR-2016-01 (2016)
15. LeMahieu, C.: Nano: a feeless distributed cryptocurrency network. https://nano.org/en/whitepaper
16. Chen, T.Y., Huang, W.N., Kuo, P.C., Chung, H., Chao, T.W.: DEXON: a highly scalable, decentralized DAG-based consensus algorithm. arXiv:1811.07525 (2018)
17. Pervex, H.: A comparative analysis of DAG-Based blockchain architectures. In: Proceedings of 12th International Conference on Open Source Systems and Technologies (ICOSST) (2018)
18. Jiang, H., Xiao, Z., Li, Z., Xu, J., Zeng, F., Wang, D.: An energy-efficient framework for internet of things underlaying heterogeneous small cell networks. IEEE Trans. Mob. Comput. **21**(1), 31–43 (2022)
19. Xiao, Z., et al.: TrajData: on vehicle trajectory collection with commodity plug-and-play OBU devices. IEEE Internet Things J. **7**(9), 9066–9079 (2020)

20. Xiao, Z., et al.: Resource management in UAV-assisted MEC: state-of-the-art and open challenges. Wirel. Netw. **28**, 3305–3322 (2022)
21. Li, J., et al.: Drive2friends: inferring social relationships from individual vehicle mobility data. IEEE Internet of Things J. **7**(6), 5116–5127 (2020)
22. Ali, T.A., Xiao, Z., Sun, J., Mirjalili, S., Havyarimana, V., Jiang, H.: Optimal design of IIR wideband digital differentiators and integrators using salp swarm algorithm. Knowl.-Based Syst. **182** (2019)
23. Dai, X., et al.: Task co-offloading for D2D-assisted mobile edge computing in industrial internet of things. IEEE Trans. Ind. Inform. (2022). https://doi.org/10.1109/TII.2022.3158974
24. Jiang, H., Dai, X., Xiao, Z., Iyengar, A.: Joint task offloading and resource allocation for energy-constrained mobile edge computing. IEEE Trans. Mob. Comput. (2022). https://doi.org/10.1109/TMC.2022.3150432
25. Long, W., et al.: Unified spatial-temporal neighbor attention network for dynamic traffic prediction. IEEE Trans. Veh. Technol. 1–15 (2022). https://doi.org/10.1109/TVT.2022.3209242
26. Hu, Z., Zeng, F., Xiao, Z., Fu, B., Jiang, H., Chen, H.: Computation efficiency maximization and QoE-provisioning in UAV-enabled MEC communication systems. IEEE Trans. Netw. Sci. Eng. **8**(2), 1630–1645 (2021)
27. Zeng, F., Li, Q., Xiao, Z., Havyarimana, V., Bai, J.: A price-based optimization strategy of power control and resource allocation in full-duplex heterogeneous Macrocell-Femtocell networks. IEEE Access **6**, 42004–42013 (2018)
28. Huang, Y., Xiao, Z., Yu, X., Wang, D., Havyarimana, V., Bai, J.: Road network construction with complex intersections based on sparsely-sampled private car trajectory data. ACM Trans. Knowl. Discov. Data **13**(3), 28, Article no. 35 (2019)
29. Xiao, Z., et al.: A joint information and energy cooperation framework for CR-enabled macro-femto heterogeneous networks. IEEE Internet of Things J. **7**(4), 2828–2839 (2020)
30. Zhang, W., Zhou, S., Yang, L., Ou, L., Xiao, Z.: WiFiMap+: high-level indoor semantic inference with WiFi human activity and environment. IEEE Trans. Veh. Technol. **68**(8), 7890–7903 (2019)
31. Zhao, P., et al.: Synthesizing privacy preserving traces: enhancing plausibility with social networks. IEEE/ACM Trans. Netw. **27**(6), 2391–2404 (2019). https://doi.org/10.1109/TNET.2019.2947452

A Detection and Information Processing Model Based on an Automatic Mechanism for Tax Payment Control in Developing Countries

Vincent Havyarimana[1], Patient Niyibikora[1], Damien Hanyurwimfura[2], and Thabo Semong[3](✉)

[1] Department of Applied Sciences, Burundi Higher Institute of Education, 6983 Bujumbura, Burundi

[2] College of Science and Technology, University of Rwanda, Kigali 3900, Rwanda

[3] Department of Computer Science and Information System, Botswana International University of Science and Technology, 10071 Palapye, Botswana

semongt@biust.ac.bw

Abstract. The foundation of humanity is nowadays based on ways of living that can take many forms including controlling living conditions, reappraising work practices and developing new technologies. However, most of these activities are done to satisfy people's needs, but they have a negative impact on their health and well-being. This is the reason why man seeks ways to develop and protect himself from fatigue and anything that can harm his health by using modern technology that reduces the consumption of resources. Recently, the most used modern technology is based on the "automatism" model which is very useful in multiple fields. The technology of automated systems is rapidly evolving in terms of components, structures, advanced control systems and application areas. The objective of this paper is to implement an automatic mechanism to ensure a better and wonderful control when collecting taxes especially in developing countries. The proposed mechanism is based on a case of paying parking tax. The mechanical part of our system is controlled by an ARDUINO micro controller under which works in parallel with a Windows application on a computer to control a servomotor that operates the barrier. The detection of the coordinates of the taxpayer is done using the radio frequency identification. This control model is composed of detection and information processing system and a mobile barrier whose structure is adapted to the opening or closing geometry of the taxpayer passage.

Keywords: Microcontroller · servomotor · RFID · automatic mechanism · tax payment control · developing country

1 Introduction

All people in the world seek to develop quickly and to protect themselves against all that can harm their health. Technology is one of the things that handle such

Z. Xiao et al. (Eds.): ICECI 2022, LNICST 478, pp. 82–96, 2023.
https://doi.org/10.1007/978-3-031-28990-3_7

human issues by reducing the consumption of resources. The field of technology is advancing so fast at an extraordinary rate. Indeed, the new era of information technology which involves for instance the transmission and storage of information in electronic formats [1] have been adapted by different institutions and organizations around the world. The "automatism" is one of the fruits of that information processing technology. The automatism is very useful in multiple fields among others, industrial, medical, military and embedded systems or even in everyday human life. The technology of automated systems is rapidly evolving in terms of components, structures, advanced control systems and application areas. Thanks to this automation technology, some countries that have reached the path of development are progressing at an exciting step and rending them extremely rich [2,3]. However, in some developing countries, this technology has not been yet developed to an appropriate level.

The developing countries are seeking to achieve sustainable development and are engaged in the fight against the squandering of national wealth, corruption, tax embezzlement and tax evasion, as these are major challenges that hinder development. For a country to prosper economically, it is very useful to use and accumulate wealth from all possible sources, including taxes, according to the law. Taxes play an important role in the economic growth of developing countries [4]; their misappropriation hinders economic decollation. Meanwhile, taxes tend to go through illegal channels and it has been observed that the taxpayer pays taxes without receiving a receipt in return. The tax collector keeps the small amount in his pocket, instead of doing the job properly assigned by the government.

In many developed countries like Brazil, after implementation of Digital Book-Keeping System (SPED) in 2009, tax collections rose at a compound annual growth rate (CAGR) of 8.7% from 2010 to 2015, as compared with a CAGR of 7.6% from 2007 to 2009 [5]. Moreover, since 2016 in China, a powerful platform for pooling tax data from all levels of tax bureaus across a country has been implemented to facilitate both taxpayer and tax authority engagement. This platform especially enables the tax authorities to closely monitor invoice creation to detect fictitious invoices, ensuring the integrity of invoice information and the authenticity of filing data [6].

Furthermore in developing country like Kenya, it was estimated through a 2015 report that Sh639 billion were lost annually in tax evasion by multinational corporations. After tax procedures became fully digitalized in 2016, the Kenya Revenue Authority (KRA) collected 1.366 trillion in the 2016/2017 financial year; an added Kshs 115 billion from its previous year's collection [7]. Based on the introduction of ICT taxpayer Department of Tanzania Revenue Authority (TRA), the revenue collection increased from TZS 204,397.5 Millions in February 2001 to TZS 1,605,751.2 Millions in 2008 while revenue contribution share rose to 41% in September 2008 from 23% in February 2001 [8].

For the case of Burundi Revenue Authority (BRA), the innovations introduced by the reform have real economic and social benefits to the citizens of Burundi. It has organized functional lines which were focused on taxpayer segmentation with the major aim of maximizing the voluntary tax payment. Therefore, the use of automated tax payment system in Burundi enabled the BRA to increase its tax collection due to the implementation of a controlled tax evasion system introduced in BRA [9].

In fact, to improve the social services, critical or poor communication infrastructures and other public sectors, the ability of each country to collect taxes is vital. The goal of this study is therefore based on the implementation of the technology in general and automation in particular for especially developing countries, with the intention of financing those services for the welfare of human being.

1.1 Literature Review

Nowadays, there exist general issues that developing countries are facing from technological changes. Some promising examples of technological innovation and application in tax administration and tax policy have been proposed in literature. During the last few years, automatic mechanism and/or intelligent systems have been developed to satisfy people's needs. Those systems have been used in multiple fields including intelligent transport systems [10], medical [11], industrial [12], internet of things (IoT) [13,14] and embedded systems [15,16] or even in everyday human life [17,18]. For instance, authors in [10] developed a hybrid approach to solve the problem of vehicle position prediction under multi-GPS failure conditions such as free and partial GPS failures as well as short and long full GPS failures. Moreover, Kuwik et al. [11] proposed a home refrigerator (which stores vaccines) that is programmed such that it continues to monitor the action of opening and closing the door to check if the patient is taking medication regularly, given that the patient takes medicine at regular and known time intervals. In [15,16], authors implemented a smart refrigerator from which information about the products remaining inside and the status of its door can be obtained using the radio frequency identification (RFID) technology. The research work in [17] proposed the realization of an electronic cane automating the detection and recognition of fixed and moving obstacles can provide more safety for blind people. Chayma Bahhar et al. [13] worked on a system to monitor the presence of a fire and the concentration of gas in real time in the atmosphere whereas authors in [18] presented the creation of a prototype of a low-cost smart home whose home automation would be controlled by mobile devices.

Although the aforementioned mechanisms have been implemented to satisfy rapidly people's needs in different fields, the country's economy is essential and should also be taken into account for a good human living. Different approaches have been developed in the literature with the intention of achieving a high-income economy, especially in developing countries. One of the strategies to enhance the country's economy is the way the taxes and the expenses are managed. The automation technology is quite primordial to reach the significant economy through the collection of the taxes. Indeed, researchers in [3]have highlighted different methods in order to collect taxes more efficiently by changing the law, giving deadlines and changing the tax collector from time to time. Moreover, authors in [19], have set up an intelligent system to monitor who pays and who does not pay taxes and to check whether tax collectors are collecting taxes properly. However, for this system, human intervention is still very important, and the more human intervention there is, the higher chances of corruption and tax evasion colluding.

1.2 Objectives and Contributions

The main objective of this study is to develop a detection and information processing model based on an automatic mechanism for parking taxes payment control especially in developing countries. To achieve this, an electronic barrier that automates the detection and recognition of the taxpayer's information is implemented. The main benefit of the proposed mechanism is that the automatic closing and opening of the taxpayer passage can bring more security in the collection of taxes. Specifically, the proposed system automates the control, payment, opening and closing of the gateway at the parking to minimize human intervention in the tax collection process. This system will improve and purify the way taxes are collected. In other words, the probability of collecting taxes using illegal channels will be highly reduced. Therefore, the taxes will be fully channeled to the public treasury.

To experimentally design and implement the proposed system, different components such as a microcontroller named ARDUINO UNO, the RFID reader, the tags and the servomotor are used to detect the information of the parking taxpayer and provide him with several types of information including the status "payment" or "non-payment". This status makes him eligible for what he is entitled to. The mechanism also presents the effectors that implement the instructions of the command to let the taxpayer passes or not.

The remainder of this paper is organized as follows. We present the description of the used circuit tools for tax payment control in Sect. 2 whereas Sect. 3 highlights the proposed detection and information processing model based on an automatic mechanism for tax payment control. Section 4 illustrates the frame design and development of the system and finally conclusion and future works are presented in Sect. 5.

2 Description of the Used Circuit Tools for Parking Tax Payment Control

In order to normally manage the collection of taxes and their routing to the public treasury, we propose an automatic tax payment controller mechanism that can automate the control, opening and closing of the taxpayer passage. The proposed mechanism is composed of several parts. It is equipped with a micro-controller (ARDUINO UNO) and a computer which are the information processing units and a sensor (RFID reader) to detect the information of the taxpayer. In order to perform a wonderful control and validate its eligibility (having paid or not the taxes), an effector (servomotor) that executes the instructions of a micro-controller (opening or closing) is taken into account. Moreover, an electric sensor (push button) is used to obtain information on the state of passage of the taxpayer. On the other hand, a light signal is implemented to ensure a communication of the system with the external environment. The whole process is summarized in the block diagram of the circuit (Fig. 1) [17].

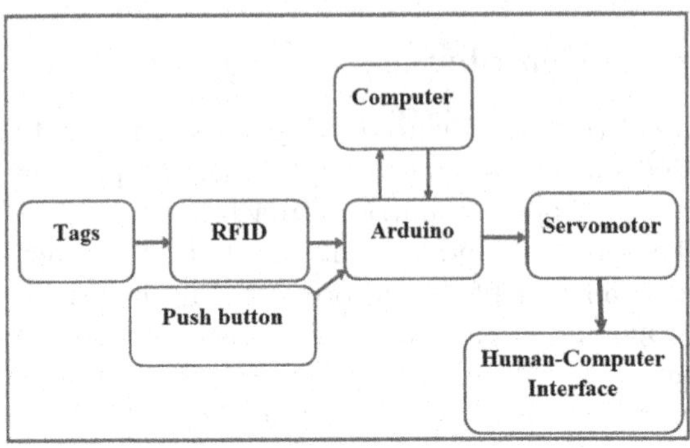

Fig. 1. Global block diagram of the circuit

2.1 The Radio Frequency Identification (RFID) Components and Operation

A complete RFID solution allows the integration of the data flow into the company's information system [20]. It includes the tag and the reader. The tag is one of the most widely used identification methods to embed a serial number or data sequence in a chip and to connect this chip to a small antenna. This pair (silicon chip + antenna) is then encapsulated in a carrier (RFID tag). The reader/writer is made of a circuit that emits electromagnetic energy through an antenna, and of an electronic that receives and decodes the information sent by the transponder and sends it to the data collection device. The RFID reader is the element responsible for reading the radio frequency tags and transmitting the information they contain (EPC code or other, status information, cryptographic key...) to the next level of the system (middleware). This communication between the reader and the label is carried out in four stages:

- The reader transmits by radio the energy necessary to activate the tag;
- It then launches a request interrogating the nearby tags;
- It listens to the answers and eliminates duplicates or collisions between answers;
- Finally, it transmits the results obtained to the applications concerned.

The communication between the reader and the tag takes place via the antennas that equip both of them, these elements being responsible for the radio frequency radiation. The power of the reader is to be combined with the appropriate antenna, which determines the optimal reading range. The RFID reader and tags are presented in Fig. 2.

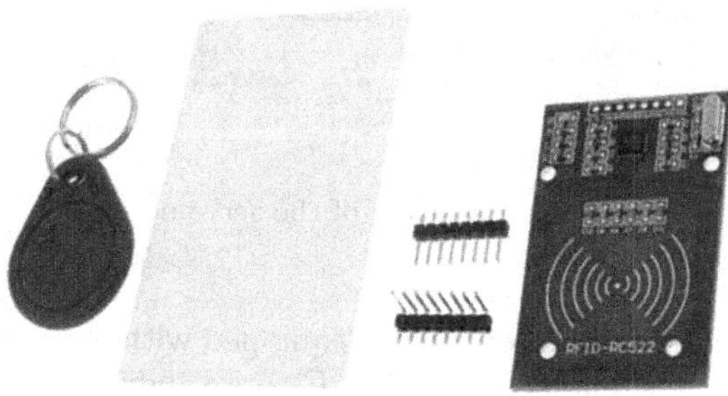

Fig. 2. RFID reader and tags

The technology of the RFID is based on the emission of electromagnetic field by a "reader", or "fixed element", which is received by the antenna of one or more labels, or "deported elements" which transmit a signal according to a given frequency towards one or more labels located in its field of reading. This electric or magnetic field serves as a vector for the information between the tag and its reader, as well as a support for the activation energy of these tags. More details related to the RFID components and its operation can be found in [17,20–23].

2.2 The Servomotor

A servomotor aims to produce a precise movement in response to an external command, it is an actuator (system producing an action) that integrates electronics, mechanics and automation. A servomotor is capable of reaching predetermined positions in the instructions given to it and then maintaining them.

As presented in Fig. 3, a servomotor consists of a DC micro motor, a gearbox at the output of this motor that decreases the speed and increases the torque, a potentiometer (acting as a resistive divider) that generates a variable voltage proportional to the angle of the output shaft, a shaft protruding out of the housing with different arms or wheels for attachment, and an electronic servo device [24].

In the ARDUINO system, the servomotor is mainly used in robotic applications. The servomotor has three wires to operate, the red and black (brown) are used for its power supply while the orange (yellow or white) receives the control signal. The servomotor has the advantage of being angularly servo-controlled, which means that the output axis of the servomotor will respect the instruction sent to its input. Even if an obstacle intervenes to change the orientation of its trajectory, the servomotor will try to keep the position. For precise position

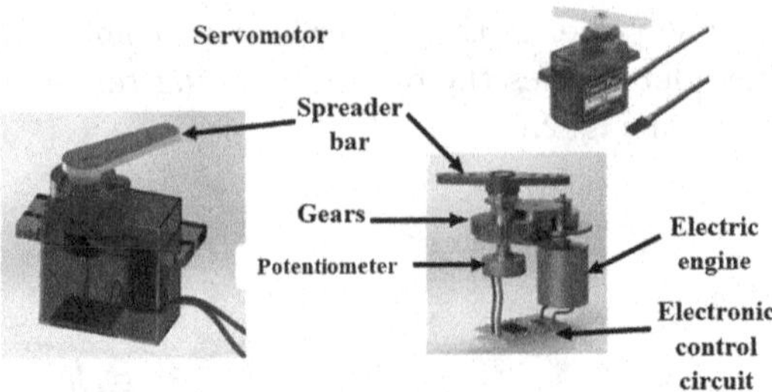

Fig. 3. Composition of the servomotor

adjustment, the motor and its control are equipped with a measurement system that determines the current position [25]. Figure 4 indicates the control signal illustration of servomotor.

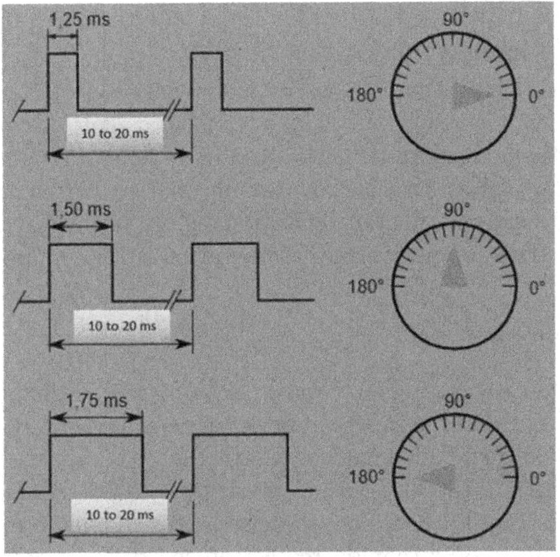

Fig. 4. Control signal illustration

2.3 The Light-Emitting Diode (LED)

In order to communicate with the users, a traffic light (monitored by LED) which plays the role of man-machine interface is used. The red, green and yellow lights of the traffic signals respectively indicate "no crossing of the signal", "authorization to pass the signal" and "forbidden to pass the signal". In the two-color system, red light means no crossing of the signal, and green light allows to pass the signal. The appearance of the red light while the green light is still on has the same meaning as the yellow light in the three-color system [26]. In this study, a two-color signal is used to ensure and facilitate a prohibition/permission to cross.

2.4 The Push Button

The N.O (Normally Open) push button, when clicked above, sends information to the control part (ARDUINO board and computer) about the passage of someone and finally the control part orders the system to close the passage.

3 The Proposed Detection and Information Processing System Based on an Automatic Mechanism for Parking Tax Payment Control

As the proposed automatic tax payment control system will need taxpayers' information on tax payments, it must be connected to the database management system, in which taxpayers are registered. The model flow chart in Fig. 5 illustrates the implementation of the detection and information processing algorithm based on an automatic mechanism for tax payment control. The model comprises of the Windows application connected to the local database management system to better perform the design and validate the model results. The main six (6) steps of the algorithm are numbered in the flow chart and are summarized as follows:
Step 1: Opening the program
Step 2: Waiting for the detection of the information by RFID
Step 3: Verification of the information by the information processing unit (valid or not)
Step 4: The servomotor initializes to apply the information from the processing unit.
Step 5: Detection of the information by the servomotor
Step 6: Implementation of the instructions that the information received by the servomotor holds

4 Frame Design and Development

With the intention of experimentally validating the effectiveness of our proposed method, a design and development of the system are carried out based on the hardware tools monitored by the Windows application (software).

4.1 Materials and Method

Model Design and Deployment. During this study, the used materials are composed of the ARDUINO board, the computer, the sensor circuit (RFID and

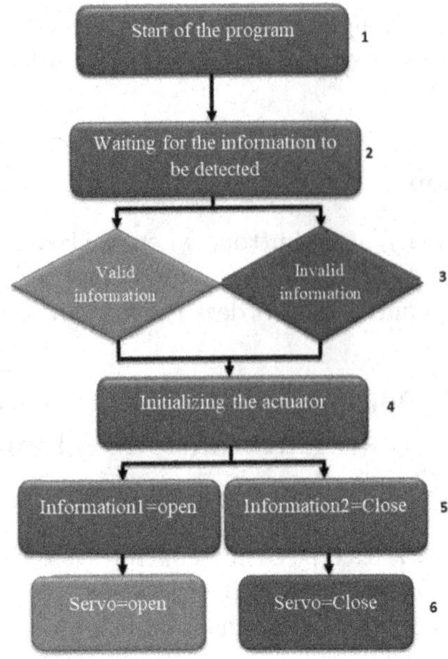

Fig. 5. The proposed model flow chart

the push-button) and the servo effector circuit. The technical parameters of the used servomotors are highlighted in Table 1.

Table 1. Technical parameters of the used servomotors

Reference and specification	$SG90$
Weight	$9g$
Torque	$1.2kgf.cm$
Operating voltage	$5V$
Stem diameter	$approx.4mm/0.2in$
Speed of rotation	$0.12/60orad/s$
Angle of rotation	$180o$

Moreover, Fig. 6 indicates the connection of the aforementioned circuit components for the control unit. Specifically, to implement the proposed system, we used an ARDUINO UNO board, sensors (RFID-RC522 reader and push button), lanes, a test plate, LEDs, an effector of rotary detecting the desired angle and the IDE ARDUINO software. The ARDUINO board is connected to the computer via USB. The communication between the ARDUINO is provided by a Windows application developed in Visual Studio 2010. Figure 7 indicates the initialization of the tax control application results.

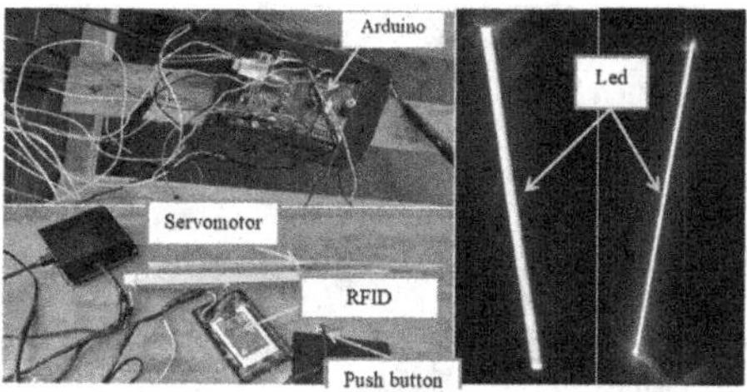

Fig. 6. Connection of the control unit

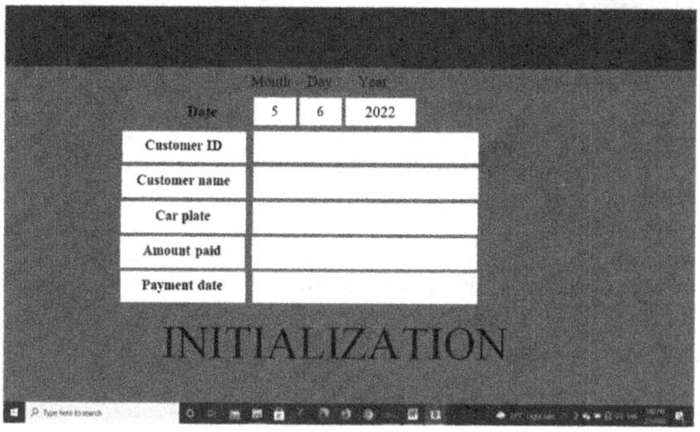

Fig. 7. Parking tax control application

After the implementation of the complete assembly of the system, ARDUINO was connected with C sharp so that there is a communication between this card and the computer holding the information corresponding to the payment or the non-payment of the taxpayer.

The Design of the Controlled System Unit. The controlled part is set in motion by the effector of the proposed control system. The proposed mechanism is subjected to three forces that are the weight of the rod that we can connect to the head of our mechanism and the two moments (the motor torque and the moment that will be developed by the rotational movement of the rod used) as shown in the Fig. 8; where P is the force developed by tripod weight, C_1 is the torque developed by the tripod and C_2 is torque developed by the movement of the rod (C_T).

By analyzing the mechanism presented in Fig. 8, we notice that all the reactions it uses to react against any force applied on it, are equal to the weight of the tripod. For this, at each support of the tripod we find $R = \frac{P}{3}$ such that $P = \sum_{i=0}^{n} R_{X,Y,Z}$ and
$C_1 = Pd_1$ where $d_1 = [(ab \times cos(35^0)) + 20]$ cm
$C_2 = C_m + C_T$ where $C_m = 1.2$ kgfcm, $C_T = Fd_T$ and $F = \frac{C_m}{r}$
For the proposed mechanism to function normally without imbalance, $\overrightarrow{P'}$ must

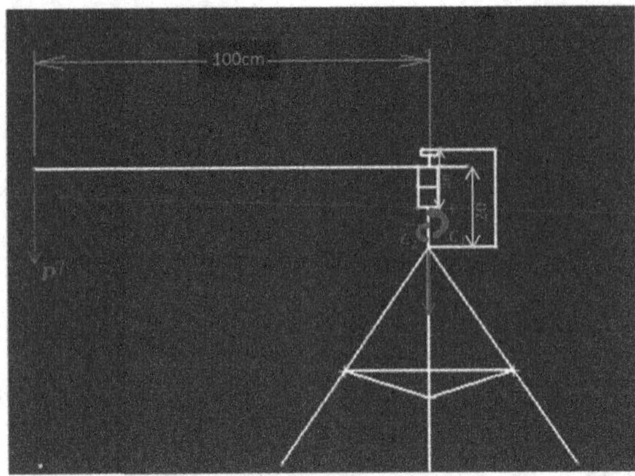

Fig. 8. Inventory of the forces applied to our mechanism that can unbalance it

be less than $\overrightarrow{P}$ ($\overrightarrow{P'} < \overrightarrow{P}$) and these two pairs must cancel each other out or C_2 must be less than C_1 ($C_2 \leq C_1$).
For the present case:
The radius $r = 17.5\,\text{mm} = 0.017\,\text{m}$
$F = \frac{1.2\,\text{kgfcm}}{1.75\,\text{cm}} = 0.6857kgf$
$C_T = 0.6857\,\text{kgf} \times 2\,\text{cm} = 1.371\,\text{kgfcm}$
$C_1 = 2\,\text{kgf} \times (65\,\text{cm} \times cos(35^0) + 20\,\text{cm}) = 146.469\,\text{kgfcm}$
$C_2 = 1.2\,\text{kgfcm} + 1.371\,\text{kgfcm} = 2.571\,\text{kgfcm}$

The torque of the presented drive motor is as small as possible. A light weight rod for our motor to drive the gate is needed. To drive a heavy rod, a high torque servomotor is used. Our motor ensures a double function, the drive and the blocking of the movement of the rod. If we use a rod of an important length, we are required to create a braking system of torque $C_{1,2}$ higher or equal to the torque of the rod. Moreover, it is important to check that the torque developed by the aforementioned rod on which we add the motor torque, is strictly lower than the resistant torque $C_T$of the tripod so that this last one does not fall over.

From the above calculations, we can notice that C_2 is less than $C_1(C_2 < C_1)$ which proves that our tripod has the power to stay in balance during the rotation of our barrier. After the calculations based on the control and controlled units, we moved to the deployment and Fig. 9 shows the mechanical part of the proposed model.

4.2 Results and Discussions

Figure 10 shows the complete mechanism where the control part to the controlled part are connected. The connection between the control system and the controlled system (mechanical), is ensured by wires that connect the ARDUINO

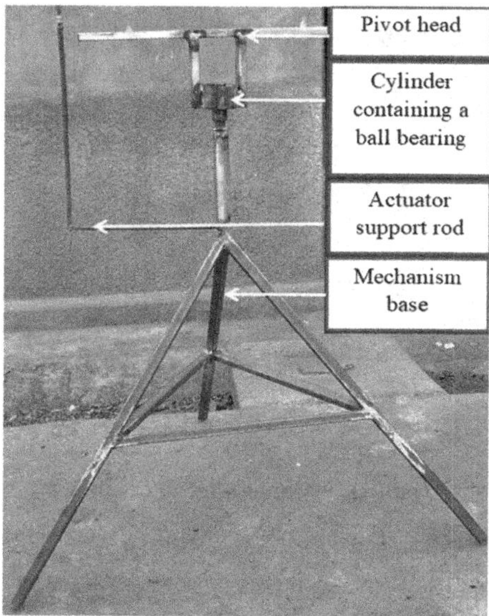

Fig. 9. The mechanical part of the mechanism

board to the servomotor. The latter executes the orders communicated by the computer via the ARDUINO board.

The servomotor describes a rotational movement on a track of a quarter circles and communicates this movement to the head of the mechanism. This head rotates from zero to 90° after checking and validating the conditions allowing the passenger to continue. The test of the automatic tax controller mechanism led us to the expected result of crossing (opening of the barrier) when we present the white card to the information reading module. A control was carried out and our system proved that the person having this card, that is to say fulfilling all the required conditions (the payment of the required month), sees the barrier opening while describing a rotation from 0 to 90° to let the passage and the green led lights up to give green light as shown in Fig. 11.

When we click on the commanded push button, the barrier closes and the red led lights up (Rotation of 90–0°). Moreover, when we present our key ring that is not in order we have seen that the system recognizes it but the barrier remains closed and the red led remains ON as presented in Fig. 12.

Although the proposed study is based on the implementation of an automatic mechanism to ensure a better and wonderful control when collecting taxes especially in developing countries, it faces some limitations. Indeed, the used tools to get to the current stage have limited capabilities. In fact, there should be an exchange of information between the tax collection authority and this automatic mechanism, as well as an exchange of information between this system and the taxpayers, so that the taxpayer is informed that the tax was paid/not paid or that someone has paid [5].

Fig. 10. Complete mechanism

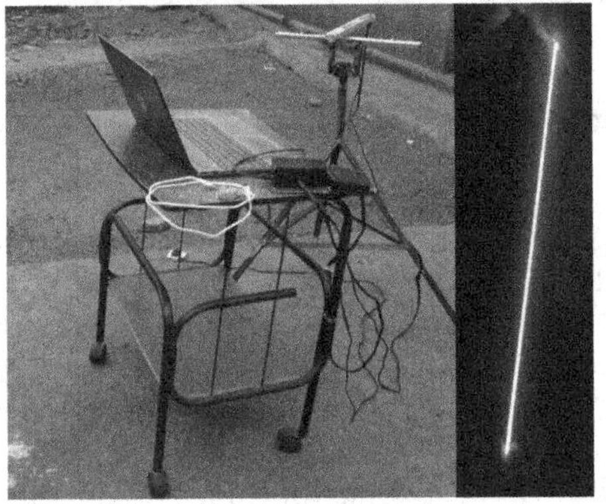

Fig. 11. Open Passage (0–90° rotation)

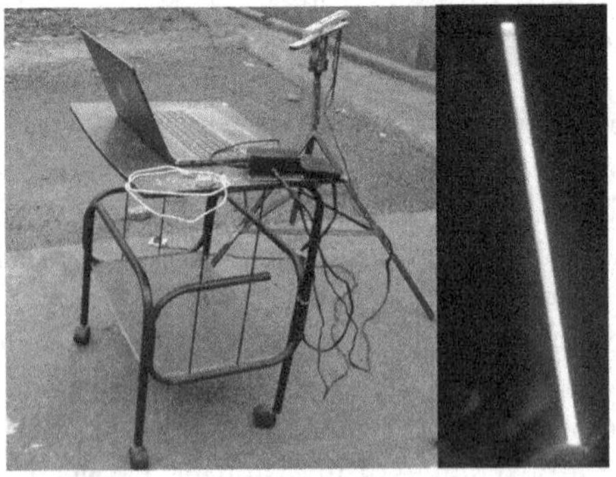

Fig. 12. Closed passage

5 Conclusion and Future Works

In this work, a detection and information processing model based on an automatic mechanism for parking taxes payment control is developed. The proposed model is implemented based on the hardware equipment and the software part was used to monitor that equipment. Specifically, the ARDUINO board enables to develop in the environment of programming IDE ARDUINO ensuring the reading of information (detection of information) and transmits this information to the computer. The latter comprises of a program of control developed in C sharp which replicates after having searched and validated the information of the taxpayer in a database, a corresponding instruction (paid = opening, not paid= closing). The proposed model detailed the practical aspects of communication between the ARDUINO UNO, its IDE and C sharp via the USB port for serial communication.

Future research will focus on the complete mechanism by extending it to a database management system of the tax administration. Indeed, additional equipment such as global positioning system (GPS), routers and other related equipment are required for allowing the proposed model to exchange information with the tax authority's database. This would enable the taxpayer receiving complete information from that agency's system.

Acknowledgements. This work was supported by the Department of Applied Sciences, Burundi Higher Institute of Education.

References

1. Mohammad, R., Maryam, R., Majid, Z., Hamidreza, A., Farid, Z.: Cooperative localization of vehicles sharing GNSS pseudoranges corrections with no base station using set inversion. In: Applied Mathematics in Engineering, Management and Technology, pp. 1208–1214 (2014)
2. Khyara, H., Amine, A., Nassih, B.: Exploratory analysis of driver and vehicle factors associated with traffic accidents in Morocco. In: Bennour, A., Ensari, T., Kessentini, Y., Eom, S. (eds.) Intelligent Systems and Pattern Recognition (ISPR 2022). CCIS, vol. 1589, pp. 119–131. Springer, Cham (2022). https://doi.org/10.1007/978-3-031-08277-1_10
3. Chaouni, H., Hassane, B.: The context of recovery of local taxes in Morocco. In: Accounting and Auditing Review (2018). ISSN: 2550-469X
4. Richard, M.-B., Eric, M.-Z.: Technology and taxation in developing countries: from hand to mouse. Natl. Tax J. **61**(4), 791–821 (2008)
5. Lachlan, W., Scott, W., Tim, G., Alexander, Z.: Transforming the tax function through technology. In: KPMG International (2018)
6. Marta, O., Prerna, P., Shimeng, L.: The digitalization of tax administration in China (People's Rep.), India and Korea (Rep.) in the fourth industrial revolution. Bull. Int. Tax. 465–480 (2020)
7. Muhia, D.-W., Francis, O.-A.: Adoption of e-procurement strategy and procurement performance in state corporations in Kenya (a case of Kenya revenue authority). Ind. Eng. Lett. **5**(6), 1–24 (2015)
8. Yuda, J.-C.: The impact of ICT on taxation: the case of large taxpayer department of Tanzania revenue authority. Dev. Ctry. Stud. **3**(2), 91–100 (2013)

9. Kieran, H., Domitien, N., Chantal, R.: For state and citizen reforming revenue administration, in Burundi. Africa Research Institute, pp. 1–32 (2013)
10. Vincent, H., Damien, H., Philbert, N., Zhu, X.: A novel hybrid approach based-SRG model for vehicle position prediction in multi-GPS outage conditions. Inf. Fusion **41**(2), 1–8 (2018)
11. Paul, K., Thomas, L., Matthew, Y., Dennis, C., David, L.-L., James, C.-S.: The smart medical refrigerator. IEEE Potentials **24**(1), 42–45 (2005)
12. Mateus, L.-A., Kamran, B.: Design, prototyping, and programming of a bricklaying robot. J. Student Sci. Technol. **8**(3), (2015)
13. Chayma, B., Chokri, B., Hedi, S.: IoT and artificial intelligence to fight fires. In: Colloquium on Connected Objects and Systems (COC 2021), IUT of Aix-Marseille (2017)
14. Ali, Z., Seyed, E.-E.: The design of a smart refrigerator prototype. Proc. EECSI **2017**, 19–21 (2021)
15. Joseph, H., Marco, Z., Chomora, M., Emmanuel, M.: Development of a TinyML based four-chamber refrigerator (TBFCR) for efficiently storing pharmaceutical products: case study: pharmacies in Rwanda. In: 2022 14th International Conference on Machine Learning and Computing (ICMLC 2022), pp. 337–346 (2022)
16. Hanshen, G., Dong, W.: A content-aware fridge based on RFID in a smart home for home healthcare. In: Proceedings of the 11th International Conference on Advanced Communication Technology, pp. 987–990 (2009)
17. Zeghoudi, A., Benoudina, H.: Study and realization of an intelligent blind stick based on ultrasonic sensors. In: National Conference on Applied Physics (CNPA 2019) (2019)
18. Kim, B., Marc, G., Sami, M., Rouwaida, K., Ayman, K.: Low cost Arduino/android-based energy-efficient home automation system with smart task scheduling. In: Fifth International Conference on Computational Intelligence, Communication Systems and Networks, pp. 296–301. IEEE (2013)
19. Wolf, M., Dale, S.: Tax administrations' adoption of new technologies to protect and ensure tax revenues. ERA Forum **19**(3), 457–464 (2019). https://doi.org/10.1007/s12027-018-0540-5
20. Karamdeep, S., Gurmeet, K.: Radio frequency identification: applications and security issues. In: IEEE Second International Conference on Advanced Computing and Communication Technologies, pp. 490–494 (2012)
21. Melanie, R.-R., Bruno, C., Andrew, S.-T.: The evolution of RFID security. IEEE Pervasive Comput. **5**(2), 62–69 (2022)
22. Divyan, M.-K., Daeyoung, K., Chan, Y.-Y., Byoungcheon, L.: Security framework for RFID-based applications in smart home environment. J. Inf. Process. Syst. **7**, 111–120 (2011)
23. Ari, J.: RFID security and privacy: a research survey. IEEE J. Sel. Areas Commun. **24**, 381–394 (2006)
24. Amirul, S.-S., Jamaludin, J., Jumad, A.-S.: A comparative study on the position control method of DC servo motor with position feedback by using Arduino. ARPN J. Eng. Appl. Sci. **11**(18), 10954–10958 (2016)
25. Maizatul, Z., Syed, A.-M.-A.-J., Zulkifli, O., Azrif, M., Mohd, M.-A.-Z.: High-efficiency dual-axis solar tracking developement using ARDUINO. In: International Conference on Technology, Informatics, Management, Engineering and Environment, pp. 43–47 (2013)
26. Sharat, G.-S.-C., Niranjan, H., Manjunatha, G.: Design and analysis of gantry robot for pick and place mechanism with Arduino Mega 2560 microcontroller and processed using Pythons. Mater. Today Proc. **45**, 377–384 (2021)

IEC-FOF: An Industrial Electricity Consumption Forecasting and Optimization Framework

Fei Teng, Yanjiao Chen(✉), and Wenyuan Xu

College of Electrical Engineering, Zhejiang University, Hangzhou, China
{tengfei118,chenyanjiao,wyxu}@zju.edu.cn

Abstract. To achieve carbon peaking and carbon neutrality goals, large-scale electricity consumption units such as factories and buildings need comprehensive solutions for energy saving and cost reduction. We propose a framework for industrial electricity consumption prediction and optimization based on multi-source information fusion named IEC-FOF. We design the electricity consumption prediction module by utilizing historical data, weather, and date info. Besides, we realize an electricity consumption optimization module based on clustering methods, including typical abnormal electricity consumption action identification, electricity consumption pattern recognition, and electricity consumption optimization suggestions.

Keywords: Industrial electricity · Electricity consumption forecasting · Time series analysis

1 Introduction

With the global warming and increase in pollution, in response to the United Nations' call to reduce carbon emissions, many countries have proposed carbon emission reduction programs suitable for their national conditions. In China, the government proposed carbon peaking and carbon neutrality goals [1]. According to the current carbon calculation scheme, a large proportion of carbon emissions come from the use of electricity. Through electricity usage optimization such as changing electricity schedule, people can achieve significant electricity savings without changing the facility infrastructure and thus reduce carbon emissions.

The existing work of electricity forecasting mainly relies on statistical methods and traditional time series forecasting models, which has achieved acceptable results in different scenarios [2–5]. In addition, in recent years, many DNN-based works have made innovations in the time series data prediction model and anomaly detection model, such as [6,16].

However, most of the existing research methods study the electricity consumption of a single area and electrical equipment, they cannot efficiently and

Z. Xiao et al. (Eds.): ICECI 2022, LNICST 478, pp. 97–110, 2023.
https://doi.org/10.1007/978-3-031-28990-3_8

precisely process the electricity consumption data under cross-industry and multi-scene conditions. In the current new scenario, we can summarize the following two technical challenges.

- The factors affecting electricity consumption are multifarious, resulting in the result that the traditional modeling and estimation methods are difficult to adapt to the current scene.
- Electricity consumers in different industries or regions have different action patterns. A unified model is difficult to model complex electricity consumption scenarios.

To address the above challenges, we propose IEC-FOF (An Industrial Electricity Consumption Forecasting and Optimization Framework). The framework is mainly composed of two parts: the data layer and application layer, the data layer includes data source collection, data preprocessing, and feature engineering module. Besides, the application layer includes electricity consumption prediction and an optimization module.

The granular data processing and feature engineering modules support the performance of the application layer. We used historical electricity usage information, weather, date, and other information to make predictions for future electricity consumption behavior, and split the model based on industry information for personalized training.

After obtaining the predicted values through a time series model, we can flexibly add application modules according to the specific business needs, such as anomaly detection based on prediction error and electricity consumption pattern recognition based on historical electricity consumption information. Based on the application layer services described above, we can generate recommendations for electricity consumption behavior, such as migrating electricity usage during peak periods to valley periods.

We summarize our main contributions as follows.

- We present a integrated electricity optimization solution for industrial scenarios that can automated response to multiple industries and multiple information sources.
- We deploy and apply the algorithm on an industrial electricity dataset. Some typical experimental results are presented to verify the universality and validity of IEC-FOF.

2 Related Work

2.1 Electricity Consumption Forecasting

There are many resultful methods for time series forecasting, and one application scene is electricity consumption forecasting. People can utilize historical information and some supplementary information like weather conditions, to predict electricity consumption levels in the future. The most widely used prediction algorithms include the following three:

- 1. Traditional sequence model like ARIMA [18], Prophet [10]. These methods decompose time series to obtain the seasonal term, trend term, noise, and other components, which are then processed and predicted respectively and then synthesize the prediction results finally.
- 2. Regression model like XGBoost [19], LightGBM [11]. This kind of method is the most widely used method in the industry. It needs to sort out data sources, conduct data preprocessing, feature engineering, and finally use the machine learning method to conduct regression modeling, and then employ future time features for prediction.
- 3. Sequence model like RNN, LSTM [7]. These models extract states from sequences using recurrent neural networks and reconstruct future sequences from the hidden state.

2.2 Time Series Pattern Recognition

Sequence pattern recognition here refers to the extraction of specific and representative pattern information from a sequence, such as recurring short curve, some segments with distinguishing effects, etc. This section focuses on techniques, anomaly detection, and operational research optimization that are relevant to the topics of our work.

As for anomaly detection, common methods include statistical methods, reconstruction error based methods, prediction error based methods [16], etc. As for pattern recognition, sequence clustering, and classification, the current prevalent method is to learn multi-dimensional data by representation, obtain fixed-length vectors and carry out subsequent applications [13–15].

3 System Overview

As is shown in Fig. 1, IEC-FOF consists of the data source layer, preprocessing layer, feature engineering layer, forecasting layer, and optimization layer. We will detail the information for each layer in the next section, and introduce a top-down structural explanation in this section.

To achieve the goal of electricity saving, we need to disassemble the target itself to get several specific business directions. This paper mainly focuses on the detection of abnormal electricity consumption behavior and the generation of suggestions for electricity consumption optimization. Such business demands need to be based on the prediction of future electricity consumption behavior, so we need the forecasting layer to support the business optimization layer at the top of the framework.

Meanwhile, predicting future electricity consumption needs to be based on historical data and information that can be accurately estimated in the future. In IEC-FOF, it refers to historical electricity consumption data, weather, date, and other information respectively.

In summary, IEC-FOF can be roughly divided into data modules with supporting functions and application modules with practical business value.

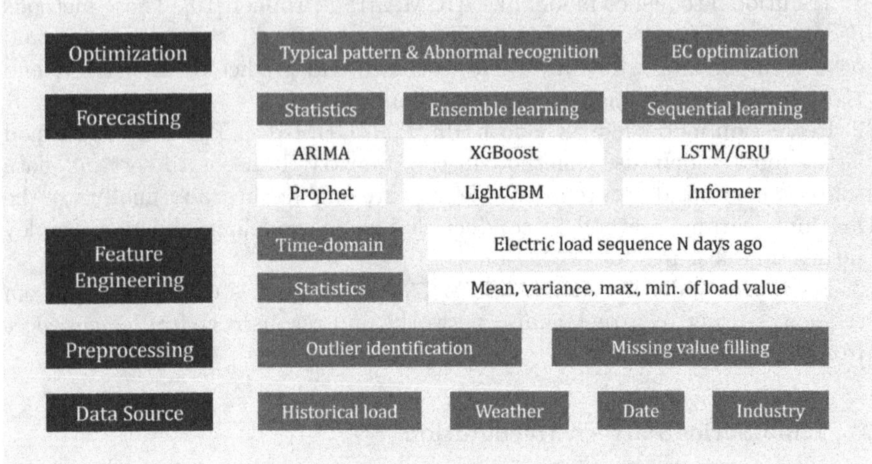

Fig. 1. Framework of IEC-FOF.

4 Methods

4.1 Electricity Consumption Forecast

Similar to a traditional data mining pipeline, we can summarize our methods into 4 steps: (The electricity consumption values mentioned below are obtained by smart electric meter, which calculate additive electricity consumption value in a period manner.)

1. Data Source Ingestion.

- **Historical data.** For most electricity consumers, the history of electricity usage is more or less indicative of habits. For example, for the apartment of an ordinary company employee, the peak of electricity consumption is after work in the evening, the electricity consumption on weekdays may be more regular, and the electricity consumption behavior on weekends will be more random, etc. We can use smart electric meter or other devices to record the amount of electricity a customer uses regularly to build up a historical time series of electricity consumption.
- **Weather info.** The weather factor is relatively easy to obtain and has a great influence on electricity consumption. By accessing external data sources, IEC-FOF can obtain key weather information such as temperature, humidity, and radiation in different geographical locations. For example, people turn on air conditioners more during high temperature and humidity, leading to a surge in electricity consumption.
- **Date characteristics.** The characteristics of a date can also serve as key features to support the model. Whether it's a workday, a holiday, a consumer goods promotion day, etc., can be used as valid information.

- **Industry categories.** Different industries have different habits of electricity consumption and different levels of regularity in electricity consumption. For example, the electricity consumption of a factory may vary greatly with the start and stop of production lines at any time, while the total electricity consumption of a school is highly correlated with holidays and weather. Industry attributes are also one of the information dimensions that must be considered. Because industry types are so broad and cross-cutting, we don't include them directly in the model as features, but rather as segment criteria for personalized models.

2. Data Preprocessing.

- Outlier identification. Obvious outliers will affect the effect of the prediction model, so they need to be filtered in the pretreatment stage. We use two simple strategies to filter outliers. One is based on distribution and the other is based on isolated forest.
- Missing value filling. Null values will be left after the above outliers are removed, and there are many null values to be dealt with in the sensor-based data. Here, IEC-FOF applies a simple forward-fill method to fill the missing values, that is, the values before the null values are used to fill the missing values.

3. Feature Engineering.

- Time-domain characteristic. In the time domain, IEC-FOF directly outputs the value of electricity consumption in certain historical periods as feature items, such as the sequence from 7 day ago can be used as a 24-dimensional feature.
- Statistical characteristic. Statistical values can also represent valid information, such as the average electricity consumption of the past day, the average electricity consumption of the last 3 days, and the variance of electricity consumption in a certain period. All of them have an impact on the value of the current moment.

Detailed features are shown in Table 1.

4. Forecasting. Since all the electricity consumption data we can collect is generated by the electricity consumption behavior that has already occurred, and many of our services are future-oriented, such as informing the approximate electricity consumption in advance, giving the electricity consumption plan for tomorrow in advance, etc., we need to make time series forecasts first. Based on the data we already have, we can use a variety of time series forecasting models, the details of which are shown below.

- Prophet [10] is a procedure for forecasting time series data based on an additive model where non-linear trends are fit with yearly, weekly, and daily seasonality, plus holiday effects. Otherwise, Prophet is robust to missing data

Table 1. A feature example. We use four major types of features, in which industry information is not directly exported to the model, but is used as a label to slice the data, and different models are used for training and deployment respectively. (EC = electricity consumption)

Feature	Example	Category
All EC value from 1 day ago	[2.88 kW, 3.88 kW, ..., 45.88 kW]	Historical
EC value average over 3 days	48.6 kW	Historical
EC value variance from 7 days ago	27.8	Historical
Max. EC value from 1 day ago	123.8kW	Historical
The current temperature	14°C	Weather
Daily temperature variance	3.75	Weather
Max. humidity from 1 day ago	67%	Weather
Is weekday or not	True	Date
Is holiday or not	False	Date
Is evening or not	True	Date
Is meal time or not	False	Date
Category of Industry	IT	Industry

and shifts in the trend, and typically handles outliers well, which is suitable for the industrial scene. The general principle can be summarized as the following formula, where g represents the trend term, s represents the seasonal term, h represents the holiday term, and ϵ represents the remaining term. A prediction example using Prophet is shown below as Fig. 2.

$$y(t) = g(t) + s(t) + h(t) + \epsilon_t \tag{1}$$

- LightGBM [11] is a gradient boosting framework that uses tree-based learning algorithms. It is designed to be distributed and efficient with many advantages, such as faster training speed and higher accuracy.
- Long short-term memory (LSTM) is a type of recurrent neural network (RNN) specially designed to prevent the neural network output for a given input from either decaying or exploding as it cycles through the feedback loops [7].

4.2 Optimization

Anomaly Detection. Since we have obtained a prediction of the future electricity use, we can directly take out the predicted value of the relatively short time, compared with the real value, if there is a very large prediction error, much greater than the prediction error of the model on the test set, it can actually represent that the real electricity consumption action is abnormal.

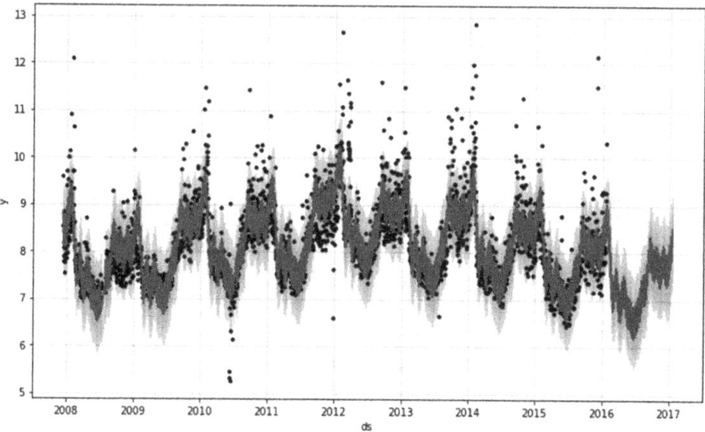

Fig. 2. A forecast example generated by Prophet [10]. Black points represent original data points, and blue lines and regions represent fitted curves and confidence intervals (Color figure online).

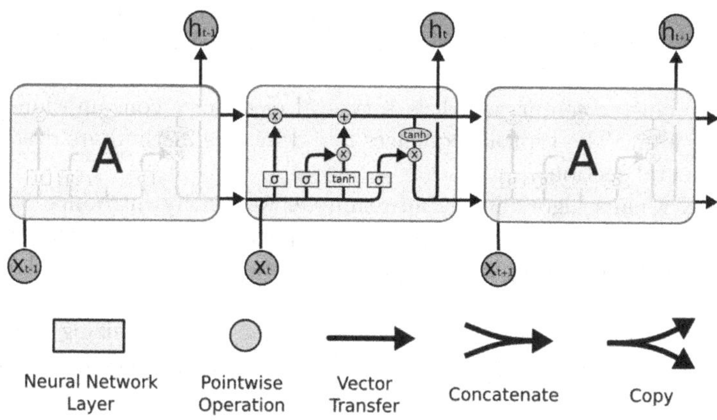

Fig. 3. Structure diagram of LSTM [7]. This structure contains forget gate, input gate and output gate, which can finally make the model remember the further sequence of information.

Typical Pattern Recognition and Optimization Recommendation Generation. We can extract typical electricity consumption patterns from historical electricity consumption sequences, so that users can quickly perceive that they have several common electricity consumption scenarios and habits. In addition, the typical electricity consumption mode can also allow us to perceive and suggest the user's electricity consumption, such as the user often uses a large amount of electricity during peak periods, as a service provider, we can inform users to reduce the consumption behavior during peak periods.

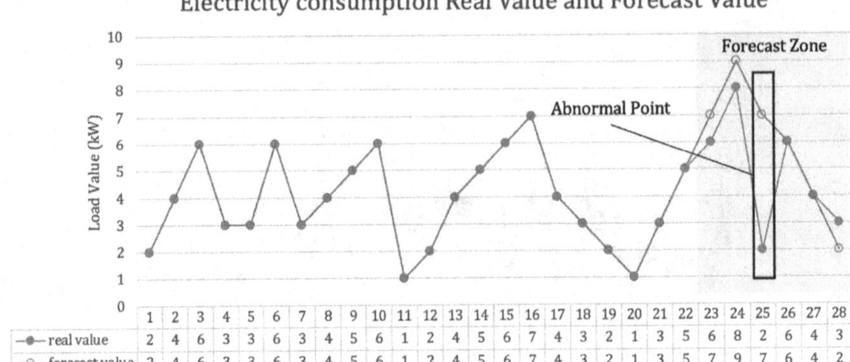

Fig. 4. A example of abnormal detection method. In the prediction area of this figure, there is a time-point whose real value differs greatly from the forecast value, and we can regard this time-point as an abnormal point.

Typical pattern recognition methods can be clustering algorithm, such as K-Means [8], DBSCAN [9], etc. We take the raw historical electricity sequence, break it down by day, and get some 24-dimensional vectors. Cluster these vectors and find the cluster center, which is a typical electricity consumption pattern sequence we want. The typical sequences found by this method are described in the experimental section.

Taking K-Means algorithm as an example, we briefly introduce its operation principle here. K-Means is a classic unsupervised learning algorithm that attempts to learn patterns in unlabeled datasets and discover similarities or regularities.

K-means groups similar data points into clusters by minimizing the average distance between geometric points. To do this, it iteratively divides the data set into a fixed number (K) of non-overlapping subgroups (or clusters), where each data point belongs to the cluster closest to the mean center of the cluster [8].

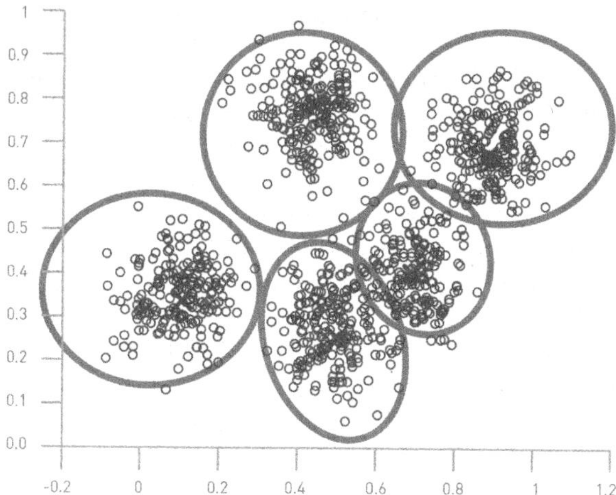

Fig. 5. A K-Means example. This figure shows the clustering effect in a two-dimensional space. The blue circle surrounding the point in the space is regarded as a cluster, and the red cross represents the center of the cluster. [12] (Color figure online)

5 Experiments

5.1 Implementation

At the data level, we used a dataset of electricity consumption that includes multiple industries and multiple electricity consumption facilities. A sample of the dataset is shown in Table 2. Each row represents the accumulated electricity consumption between the current point in time and the previous point in time. The sampling period of electricity consumption is 1 h, and the unit of electricity consumption is kW. At the model level, we used the following models, i.e. Prophet, Logistic Regression, XGBoost, LightGBM, and LSTM, using the frameworks of the native framework, sklearn, and Keras.

5.2 Forecasting Performances

We used SMAPE [17] indicators to quantify the effect of the prediction. A larger SMAPE value represents a larger error, and a smaller SMAPE value represents a better prediction accuracy. The specific formula of SMAPE is shown below, where A_t is the actual value and F_t is the forecast value. The reason why we chose SMAPE instead of MAPE, MSE, etc. is that the denominator of SMAPE takes into account the predicted value and has the characteristic of normalization, which brings fairer judgment in our scene.

In addition to verifying the accuracy of the predictions, we also recorded the training and testing time cost of the model, and the overall performance of LightGBM is the best, which achieves SMAPE = 27.32% and prediction time cost = 19.83 s over 7 days forecasting task.

Table 2. A sample of electricity consumption dataset

timestamp	electricity consumption	user id	industry category
2022-01-03 19:00:00	44.94	F238FIYL8	IT
2022-01-03 20:00:00	48.63	F238FIYL8	IT
2022-01-03 21:00:00	NaN	F238FIYL8	IT
2022-01-03 22:00:00	67.33	F238FIYL8	IT
2022-01-03 19:00:00	2.94	A238FI88U	Agri.
2022-01-03 20:00:00	4.88	A238FI88U	Agri.
2022-01-03 21:00:00	55.23	A238FI88U	Agri.
2022-01-03 22:00:00	9.13	A238FI88U	Agri.

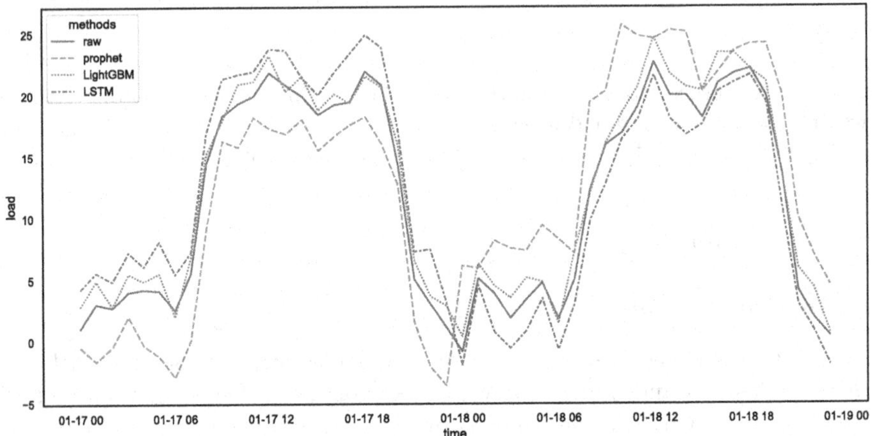

Fig. 6. A electricity consumption forecast example. We show the forecast sequence from various models, which can show forecasting performance to some extent. The predicted value can be negative and is set to 0 when used.

As to why the Prophet and LSTM didn't get the best performance, based on the experience, they are more suited to capture trends and laws, have the obvious time depend on the time series prediction scenarios, and very many scenes for influence factors, such as the industrial scenario described in this article, their performance may not be as feature engineering + tree model of the scheme. Due to different scenarios having different prediction effects and performance requirements, we reserved these various algorithms in IEC-FOF.

$$\text{SMAPE} = \frac{100\%}{n} \sum_{t=1}^{n} \frac{|F_t - A_t|}{(|A_t| + |F_t|)/2} \tag{2}$$

5.3 Optimization Effectiveness Evaluation

Based on the prediction error comparison, we present the anomaly detection service in Fig. 7; Based on K-Means clustering, we demonstrate typical electricity consumption pattern recognition services in Fig. 8; Based on sequence comparison and prior domain knowledge, we present the optimization recommendation service in Fig. 9.

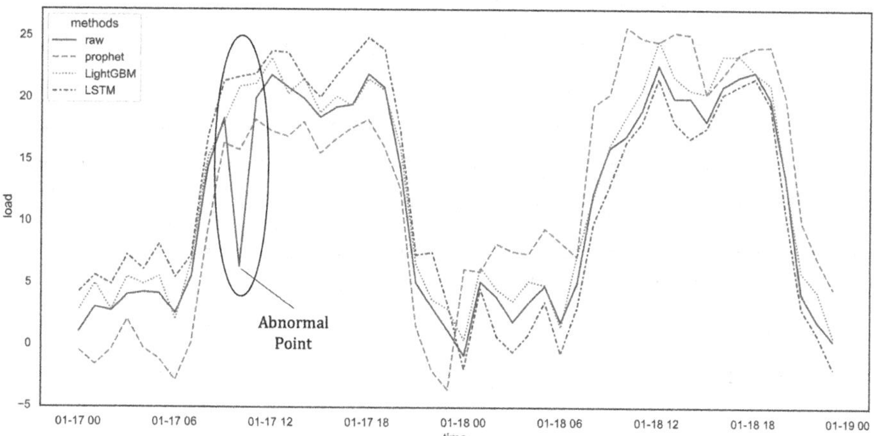

Fig. 7. An anomaly detection sample. The circled part of the figure has a large prediction error and is marked by the anomaly detection service of the IEC-FOF application layer. Note that some of the pictures in this article may be uniform in time, but do not correspond to the same electric customer, so the curve may be different. The predicted value can be negative and is set to 0 when used.

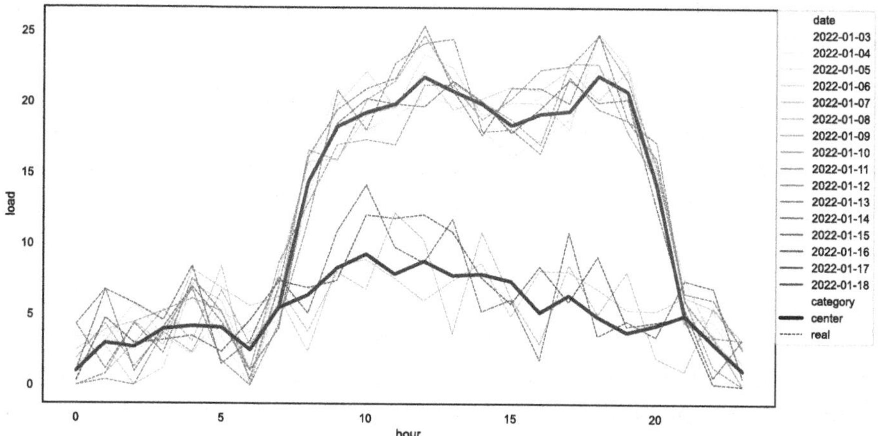

Fig. 8. A typical pattern recognition case. The dashed lines in the figure are the electricity consumption curves for several days, and the two solid lines are two typical electricity consumption modes, corresponding to weekdays and weekends.

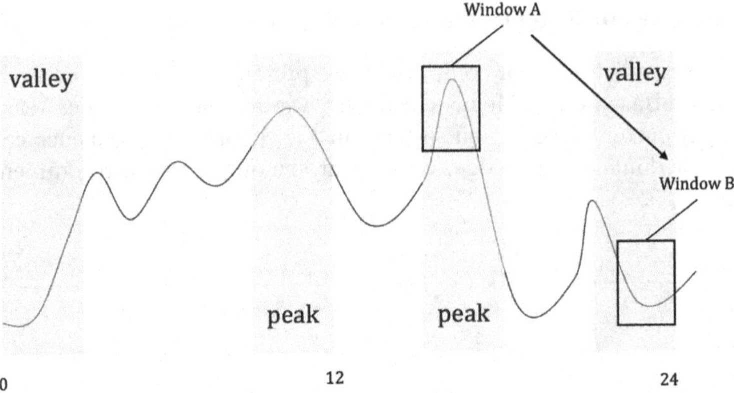

Fig. 9. An example of electricity consumption optimization. The yellow area is the peak of electricity consumption, the most expensive electricity price, and the light blue area is the electricity valley value, the lowest electricity price. The IEC-FOF application layer recommendation generation service informs the user to shift electricity consumption from window A to window B to reduce the cost of electricity. (Color figure online)

6 Discussion

In the industrial electricity consumption scenario described in this paper, through the capture of historical information, we can obtain a prediction of future conditions, so as to obtain more effective services. Forecasting electricity consumption and behavior not only plays a role in enterprises and households but also plays a significant role in electricity distribution and abnormal location.

However, the research application framework proposed by us is not perfect enough. For example, the time series prediction model used is not good at compensating for the long-time dependence. Such task scenarios may require a similar architecture to Transformer to complete, such as the Informer model.

For the design and application of top-level services, we believe that researchers are worthy of further research on the optimization of electricity consumption behavior, such as using operational optimization methods to guide users to make optimal adjustments to electricity consumption. A qualified recommendation needs to measure the elasticity of electricity demand, detect and warn of possible anomalies, and much more can be done.

7 Conclusion

In this paper, we introduce an algorithmic application framework for industrial electricity consumption prediction and optimization, called IEC-FOF, which can provide a variety of electricity consumption-related derivative services. We explained its principles and ideas in detail, and the evaluation result also confirmed the practicality of IEC-FOF.

References

1. Wei, Y.M., Chen, K., Kang, J.N., Chen, W., Wang, X.Y., Zhang, X.: Policy and management of carbon peaking and carbon neutrality: a literature review. Engineering (2022)
2. Vivas, E., Allende-Cid, H., Salas, R.: A systematic review of statistical and machine learning methods for electrical power forecasting with reported MAPE score. Entropy **22**(12), 1412 (2020)
3. Ugurlu, U., Oksuz, I., Tas, O.: Electricity price forecasting using recurrent neural networks. Energies **11**(5), 1255 (2018)
4. Akhter, M.N., Mekhilef, S., Mokhlis, H., et al.: Review on forecasting of photovoltaic power generation based on machine learning and metaheuristic techniques. IET Renew. Power Gener. **13**(7), 1009–1023 (2019)
5. Demolli, H., Dokuz, A.S., Ecemis, A., et al.: Wind power forecasting based on daily wind speed data using machine learning algorithms. Energy Convers. Manage. **198**, 111823 (2019)
6. Zhou, H., et al.: Informer: beyond efficient transformer for long sequence time-series forecasting. In: Proceedings of the AAAI Conference on Artificial Intelligence, vol. 35, No. 12, pp. 11106–11115 (2021)
7. Yu, Y., Si, X., Hu, C., et al.: A review of recurrent neural networks: LSTM cells and network architectures. Neural Comput. **31**(7), 1235–1270 (2019)
8. Krishna, K., Murty, M.N.: Genetic K-means algorithm. IEEE Trans. Syst. Man Cybern. Part B **29**(3), 433–439 (1999)
9. Schubert, E., Sander, J., Ester, M., et al.: DBSCAN revisited, revisited: why and how you should (still) use DBSCAN. ACM Trans. Database Syst. **42**(3), 1–21 (2017)
10. Taylor, S.J., Letham, B.: Forecasting at scale. Am. Stat. **72**(1), 37–45 (2018)
11. Ke, G., et al.: LightGBM: a highly efficient gradient boosting decision tree. In: Proceedings of the 31st International Conference on Neural Information Processing Systems (NIPS 2017), pp. 3149–3157. Curran Associates Inc., Red Hook, NY, USA (2017)
12. Nvidia data-science page: https://www.nvidia.com/en-us/glossary/data-science/k-means/. Accessed 21 July 2022
13. Li, W., et al.: FingFormer: contrastive graph-based finger operation transformer for unsupervised mobile game bot detection. In: Proceedings of the ACM Web Conference 2022, pp. 3367–3375 (2022)
14. Pu, J., et al.: Unsupervised representation learning of player behavioral data with confidence guided masking. In: Proceedings of the ACM Web Conference 2022, pp. 3396–3406 (2022)
15. Wu, R., Deng, H., Tao, J., Fan, C., Liu, Q., Chen, L.: Deep behavior tracing with multi-level temporality preserved embedding. In: Proceedings of the 29th ACM International Conference on Information & Knowledge Management, pp. 2813–2820 (2020)
16. Xu, J., Wu, H., Wang, J., et al.: Anomaly transformer: time series anomaly detection with association discrepancy. arXiv preprint arXiv:2110.02642 (2021)

17. Chicco, D., Warrens, M.J., Jurman, G.: The coefficient of determination R-squared is more informative than SMAPE, MAE, MAPE, MSE and RMSE in regression analysis evaluation. PeerJ Comput. Sci. **7**, e623 (2021)
18. Ho, S.L., Xie, M.: The use of ARIMA models for reliability forecasting and analysis. Comput. Ind. Eng. **35**(1–2), 213–216 (1998)
19. Chen, T., He, T., Benesty, M., et al.: Xgboost: extreme gradient boosting. R Package Version 0.4-2 **1**(4), 1–4 (2015)

Demons Hidden in the Light: Unrestricted Adversarial Illumination Attacks

Kaibo Wang, Yanjiao Chen(✉), and Wenyuan Xu

College of Electrical Engineering, Zhejiang University, Hangzhou, China
{kaibo,chenyanjiao,wyxu}@zju.edu.cn

Abstract. As deep learning-based computer vision is widely used in IoT devices, it is especially critical to ensure its security. Among the attacks against deep neural networks, adversarial attacks are a stealthy means of attack, which can mislead model decisions during the testing phase. Therefore, the exploration of adversarial attacks can help to understand the vulnerability of models in advance and make targeted defense.

Existing unrestricted adversarial attacks beyond the ℓ_p norm often require additional models to be both adversarial and imperceptible, which leads to a high computational cost and task-specific design. Inspired by the observation that models exhibit unexpected vulnerability to changes in illumination, we develop Adversarial Illumination Attack (AIA), an unrestricted adversarial attack that imposes large but imperceptible alterations to the image.

The core of the attack lies in simulating adversarial illumination through Planckian jitter, of which the effectiveness comes from a causal chain where the attacker misleads the model by manipulating the confusion factor. We propose an efficient approach to generate adversarial samples without additional models by image gradient regularization. We validate the effectiveness of adversarial illumination in the face of black-box models, data preprocessing, and adversarially trained models through extensive experiments. Experiment results confirm that AIA can be both a lightweight unrestricted attack and a plug-in to boost the effectiveness of other attacks.

Keywords: Unrestricted adversarial attacks · Adversarial illumination

1 Introduction

Deep neural networks (DNNs) are widely used in IoT devices for tasks such as vehicle data analysis [1–4] and resource allocation [5–9]. However, DNNs have been found to be vulnerable to adversarial attacks [10–12], which hinder their applications in security-critical scenarios in IoT, e.g., autonomous driving. Adversarial examples mislead the decision of DNNs in an imperceptible manner, which is conventionally achieved by bounding the modifications by

Z. Xiao et al. (Eds.): ICECI 2022, LNICST 478, pp. 111–127, 2023.
https://doi.org/10.1007/978-3-031-28990-3_9

the ℓ_p norm [13–15]. However, pixel-level similarity imposed by the ℓ_p norm is unnecessary as adversarial examples only need to be natural and unsuspicious [16,17]. Therefore, unrestricted adversarial attacks, which aim to generate visually natural perturbations, have attracted extensive attention [18–20].

Existing unrestricted adversarial attacks usually contain a model for generating adversarial noises or an additional model for concealing the noises. For instance, in unrestricted adversarial attacks, encoders are often leveraged to transform generated adversarial noises into imperceptible image styles [21,22], and perceptual models are often used as perceptual metrics to assist attackers in concealing the noises [23]. However, this model-based setting incurs extra computational cost, and the noise-concealing model is often task-specific.

To realize unrestricted adversarial attacks with a lightweight framework, we propose to use illuminations to apply large but imperceptible modifications to images. We find that images under carefully-designed illumination are more vulnerable to adversarial attacks. We explain this vulnerability from a causal perspective, i.e., a spurious association between the label and the illumination in the learning process. The attacker can simulate adversarial illumination by Planckian jitter, which makes even tiny noises hidden at the image edges sufficient to mislead the model. The adversarial illumination can be obtained by solving an optimization problem with an image gradient regularization term. Integrating the Planckian jitter and the image gradient regularization, we can obtain a lightweight unrestricted adversarial attack framework named Adversarial Illumination Attack (AIA), which can also be used as a plug-in to boost the effectiveness of other attacks. We summarize our main contributions as follows:

- We explore the vulnerability of learning models in the face of adversarial illumination noises and provide a causal explanation.
- We propose a lightweight unrestricted adversarial attack method AIA using adversarial illumination and image gradient regularization.
- We validate the effectiveness of the AIA in the face of black-box models, data preprocessing, and adversarially trained models with comprehensive experiments.

2 Related Works

2.1 Adversarial Attacks with ℓ_p-norm Constraints

Due to the nice theoretical properties of ℓ_p-norm, it is often used as a perceptibility metric for adversarial examples. The attacker either designs the adversarial noise within the ℓ_p-norm ball [11,13] or designs the successful adversarial noise with a minimum ℓ_p-norm [24]. Many algorithms are designed based on ℓ_∞-norm constraints, including single-step FGSM [11] and iterative PGD [13]. There are also algorithms aiming at minimizing ℓ_2-norm, such as L-BFGS [10] and C&W [14]. Adversarial attacks with ℓ_1-norm constraints for the sake of noise sparsity have also been studied [25]. ℓ_0-attacks target at modifying the minimum number of pixels [26,27]. Patch attacks, which are widely used in physical world attacks, can also be regarded as special ℓ_0-attacks [28,29].

2.2 Unconstrained Adversarial Attacks

As ℓ_p-norm oversimplifies the perceptual condition of adversarial examples, unconstrained attacks beyond the ℓ_p-norm constraint have been proposed recently. Unconstrained adversarial attacks can be implemented by color adjustment [20,30] and geometric transformation [31,32]. Unrestricted adversarial attacks usually adopt an extra generative model to make the modifications non-suspicious. For example, GANs [19] and encoders [21] can be used to generate natural adversarial examples; perceptual models [33] can be used as a perceptual metric to transform the generation of adversarial samples into a multi-objective optimization problem [23]; and semantic segmentation models can segment images to attack separately [34–36]. However, all these approaches require task-specific design before attacking and additional computation during attacking.

2.3 Defense Against Adversarial Attacks

As the threat of adversarial attacks becomes more prominent, defending against them is especially critical. Both data preprocessing and adversarial training are commonly used as defenses. Data preprocessing are used to corrupt adversarial noise, including JPEG compression [37], bit-depth compression [38], and autoencoder-based reconstruction [39]. Adversarial training is one of the most effective means to defend against ℓ_p-norm adversarial examples [13,40]. The variants of adversarial training may consider accuracy trade-offs [41], adversarial perturbations to weights [42], and hypersphere embedding [43]. However, these defenses are usually designed for ℓ_p-norm adversarial examples and may not work for unrestricted attacks.

3 Adversarial Illumination Attack (AIA)

Threat Model. Given an image $x \in \mathbb{R}^{CHW}$ with width W, height H and C channels and its label y, a classifier $f : \mathbb{R}^{CHW} \rightarrow \mathbb{R}^N$ will classify it as $f(x) = \arg\max_{n=1,\dots,N} f_n(x)$, where N is the number of classes. The attacker aims to find an adversarial mapping $r : \mathbb{R}^{CHW} \rightarrow \mathbb{R}^{CHW}$ so that $r(x)$ is misclassified, i.e., $f[r(x)] \neq y$. Unlike the ℓ_p-norm constrained adversarial attack that constrains $\|r(x) - x\|_p \leq \epsilon$, the unrestricted attack only requires that the semantic information of the images remains consistent. It is worth noting that semantic information consistency does not require images $r(x)$ and x to be similar since the model knows nothing about the original image x.

Attack Algorithm Overview. We design a lightweight algorithm that ensures the effectiveness of the attack with a unified model. We explicitly decouple $r(x)$ into two parts, a global transformation $I(x;\theta)$ with a few parameters to maintain the semantic information of the image and an adversarial noise δ:

$$r(x) = I(x;\theta) + \delta. \tag{1}$$

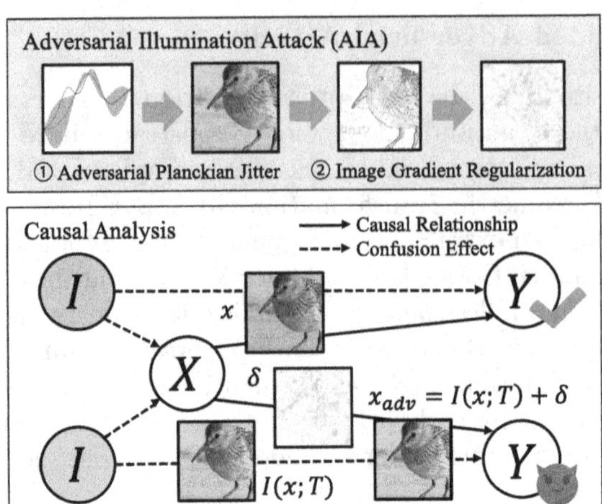

Fig. 1. The diagram of Adversarial Illumination Attacks (AIA). **Top:** Illustration of the AIA algorithm flow; **Bottom:** Causal analysis of AIA.

$I(x;\theta)$ can be seen as a "low-frequency" noise applied to the entire image, giving a large but not suspicious transformation to the image and making the model's decisions fragile. Therefore, the generation of δ can be simplified without relying on other models. As shown in Fig.1, the design of our algorithm for $I(x;\theta)$ and δ can be briefly described as:

- **Adversarial Planckian Jitter (APJ):** We note that images under different illumination conditions vary greatly and are found to potentially mislead the model's decisions, which may be due to the model's bias towards illumination during training. Therefore, we manipulate the causal relationship between images and labels by simulating adversarial illumination as $I(x,\theta)$ through adversarial Planckian jitter.
- **Image Gradient Regularization:** Model's decisions under adversarial illumination are more fragile so that the adversarial noise hidden in the image texture is sufficient to rival the effect of model-based unrestricted attacks. Therefore, we regularize the generation of adversarial noise δ by image gradients.

3.1 Adversarial Planckian Jitter

In reality, changes in lighting conditions can bring different tones to an image, such as images taken at dusk or dawn will have a warm tone, while images under artificial light may lean toward cooler tones. DNNs deployed in safety-critical scenarios, such as autonomous driving, are supposed to be invariant to illumination transformation but have been found to be unexpectedly vulnerable under carefully crafted illumination transformation. Attackers can simulate such illumination by Planckian jitter, which consists of the following steps: 1) obtaining a spectrum of a given temperature based on the physical description of blackbody radiation; 2) converting the spectrum into an sRGB representation; 3) jittering the image illumination by making channel-wise products of this representation and the image.

According to Planck's law, a blackbody radiates a different spectrum $\sigma_T(\lambda)$ at different temperatures T, which can be expressed as

$$\sigma_T(\lambda) = \frac{2\pi hc^2}{\lambda^5[\exp(hc/kT\lambda) - 1]}, \tag{2}$$

where c, h, k are the speed of light, Planck's constant, and Boltzmann's constant, respectively.

Following the method proposed in [44], we convert the spectrum at temperature T to its sRGB representation $A(T) \in \mathbb{R}^3$, then based on which jitter the illumination of the image as:

$$I(x;T) = 0.8\,A(T) \circ x + 0.2\mu[A(T) \circ x], \tag{3}$$

where $\circ$ represents channel-wise product, $\mu(\cdot)$ is a spatial average function.

Attackers aim to find a re-illumination transformation that maximizes the adversarial of $r(x)$ by varying its temperature T. For the realism of the transformation, T is constrained to be in the interval $3 \times 10^4 K$ to $15 \times 10^4 K$. For convenience, we scale it to the interval $[0, 1]$. For the efficiency and generality of the solution, we choose δ as a ℓ_∞ bounded single-step adversarial noise, which is known as FGSM [11]. Therefore, T can be obtained by solving the optimization problem:

$$T^* = \arg\max_T \mathcal{L}\{I_x + \epsilon\,\text{sign}[\nabla_{I_x}\mathcal{L}(I_x)]\} \quad s.t. \;\; T \in [0, 1], \tag{4}$$

where I_x is an abbreviation for $I(x;T)$, $\mathcal{L}(x)$ is a loss function w.r.t x.

In practice, it is found that the objective function is often multi-peaked w.r.t T, which may make the gradient-based optimization method converge to a local optimum. So we adopt the Bayesian optimization algorithm as the solver, the advantage of which is that it allows more exploration in the interval to obtain an approximate solution closer to the global optimum.

3.2 Effectiveness of AIA: A Causal Perspective

We selected the commonly used margin loss as the objective function and did preliminary experiments on CIFAR10, ImageNet, and ImageNette. We report the success rate and margin loss of FGSM attacks under adversarial illumination for three datasets in Fig.2(a). Even if only one parameter is adjusted to change the illumination of the image, the attack success rate and margin loss of FGSM attacks improve significantly.

Although the change in illumination can be seen as a shift in the data distribution, unlike a distribution that has not been seen by a model such as data corruption [45], the model has seen different illumination during training. This vulnerability to seen distribution shifts is counterintuitive. We give an explanation from a causality perspective:

The illumination acts as a confounding factor, establishing a spurious association with the label, which can be exploited by attackers.

Using X, Y, and I to denote the image, label, and illumination, respectively, the causal map can be drawn as shown in Fig.1, where I is a confounding factor. An intuitive example is that we want the model to learn the causal mapping of lion images to labels, i.e., $X \rightarrow Y$. Whereas lions often appear in warm grassland backgrounds, the model may unthinkingly associate illumination to labels, i.e., $X \leftarrow I \rightarrow Y$, which is considered a predictive but not robust feature in [46]. By manipulating the illumination, the attacker can maximize the effect of path $I \rightarrow Y$, whose contradiction with $X \rightarrow Y$ can make the model's decision hesitant. This explains the unintended vulnerability of the model to simple attacks under adversarial illumination: attackers can manipulate the causality of both $X \rightarrow Y, I \rightarrow Y$ to lead to the wrong prediction, as shown in Fig.1.

We designed a toy dog and cat classification task with biased illumination transformation to verify this idea, where the illumination temperature of the cat's picture is sampled from Beta(3, 7), while the dog's is sampled from Beta(7, 3), as shown in Fig.2b (top). The model can achieve a test accuracy of 94% with the same distribution. Once the illumination distributions of dogs and cats are exchanged, the model's test accuracy plummets to 68%, implying that the model exploits the causality of $I \rightarrow Y$. The results of adversarial illumination similarly validate this result, as the temperature obtained for cat's images is significantly biased towards one and vice versa, which is shown in Fig.2(b) (bottom).

3.3 Image Gradient Regularization

Optimization Problem with Regularization. The presence of adversarial illumination makes it easier to generate adversarial noise without the need for other models. Intuitively high-frequency noise added to a monochromatic surface is easily detected, while noise at the edges of the image is more subtle. In other words, the variation pattern of the noise should be consistent with the variation pattern of the image. A straightforward idea is to use the image's gradient to regularize the noise's gradient.

The image gradient can be obtained by the first- or second-order derivative operator. We use Sobel and Laplacian operators as estimators of the image gradient, and both are implemented based on convolution. Specifically, with the following convolution kernel, we can obtain three post-convolution results $G_1^{(1)}(x)$, $G_2^{(1)}(x)$, $G^{(2)}(x) \in \mathbb{R}^{CHW}$:

$$G_1^{(1)}(x) = \begin{bmatrix} -1 & 0 & 1 \\ -2 & 0 & 2 \\ -1 & 0 & 1 \end{bmatrix} * x, \; G_2^{(1)}(x) = \begin{bmatrix} -1 & -2 & -1 \\ 0 & 0 & 0 \\ 1 & 2 & 1 \end{bmatrix} * x, \; G^{(2)}(x) = \begin{bmatrix} 0 & 1 & 0 \\ 1 & -4 & 1 \\ 0 & 1 & 0 \end{bmatrix} * x, \tag{5}$$

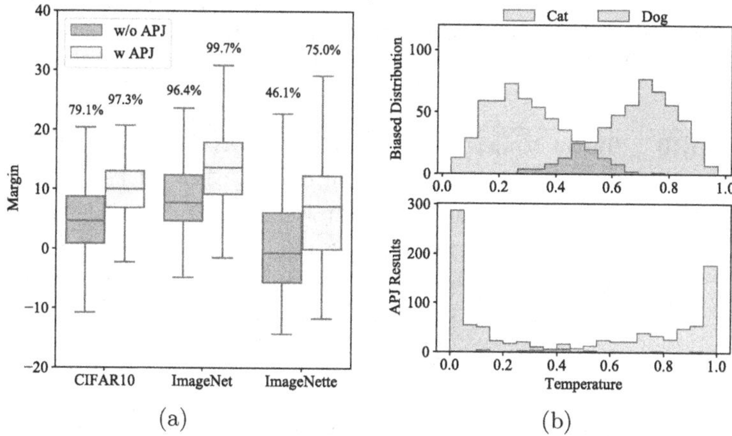

Fig. 2. (a) Experimental results of FGSM attacks with and without APJ on three datasets. The box plot shows margin loss, and the success rate of the attack is annotated above. (b) **Top:** Biased light distribution applied during training of toy models. Cats: Beta(3, 7), dogs: Beta(7, 3); **Bottom:** Distribution of adversarial Planckian jitter in different categories

where $*$ denotes the convolution operation. The Sobel and Laplacian gradients $S(x), L(x)$ can be obtained as follows:

$$S(x) = \sqrt{G_1^{(1)}(x)^2 + G_2^{(1)}(x)^2}, \quad L(x) = |G^{(2)}(x)|, \tag{6}$$

where the operations here are all element-wise operations.

The regularization should provide a high loss when the image gradient is small while the noise gradient is large and a low loss for the rest of the cases, which can be expressed as:

$$\max_{\delta} \mathcal{L}(I_x + \delta; \alpha) := \mathcal{L}(I_x + \delta) - \alpha\{[1 - S(I_x)^2]S(\delta)^2 + [1 - L(I_x)^2]L(\delta)^2\} \tag{7}$$

where α is the weight of the regularization.

Warm-up and Early Stop. The regularization term is derivable, so any adversarial attack algorithm can be used to generate δ, simply by replacing the loss function $\mathcal{L}(I_x + \delta)$ with $\mathcal{L}(I_x + \delta; \alpha)$. Here we use the PGD algorithm with momentum [15] to generate the adversarial noise, where we remove the projection operation to make the noise unrestricted. To avoid generating too large noise, we limit the noise amplitude by choosing a small step ξ. In addition, we gradually increase the regularization weights as the number of iterations increases, i.e., $\alpha = \alpha_0 t$, which constrains excessive noise in the later stages and provides a direction to maximize the loss function in the earlier stages. To generate moderate adversarial noise, we stop the optimization early after the margin loss is greater than a given threshold κ. Therefore, the adversarial noise can be obtained by the following iterative algorithm:

Table 1. The success rate of attacks against white-box (denoted by superscript *) and black-box models. The model architectures include ResNet (RN) [47], WideResNet (WRN) [48], DenseNet (DN) [49], MobileNetv2 (MNv2) [50] and EfficientNet (EN) [51].

CIFAR10	Target Model	WRN28*	RN18	DN161	MNv2	Avg
	PGD	100.0%	66.7%	68.5%	91.1%	81.6%
	FSA	98.9%	71.3%	68.9%	71.7%	77.7%
	PPA	100.0%	17.1%	17.1%	38.6%	43.2%
	AIA (ours)	100.0%	66.6%	68.1%	76.7%	77.8%
	PGD+APJ	100.0%	76.8%	82.2%	93.4%	88.1%
	FSA+APJ	99.8%	79.2%	77.3%	78.1%	83.6%
	PPA+APJ	100.0%	35.0%	33.5%	49.8%	54.6%
ImageNet	Target Model	RN50*	WRN50	EN	DN201	Avg
	PGD	100.0%	73.2%	55.4%	70.0%	74.6%
	FSA	99.6%	85.0%	75.8%	78.0%	84.6%
	PPA	100.0%	36.4%	34.8%	38.1%	52.3%
	AIA (ours)	100.0%	78.2%	61.3%	72.0%	77.9%
	PGD+APJ	100.0%	85.5%	69.9%	79.2%	83.7%
	FSA+APJ	99.9%	91.1%	84.2%	84.6%	90.0%
	PPA+APJ	100.0%	55.6%	46.9%	51.2%	63.4%
ImageNette	Target Model	RN50*	WRN50	EN	DN201	Avg
	PGD	100.0%	30.1%	16.0%	19.4%	41.4%
	FSA	78.0%	33.6%	25.9%	27.9%	41.4%
	PPA	98.4%	6.1%	4.1%	5.1%	28.4%
	AIA (ours)	97.2%	22.6%	14.6%	22.7%	39.3%
	PGD+APJ	100.0%	46.0%	24.1%	33.0%	50.8%
	FSA+APJ	89.1%	41.8%	36.1%	35.7%	50.7%
	PPA+APJ	98.5%	16.1%	10.1%	13.9%	34.7%

$$\delta^{(t+1)} = \begin{cases} \delta^{(t)} + \xi \text{sign}[g^{(t+1)}] & \mathcal{L}(I_x + \delta^{(t)}) < \kappa \\ \delta^{(t)} & \text{else} \end{cases}, \tag{8}$$

$$g^{(t+1)} = g^{(t)} + \frac{\nabla_\delta \mathcal{L}(I_x + \delta^{(t)}; \alpha_0 t)}{\|\nabla_\delta \mathcal{L}(I_x + \delta^{(t)}; \alpha_0 t)\|_1} \quad t = 1, ...T_{max}. \tag{9}$$

The convolution-based regularization imposes almost no additional burden on the gradient computation and is task-independent, requiring no specific design for different tasks.

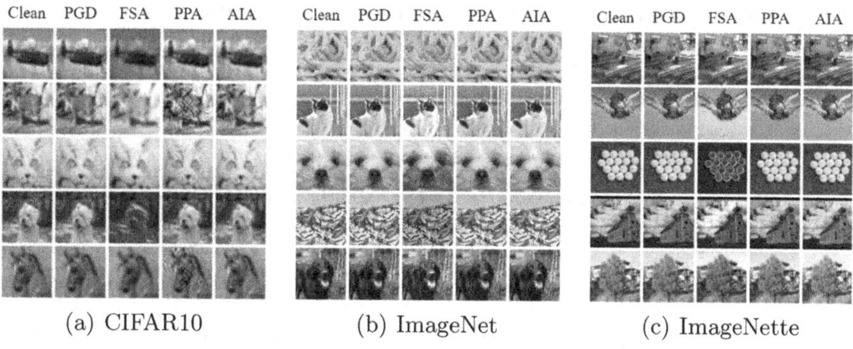

(a) CIFAR10 (b) ImageNet (c) ImageNette

Fig. 3. Example of adversarial samples $r(x)$ generated by different attack methods.

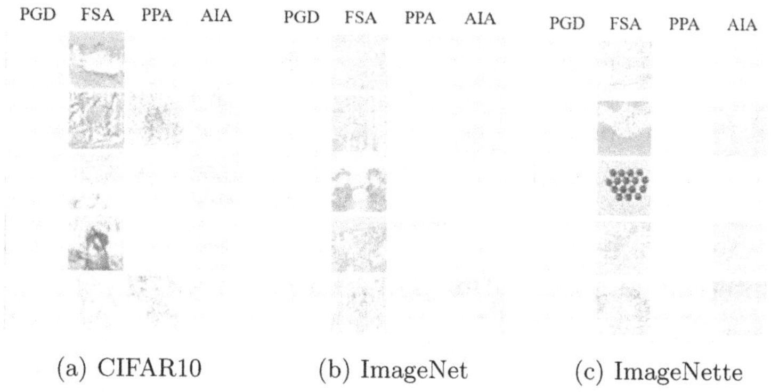

(a) CIFAR10 (b) ImageNet (c) ImageNette

Fig. 4. Example of adversarial noise $|r(x) - x|$.

4 Experiments

4.1 Experimental Setup

We tested the performance of AIA on three datasets, including CIFAR10 [52], ImageNet [53] and Imagenette (a subset of 10 easily classified classes from Imagenet). We chose L_∞-constrained projected gradient descent (PGD) [13] as the baseline. For the unrestricted attack, we chose the encoder-based feature space attack (FSA) [21] and the perceptual model-based perceptual PGD attack (PPA) [23] as a comparison. Following the conventional settings, the ℓ_∞-norm constraint of PGD is set to 8/255, and the bounds of FSA and PPA are set to 2 and 0.5, respectively. The parameters in AIA are set to $\xi = 0.0025, \alpha_0 = 0.75\sqrt{HW}, \kappa = 15$. The number of iterations for all attacks is set to 50. We randomly selected 1000 samples in the test set for each attack and reported their attack success rates (ASR).

Table 2. Results of image quality quantification for the adversarial samples. The metrics include Peek Signal to Noise Ratio (PSNR), Structural Similarity (SSIM), BRISQUE (BQ), and Total Variation (TV), where ↑ indicates that the higher the metric is, the better the image quality is, and vice versa.

	Attack Methods	PSNR↑	SSIM↑	BQ↓	TV↓	Avg↑
CIFAR10	PGD	31.78	0.90	58.94	0.39	0.82
	FSA	18.27	0.71	59.66	0.28	0.71
	PPA	31.90	0.94	58.99	0.38	0.83
	AIA (ours)	30.34	0.90	55.91	0.33	0.84
ImageNet	PGD	32.61	0.86	24.29	0.32	0.78
	FSA	19.02	0.72	16.34	0.27	0.77
	PPA	39.04	0.96	15.99	0.30	0.95
	AIA (ours)	35.79	0.96	17.91	0.26	0.91
ImageNette	PGD	31.78	0.90	58.94	0.39	0.66
	FSA	18.27	0.71	59.66	0.28	0.56
	PPA	31.90	0.94	58.99	0.38	0.68
	AIA (ours)	30.34	0.90	55.91	0.33	0.67

4.2 White-Box and Black-Box Adversarial Attack

We tested the effectiveness of the four attacks under white-box and transfer-based black-box settings, as shown in Table 1. We chose three models with different structures and FLOPs as the target models. It can be found that each attack in the white-box setting achieves extremely high ASR. In transfer-based black-box attacks, FSA achieves a high ASR, and its performance stems from the significant changes brought to the image style based on the encoder. Our proposed AIA achieves comparable results to FSA on CIFAR10 and better results than PGD on ImageNet without additional models. In comparison, the low transferability of PPA may be due to a focus on imperceptibility leading to convergence to model-specific noise.

We also tested the attack performance of other attacks with an adversarial illumination plug-in (+APJ). It can be seen that the success rates of the attacks with APJ are all significantly improved (∼8.2%), which means that the adversarial illumination can be used as a plug-in to enhance the transferability of other attacks by exploiting the bias of the training data, a vulnerability that is common across models.

4.3 Image Quality

Here, we show samples and noise generated by different attacks, as shown in Fig.3 and Fig.4. Encoder-based FSA brings image adversarial style transformation, but such transformation is sometimes unrealistic. Perceptual model-based PPA produces adversarial noise that is more realistic on high-resolution images but

Table 3. The success rate of the attack in the face of different data preprocessing defenses. The preprocessing defenses include: JPEG compression (JPEG) [37], Bit-Depth compression (BitDepth) [38], Blur, and Auto-Encoder Reconstruction (AE).

	Attack Methods	JPEG	BitDepth	Blur	AE	Avg
CIFAR10	PGD	78.1%	100.0%	83.0%	66.2%	85.4%
	FSA	89.2%	97.1%	94.2%	81.4%	91.0%
	PPA	26.8%	81.2%	32.5%	38.2%	47.2%
	AIA (ours)	93.9%	100.0%	99.5%	89.3%	96.5%
	PGD+APJ	93.5%	100.0%	96.2%	81.7%	94.3%
	FSA+APJ	96.4%	99.4%	97.2%	89.3%	96.1%
	PPA+APJ	56.1%	93.2%	63.7%	65.2%	72.0%
ImageNet	PGD	99.7%	100.0%	98.8%	87.2%	97.1%
	FSA	99.6%	85.0%	75.8%	78.0%	84.6%
	PPA	50.9%	69.7%	52.0%	57.4%	58.0%
	AIA (ours)	99.8%	99.8%	99.8%	94.8%	98.8%
	PGD+APJ	99.9%	100.0%	99.3%	94.3%	98.7%
	FSA+APJ	99.3%	99.1%	96.8%	92.4%	97.3%
	PPA+APJ	73.4%	89.2%	73.1%	76.4%	79.0%
ImageNette	PGD	94.9%	99.9%	98.1%	89.6%	87.0%
	FSA	68.4%	72.2%	66.6%	61.4%	61.8%
	PPA	19.7%	38.8%	27.8%	17.6%	23.4%
	AIA (ours)	95.3%	94.8%	94.4%	95.6%	87.3%
	PGD+APJ	96.9%	99.9%	98.9%	93.6%	90.4%
	FSA+APJ	81.3%	85.8%	81.2%	73.4%	74.3%
	PPA+APJ	41.9%	67.8%	58.4%	34.5%	46.5%

conspicuous on low-resolution images. The adversarial samples generated by AIA can be disguised as the result of illumination changes, which avoids adding noise in monochromatic regions like PGD by image gradient regularization.

We also quantified the image quality of the adversarial samples. In image quality metrics, different metrics have different meanings and different scales. Among them, PSNR measures the ratio of signal to noise, and a higher signal-to-noise ratio indicates that less noise is added. It is generally believed that images with PSNR greater than 40 dB have higher quality, so we rescale PSNR with PSNR/40. SSIM measures the structural similarity of the image to the original image, a higher SSIM means the modified image is more similar to the original image. SSIM takes a value between 0 and 1, so we do not scale it. TV indicates the smoothness of the image and is obtained by averaging the differences between adjacent pixel values. A lower TV indicates a smoother image and takes a value between 0 and 1, so we scale it with $1 - \text{TV}$. BRISQUE is a measure of the naturalness of an image, and a lower value indicates a higher quality image.

Table 4. Attack success rate on an adversarially trained model. The methods of adversarial training include: Hypersphere Embedding (HE) [43], Adversarial Weight Perturbation (AWP) [42], Feature Scatter (FS) [54], Robust Self-Training (RST) [40], and TRADES [41].

Defense	HE	AWP	FS	RST	TRADES	Avg
PGD	40.3%	35.8%	34.5%	34.0%	42.3%	37.4%
FSA	96.6%	96.3%	53.7%	96.4%	97.5%	88.1%
PPA	94.9%	99.1%	49.9%	98.7%	99.4%	88.4%
AIA (ours)	73.9%	82.9%	79.5%	83.7%	89.1%	81.8%
PGD+APJ	80.9%	76.4%	78.0%	75.6%	83.0%	78.8%
FSA+APJ	98.8%	99.0%	84.0%	99.0%	99.3%	96.0%
PPA+APJ	99.7%	99.9%	86.7%	100.0%	100.0%	97.3%

The value of BRISQUE varies across datasets, so we scale it with the average of BRISQUE over the dataset. Therefore, the average value can be obtained by:

$$\mathbf{Avg} = \frac{1}{4}[\frac{\text{PSNR}}{40} + \text{SSIM} + 1 - \text{TV} + \frac{\overline{\text{BRISQUE}}}{\text{BRISQUE}}]. \tag{10}$$

where $\overline{\text{BRISQUE}}$ is the average of BRISQUE on the dataset. Note that the average value here is only for the convenience of comprehensive comparison. The results are shown in Table.2.

We can find that the imperceptibility of AIA is comparable to that of PPA and better than that of PGD and FSA, especially in the case of unreferenced metrics, which is a more reasonable scenario of adversarial sample quality assessment.

4.4 Attack Effect Under Data Preprocessing

We selected four representative defenses to test the effectiveness of the attack under preprocessing, as shown in Table.3. We can find that AIA achieves the highest ASR in the face of preprocessing, especially in AE. This is due to the global noise brought to the images by the adversarial illumination, which is difficult to corrupt by data preprocessing, even after reconstruction. As shown in Fig.3, the more significant noise generated by AIA gains the robustness of the adversarial sample, which can also be verified from the boosted ASR ($\sim$10.9%) of the other attacks with APJ in Table.3.

4.5 Attack Effect Facing Defense Models

Since the adversarial training was mostly evaluated on the CIFAR10, we selected five adversarially trained models on the CIFAR10 dataset to test the ASR of each attack, as shown in Table.4. It can be seen that PPA and FSA have higher attack

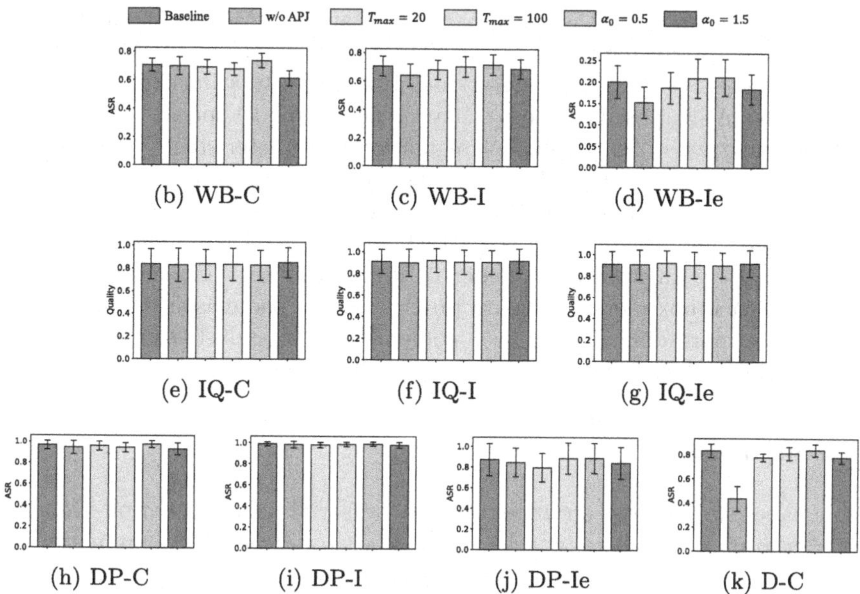

Fig. 5. Results of ablation experiments in four tasks, including white-box and black box attacks (WB), image quality (IQ), data preprocessing (DP) and defense (D). Datasets CIFAR10, ImageNet and ImageNette are abbreviated by C, I, Ie, respectively. The baseline setting is $\alpha_0 = 0.75, T_{max} = 50$ with APJ. The mean and standard deviation of different metrics were plotted.

success rates in the face of adversarially trained models, while AIA is slightly weaker, probably due to its more conservative constraint on noise. Note that APJ plays a crucial role in breaking some defenses, such as FS, and thus APJ is suitable as a complement to other attacks. We speculate that the reason is that the adversarial training model smooths the decision boundaries under normal data distribution. However, the data distribution under adversarial illumination is not considered during the adversarial training. It is also evident from the significant ASR improvement brought by APJ for PGD: adversarial training focuses too much on the ℓ_∞ neighborhoods of the training data. Simply changing the illumination of the samples is enough to break through the adversarial training model even if it is still ℓ_∞-bounded adversarial noise.

4.6 Ablation Study

we investigated the performance of AIA with different parameter settings, including with and without APJ, different number of iterations T_{max}, and different image gradient regularization weights α_0. From the results shown in Fig.5, we can find that 1) APJ is more critical to breaking through the defense model and improving ASR in the face of black-box models and data preprocessing. The reason for the improvement is not apparent is that the attacker exploits tremendous noise, i.e., sacrificing image quality for ASR improvement. 2) AIA does not require an excessive number of iterations. Too many iterations can sometimes lead to worse ASR, possibly due to convergence to model-specific noise on the one hand and greater image gradient regularization in later stages on the other. 3) Different α_0 regulate the ASR and image quality trade-offs. The difference brought by α_0 is milder, so it is not difficult to find a moderate parameter.

On ImageNette, the effect of the attack without APJ is significantly lower, and the attack with a higher number of iterations has a higher ASR in the face of the black box model and data preprocessing. The reason for this is that ImagNette is more difficult to attack compared to ImageNet, so the APJ and more iterations which is used to improve the effectiveness are more important.

5 Conclusion

In this paper, we propose an unrestricted adversarial attack based on illumination transformation, where attackers can generate adversarial illumination by Planckian jitter and manipulate the causal relationship between illumination and labels to mislead the model. We design an unrestricted adversarial noise optimization algorithm based on this by image gradient regularization, which achieves significant attack results without additional models. Comprehensive experiments validate the effectiveness of adversarial illumination.

References

1. Xiao, Z., et al.: Trajdata: on vehicle trajectory collection with commodity plug-and-play OBU devices. IEEE Internet Things J. **7**(9), 9066–9079 (2020)
2. Li, J., et al.: Drive2friends: inferring social relationships from individual vehicle mobility data. IEEE Internet Things J. **7**(6), 5116–5127 (2020)
3. Long, W., et al.: Unified spatial-temporal neighbor attention network for dynamic traffic prediction. IEEE Trans. Veh. Technol. (2022)
4. Huang, Y., Xiao, Z., Yu, X., Wang, D., Havyarimana, V., Bai, J.: Road network construction with complex intersections based on sparsely sampled private car trajectory data. ACM Trans. Knowl. Discov. Data (TKDD) **13**(3), 1–28 (2019)
5. Jiang, H., Xiao, Z., Li, Z., Xu, J., Zeng, F., Wang, D.: An energy-efficient framework for internet of things underlaying heterogeneous small cell networks. IEEE Trans. Mob. Comput. **21**(1), 31–43 (2020)
6. Xiao, Z., et al.: Resource management in UAV-assisted MEC: state-of-the-art and open challenges. Wireless Netw. **28**(7), 3305–3322 (2022)
7. Dai, X.: Task co-offloading for d2d-assisted mobile edge computing in industrial internet of things. IEEE Trans. Ind. Inform. **19**(1), 480–490 (2022)
8. Zeng, F., Li, Q., Xiao, Z., Havyarimana, V., Bai, J.: A price-based optimization strategy of power control and resource allocation in full-duplex heterogeneous macrocell-femtocell networks. IEEE Access **6**, 42004–42013 (2018)
9. Xiao, Z., et al.: A joint information and energy cooperation framework for CR-enabled macro-femto heterogeneous networks. IEEE Internet Things J. **7**(4), 2828–2839 (2019)

10. Szegedy, C.: Intriguing properties of neural networks. arXiv preprint arXiv:1312.6199 (2013)
11. Goodfellow, I.J., Shlens, J., Szegedy, C.: Explaining and harnessing adversarial examples. arXiv preprint arXiv:1412.6572 (2014)
12. Carlini, N., Wagner, D.: Audio adversarial examples: targeted attacks on speech-to-text. In: 2018 IEEE Security and Privacy Workshops (SPW), pp. 1–7. IEEE (2018)
13. Madry, A., Makelov, A., Schmidt, L., Tsipras, D., Vladu, A.: Towards deep learning models resistant to adversarial attacks. arXiv preprint arXiv:1706.06083 (2017)
14. Carlini, N., Wagner, D.: Towards evaluating the robustness of neural networks. In: 2017 IEEE Symposium on Security and Privacy (SP), pp. 39–57. IEEE (2017)
15. Dong, Y., et al.: Boosting adversarial attacks with momentum. In: Proceedings of the IEEE Conference on Computer Vision and Pattern Recognition, pp. 9185–9193 (2018)
16. Johnson, J., Alahi, A., Fei-Fei, L.: Perceptual losses for real-time style transfer and super-resolution. In: Leibe, B., Matas, J., Sebe, N., Welling, M. (eds.) ECCV 2016. LNCS, vol. 9906, pp. 694–711. Springer, Cham (2016). https://doi.org/10.1007/978-3-319-46475-6_43
17. Sharif, M., Bauer, L., Reiter, M.K.: On the suitability of LP-norms for creating and preventing adversarial examples. In: Proceedings of the IEEE Conference on Computer Vision and Pattern Recognition Workshops, pp. 1605–1613 (2018)
18. Liu, F., Zhang, C., Zhang, H.: Towards transferable unrestricted adversarial examples with minimum changes. arXiv preprint arXiv:2201.01102 (2022)
19. Xiang, T., Liu, H., Guo, S., Gan, Y., Liao, X.: Egm: an efficient generative model for unrestricted adversarial examples. ACM Trans. Sens. Netw. (TOSN) **18**(4), 1–25 (2022)
20. Zhao, Z., Liu, Z., Larson, M.: Adversarial color enhancement: generating unrestricted adversarial images by optimizing a color filter. arXiv preprint arXiv:2002.01008 (2020)
21. Xu, Q., Tao, G., Cheng, S., Zhang, X.: Towards feature space adversarial attack by style perturbation. In: Proceedings of the AAAI Conference on Artificial Intelligence, vol. 35, pp. 10523–10531 (2021)
22. Duan, R., Ma, X., Wang, Y., Bailey, J., Qin, A.K., Yang, Y.: Adversarial camouflage: hiding physical-world attacks with natural styles. In: Proceedings of the IEEE/CVF Conference on Computer Vision and Pattern Recognition, pp. 1000–1008 (2020)
23. Laidlaw, C., Singla, S., Feizi, S.: Perceptual adversarial robustness: defense against unseen threat models. In: ICLR (2021)
24. Moosavi-Dezfooli, S.-M., Fawzi, A., Frossard, P.: Deepfool: a simple and accurate method to fool deep neural networks. In: Proceedings of the IEEE Conference on Computer Vision and Pattern Recognition, pp. 2574–2582 (2016)
25. Chen, P.-Y., Sharma, Y., Zhang, H., Yi, J., Hsieh, C.-J.: Ead: elastic-net attacks to deep neural networks via adversarial examples. In: Proceedings of the AAAI Conference on Artificial Intelligence, vol. 32 (2018)
26. Papernot, N., McDaniel, P., Jha, S., Fredrikson, M., Celik, Z.B., Swami, A.: The limitations of deep learning in adversarial settings. In: 2016 IEEE European Symposium on Security and Privacy (EuroS&P), pp. 372–387. IEEE (2016)
27. Su, J., Vargas, D.V., Sakurai, K.: One pixel attack for fooling deep neural networks. IEEE Trans. Evol. Comput. **23**(5), 828–841 (2019)
28. Brown, T.B., Mané, D., Roy, A., Abadi, M., Gilmer, J.: Adversarial patch. arXiv preprint arXiv:1712.09665 (2017)

29. Liu, X., Yang, H., Liu, Z., Song, L., Li, H., Chen, Y.: Dpatch: an adversarial patch attack on object detectors. arXiv preprint arXiv:1806.02299 (2018)
30. Laidlaw, C., Feizi, S.: Functional adversarial attacks. In: Advances in Neural Information Processing Systems, vol. 32 (2019)
31. Alaifari, R., Alberti, G.S., Gauksson, T.: Adef: an iterative algorithm to construct adversarial deformations. arXiv preprint arXiv:1804.07729 (2018)
32. Xiao, C., Zhu, J.-Y., Li, B., He, W., Liu, M., Song, D.: Spatially transformed adversarial examples. arXiv preprint arXiv:1801.02612 (2018)
33. Zhang, R., Isola, P., Efros, A.A., Shechtman, E., Wang, O.: The unreasonable effectiveness of deep features as a perceptual metric. In: Proceedings of the IEEE Conference on Computer Vision and Pattern Recognition, pp. 586–595 (2018)
34. Hosseini, H., Poovendran, R.: Semantic adversarial examples. In: Proceedings of the IEEE Conference on Computer Vision and Pattern Recognition Workshops, pp. 1614–1619 (2018)
35. Shamsabadi, A.S., Sanchez-Matilla, R., Cavallaro, A.: Colorfool: semantic adversarial colorization. In: Proceedings of the IEEE/CVF Conference on Computer Vision and Pattern Recognition, pp. 1151–1160 (2020)
36. Bhattad, A., Chong, M.J., Liang, K., Li, B., Forsyth, D.A.: Unrestricted adversarial examples via semantic manipulation. arXiv preprint arXiv:1904.06347 (2019)
37. Das, N.: Shield: fast, practical defense and vaccination for deep learning using jpeg compression. In: Proceedings of the 24th ACM SIGKDD International Conference on Knowledge Discovery & Data Mining, pp. 196–204 (2018)
38. Guo, C., Rana, M., Cisse, M., Van Der Maaten, L.: Countering adversarial images using input transformations. arXiv preprint arXiv:1711.00117 (2017)
39. Meng, D., Chen, H.: Magnet: a two-pronged defense against adversarial examples. In: Proceedings of the 2017 ACM SIGSAC Conference on Computer and Communications Security, pp. 135–147 (2017)
40. Raghunathan, A., Xie, S.M., Yang, F., Duchi, J., Liang, P.: Understanding and mitigating the tradeoff between robustness and accuracy. arXiv preprint arXiv:2002.10716 (2020)
41. Zhang, H., Yu, Y., Jiao, J., Xing, E., El Ghaoui, L., Jordan, M.: Theoretically principled trade-off between robustness and accuracy. In: International Conference on Machine Learning, pp. 7472–7482. PMLR (2019)
42. Wu, D., Xia, S.-T., Wang, Y.: Adversarial weight perturbation helps robust generalization. Adv. Neural. Inf. Process. Syst. **33**, 2958–2969 (2020)
43. Pang, T., Yang, X., Dong, Y., Xu, K., Zhu, J., Su, H.: Boosting adversarial training with hypersphere embedding. Adv. Neural. Inf. Process. Syst. **33**, 7779–7792 (2020)
44. Zini, S., Buzzelli, M., Twardowski, B., van de Weijer, J.: Planckian jitter: enhancing the color quality of self-supervised visual representations. arXiv preprint arXiv:2202.07993 (2022)
45. Hendrycks, D., Dietterich, T.: Benchmarking neural network robustness to common corruptions and perturbations. arXiv preprint arXiv:1903.12261 (2019)
46. Ilyas, A., Santurkar, S., Tsipras, D., Engstrom, L., Tran, B., Madry, A.: Adversarial examples are not bugs, they are features. In: Advances in Neural Information Processing Systems, vol. 32 (2019)
47. He, K., Zhang, X., Ren, S., Sun, J.: Deep residual learning for image recognition. In: Proceedings of the IEEE Conference on Computer Vision and Pattern Recognition, pp. 770–778 (2016)
48. Zagoruyko, S., Komodakis, N.: Wide residual networks. arXiv preprint arXiv:1605.07146 (2016)

49. Huang, G., Liu, Z., Van Der Maaten, L., Weinberger, K.Q.: Densely connected convolutional networks. In: Proceedings of the IEEE Conference on Computer Vision and Pattern Recognition, pp. 4700–4708 (2017)
50. Sandler, M., Howard, A., Zhu, M., Zhmoginov, A., Chen, L.-C.: Mobilenetv2: inverted residuals and linear bottlenecks. In: Proceedings of the IEEE Conference on Computer Vision and Pattern Recognition, pp. 4510–4520 (2018)
51. Tan, M., Le, Q.: Efficientnet: rethinking model scaling for convolutional neural networks. In: International Conference on Machine Learning, pp. 6105–6114. PMLR (2019)
52. Krizhevsky, A., Hinton, G., et al.: Learning multiple layers of features from tiny images (2009)
53. Deng, J., et al.: Imagenet: a large-scale hierarchical image database. In: 2009 IEEE Conference on Computer Vision and Pattern Recognition, pp. 248–255. IEEE (2009)
54. Zhang, H., Wang, J.: Defense against adversarial attacks using feature scattering-based adversarial training. In: Advances in Neural Information Processing Systems, vol. 32 (2019)

Edge Intelligence Based Garbage Classification Detection Method

Ruijia Zhu[1], Yiwen Liu[1,2,3], Yanxia Gao[1,2,3](✉), Yuanquan Shi[1,2,3], and Xiaoning Peng[1,2,3]

[1] School of Computer and Artificial Intelligence, Huaihua University, Huaihua 418000, China
2877464155@qq.com

[2] Key Laboratory of Wuling-Mountain Health Big Data Intelligent Processing and Application in Hunan Province Universities, Huaihua 418000, China

[3] Key Laboratory of Intelligent Control Technology for Wuling-Mountain Ecological Agriculture in Hunan Province, Huaihua 418000, China

Abstract. To address the problem that the classification and cleaning of garbage in city streets is always ineffective nowadays, the paper proposes a garbage detection method based on edge intelligence. The edge intelligence not only reduces the computational load of the cloud and speeds up the data transmission, but also greatly reduces the data transmission cost. First, images of city streets are collected and uploaded to the edge device via mobile devices in various locations in the city. Then, the edge server is used to temporarily store the image information, and the PeleeNet model deployed on it is used to identify and classify various kinds of garbage, and then visualize the information of each street. Finally, the street garbage information is transmitted to the cloud, which provides a detailed picture of the city's garbage situation and facilitates city management.

In this paper, the PeleeNet model is compared with ResNet, DenseNet and MobileNet models. The results show that the edge devices equipped with PeleeNet model not only have the fastest computation speed and the highest accuracy, but also occupy the least memory. It is fully demonstrated that the method studied in the paper can be applied to the problem of litter detection in urban streets.

Keywords: Edge Intelligence · Waste Classification · Convolutional Neural Network · Smart City

1 Introduction

With the further development of smart cities, the issue of urban street trash cleaning has once again come into focus. Traditionally, street cleaning has required manual intervention at various levels [1], and in many cities, garbage is taken by city citizens to designated garbage collection points and then collected by sanitation workers. There are also cities that install cameras at street intersections to observe the presence of trash within this area. However, these are not able to keep the city streets clean for a long time, and they do not know the status of the city's garbage in real time. Therefore, some

Z. Xiao et al. (Eds.): ICECI 2022, LNICST 478, pp. 128–141, 2023.
https://doi.org/10.1007/978-3-031-28990-3_10

scholars have studied an automated system based on edge computing [2], which collects information from edge devices, stores and simply processes the street image information using edge servers, transfers the data to a cloud center and then classifies and counts the garbage using a neural network model in deep learning. However, with the rapid development of 5G networks, network-dependent and inflexible cloud computing is no longer able to efficiently process massive amounts of data, and deploying neural network models to cloud centers for data processing can no longer yield analysis results in a very short period of time.

Based on this, this paper proposes a garbage classification detection method based on edge intelligence. It not only reduces the pressure of data transmission between edge devices and cloud center, improves the accuracy and intelligence of garbage classification, reduces the time delay of data transmission, but also protects the privacy and security of users. Images of city streets are first collected through cameras and portable mobile devices installed at street intersections. The data is then stored on an edge server, and the PeleeNet model on which it is based is used to identify and visualize the garbage images. Finally, the data is transmitted to the cloud center through the city network, and finally the garbage visualization information of the whole city is obtained. It is convenient for city managers to manage the city, arrange cleaning staff and coordinate waste management.

The rest of the paper is divided into the following parts: Sect. 2 contains a review of related work. In Sect. 2.3, the PeleeNet model is described specifically. In Sect. 3, the experimental approach is described, including the model, the image database, and the specific methods. In Sect. 4, the results of the experiments are presented. The study is concluded in Sect. 5.

2 Related Work

2.1 Edge Intelligence Research

Edge Intelligence (EI) [3] refers to the combination of endpoint intelligence, EC and AI. This new intelligence paradigm is also known as mobile intelligence [4]. Zhang et al. define edge intelligence as the ability to enable edge devices to execute AI algorithms [5]. Ken Li et al. define EI as an open platform that incorporates the core capabilities of networking, computing, storage, and applications [6]. Compared with traditional cloud-based smart end devices that upload generated data to cloud centers, edge intelligence processes and analyzes data locally, which can effectively protect user privacy, reduce response time, and save bandwidth resources [7]. Deploying intelligence on edge devices can provide intelligent services to users faster and better.

To solve the computational speed problem and resource problem in edge devices and edge networks, Hu [8] et al. proposed an algorithm that can maximize computational efficiency and optimize quality allocation. Zeng et al. proposed a resource allocation algorithm that eliminates cross-layer interference and reduces latency [9], and also proposed a solution on how to maximize the total rate at optimal power [10]. Jiang et al. proposed a solution to the task offloading and resource allocation problem in mobile edge computing [11], and to achieve the above results with limited resources, they also proposed a framework that can improve the energy efficiency of the network [12] and a method to guarantee the accuracy [13]. Liu et al. also proposed a covalent organic framework that can significantly improve the energy efficiency [14] and practical network protocols that can achieve concurrency and low power consumption [15], and also give very good approaches for transmission stability [16] and how to optimize the data transmission throughput in the network [17].

For the problem of poor signal in some areas, Zhu et al. proposed how to get accurate information under noise interference [18]. Hu et al. proposed a method to use radar signals for data enhancement [19]. In order to optimize the user experience and reduce the energy consumption at the user side, Qian [20] et al. presented the results of their study. Finally, in order to count various information, Talal [21] et al. gave very excellent statistical methods.

Finally, there are many applications that apply the edge intelligence paradigm to real life, proving the feasibility of edge intelligence. It is applied in various aspects such as industrial technology [22, 23], precision agriculture [24, 25], smart healthcare [26, 27], and smart home [28, 29].

2.2 Smart City Research

The term "smart city" has attracted worldwide attention since its emergence, and there is a boom in the construction of urban information technology with it as the core in China. However, there has been no research on urban street garbage in the construction of smart cities, which is an important reason for us to study garbage classification based on edge intelligence.

The British Standards Institute describes smart cities as "the effective integration of physical, digital and human systems in the built environment to provide a sustainable, prosperous and inclusive future for citizens" [30]. In China, there are already successful examples of smart cities as well. Alibaba's cloud computing project "City Brain" used data collected from video feeds of traffic signals to alleviate traffic congestion in Hangzhou, China, where traffic management was 92% accurate in identifying traffic violations. It helped emergency vehicles reach their destinations 50% faster than before and increased traffic speeds by 15% [31]. City government leaders and planners can also use the city brain to overcome other pressing problems, such as alleviating the problem of diminishing water supplies.

2.3 Convolutional Neural Network Model

With the continuous development of deep learning, garbage classification has gradually become intelligent, and the use of deep learning to classify garbage has become a key research direction in academia and industry. As the authoritative network structure in deep learning, convolutional neural network model has made great achievements in the field of image processing, so this paper uses convolutional neural network for urban street garbage classification processing.

The first convolutional neural network was proposed by Wei Zhang and was successfully applied in the field of medical image detection [32]. Subsequently, Yann LeCun proposed LeNet, a model that has made remarkable contributions in the field of computer vision [33]. Based on this, Yann et al. successfully solved the problem of handwritten digit recognition in 1998 [34]. Since then the research area of convolutional neural networks has become the focus. Medical image classification [35], handwritten digital image [36], coronary virus detection [37] are all successful applications of convolutional neural networks. The following is a brief description of each neural network model that will be used in this paper.

ResNet

With the exploration of the majority of researchers in the field of convolutional neural networks, we find that improving the performance of the network can increase the depth of the network. However, many experiments have proved that simply increasing network depth in a certain depth range cannot effectively improve network performance. If the number of neural network layers is within 20, increasing the number of network layers will bring improvement of network performance, and the category accuracy will decrease. This is because the deepening of the network will cause the problem of gradient explosion and gradient disappearance. In order to make a deeper network training good results, in 2016, HE [38] and others proposed a 34-layer residual network. The problem. However, deep neural networks still face the dilemma of gradient disappearance and degeneration, and network training has become a difficult problem.

DenseNet

To address this problem, the DenseNet model [39] was born. The two main advantages of the DenseNet model are the implementation of dense connectivity and feature reuse. These advantages allow DenseNet to achieve better performance with few parameters and lower cost. DenseNet also has very good generalization performance, which is especially suitable for training small data set applications. At this time, the performance of the network has been greatly improved. However, new issues arise, one is whether the device can successfully store our model, and the other is the time consumption of the model for computation. Therefore, in order to meet the practical application criteria, the only options are to optimize the processor performance or to reduce the amount of computation. Due to the time problem, reducing the amount of computation becomes the main technical tool. Solving the above problems, neural network models can be widely used in mobile.

MobileNet

Therefore, Google proposed MobileNet, a lightweight neural network model, in 2017 [40]. It is mainly deployed on resource-limited mobile and embedded devices. MobileNet requires fewer parameters, the whole model is very lightweight and computationally fast, easily meeting the requirements of these portable devices. But it also has a fatal problem of being very dependent on deep separable convolutions, which prevents it from being deployed in most frameworks.

PeleeNet

Therefore, researchers from the University of Western Ontario, Canada, have proposed PeleeNet, which requires only ordinary convolution for real-time operation on mobile devices [41]. PeleeNet has the same excellent performance as MobileNet and is applicable to almost all frameworks. It has a very good performance in terms of accuracy, speed, and power consumption. We will also introduce the PeleeNet model in detail in later sections.

In summary, the PeleeNet model is chosen as the training network in this paper.

3 Experimental Model

The PeleeNet model borrows the cascade model and architecture from the DenseNet model. On its basis, it solves the problem of limited both storage capacity and computational power. The following are the main improvement features of PeleeNet and the general structure of the PeleeNet model.

3.1 Stem Block

The Stem Block structure is the method used for downsampling in PeleeNet. This module ensures a good feature representation of the model and reduces a large number of parameters (Fig. 1).

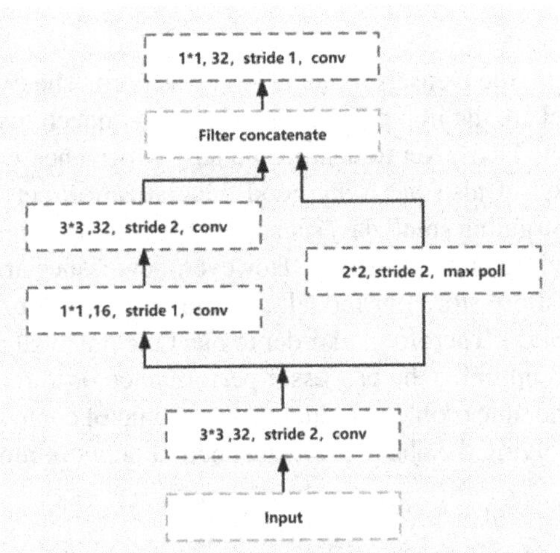

Fig. 1. The convolution operation is performed by Stem Block to enrich the feature layers and reduce the number of weight parameters.

The structure first performs a 3×3 convolution operation on the input image, the main purpose of which is to change the number of channels of the feature map. Then the network structure is divided into two branches, and the feature map is divided into two parts. One part of the feature map is pooled for maximum value, and the other part of the feature map is convolved by a 1×1 operation to halve the number of channels, followed by a 3×3 convolution with a step size of 2 to achieve the second downsampling. The outputs of the two branches are stitched together in the channel dimension, and finally the number of channels is reduced by another 1×1 convolution. Compared with the original convolution operation, the main operation of Stemblock structure to reduce the number of parameters is to introduce a bottleneck layer in one branch to reduce the number of channels before downsampling, and the other branch to pool the original input to the maximum value before stitching, in order to pass some of the information in the input and ensure that the final result still has enough semantic information based on the reduced number of parameters, without excessive loss of information. The purpose is to pass some of the information in the input to ensure that the final result still has enough semantic information on the basis of the reduced number of parameters, without excessive loss of information. In general, the Stem Block not only enriches the feature layer, but also greatly reduces the number of weight parameters.

3.2 Two-Way Dense Layer

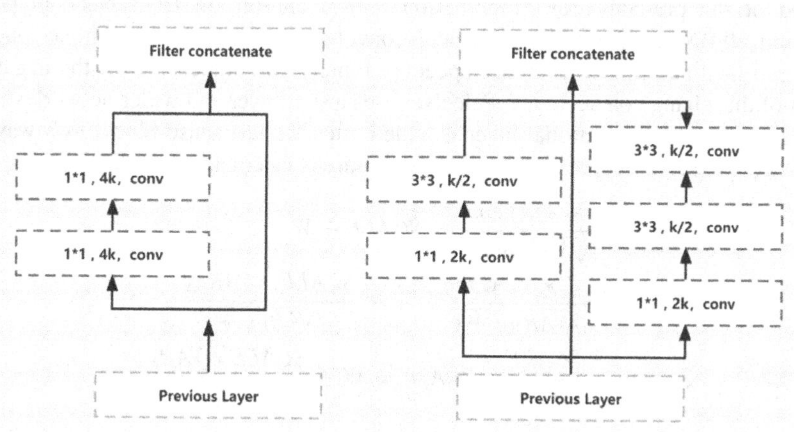

Fig. 2. The filter is convolved in two ways by Two-Way Dense Layer to achieve the effect of taking into account the size of the target.

The left (a) diagram above shows the basic module designed in DenseNet, where k and 4k represent the number of filters. The right (b) figure represents the basic module designed in PeleeNet, in addition to halving the filter of the original backbone branch (the perceptual field of the backbone branch is 3 × 3), a new branch is added, in which two 3 × 3 convolutions are used, and the perceptual field of this branch is 5 × 5. This ensures that the extracted features are not just single-scale, but can take into account both Small and large targets.

3.3 Transition Layer Without Compression

In DenseNet, the transition layer is used to reduce the spatial resolution of the feature map, and the number of channels in the transition layer will be smaller than the number of channels in the previous layer. However, experiments show that the compression factor proposed by DenseNet can damage the feature representation. And setting the number of channels in the transition layer and the previous layer to the same value in PeleeNet can solve this problem.

3.4 Dynamic Number of Channels of Bottleneck Layer

In DenseNet, the number of channels in the bottleneck layer of each Dense Block is fixed, but this causes the number of channels in the bottleneck in some layers at the beginning of the network to far exceed the number of input channels, resulting in an increase in computation. In PeleeNet, the dynamic setting of the number of channels in the bottleneck layer solves this problem.

3.5 Composite Function

Also, to increase the speed, the PeleeNet model uses the combination of conv+bn+relu (instead of the pre-activation combination (conv+relu+bn) in DenseNet). In post-activation, all BN layers can be merged with convolutional layers in the inference phase, which can facilitate model inference speedup. Finally, to compensate for the negative impact of this change on accuracy, PeleeNet uses a shallower and wider network structure, i.e., a 1×1 convolutional layer is added after the last sense block, as a way to obtain stronger feature representation. The structure is calculated as follows:

$$\begin{aligned} Y &= \frac{X - AVE_{BN}}{\sqrt{VAR_{BN} + \varepsilon}} * SCALE + W \\ &= \frac{X * SCALE}{\sqrt{VAR_{BN} + \epsilon}} + W - \frac{SCALE * VAR_{BN}}{\sqrt{VAR_{BN} + \varepsilon}} \end{aligned} \tag{1}$$

$$Z_{BN} = \frac{SCALE}{\sqrt{VAR_{BN} + \varepsilon}} * A_{BN} = W - \frac{SCALE * VAR_{BN}}{\sqrt{VAR_{BN} + \varepsilon}} \tag{2}$$

Substituting Eq. (2) into Eq. (1) yields:

$$Y = Z_{BN} * X + A_{BN} \tag{3}$$

$$X = Z_{Conv} * X_{conv} + A_{Conv} \tag{4}$$

Combining Eq. (3) with (2) yields.

$$Y = Z_{BN} * (Z_{Conv} * X_{Conv} + A_{Conv}) + A_{BN} \tag{5}$$

The final results are as follows:

$$Weighting : Z = Z_{BN} * Z_{Conv}$$

$$Offset : A = Z_{BN} * Z_{Conv} + A_{BN}$$

The input X is normalized in the BN layer. AVE_{BN} is the mean of the input, VAR_{BN} is the variance of the input, SCALE is the scaling, W is the displacement, the convolution kernel size is K, the weight is Z_{Conv}, the bias is A_{Conv}. And the number of channels is B_{Conv}.

3.6 General Structure of the PeleeNet

(See Fig. 3).

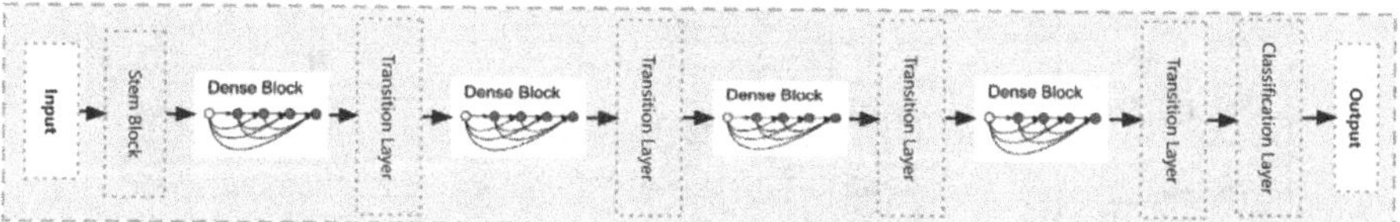

Fig. 3. The structure of each level of the PeleeNet model

4 Process Design

4.1 Method Overview

The architecture of the method model consists of three parts: the first part is the data collection from the edge devices, the second part is the analysis and processing of the data by the edge server, and the third part is the cloud server presenting the whole city garbage information status.

When the garbage images taken by edge devices are transmitted to the edge server, the edge server uses the PeleeNet model deployed on it to analyze and process the image data temporarily stored in the server, delete the images with garbage and classify and count the garbage in them in order to present the city's street garbage data quickly and accurately in the cloud server center. In the local management, the edge data center not only stores and uploads the garbage classification results accurately processed by the PeleeNet model, but also stores the initial data from the edge servers locally for a long time, which not only prevents data loss due to the failure of the edge devices, but also protects user privacy. City administrators can allocate human resources according to the visualization results of garbage and realize intelligent garbage disposal. Figure 2 shows the process of building a garbage detection model for city streets (Fig. 4).

4.2 Data Collection

The main source of city street spam information images is from edge devices such as cameras, sensors, smartphones, etc. spread all over the city, as well as information from local management centers.

For the information uploaded by edge devices, the edge server needs to set certain criteria: 1) fixed image resolution; 2) fixed number of photos taken by each edge device; 3) fixed shooting area.

For the local data center, it needs to transmit the garbage classification data to the city administrator at a fixed time, while the city administrator makes timely responses through the reports from the data center and arranges the cleaning staff to clean it in time.

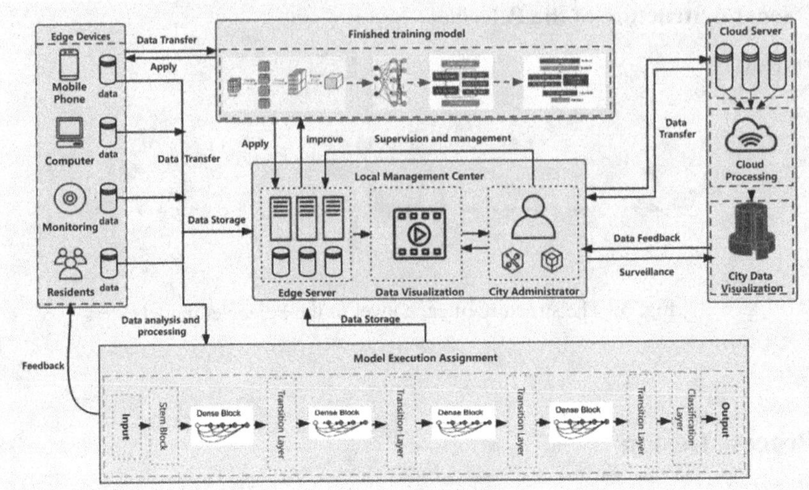

Fig. 4. Overall framework of edge intelligence-based waste sorting monitoring model

4.3 Mobile Edge Processing

Sometimes, the information uploaded by the edge devices may be useless information. For example, in one of the pictures collected by an edge device, there are obstacles such as cars and houses blocking causing incomplete information of garbage in the captured garbage images, or garbage does not appear in the captured photos. These photos are obviously useless, and the edge data processing layer is essential in order to reduce the workload and time consumption of the edge server. This layer accepts the information of garbage images from the edge devices and filters out the complete photos containing garbage images before analyzing and processing them. Figure 5 shows the basic architecture of mobile edge computing, which mainly consists of the following parts.

Edge devices: Every camera and sensor in the city streets are edge devices that can collect information, while every resident is able to take pictures of the streets with his or her own device, and this data is transmitted to the edge server.

Edge server: It is an edge device that can provide a data transmission channel and establishes a reliable connection with nearby mobile devices. Its role is to process service requests from mobile devices and store the information uploaded by mobile devices, and analyze and process the data through the neural network model mounted on it.

Cloud Center: Processes service requests from the edge servers and stores the information uploaded by the servers, and visualizes the final city street waste information.

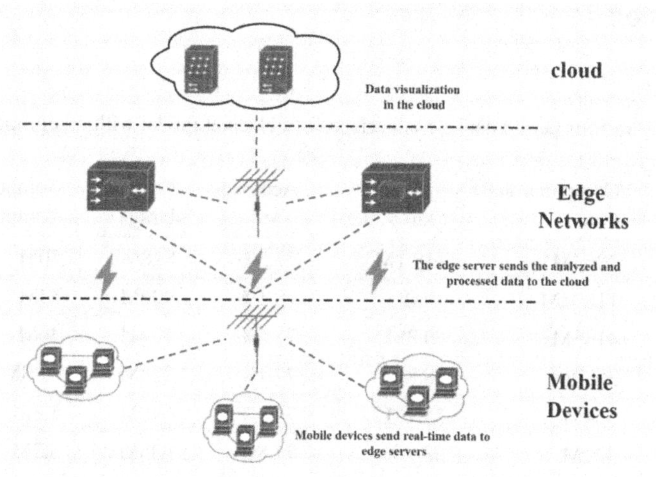

Fig. 5. Foundational Framework for Edge Computing

4.4 Image Detection Based on Pelee Model

The experiments are based on Window10 environment and simulated using iFogSim, a virtual simulation platform for edge computing.

Data Preparation

In this training, we collected more than 20,000 garbage images. These images were divided into four major categories, namely food waste, recyclable waste, hazardous waste, and other waste. In total, there are forty sub-categories, including scraps of left-overs, newspapers, shopping paper bags, foam boxes, batteries, pharmaceuticals, etc. A total of 15,000 images were used as the training set and 5,000 images were used as the test set with a ratio of (7:3).

Model Construction and Training

First, a convolutional layer is built to perform feature extraction and then normalization. Next, an activation function is chosen to introduce nonlinearities to enable the model to solve nonlinear problems. Then the first Stem Block module is built to preserve the feature representation and reduce the parameters. Then the most critical Two-Way Dense Layer is built, which makes the model very flexible and can detect both large and small shapes. Then the Two-Way Dense Layer is repeated to form the Dense Block, and each Dense Block is directly built with a transition layer for dimensionality reduction. After repeating these operations, we finally add a classification layer to complete the model construction.

Evaluation Model

In this paper, we use the following performance metrics to measure the performance of a model: Computational Cost, Speed, Accuracy, Memory Usage, Computational Complexity.

5 Conclusion

Table 1. Various performance comparisons of PeleeNet model with other models

Model	Computational Cost	Speed (320 × 320)	Accuracy	Memory Usage	Computational Complexity
ResNet-101	7864M	118.1M	77.5%	818M	50M
ResNet-152	11832M	70M	78.1%	906M	53M
DenseNet-161	4145M	60.3M	77.6%	774M	36M
DenseNet-201	3680M	58.8M	77.1%	724M	32.3M
MobileNet-v1	569M	75.7M	70.1%	648M	5.3M
MobileNet-v2	321M	68.9M	71.8%	635M	5.2M
PeleeNet	507M	129.2M	74.3%	362M	2.8M

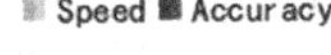

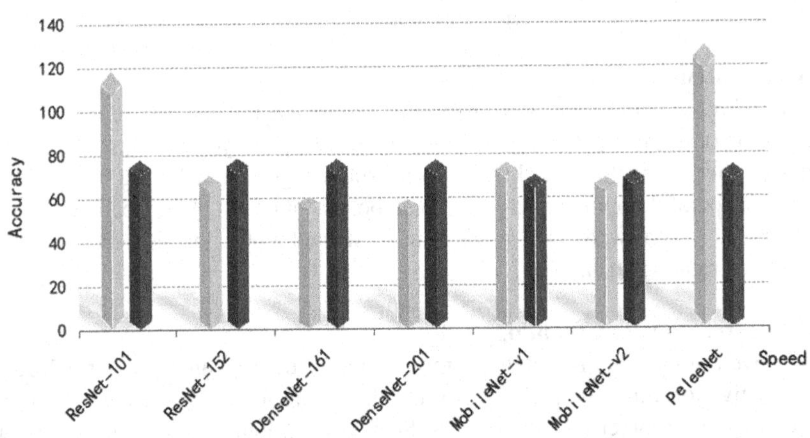

Fig. 6. Comparison of speed and accuracy of each model on edge devices

Putting each model on the virtual simulation platform iFogSim (Table 1 and Figs. 6, 7).

From the above tables and charts, we can clearly observe that PeleeNet, with its lightweight architecture, not only occupies little memory and has low computational complexity, but also has good accuracy and computational speed. It is well proven that it is suitable for deployment on edge devices.

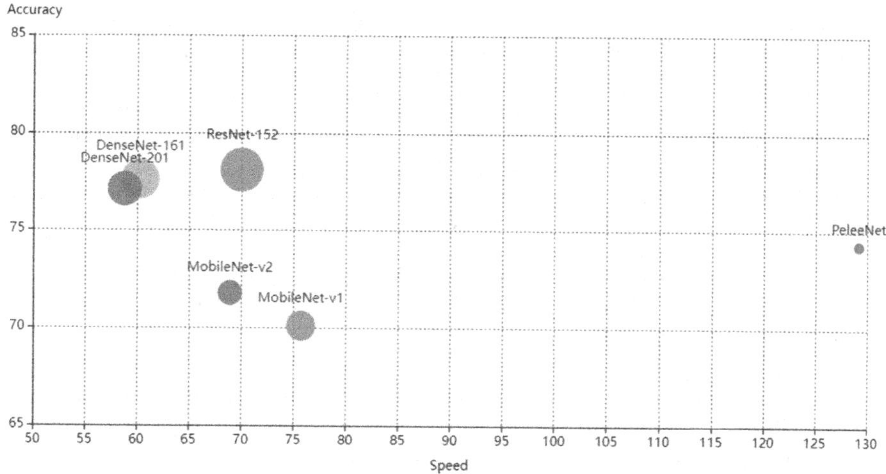

Fig. 7. Comparison of computational complexity with accuracy and speed of different models

Acknowledgment. This work was supported in part by the Scientific research projects funded by the Department of education of Hunan Province (No. 21C0628, No. 20C1472 and No. 22C0668), the Huaihua University Double First-Class initiative Applied Characteristic Discipline of Control Science and Engineering (No. ZNKZN2021-10) ,the National Natural Science Foundation of China (No. 62172182), the Hunan Provincial Natural Science Foundation of China (No. 2020JJ4490), the Project of Hunan Provincial Social Science Foundation (NO.21JD046), the Huaihua University Project (No. HHUY2019-25), the Philosophy and Social Science Achievement Evaluation Committee of Huaihua (No. HSP2022YB40) and the Science and Technology Innovation 2030 Special Project Sub-Topics (No. 2018AAA0102100).

References

1. Balchandani, C., Hatwar, K., Makkar, P., et al.: A deep learning framework for smart street cleaning. In: IEEE Third International Conference on Big Data Computing Service and Applications, pp. 112–117. IEEE, Redwood City (2017)
2. Begur, H., Dhawade, M., Gaur, N., et al.: An edge-based smart mobile service system for illegal dumping detection and monitoring in San Jose. In: IEEE International Conference on Smart City and Innovation, pp. 1–6. IEEE, San Francisco (2017)
3. Wang, X., Han, Y., Wang, C., Zhao, Q., Chen, X., Chen, M.: In-edge AI: intelligentizing mobile edge computing, caching and communication by federated learning. IEEE Netw. **33**(5), 156–165 (2019)
4. Wang, Z., Cui, Y., Lai, Z.: A first look at mobile intelligence: architecture, experimentation and challenges. IEEE Netw. **33**, 120–125 (2019)
5. Zhang, X., Wang, Y., Lu, S., et al.: Open EI: an open framework for edge intelligence. In: IEEE 39th International Conference on Distributed Computing Systems, pp. 1840–1851 (2019)
6. Li, K.L., Liu, C.B.: Edge intelligence: state-of-the-art and expectations. Big Data Res. 69–75 (2019)
7. Khelifi, H., et al.: Bringing deep learning at the edge of information-centric internet of things. IEEE Commun. Lett. **23**(1), 52–55 (2018)

8. Hu, Z., Zeng, F., Zhu, X., Fu, B., Jiang, H., Chen, H.: Computation efficiency maximization and QoE-provisioning in UAV-enabled MEC communication systems. IEEE Trans. Netw. Sci. Eng. **8**(2), 1630–1645 (2021)
9. Zeng, F., Li, Q., Zhu, X., Havyarimana, V., Bai, J.: A price-based optimization strategy of power control and resource allocation in full-duplex heterogeneous Macrocell-Femtocell networks. IEEE Access **6**, 42004–42013 (2018)
10. Zeng, F., et al.: Resource allocation and trajectory optimization for QoE provisioning in energy-efficient UAV-enabled wireless networks. IEEE Trans. Veh. Technol. **69**(7), 7634–7647 (2020)
11. Jiang, H., Dai, X., Zhu, X., Iyengar, A.: Joint task offloading and resource allocation for energy-constrained mobile edge computing. IEEE Trans. Mob. Comput. (2022). https://doi.org/10.1109/TMC.2022.3150432
12. Jiang, H., Zhu, X., Li, Z., Xu, J., Zeng, F., Wang, D.: An energy-efficient framework for internet of things underlaying heterogeneous small cell networks. IEEE Trans. Mob. Comput. **21**(1), 31–43 (2022)
13. Jiang, H., Cao, H., Liu, D., Xiong, J., Cao, Z.: SmileAuth: using dental edge biometrics for user authentication on smartphones. Proc. ACM Interact. Mob. Wearable Ubiquitous Technol. **4**(3), 84:1–84:24 (2020)
14. Liu, D., Cao, Z., He, Y., Ji, X., Hou, M., Jiang, H.: Exploiting concurrency for opportunistic forwarding in duty-cycled IoT networks. ACM Trans. Sens. Networks **15**(3), 31:1–31:33 (2019)
15. Liu, D., Hou, M., Cao, Z., He, Y., Ji, X., Zheng, X.: COF: exploiting concurrency for low power opportunistic forwarding. In: ICNP, pp. 32–42 (2015)
16. Liu, D., Wu, X., Cao, Z., Liu, M., Li, Y., Hou, M.: CD-MAC: a contention detectable MAC for low duty-cycled wireless sensor networks. In: SECON, pp. 37–45 (2015)
17. Liu, D., Cao, Z., Hou, M., Rong, H., Jiang, H.: Pushing the limits of transmission concurrency for low power wireless networks. ACM Trans. Sens. Netw. **16**(4), 40:1–40:29 (2020)
18. Zhu, X., et al.: Toward accurate vehicle state estimation under non-Gaussian noises. IEEE Internet Things J. **6**(6), 10652–10664 (2019)
19. Hu, J., et al.: BlinkRadar: non-intrusive driver eye-blink detection with UWB radar. In: Proceedings of IEEE ICDCS (2022)
20. Qian, C., Liu, D., Jiang, H.: Harmonizing energy efficiency and QoE for brightness scaling-based mobile video streaming. In: IWQoS, pp. 1–10 (2022)
21. Talal, A., Zhu, X., Sun, J., Seyedali, M., Vincent, H., Jiang, H.: Optimal design of IIR wideband digital differentiators and integrators using salp swarm algorithm. Knowl.-Based Sys. **182**(15), 104834 (2019). https://doi.org/10.1016/j.knosys.2019.07.005
22. Morán, A., et al.: Hardware-optimized reservoir computing system for edge intelligence applications. Cogn. Comput. 1–9 (2021)
23. Foukalas, F., Tziouvaras, A.: Edge artificial intelligence for industrial internet of things applications: an industrial edge intelligence solution. IEEE Industr. Electron. Mag. **15**, 28–36 (2021)
24. Liu, J., et al.: Boost precision agriculture with unmanned aerial vehicle remote sensing and edge intelligence: a survey. Remote. Sens. **13**, 4387 (2021)
25. Friha, O., et al.: Internet of things for the future of smart agriculture: a comprehensive survey of emerging technologies. IEEE/CAA J. Autom. Sinica **8**, 718–752 (2021)
26. Kamruzzaman, M. M.: New opportunities, challenges, and applications of edge-AI for connected healthcare in smart cities. In: IEEE Globecom Workshops, pp. 1–6 (2021)
27. Amin, S.U., Hossain, M.S.: Edge intelligence and internet of things in healthcare: a survey. IEEE Access **9**, 45–59 (2021)
28. Yar, H., et al.: Towards smart home automation using IoT-enabled edge-computing paradigm. Sens. (Basel Switz.) **21** (2021)

29. Yuan, D., et al.: Intrusion detection for smart home security based on data augmentation with edge computing. In: ICC 2020 - 2020 IEEE International Conference on Communications (ICC), pp. 1–6 (2020)
30. Smart Cities Overview—Guide, BSI Standards Publication. http://shop.bsigroup.com/upload/Shop/Download/PAS/30313208-PD8100-2015.pdf. Accessed 7 Aug 2020
31. Hasija, S., Shen, Z.J.M., Teo, C.P.: Smart city operations: modeling challenges and opportunities. Manuf. Serv. Oper. Manage. **22**, 203–213 (2020)
32. Zhang, W.: Shift-invariant pattern recognition neural network and its optical architecture. In: Proceedings of Annual Conference of the Japan Society of Applied Physics, pp. 2147–2151 (1988)
33. LeCun, Y., et al.: Backpropagation applied to handwritten zip code recognition. Neural Comput. **1**, 541–551 (1989)
34. LeCun, Y., Bottou, L., Bengio, Y., Haffner, P.: Gradient-based learning applied to document recognition. Proc. IEEE **86**, 2278–2324 (1998)
35. Jiang, Y., Chen, L., Zhang, H., Xiao, X.: Breast cancer histopathological image classification using convolutional neural networks with small SE-ResNet module. PloS One **14**(3) (2019)
36. Xu, X., et al.: 11 TOPS photonic convolutional accelerator for optical neural networks. Nature **589**, 44–51 (2021)
37. Narin, A., Kaya, C., Pamuk, Z.: Automatic detection of coronavirus disease (COVID-19) using X-ray images and deep convolutional neural networks. Pattern Anal. Appl. **24**(3), 1207–1220 (2021). https://doi.org/10.1007/s10044-021-00984-y
38. He, K., et al.: Deep residual learning for image recognition. In: Proceedings of the IEEE Conference on Computer Vision and Pattern Recognition, pp. 770–778 (2016)
39. Huang, G., et al.: Densely connected convolutional networks. In: Proceedings of the IEEE Conference on Computer Vision and Pattern Recognition, pp. 4700–4708 (2017)
40. Conference on Computer Vision and Pattern Recognition (CVPR), Honolulu, HI, USA, pp. 21–26 (2017)
41. Mahmud, R., Buyya, R.: Modelling and simulation of fog and edge computing environments using iFogSim toolkit. Fog Edge Comput. Principles Paradigms 1–35 (2019)

Mobile Computing in Wireless Networks

Evaluation of Higher Education System

Zhonglin Wang(✉)

Ningbo University of Finance and Economics, Haishu District, Ningbo, Zhejiang, China
279032562@qq.com

Abstract. By the analytic hierarchy process. Suggestions and policies for the construction of a healthy and sustainable higher education system are put forward. Firstly, after analyzing the two evaluation models of grey comprehensive evaluation and analytic hierarchy process (AHP), the analytic hierarchy process (AHP) was selected to construct the model. Next, we selected 14 indicators related to the higher education system and conducted a data search. The weight of each index is calculated by analytic hierarchy process and the basic evaluation model is constructed. Second, we take data from 17 countries and use the model to evaluate. It is found that the final ranking is very similar to the current ranking of higher education level in the world, which verifies the correctness of the model. Then, we use multiple linear regression method to calculate the index corresponding coefficient and compare it with the weight, and find the shortcomings of the selected country, the United States. In view of the shortcomings, we put forward some policies and implementation schedule. The effectiveness of the policy is verified by model evaluation. Finally, we discussed some practical problems in the process of implementing the policy from the aspects of students, teachers, schools, communities and countries.

Keywords: higher education · analytic hierarchy process · health · sustainable

1 Introduction

1.1 Problem of Background

Higher education is a concept of education level. In a broad sense, it refers to all professional education based on secondary education [1–7].

The higher education system is an important element in a country's efforts to provide its citizens with further education beyond primary and secondary education. Thus, the higher education system not only has the value of the industry itself, but also the value of producing trained and educated citizens for the national economy. The development of globalization is not only economic cooperation, but also the integration of education. Every country not only educates its own students, but also attracts a large number of international students every year [8–15]. At the same time, the development of economy drives the progress of science and technology, people's educational ideas, living needs and so on have undergone great changes. How to make effective adjustment in the current pandemic period, taking the essence and discarding the dross, so that the higher education

Z. Xiao et al. (Eds.): ICECI 2022, LNICST 478, pp. 145–165, 2023.
https://doi.org/10.1007/978-3-031-28990-3_11

system can move forward steadily with the development of The Times, is the primary consideration of all countries in the world. Countries can determine whether the higher education system is healthy and sustainable according to the specific situation of their own country [16–24]. If so, how to make it better and how to improve the current higher education system if there are still shortcomings. All these need to be implemented in a relatively long period of time.

1.2 Restatement of Problem

To address this problem, we will develop a model to measure and evaluate the national higher education system, determine a healthy and sustainable state for the higher education system in a given country, and propose recommendations and improvement measures.

Specifically, we first need a model that can assess the health of the higher education system in any country;

In addition, according to the countries analyzed, the choice of a higher education system has room for improvement;

Propose a realistic vision for the country that supports a healthy and sustainable higher education system;

Use our model to assess the state of the country. Propose targeted policies and implementation timelines to support migration from the current state to your proposed state;

Use your models to shape and/or evaluate the effectiveness of your policies;

Discuss the real-world impact of implementing the plan during the transition and final state, recognizing that change is difficult.

1.3 Overview of Our Work

First, we analyzed the questions to find out the factors affecting the health and sustainability of the higher education system and related data.

Secondly, we searched literature and considered various evaluation methods, including grey comprehensive evaluation, analytic hierarchy process, etc. And finally chose the data obtained by analytic hierarchy process. Analytic Hierarchy Process (AHP) does not separate the influence of each factor on the evaluation of higher education system. The weight setting of each level will directly or indirectly affect the result at last, and the influence degree of each factor on the evaluation in each level is quantified. The evaluation method is used to obtain the national education model. The model is applied to 16 selected countries to make country-to-country comparisons.

Then, regression fitting analysis is carried out on the data and rankings of each country to obtain the coefficients of each factor data, which are compared with the weight value to obtain the implementation status and deficiencies of each factor in each country, so as to provide some suggestions for the implementation of healthy and sustainable higher education system in the current selected countries. This paper focuses on the analysis of the United States and Mexico.

Then, using multiple linear regression method, the existing weights are compared with the obtained factor coefficients to obtain the deficiencies of the education system.

In addition, clear policies and suggestions are put forward to address the deficiencies, and the implementation schedule of migration from the current state to the proposed state is drawn.

Finally, our model is used to determine and evaluate the effectiveness of policies, and the impact of policy implementation on reality is discussed (Fig. 1).

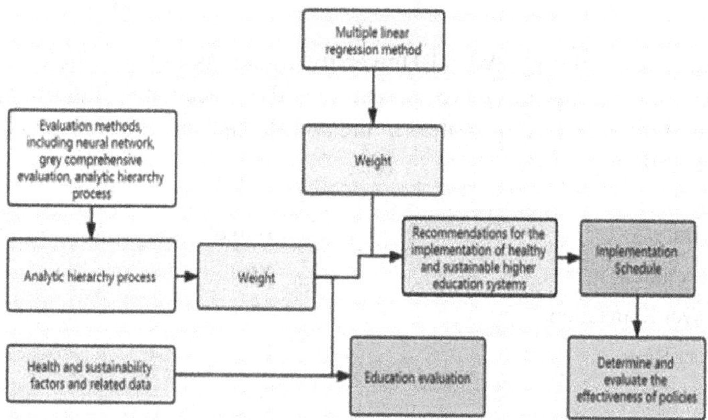

Fig. 1. The structure of our paper.

2 Assumptions

We assume that our field of study is about higher education systems. The higher education system is a global problem that touches every region, so we expect the authorities to take positive measures.

In order to facilitate the analysis, we temporarily do not consider the subjective factors such as human nature hypothesis and ethical orientation behind the evaluation.

We assume that the data obtained are accurate and reliable. We get our data from credible international websites and newspapers.

3 Establishing an Evaluation Model

3.1 Index Selection

Considering the large number of indicators to evaluate higher education, we establish a two-level index system.

As for the first-level index, it draws on the reference factors of the ranking of world universities recognized at home and abroad. Times Higher Education's world university rankings are based on the following factors:

Ranking criteria	Weight (%)
Teaching (Learning Environment)	30
Research (number of publications, revenue and reputation)	30
Citation (Research Impact)	30
Internationalization (Staff, Students and research)	7.5
Industrial income (knowledge transfer)	2.5

At the same time, the QS World University Rankings are considered. Since the ranking mainly adopts questionnaire survey, a series of academic indicators are used to measure the influence of universities in the world. The specific indicators and their weights are as follows:

Ranking criteria	Weight (%)
Academic Reputation	40
Global Employer Reputation	10
Faculty/Student Ratio	20
Citations per faculty	20
International Faculty Ratio	5
International Student Ratio	5

However, considering that the QS ranking has too many subjective indicators and commercialization indicators, many countries have a serious lack of data on reputation and commercialization indicators. Therefore, in this paper, we do not focus on the reference of this index and weight.

In addition, considering the U.S. News World University Rankings:

Ranking criteria	Weight (%)
Global Academic Reputation	12.50
Regional Academic Reputation	12.50
Papers published	10
The book	2.50
The meeting	2.50
Standardized paper citation impact index	10
Number of citations	7.50
Number of citations in the "maximum 10% of publications cited" list	12.50
Publications account for the percentage of "top 10% cited publications"	10
International collaboration	5
Percentage of total publications with international cooperation	5

(continued)

(*continued*)

Ranking criteria	Weight (%)
The number of papers cited in the "top 1% of cited papers in all publications" representing the field	5
Publications account for the "top 1% of papers cited in all publications"	5

Combined with the query data and the first-level indicators we determined, we gave the following weights:

Ranking criteria	Weight (%)
Education level	30
Research level	30
Educational resources	15
The value of degree	15
Opportunity	10

The design of higher education internationalization evaluation index system is closely related to the internationalization goal, which is rooted in the development level and stage of regional higher education and the system form of higher education.

The index system design highlights three principles:

One is the guiding principle. In internationalization of higher education assessment, which is based on the development of higher education internationalization level on the basis of the judgment, to grasp the future development direction, target oriented, based on the data, with the facts to prove, found in the process of development of higher education internationalization, guide the institutions of higher learning for short, strong or weak, realize the innovation of higher education development and quality improvement.

Second, the principle of development. Internationalization of higher education is the process of integrating international dimension and cross-cultural dimension into the function of talent cultivation, scientific research and social service of higher education. Therefore, the evaluation process of internationalization of higher education must pay attention to the relationship among goals, processes, activities and results, and pay attention to the improvement of process and the enhancement of connotation.

Third, the principle of diversity. Different types and levels of colleges and universities have different goals, approaches and emphases of internationalization development. Therefore, it is necessary to take into account the characteristics of different types of colleges and universities' internationalization status and differences in goals, and pay attention to hierarchical and classified evaluation.

Based on this problem, we initially consider two evaluation methods – grey comprehensive evaluation method and analytic hierarchy process (AHP).

Grey comprehensive evaluation method: there will be incomplete, incomplete and insufficient information when evaluating the effectiveness of complex large-scale systems. The relevant principles and methods of grey theory are just suitable for this problem. The grey vernacular weight function clustering method is a kind of grey comprehensive evaluation method. It aggregates some observation indexes or objects into several categories that can be defined according to the whitening weight function of the grey number. The process of classifying the system into a certain grey category is used to detect whether the objects belong to different categories set in advance. The grey whitening weight function clustering method can evaluate the efficiency of complex large-scale systems.

Analytic hierarchy process (AHP), analytic hierarchy process (AHP) is a complicated multi-objective decision-making problem as a system, the target is decomposed into multiple objectives or principles, or rules, constraints, and multiple index of several levels, through qualitative index fuzzy quantification method to calculate hierarchical single sort (weight) and total ordering, as the target (index), scheme optimization decision method of system.

Analytic hierarchy process (AHP) is a decision-making problem according to the general objective, the each layer sub-targets, evaluation criteria and the order of the specific for voting scheme is decomposed into different hierarchies, and then, by solving the judgement matrix eigenvector calculated for each element of each level on a hierarchy of an element of priority weights, finally, the method of weighted sum hierarchical merging each alternative solution on the final total target weight, the final weight so much as the optimal solution. Grey comprehensive evaluation method requires sample data and has the characteristics of time series. It only identifies the merits and demerits of the evaluation object, but does not reflect the absolute level, which is suitable for the problem of a small amount of observation data.

Based on the existing data and analysis of various aspects, we choose the analytic hierarchy process (AHP).

3.2 Analytic Hierarchy Process

3.2.1 Model Description

Analytic hierarchy process (AHP) is a complicated multi-objective decision-making problem as a system, the target is decomposed into multiple targets and multiple index (or rule, constraints) several levels, through qualitative index fuzzy quantification method to calculate hierarchical single sort (weight) and total ordering, as the target (index), scheme optimization decision method of system.

Analytic hierarchy process (AHP) is a decision-making problem according to the general objective, the each layer sub-targets, evaluation criteria and the order of the specific for voting scheme is decomposed into different hierarchies, and then, by solving the judgement matrix characteristic vector calculated for each element of each level on a hierarchy of an element of priority weights, finally, the method of weighted sum hierarchical merging each alternative solution on the final total target weight, the final weight so much as the optimal solution. Analytic Hierarchy Process (AHP) is more suitable for the decision-making problem with the objective system with stratified and staggered evaluation indexes, besides the target value is difficult to describe quantitatively.

3.2.2 Modeling

The Main Steps are as Follows:

1) *Build a hierarchy model.* Decision-making objectives, factors to be considered (decision criteria) and decision objects are divided into the highest level, middle level and lowest level according to their mutual relations, and the hierarchy chart is drawn. The highest level is the purpose of the decision, the problem to be solved. The lowest level refers to the alternatives when making a decision. The middle layer refers to the factors that are considered and the criteria for decision making. For two adjacent layers, the upper layer is called the target layer and the lower layer is called the factor layer (Fig. 2).

Level indicators	The secondary indicators	Level 3 indicators
Educational resources	General conditions	1. Total area of school buildings
		2. The average size of the school building per student
		3. Total amount of equipment
		4. The average amount of equipment per student
		5. Books in total
		6. Number of books per student
	Educational fund	7. Total educational expenditure this year
		8. Per student expenditure on education this year
	Teachers	9. Phenom
		10. Number of doctoral supervisors
		11. Proportion of the total number of teachers with senior titles
		12. Teacher-student ratio
Teaching level	Graduate	13. Number of PhD graduates
		14. Number of Master Graduates
		15. One-time employment rate of graduates
	Quality of teaching	16. Number of outstanding doctoral dissertations
		17. Number of prizes won in various international competitions
Scientific research	Research team and base	18. State key laboratories, research centers and scientific research bases
		19. Proportion of full-time R&D personnel in teachers
	Scientific research output	20. Number of patent applications and grants
		21. Number of papers indexed by SCI, SSCI, A&HCI
		22. EI, ISTP, ISSHP papers
		23. CSTPC, CSSCI papers
		24. Social Science Monograph (Part)
	Efficiency and benefit	25. Output per capita
		26. Output rate of ten thousand yuan

Fig. 2. The table of factors

2) *Construction of Pairwise Comparison Matrix.* According to the established indicators, we respectively made pairwise comparison of the indicators at the unified level to construct judgment matrices at different levels.

$$A = (a_{ij}) = \begin{pmatrix} a_{11} & \cdots & a_{1n} \\ \vdots & \ddots & \vdots \\ a_{n1} & \ldots & a_{nn} \end{pmatrix}$$

where a_{ij} is the value of the i index compared with the j index.

3) *Consistency index and consistency test.* The eigenvector corresponding to the largest characteristic root of the judgment matrix is denoted by W after normalization (making the sum of each element in the vector equal to 1). The element of W is the ranking weight of a factor of the same level to the relative importance of a factor of the upper level. This process is called hierarchical single sorting. Consistency test is needed to confirm whether the hierarchical single ordering can be confirmed. The so-called consistency test refers to determining the allowable range of inconsistencies for A. Wherein, the unique non-zero characteristic root of a uniform matrix of order n is n; The maximum characteristic root of the positive reciprocal matrix A of order n is $\lambda \geq n$, and A is a uniform matrix if and only if $\lambda = n$.

Since λ continuously depends on A, the more λ is greater than N, the more serious the inconsistency of A is. The consistency index is calculated by Ci, and the smaller Ci, the greater the consistency is. The eigenvector corresponding to the maximum eigenvalue is used as the weight vector of the influence degree of the factors being compared on the upper layer of a factor. The greater the degree of inconsistency, the greater the judgment error will be. Therefore, the degree of inconsistency of A can be measured by the value of $\lambda - n$.

The consistency index was defined as:

$$CI = \frac{\lambda - n}{n - 1}$$

The random consistency index RI is as follows.

n	**3**	**4**	**5**	**6**	**7**	**8**	**9**	**10**
RI	0.58	0.90	1.12	1.14	1.32	1.42	1.45	1.49

Define Consistency Ratio

$$CR = \overline{RI}$$

When $Cr = 0$, it indicates that the judgment matrix has good consistency.

When $Cr < 0.\ 1$, it indicates good consistency.

Otherwise, it indicates that the consistency of the judgment matrix is not good, and the values of the matrix should be modified until $CR < 0.\ 1$.

According to the importance of each index in the mind of the decision maker, the value is assigned, and the pairwise comparison of each index in the same level is made. Numbers 1–9 and their reciprocal are used as the scale. The greater the value is, the greater the degree of importance it represents. Moreover, it is judged that matrix A is A positive reciprocal matrix, with the diagonal as the axis, and the symmetric value is the reciprocal relationship.

Analytic Hierarchy Scale (Note: 2, 4, 6 and 8 are the middle values of two adjacent grades).

Meaning	**Equally important**	**Somewhat important**	**Obviously important**	**Highly important**	**Extremely important**
Scale value	1	3	5	7	9

By referring to literature and data, various evaluation systems are referred, and some more important factors are selected for calculation (Fig. 3).

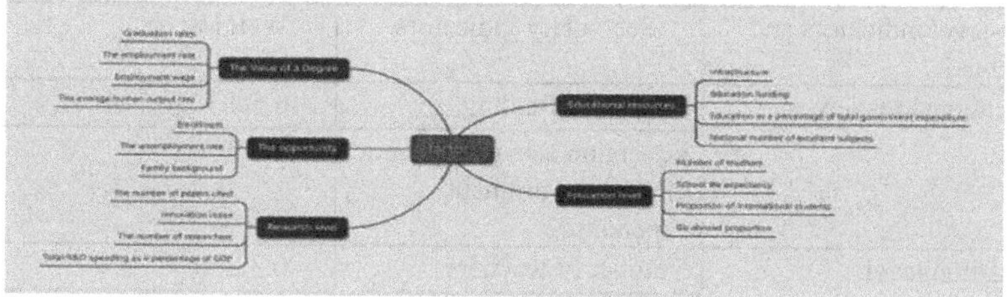

Fig. 3. The table of necessary factors.

The importance of the factors we set up was evaluated, and the results were as follows (Fig. 4):

index	significance
The percentage of education expenditure in GDP	2
The percentage education expenditure of in total expenditure	3
Government expenditure on higher education	7
Enrollment rate	6
Dropout rates	4
The number of higher education teachers	7
Innovation Index	9
The percentage of Total R&D spending in GDP	4
The number of researchers	8
Employment rate	5
Graduation rate	6
School life expectancy	4
Proportion of international students	8
Go abroad proportion	2
Employment wage	4
The average human output rate	5
Family background	3
The number of papers cited	3
Infrastructure	1
Number of national excellent papers	4

Fig. 4. .

The weight value of education system was obtained by AHP (Fig. 5):

In order to make the importance index obtained by AHP more reliable. Reference serves as a rough guide by looking at how countries rank in terms of education. We used SPSS to carry out the similarity analysis between the values of various factors of the selected countries and the negative rankings, and the results are as follows (Fig. 6):

And the importance of analytic hierarchy process is more consistent.

First-level indicators and weights	Secondary indicators	Weights
Educational resources 0.15	Education funding	0.5833
	Education as a percentage of total government expenditure	0.4167
Education level 0.3	Number of teachers	0.3333
	School life expectancy	0.1905
	Proportion of international students	0.3810
	Go abroad proportion	0.0952
The value of a degree 0.15	Graduation rates	0.5455
	The employment rate	0.4545

Fig. 5. .

index	Weight
The percentage of education expenditure in GDP	0.203
The percentage education expenditure of in total expenditure	0.311
Government expenditure on higher education	0.568
Enrollment rate	0.521
Dropout rates	0.415
The number of higher education teachers	0.541
Innovation Index	0.683
The percentage of Total R&D spending in GDP	0.361
The number of researchers	0.630
Employment rate	0.446
Graduation rate	0.583
School life expectancy	0.370
Proportion of international students	0.630
Go abroad proportion	0.260

Fig. 6. The similarity analysis.

By calculating the matrix of analytic hierarchy process (AHP) under each first-level index, the results obtained meet the consistency test. Considering that the consistency ratio of the matrix CR is very close to 0, we directly take the ratio of importance as an important index of weight. Different units and orders of magnitude are taken into account for each country's data indicators. To facilitate calculation and reduce the impact of different units and orders of magnitude. For example, the innovation index is on the order of 10^1, and the number of teachers is on the order of 10^4. Even if the weights are different, direct multiplication will result in an effect of a larger order of magnitude overriding a change in a smaller order of magnitude. So, we're going to standardize the data.

4 Evaluation of Higher Education System Evaluation Model

4.1 Example: American

In order to illustrate our model more intuitively, we choose the United States as a case.

According to the 2016 Open Doors Report released by IIE, the number of students studying in the United States reached a new high in 2016, exceeding one million for the first time. Among them, 328,547 students were from China, an increase of 8. 1% year on year, accounting for 31.5% of the total number of students in the United States. According to the 2015 Chronicle of Higher Education, there are 4,810 colleges and universities in the United States, of which 3, 120 are four-year colleges and universities and 1,690 are two-year colleges and universities, with 20.417,500 students. Each university has a clear position, plays its own role, depends on each other, and has its own characteristics. It shoulders the mission and responsibility of cultivating and absorbing talents, promoting social and economic development, maintaining values and exerting international influence.

We believe that the United States has one of the world's leading higher education systems (Fig. 7).

Category	Number	Percentage	Category	Number	Percentage
Teaching	719873	28 52	Community service	140621	5.79
Professional scientific research	75620	3.00			
Public services	20267	0.80	Health care workers	94899	3.76
Library management and archives	35832	1.42	Service professional	202931	8.04
Student affairs	121296	4.81	Sales and related occupations	10521	0.42
Management	252156	9.99	Administrat-ion	347181	13.76
Business and financial operations	197107	7.81	Natural resources	70156	2.78
Computer science	2194249	8.49	Production	15871	0.63

Fig. 7. Full-time faculty structure in American universities

4.2 Example: Mexico

Mexico can simply represent a developing country.

Mexico is not only the second largest economy, population and education country in Latin America after Brazil, but also the world's largest country in higher education. At present, Mexico has 2,847 undergraduate institutions (including university campuses), with an enrollment of 2,384,800 students. Graduate education, which started earlier but developed relatively slowly, has also made great progress. There are 1,361 universities offering graduate education annually, with 150,800 postgraduate students and 280 million full-time faculty members, or 105.6 million, ranking 11th in the world. In terms of the size of higher education, Mexico ranks eighth among developing countries.

Based on the model data and the factor weight data derived from the model, the evaluation scores for American higher education were obtained as follows:

Score = Σ (Σ (Index * Secondary weights)) * First - level weights = 3.3736 The other countries' evaluation scores are shown below (Fig. 8):

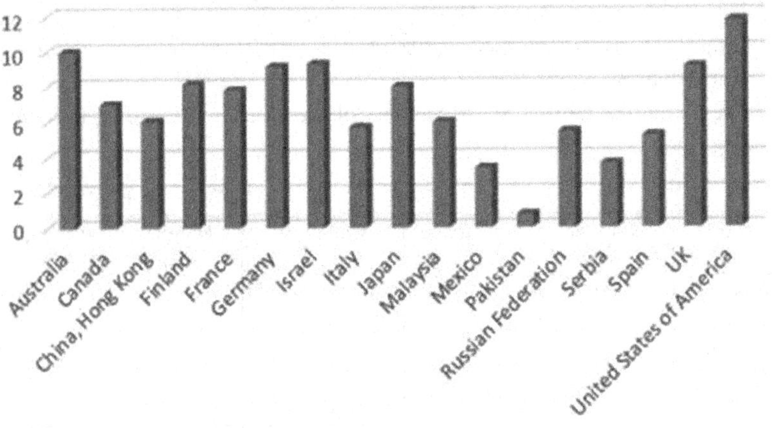

Fig. 8. All countries's evaluation scores.

5 Attainable and Reasonable System of Higher Education for UK

5.1 Evaluation Model Design

We have established the criteria for a healthy and sustainable higher education system based on the factor weights calculated by AHP.

(1) The level of education: as an important subject in the process of higher education, tutors are the key to the high-quality development of higher education. Good quality of teachers can provide a strong intellectual support and impetus for the development of graduate students. As the main body and personality shaper guiding students' academic development, mentors' own ideological and moral cultivation and

professional quality play an imperceptible role in shaping students' personalized development. A competent mentor team can effectively make up for the deficiency of single mentor training. It is very important to cultivate a team of leaders who are responsible for the cultivation of students' academic ability as well as the shaping of students' values and the leading of their thoughts.

(2) The level of research: dissertation as students investigation and feedback of quality, is the last line of defense education checks. It includes strict requirements in the whole process of initial proposal, mid-term examination, "double-blind" evaluation and defense of the thesis, and firmly holds the red line of degree quality.

(3) School resources: the critical path to improve the quality of students in learning links in resources platform construction and ascension. Library, management services and infrastructure, as an important factor in the training process, provide students with a good study and life logistics support and resource access platform, so that students can better devote themselves to scientific research. By improving the training mode, we can realize link connection, carrier combination and internal and external linkage, so as to continuously improve students' learning quality and participation, and further promote the improvement of teaching and training quality.

(4) Degree value: end continuously shunt elimination mechanism, establish and improve the students time and misconduct zero tolerance mechanism. In order to overcome the tendency of "five only" among students, a new degree evaluation standard system should be established through the revision of the degree evaluation standard. According to their research characteristics, targeted classification guidance should be given to avoid professional degree graduate students from too "academic" research and deviate from reality, so as to promote the high-quality development of different types of students

(5) Access: students, as an important subject throughout the process of education, are the starting point and foundation of high-quality development of education. A good source of students can guarantee the quality of education from the source. The methods of classified examination, comprehensive evaluation and multiple admission provide a good reference for scientific selection of graduate students. At the same time, it actively promotes the construction of practice-oriented courses, the construction of professional practice bases, and adopts diversified and targeted training models to make it more competitive when facing the main battlefield of national economy.

The ideal weight of specific factors in the higher education system is shown below:

The percentage of education expenditure in GDP	0.203
The percentage education expenditure of in total expenditure	0.311
Government expenditure on higher education	0.568
Enrollment rate	0.521
Dropout rates	0.415
The number of higher education teachers	0.541
Innovation Index	0.683

(*continued*)

(*continued*)

The percentage of Total R&D spending in GDP	0.361
The number of researchers	0.630
Employment rate	0.446
Graduation rate	0.583
School life expectancy	0.370
Proportion of international students	0.630
Go abroad proportion	0.260

5.2 Evaluate the Results and Compare Them

The evaluation score was obtained by fitting the weighted value obtained by the analytic hierarchy process with the real value of the factors of the higher education system, and the evaluation score was compared with the official national higher education ranking (Fig. 9):

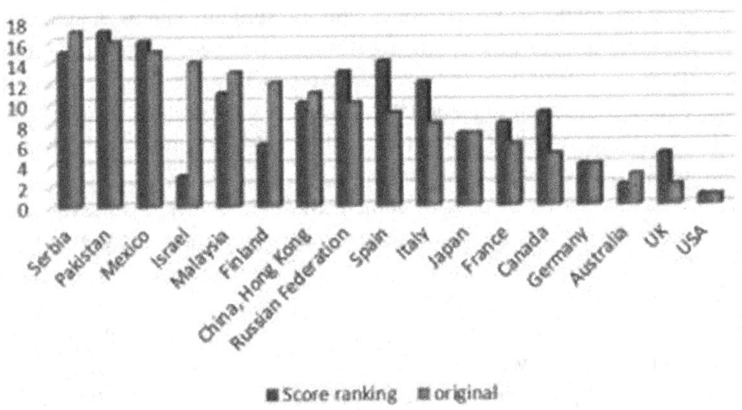

Fig. 9. Contrast.

It can be concluded that most countries' evaluation scores and rankings are consistent. In order to illustrate the feasibility and scientificity of our model more directly, we use the British higher education evaluation method as an example.

The Higher Education Quality Assurance Agency (QAA) is an educational assessment body independent of the government and institutions of higher learning. Its mission is to provide comprehensive quality assurance services to British universities to ensure and improve the quality of higher education, and to promote the continuous reform and deepening of the quality of higher education.

The assessment content of QAA covers two aspects of school quality assessment and discipline quality assessment, including six assessment indicators, which are: curriculum design, content and organization; Teaching quality and learning quality; Student progress and achievement; Student assistance and guidance; Learning resources; Quality management and improvement. As a reference for the government to formulate education policies and implement education quality management, the evaluation results have strong authority and fairness.

The analytic hierarchy process (AHP) adopted in this paper is the same as its evaluation method, which uses multiple indicators to evaluate the higher education system in different countries. At the same time, due to the diversity of evaluation indicators and wide coverage, the model can provide different levels of evaluation services, so as to adapt to different countries with different levels and situations. It also shows that the analytic hierarchy process (AHP) we use to construct the evaluation model is scientific and adaptable.

6 Policy Proposal and Implementation Schedule

6.1 Multiple Linear Regression for the Coefficient

First of all, we use MATLAB to use multiple linear regression to figure out the coefficient before each impact factor.

Use the regress function:

```
x = data (:, 1:14); %input.
Y = data (:, 15);
X = [ones (17, 1), x];
[b, bint,r, rint, stats] = regress(Y, X).
```

The required coefficients are as follows (marked in yellow) (Fig. 10):

Education spending as a	0.3	0.166667		
Education expenditure a	0.45	0.25		
Education spending	1.05	0.583333	1.8	0.10557
Enrollment rate	0.6	0.6		
Dropout rates	0.4	0.4	1	0.05865
Go abroad proportion	0.6	0.11764		
Number of teachers	2.1	0.41176		
Proportion of internati	2.4	0.47058	5.1	0.29912
Life expectancy at schc	1.2	0.42105		
Graduation rate	0.9	0.31578		
Employment rate	0.75	0.26315	2.85	0.16715
Innovation index	2.7	0.42857		
R&D spending as a perce	3.6	0.57142		
Number of researchers	0	0	6.3	0.3695

Fig. 10. The required coefficients. (Color figure online)

The 14 values on the left are the coefficients of the second-level indicators, and the 5 values on the right are the coefficients of the first-level indicators.

6.2 Multiple Linear Regression for the Coefficient

The data used to evaluate the indicators came from a number of databases, including the World Bank, UNESCO, the National Bureau of Statistics, and others.

Based on factors related to education level, we cut and integrated them. This reduces redundancy and noise due to excessive factors. International data is difficult to find, and if data is missing in an area, we do not evaluate that area in order to get the most accurate results. We got four years' worth of data from 162 countries and territories. Countries may be affected by political, natural or uncertain factors, given the different years. Educational indicators have also been affected. So we averaged the data for different countries over four years. Even if one indicator is up, fluctuating or down, averaging doesn't have much effect on the country's indicators. The indicators we selected are all positive ones, but there are dimensional differences between most of them, so we use the normalization of the interval [0, 1].

The formula should be:

$$ri = \frac{xi - rmin}{rmax - rmin}$$

ri is the normalized value, rmin is the maximum and rmax is the minimum of the factor. Considering that the weights obtained by the original AHP are inconsistent with the orders of magnitude of the coefficients, they cannot be compared, so the weight is normalized.

Fill the following table with the normalized weight and the desired coefficient:

Impact factor	Coefficient	Normalized weights
Education spending as a percentage of GDP	0. 1667	0
Education expenditure as a percentage of total expenditure	0.2500	0. 1428
Government expenditure on higher education	0.5833	0.7142
Enrollment rate	0 6000	0 5714
Dropout rates	0.4000	0.2857
Number of higher education teachers	0 4117	0 7143
Innovation Index	0.4285	1.0000
Total R&D spending as a percentage of GDP	0.5714	0.2857
Number of researchers	0	0.8571
Employment rate	0.2631	0.4286
Graduation rate	0 3157	0 5714
School's life expectancy	0.4210	0.2857
Proportion of international students	0 4705	0 8571
Go abroad proportion	0. 1176	0

6.3 Policy Presentation

As can be seen from the table, the coefficients and weights of education expenditure, number of teachers, innovation index, number of researchers, employment rate and proportion of overseas students are relatively low. It shows that the United States has shortcomings in these aspects, and the following policies need to be put forward to improve the higher education system:

1. Government spending on higher education increased to $27.0 million.
2. Actively introduce foreign talents and encourage participation in the construction of higher education. It is estimated that the number of teachers in higher education will reach 1600000.
3. Encourage universities to conduct innovative research and give certain amounts of government subsidies.
4. Encourage teachers and students to participate in research and development work, and provide subsidies for research and development projects.
5. Encourage foreign talents to study abroad, and provide necessary social security, and monthly social subsidies.

6.4 Implementation Schedule

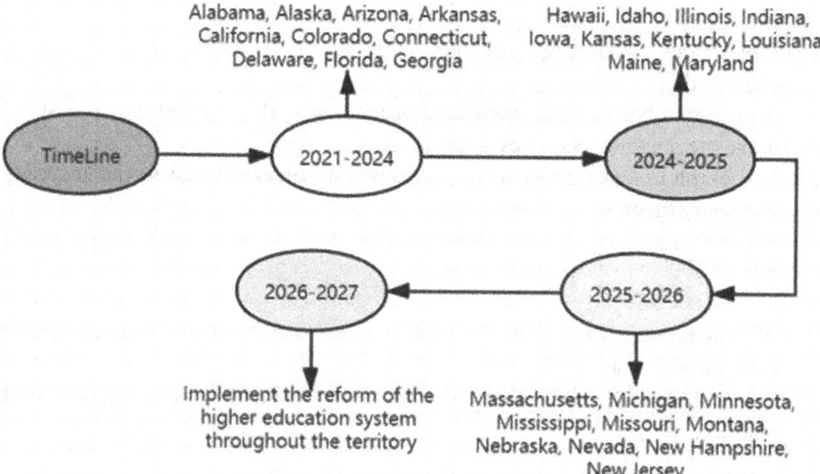

The first phase (2021–2024) is a pilot phase, which will be implemented in several states first. The second phase (2024–2025) expands the pilot scope and further expands the scope; The third stage (2025–2026) is the upgrading and reform stage, which will continue to expand the scope; The fourth stage (2026–2027) is the comprehensive implementation stage, in which policies are implemented throughout the territory to deepen the reform of the higher education system.

7 First Section Validation of Policy Effectiveness and Its Impact on Reality

7.1 Validation of Effectiveness

The implementation of these policies has greatly improved the inadequacies of the US higher education system. At the same time, the amount of the above impact factors also changed accordingly.

Repeat the operation of the second step, normalize each factor and put it into the evaluation model. The current health score of the higher education system is calculated as 12.8411, which is 1 point higher than the health score of 11.7235 before the release of the policy, proving that the release of the policy has a positive impact on the health of the higher education system in the United States.

Therefore, it can be proved that the release of the policy plays an effective role in improving the health of the higher education system.

7.2 The Impact on Reality

(1) Students

1. Preferences for foreign students studying in the United States have been enhanced.
2. As the number of overseas students increases, the competition pressure for domestic students becomes greater.
3. The employment rate of local students may decrease due to the increase of overseas students.

(2) Teachers

1. As the number of teachers introduced increases, the distribution of public education resources decreases.
2. The high subsidy for imported teachers may lead to the dissatisfaction of local teachers.

(3) School

1. The introduction of overseas students and foreign talents increases the management pressure of the school.
2. The inherent resources of the school have reached saturation.

(4) Community

1. The introduction of a large number of foreign personnel and cultural differences may increase the number of conflicts in communities.
2. The increase of personnel makes community management more difficult.

(5) Countries

1. The increase of education expenditure reduces the expenditure on industry, high technology and so on.
2. Subsidies for foreign students and teachers eat up a portion of government spending and slow down economic growth.

8 Vision of the Future

The internationalization of higher education, as a significant feature of the development of higher education in the world, has become an important way to improve the quality of national higher education, national innovation ability and international influence of culture.

University of the United Nations educational, scientific and cultural organization of the international federation of given is defined as: "the higher education internationalization is across national borders and the perspective of cross-cultural and atmosphere and university teaching, scientific research and social service and the main function of the combination of process, it is a comprehensive process, the change of the school internal, external changes and school; There are both bottom-up and top-down; And the schools themselves are changing".

(1) The third-party educational evaluation institutions run by the government and assisted by the public are not dependent on the government or other organizations, and are not subject to interference from any interested parties. They are conducive to carrying out the evaluation work independently and objectively and performing the function of quality assurance. This practice encourages third-party education evaluation institutions to operate independently based on market demand and provide different levels and various types of evaluation services to meet social needs, thus gaining broad credibility and more evaluation funds. This evaluation system can give full play to the professionalism and authority of the third-party evaluation agencies, while not affecting the government's indirect guidance and management of higher education.

(2) The scientificity of the evaluation is mainly reflected in the diversity of the evaluation indexes, the diversity of the participants, the standardization of the admittance system and the scientific technical means. The professional evaluation experts and teams are committed to the establishment of the evaluation index system, the setting of the evaluation procedures and the development and implementation of the evaluation work. They can provide different levels of evaluation services oriented by the market, so as to adapt to the various colleges and universities with different levels and different situations. This kind of "target adaptability" diversified evaluation index system is beneficial to comprehensively consider the quality of higher education and promote the smooth progress of higher education evaluation. In addition, the student participation mechanism in higher education evaluation is one of the important guarantees of higher education quality. The concept of "student-centered"

runs through the whole process of higher education evaluation. Student representatives, as members of the evaluation group, participate in the evaluation work, feedback quality information, and provide suggestions and opinions, so as to comprehensively and objectively evaluate the quality of higher education. Admittedly, sometimes the limited ability of students to understand information and literature may affect the accuracy of information feedback in educational quality assessment, but the positive effect of student participation in assessment is beyond doubt.

(3) The public disclosure of the education quality assessment information provided by the continuous strengthening of the competition mechanism of college evaluation will directly affect the reputation, enrollment, employment and the amount of funds obtained by each university. Therefore, each university attaches great importance to the improvement of the quality of teaching and research, in order to obtain better evaluation results. This competition mechanism is conducive to the self-regulation, self-protection and self-improvement of colleges and universities, and is an effective means to promote the quality of higher education.

Acknowledgement. This work was supported in part by Natural Science Foundation of Ningbo (2021J233), in part by the 2022 Ningbo philosophy and Social Sciences Planning Project (G2022-2-76), in part by Zhejiang philosophy and Social Sciences Planning Project (23NDJC049Z).

References

1. Ma, Y.: Performance Evaluation and index system construction of higher education internationalization in Shanxi Province (2019)
2. Wang, L.: Steady progress towards universal Mexican higher education (2007)
3. Li, W.: The construction of high quality development evaluation system for graduate education in the new era (2020)
4. Li, M.: The construction and thinking of higher education internationalization evaluation index system -- based on the practice analysis of L province (2020)
5. Zhou, H.: The basic characteristics and perfecting path of the third-party evaluation of higher education (2020)
6. Lin, H.: Accelerate the formation of higher education evaluation system with Chinese characteristics (2020)
7. Liu, Y.: British higher education evaluation model and its enlightenment (2020)
8. Zhang, H.: Exploration on the construction of undergraduate curriculum evaluation system based on diversification-process and development (2020)
9. Institute of Statistics. http://data.uis.unesco.org/. Accessed 9 Nov 2022
10. State Statics Cureau. http://www.stats.gov.cn/. Accessed 19 Nov 2022
11. Jiang, H., Xiao, Z., et al.: An energy-efficient framework for internet of things underlaying heterogeneous small cell networks. IEEE Trans. Mob. Comput. **21**(1), 31–43 (2022)
12. Xiao, Z., Li, F., et al.: TrajData: on vehicle trajectory collection with commodity plug-and-play OBU devices. IEEE Internet Things J. **7**(9), 9066–9079 (2020)
13. Xiao, Z., Chen, Y., et al.: Resource management in UAV-assisted MEC: state-of-the-art and open challenges. Wirel. Netw. **28**, 3305–3322 (2022)
14. Li, J., Zeng, F., et al.: Drive2friends: inferring social relationships from individual vehicle mobility data. IEEE Internet Things J. **7**(6), 5116–5127 (2020)

15. Ali, T.A.A., Xiao, Z., et al.: Optimal design of IIR wideband digital differentiators and integrators using salp swarm algorithm. Knowl.-Based Syst. **182** (2019)
16. Dai, X., Xiao, Z., et al.: Task co-offloading for D2D-assisted mobile edge computing in industrial internet of things. IEEE Trans. Industr. Inform. (2022). https://doi.org/10.1109/TII.2022.3158974
17. Jiang, H., et al.: Joint task offloading and resource allocation for energy-constrained mobile edge computing. IEEE Trans. Mob. Comput. (2022). https://doi.org/10.1109/TMC.2022.3150432
18. Long, W., et al.: Unified spatial-temporal neighbor attention network for dynamic traffic prediction. IEEE Trans. Veh. Technol. (2022). https://doi.org/10.1109/TVT.2022.3209242
19. Hu, Z., Zeng, F., et al.: Computation efficiency maximization and QoE-provisioning in UAV-enabled MEC communication systems. IEEE Trans. Netw. Sci. Eng. **8**(2), 1630–1645 (2021)
20. Zeng, F., Li, Q., et al.: A price-based optimization strategy of power control and resource allocation in full-duplex heterogeneous macrocell-femtocell networks. IEEE Access **6**, 42004–42013 (2018)
21. Huang, Y., Xiao, Z., et al.: Road network construction with complex intersections based on sparsely-sampled private car trajectory data. ACM Trans. Knowl. Discov. Data **13**(3), 1–28 (2019)
22. Xiao, Z., Li, F., et al.: A joint information and energy cooperation framework for CR-enabled macro-femto heterogeneous networks. IEEE Internet Things J. **7**(4), 2828–2839 (2020)
23. Zhang, W., Zhou, S., et al.: WiFiMap+: high-level indoor semantic inference with WiFi human activity and environment. IEEE Trans. Veh. Technol. **68**(8), 7890–7903 (2019)
24. Zhao, P., et al.: Synthesizing privacy preserving traces: enhancing plausibility with social networks. IEEE/ACM Trans. Netw. **27**(6), 2391–2404 (2019)
25. Huang, Y., et al.: Exploring individual travel patterns across private car trajectory data. IEEE Trans. Intell. Transp. Syst. **21**(12), 5036–5050 (2019)
26. Jiang, H., et al.: RobloP: towards robust privacy preserving against location dependent attacks in continuous LBS queries. IEEE/ACM Trans. Netw. **26**(2), 1018–1032 (2018)
27. Ma, X., et al.: Exploring sharing patterns for video recommendation on You Tube-like social media. Multimed. Syst. **20**(6), 675–691 (2014)
28. Jiang, H., et al.: Continuous multi-dimensional top-k query processing in sensor networks. In: 2011 Proceedings IEEE INFOCOM, pp. 793–801 (2011)
29. Wang, S., Vasilakos, A., et al.: Energy efficient broadcasting using network coding aware protocol in wireless ad hoc network. In: ICC, Kyoto, Japan (2011)
30. Jiang, H., et al.: Load balancing for SIP server clusters. In: IEEE INFOCOM, pp. 2286–2294 (2009)

Defense Mechanisms Against Audio Adversarial Attacks: Recent Advances and Future Directions

Routing Li[1(✉)] and Meng Xue[2]

[1] School of Software Engineering, Huazhong University of Science and Technology, Wuhan, China
routingli@hust.edu.cn
[2] School of Computer Science, Wuhan University, Wuhan, China
xuemeng@whu.edu.cn

Abstract. With the popularity of speech and speaker recognition systems in recent years, voice interfaces are increasingly integrated into various Internet of Things (IoT) devices. However, studies have demonstrated that such systems are vulnerable to attacks using manipulated inputs. During the last few years, defense mechanisms have been studied and discussed from various aspects to protect voice systems from such attacks. Notwithstanding, there is lacking survey focus on the defense mechanism of audio adversarial examples. In this paper, we provide a comprehensive survey on state-of-the-art defense methods by illuminating their main concepts, reviewing the recent progress with a novel taxonomy, and discussing the future directions. It promises to bring awareness to the security problems in speech and speaker recognition systems and encourages people to propose more robust defenses against audio adversarial examples.

Keywords: Adversarial defenses · Deep learning · Speech recognition · Speaker recognition

1 Introduction

In recent year, the Internet of Things (IoT) has drawn significant research attention [12,21,31,32,37]. Automatic speech recognition (ASR) and speaker recognition (SR) systems, which are critical interfaces for many IoT devices [7,9], have made significant progress over the past decade[1]. In particular, voice assistants, like Amazon Alexa and Apple Siri, have been integrated into all kinds of platforms, giving people convenience over all aspects of their daily lives.

With the advent of the deep learning era, deep neural networks (DNNs) are playing a crucial role in ASR and SR systems. However, studies [1,6,10,13]

[1] In the following discussions, we refer to automatic speech recognition and speaker recognition as ASR and SR, respectively, for ease of distinction.

Z. Xiao et al. (Eds.): ICECI 2022, LNICST 478, pp. 166–175, 2023.
https://doi.org/10.1007/978-3-031-28990-3_12

have demonstrated that these models could be easily fooled by so-called adversarial examples (AEs). In AE attacks, the adversary intentionally adds subtle interference to the input samples to cause the model gives an incorrect output [28]. Specifically, in the audio realm, adversarial samples should meet two objectives simultaneously: 1) causing the voice system to make a wrong prediction; 2) being undetectable to humans. Over the past few years, we have witnessed a rapid growth of works regarding defense against AE attacks [14,20,30]. Meanwhile, several survey papers [8,18,38,39] have been proposed for introducing adversarial perturbations and corresponding defense methods on DNNs. However, these papers mainly focus on the image domain [16,17,19]. Because of the particularity of voice signal and voice processing pipeline, we cannot directly use the attack and defense mode for the image domain to ASR and SR systems. Abdullah et al. [2], and Chen et al. [11] analyze the security threats to voice systems from different perspectives. Notwithstanding, the content of the existing works on defense methods against audio adversarial attacks is limited. Despite its potential significance, there is a lack of discussion that focuses on audio AE defenses. Hence, the primary motivation of this paper is to provide a comprehensive survey on state-of-the-art defense mechanisms against AE by illuminating their main concepts, reviewing the recent progress with a novel taxonomy, and discussing the future direction.

2 Background

2.1 Automatic Speech and Speaker Recognition Systems

Automatic Speech Recognition Systems. ASR systems usually consist of four processes: pre-processing, feature extraction, inference, and decoding.

Pre-processing. The purpose of the pre-processing phase is to extract the speech portion of the signal to produce a "clean" signal. This stage usually contains two components: a noise filter and a low-pass filter. The noise filter removes noise from speech signals. Since most frequencies in human speech range from 300 Hz to 3000 Hz, the low-pass filter discards high-frequency signals.

Feature Extraction. The pre-processed speech signal is divided into frames and input to the feature extraction module. The most common method in this phase is Mel Frequency Cepstral Coefficient (MFCC) [26], as it is closest to the human auditory system. MFCC consists of four steps: Discrete Fourier Transform (DFT), Mel Filtering, Log Scaling, and Discrete Cosine Transform (DCT). DFT converts time domain signals into frequency domain signals. The loudness of the sound perceived by the human ear has a logarithmic relationship with the intensity of the sound signal rather than a simple linear relationship. The purpose of Mel Filtering and Log Scaling is to scale the intensity of the frequencies accordingly to this phenomenon. Finally, the DCT breaks down the input into many cosine components, leaving the part with most of the information and discarding the rest.

Inference. Hidden Markov Model (HMM) is the most commonly used inference model in early ASR systems. With the advent of the deep learning era, DNNs have become the main choice in this field. The most commonly used DNN models are convolutional neural network (CNN) and recurrent neural network (RNN). One limitation of CNNs is that their input and output sizes are fixed, whereas RNNs have flexible input and output sizes and can handle context information. Since speech recognition is a sequence-to-sequence task, it is more suitable to use RNNs in the inference phase.

Decoding. As described in [24], a decoding technique uses an acoustic model, a language model, and the spoken utterance to translate the inference result into the most likely sequence of words. The most commonly used decoding techniques are Viterbi search and N-Best search.

Speaker Recognition System. Speaker recognition systems and speech recognition systems have similar pipelines. The is that SR systems do not require decoding. Instead, they make judgments directly based on the results of the inference stage. As described in [6], SR systems can be classified into three categories based on the task: close-set identification (CSI), open-set identification (OSI), and speaker verification (SV).

Multiple enrolled speakers in a CSI system form a speaker group G. For any input voice x, the inference result contains the scores of all the enrolled speakers $[S(x)]_i$ for $i \in G$, which represents the probability that x is uttered by the speaker i. Finally, the CSI system outputs the speaker with the highest score. OSI systems have a similar task to CSI systems, which is to determine who made the input sound. The difference is that OSI has a preset threshold θ. Instead of directly outputting the speaker with the highest score, it compares the highest score to the threshold θ and rejects the voice if the score is less than θ. SV systems have only one enrolled speaker, unlike CSI and OSI systems. Therefore, the inference result contains only one score. The task is to determine if the enrolled speaker utters an input voice. Similar to the OSI system, the SV system rejects the voice with a score below the threshold θ.

2.2 Adversarial Example

An AE attack is to manipulate the input so that the model makes incorrect predictions. Meanwhile, to make the attack imperceptible, the difference between the adversarial sample and the original sample must not be too large. According to the adversary's knowledge, we categorize AE construction methods into two groups: white-box and black-box attacks. In white-box attacks, the whole model is accessible to the adversary. In other words, the attacker not only has access to the input data but also has full knowledge of the structure of the model and the specific parameters of each layer. Compared with white-box attacks, the adversary in black-box attacks is stronger. They treat the target model as a black box. That is to say, the attacker knows nothing about the model other than the input data.

AE attacks can also be divided into two categories depending on the outcome of the attack: untargeted and targeted attacks. The goal of untargeted attacks is to add a perturbation to the input sample so that the model output changes, while the targeted attacks specify the output of the model input AE.

Although AE is first proposed in the field of image recognition, studies in recent years have also proved that it got practical success in the audio domain. Both untargeted and targeted AEs can be constructed in black-box settings. For instance, DolphinAttack [35] and CommanderSong [34] inject hidden voice commands into the audio without catching the victims' attention. Kenansville Attack [1] develops signal processing methods to construct AE. Chen et al. [6] calculate adversarial perturbations by gradient estimation. In paper [13], Du et al. propose an audio AE generation mechanism based on the Particle Swarm Optimization (PSO) algorithm and the fooling gradient method. Chen et al. [10] strive to build a local substitute model with a handful of strategic queries, and the audio AE is constructed with the white-box substitute model to attack the black-box commercial speech recognition system. Unlike methods that rely on the knowledge of prediction/confidence scores, Zheng et al. [40] formulate the decision-only AE generation as a discontinuous large-scale global optimization problem and develop a novel technique called CC-CMA-ES to solve the problem.

Besides AE discussed above, universal adversarial perturbation (UAP) attacks in the audio domain [4]. UAP is in a completely black-box setting, where the attacker has no access to either the model or the input data. It is more practical than AE attacks because the input data is sometimes not easily accessible.

Table 1. Overview of the current defenses for ASR and SR systems

Defense method	Category	Subcategory	Phase	Target system
Sun et al. [27]	AE preservation	Adversarial training	Inference	ASR
Dompteur [14]	AE preservation	Model optimization	Inference	ASR
Esmaeilpour et al. [15]	AE preservation	Perturbation conversion	Pre-processing	ASR
Joshi et al. [22]	AE preservation	Perturbation conversion	Pre-processing	SR
Li et al. [23]	AE rejection	Model-based detection	Before inputting	SR
Samizade et al. [25]	AE rejection	Model-based detection	Before inputting	ASR
WaveGuard [20]	AE rejection	Model-free detection	Before inputting	ASR
Tramer et al. [29]	AE rejection	Model-free detection	Before inputting	ASR
Yang et al. [33]	AE rejection	Model-free detection	Before inputting	ASR

3 Defenses Against Audio Adversarial Attacks

Based on the results of processing AE, the existing defenses can be divided into two categories, including adversarial example preservation and adversarial example rejection. AE preservation defenses aim to make the ASR/SR system output the correct result of AEs, while AE rejection methods attempt to detect AEs and reject them before inputting the ASR/SR system.

Figure 1 summarizes the realization of the two classes of defense methods, and a brief overview is given in Table 1. We discuss the latest defense mechanisms from these perspectives as follows.

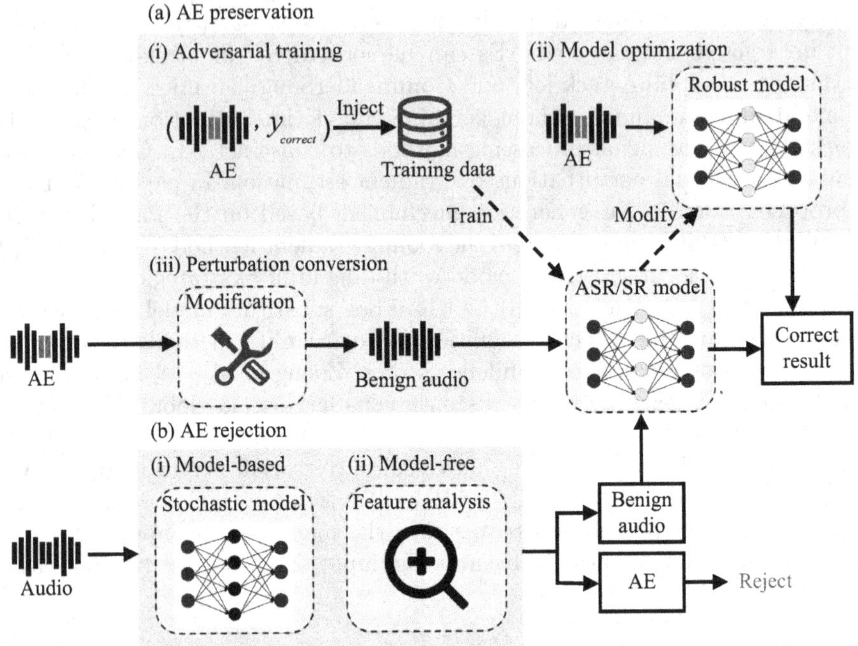

Fig. 1. The framework diagram of defenses against audio adversarial attacks.

3.1 Adversarial Examples Preservation

In AE preservation defenses, AEs are correctly recognized by the target system instead of being rejected. There are three ways to achieve this goal: adversarial training, model optimization, and perturbation conversion.

Adversarial Training. Adversarial training is a method to improve the robustness of recognition models by injecting correctly labeled AEs into the training set as new training samples in the model training stage. This method has been proven effective in resisting specific AE attacks [27]. However, adversarial training will reduce the accuracy of the recognition model, which is a great loss for the model owner. Moreover, adversarial training needs prior knowledge of the attack and adequate AE audio for training and is weak in preventing unknown attacks. Finally, according to [2], it is not effective in defending against signal processing attacks such as Kenansville Attack [1].

Model Optimization. Unlike the adversarial training approach, model optimization methods focus on improving the internal structure of the recognition model rather than enriching the training data. For example, in Dompteur [14], the authors exploit a psychoacoustic filter and a band-pass filter to make the recognition system closer to the human auditory system. This approach does not eliminate AEs but makes the perturbations in AEs easily identified by humans. In other words, Dompteur breaks the stealthy feature of AE.

Perturbation Conversion. Compared with adversarial training and model optimization methods, perturbation conversion defenses do not need to retrain the recognition model. Instead, it processes the input speech signal to remove the adversarial disturbance and converse the AE to benign audio.

For example, Esmaeilpour et al. [15] use a class-conditional Generative Adversarial Network (GAN) to pre-process the input signal to defend for DeepSpeech and Lingvo-based speech recognition systems. As for SR systems, Joshi et al. [22] analyze four perturbation conversion defenses, namely randomized smoothing, defense-GAN, variational autoencoder (VAE), and parallel waveGAN vocoder (PWG). They finally found that PWG combined with randomized smoothing is the best defense among them.

3.2 Adversarial Examples Rejection

Some studies [23,25] distinguish AE from benign samples by training stochastic (or machine learning) models since AE detection can be regarded as a classification problem. Besides, there are methods to detect AE by simply analyzing specific features without an additional model [20,33]. Therefore, we can divide AE rejection defense methods into two categories: model-based and model-free methods.

Model-Based Detection. The detection of adversarial examples can be treated as a classification problem. With a stochastic model, we can reject AEs before inputting the recognition system with high accuracy. For instance, Li et al. [23] introduced a VGG-like binary classification detector to detect AEs effectively. Samizade et al. [25] train a CNN model with three convolutional layers to detect AE. They present that this method has high accuracy for defending against the attacks proposed by Carlini et al. [5] and Alzantot et al. [3]. However, these methods require a large amount of AE audio. Moreover, similar to adversarial training, it requires the defender to know the attack algorithm's details, and such defenses' performance may degrade dramatically for unknown attacks. Worse, the stochastic model is vulnerable to many attacks, introducing additional security risks to the system.

Model-Free Detection. Yang et al. [33] leverage temporal dependency in speech signals to detect audio AE. They check whether the transcription of the first half of the speech sample $f(x_{pre})$ is similar to the first half transcription of the whole audio $[f(x)]_{pre}$. If the two transcripts are not similar, the input is identified as an adversarial sample, and the system will reject it. Unfortunately, recent studies have proved that the temporal dependency framework is not effective in detecting AE. Tramer et al. [29] find an attack method to bypass the detection perfectly and prove that the adaptive evaluation in [33] is incomplete. Zhang et al. [36] propose an Iterative Proportional Clipping (IPC) algorithm to construct audio AE with the temporal dependency feature, which is also robust against the defense in [33].

In WaveGuard [20], the speech is input into the transform function, and AE is detected by comparing the differences between the two translations of the original audio and the transformed audio. This approach is similar to pre-processing defense, except that it rejects AE and feeds the benign raw audio into the ASR system instead of the converted one. The authors analyze the defense results of several candidate transform functions, such as quantization-dequantization, down-sampling, noise filtering, Mel extraction-inversion, and Linear Predictive Coding (LPC). They conclude that the transform-based defense can successfully reject AE, and Mel extraction-inversion is the best choice among them in an adaptive attack scenario. However, they also deduce that the detection accuracy of this mechanism will decrease when facing UAP attacks.

4 Future Direction

As shown in Table 1, only a tiny subset of the existing work has focused on defending against adversarial attacks in SR systems. Though ASR and SR systems have similar pipelines, some differences cannot be ignored. For example, as mentioned in Sect. 2.1, OSV and SI systems have a preset threshold θ, and the input voice will be rejected if the (highest) prediction/confidence score is less than θ, while ASR systems output the prediction result of any input audio and never rejected them. Besides, the prediction result of SR systems is limited to the enrolled speaker, while there are a tremendous number of predictions in ASR systems. For these and many other reasons, the defense methods may have limited effects on SR systems, although they are reported to be promising in the speech recognition domain. Therefore, it is urgent to explore more defense methods for SR systems.

Compared to other AE attacks, signal processing attacks have better transferability, which makes them more robust against some defenses. However, the existing works mainly focus on defending against optimization-based AE attacks and ignore evaluating the defense effectiveness on signal processing attacks. Thus, we advise more studies to explore mechanisms to defend against signal processing attacks.

5 Conclusion

With the rise of adversarial attacks on deep-learning-based speech and speaker recognition systems, it is of great importance to study the defense strategy against this kind of attack. In this paper, we analyze the latest defense mechanisms from two aspects of adversarial examples rejection and preservation. All these defense methods can protect voice systems to some extent. However, they may not be so perfect when the attack setting changes. Compared with the field of image classification, the defense and detection methods of adversarial samples in the audio domain are not mature enough. It is promising that this paper can help people realize the security problems faced by speech and speaker recognition systems and encourage people to propose more robust defense methods.

References

1. Abdullah, H., et al.: Hear "no evil", see "kenansville"*: efficient and transferable black-box attacks on speech recognition and voice identification systems. In: 2021 IEEE Symposium on Security and Privacy (SP), pp. 712–729. IEEE (2021)
2. Abdullah, H., Warren, K., Bindschaedler, V., Papernot, N., Traynor, P.: SoK: the faults in our ASRs: an overview of attacks against automatic speech recognition and speaker identification systems. In: 2021 IEEE Symposium on Security and Privacy (SP), pp. 730–747. IEEE (2021)
3. Alzantot, M., Balaji, B., Srivastava, M.: Did you hear that? Adversarial examples against automatic speech recognition. arXiv preprint arXiv:1801.00554 (2018)
4. Bahramali, A., Nasr, M., Houmansadr, A., Goeckel, D., Towsley, D.: Robust adversarial attacks against DNN-based wireless communication systems. In: Proceedings of the 2021 ACM SIGSAC Conference on Computer and Communications Security, pp. 126–140 (2021)
5. Carlini, N., Wagner, D.: Audio adversarial examples: targeted attacks on speech-to-text. In: 2018 IEEE Security and Privacy Workshops (SPW), pp. 1–7. IEEE (2018)
6. Chen, G., et al.: Who is real bob? Adversarial attacks on speaker recognition systems. In: 2021 IEEE Symposium on Security and Privacy (SP), pp. 694–711. IEEE (2021)
7. Chen, Y., Gong, X., Ou, R., Duan, L., Zhang, Q.: CrowdCaching: incentivizing D2D-enabled caching via coalitional game for IoT. IEEE Internet Things J. **7**(6), 5599–5612 (2020)
8. Chen, Y., Gong, X., Wang, Q., Di, X., Huang, H.: Backdoor attacks and defenses for deep neural networks in outsourced cloud environments. IEEE Netw. **34**(5), 141–147 (2020)
9. Chen, Y., Ran, Y., Zhou, J., Zhang, J., Gong, X.: MPCN-RP: a routing protocol for blockchain-based multi-charge payment channel networks. IEEE Trans. Netw. Serv. Manage. **19**, 1229–1242 (2021)
10. Chen, Y., et al.: {Devil's} whisper: a general approach for physical adversarial attacks against commercial black-box speech recognition devices. In: 29th USENIX Security Symposium (USENIX Security 2020), pp. 2667–2684 (2020)
11. Chen, Y., et al.: SoK: a modularized approach to study the security of automatic speech recognition systems. ACM Trans. Priv. Secur. **25**(3), 1–31 (2022)
12. Dai, X., et al.: Task co-offloading for D2D-assisted mobile edge computing in industrial internet of things. IEEE Trans. Industr. Inform. **19**, 480–490 (2022)
13. Du, T., Ji, S., Li, J., Gu, Q., Wang, T., Beyah, R.: SirenAttack: generating adversarial audio for end-to-end acoustic systems. In: Proceedings of the 15th ACM Asia Conference on Computer and Communications Security, pp. 357–369 (2020)

14. Eisenhofer, T., Schönherr, L., Frank, J., Speckemeier, L., Kolossa, D., Holz, T.: Dompteur: taming audio adversarial examples. In: 30th USENIX Security Symposium (USENIX Security 2021), pp. 2309–2326 (2021)
15. Esmaeilpour, M., Cardinal, P., Koerich, A.L.: Class-conditional defense GAN against end-to-end speech attacks. In: ICASSP 2021–2021 IEEE International Conference on Acoustics, Speech and Signal Processing (ICASSP), pp. 2565–2569. IEEE (2021)
16. Gong, X., Chen, Y., Huang, H., Liao, Y., Wang, S., Wang, Q.: Coordinated backdoor attacks against federated learning with model-dependent triggers. IEEE Netw. **36**(1), 84–90 (2022)
17. Gong, X., et al.: Defense-resistant backdoor attacks against deep neural networks in outsourced cloud environment. IEEE J. Sel. Areas Commun. **39**(8), 2617–2631 (2021)
18. Gong, X., Chen, Y., Wang, Q., Kong, W.: Backdoor attacks and defenses in federated learning: state-of-the-art, taxonomy, and future directions. IEEE Wirel. Commun. (2022)
19. Gong, X., Chen, Y., Yang, W., Mei, G., Wang, Q.: InverseNet: augmenting model extraction attacks with training data inversion. In: IJCAI, pp. 2439–2447 (2021)
20. Hussain, S., Neekhara, P., Dubnov, S., McAuley, J., Koushanfar, F.: {WaveGuard}: understanding and mitigating audio adversarial examples. In: 30th USENIX Security Symposium (USENIX Security 2021), pp. 2273–2290 (2021)
21. Jiang, H., Xiao, Z., Li, Z., Xu, J., Zeng, F., Wang, D.: An energy-efficient framework for internet of things underlaying heterogeneous small cell networks. IEEE Trans. Mob. Comput. **21**(1), 31–43 (2020)
22. Joshi, S., Villalba, J., Żelasko, P., Moro-Velázquez, L., Dehak, N.: Study of preprocessing defenses against adversarial attacks on state-of-the-art speaker recognition systems. IEEE Trans. Inf. Forensics Secur. **16**, 4811–4826 (2021)
23. Li, X., et al.: Investigating robustness of adversarial samples detection for automatic speaker verification. arXiv preprint arXiv:2006.06186 (2020)
24. Malik, M., Malik, M.K., Mehmood, K., Makhdoom, I.: Automatic speech recognition: a survey. Multimed. Tools Appl. **80**(6), 9411–9457 (2021)
25. Samizade, S., Tan, Z.H., Shen, C., Guan, X.: Adversarial example detection by classification for deep speech recognition. In: ICASSP 2020–2020 IEEE International Conference on Acoustics, Speech and Signal Processing (ICASSP), pp. 3102–3106. IEEE (2020)
26. Sigurdsson, S., Petersen, K.B., Lehn-Schiøler, T.: Mel frequency cepstral coefficients: an evaluation of robustness of MP3 encoded music. In: ISMIR, pp. 286–289 (2006)
27. Sun, S., Guo, P., Xie, L., Hwang, M.Y.: Adversarial regularization for attention based end-to-end robust speech recognition. IEEE/ACM Trans. Audio Speech Lang. Process. **27**(11), 1826–1838 (2019)
28. Szegedy, C., et al.: Intriguing properties of neural networks. arXiv preprint arXiv:1312.6199 (2013)
29. Tramer, F., Carlini, N., Brendel, W., Madry, A.: On adaptive attacks to adversarial example defenses. Adv. Neural. Inf. Process. Syst. **33**, 1633–1645 (2020)
30. Wang, S., Cao, J., He, X., Sun, K., Li, Q.: When the differences in frequency domain are compensated: understanding and defeating modulated replay attacks on automatic speech recognition. In: Proceedings of the 2020 ACM SIGSAC Conference on Computer and Communications Security, pp. 1103–1119 (2020)

31. Xiao, Z., et al.: A joint information and energy cooperation framework for CR-enabled macro-femto heterogeneous networks. IEEE Internet Things J. **7**(4), 2828–2839 (2019)
32. Xiao, Z., et al.: TrajData: on vehicle trajectory collection with commodity plug-and-play OBU devices. IEEE Internet Things J. **7**(9), 9066–9079 (2020)
33. Yang, Z., Li, B., Chen, P.Y., Song, D.: Characterizing audio adversarial examples using temporal dependency. arXiv preprint arXiv:1809.10875 (2018)
34. Yuan, X., et al.: {CommanderSong}: a systematic approach for practical adversarial voice recognition. In: 27th USENIX Security Symposium (USENIX Security 2018), pp. 49–64 (2018)
35. Zhang, G., Yan, C., Ji, X., Zhang, T., Zhang, T., Xu, W.: DolphinAttack: inaudible voice commands. In: Proceedings of the 2017 ACM SIGSAC Conference on Computer and Communications Security, pp. 103–117 (2017)
36. Zhang, H., Yan, Q., Zhou, P., Liu, X.Y.: Generating robust audio adversarial examples with temporal dependency. In: Proceedings of the Twenty-Ninth International Conference on International Joint Conferences on Artificial Intelligence, pp. 3167–3173 (2021)
37. Zhang, W., Zhou, S., Yang, L., Ou, L., Xiao, Z.: WiFiMap+: high-level indoor semantic inference with WiFi human activity and environment. IEEE Trans. Veh. Technol. **68**(8), 7890–7903 (2019)
38. Zhang, W.E., Sheng, Q.Z., Alhazmi, A., Li, C.: Adversarial attacks on deep-learning models in natural language processing: a survey. ACM Trans. Intell. Syst. Technol. (TIST) **11**(3), 1–41 (2020)
39. Zhang, X., Zheng, X., Mao, W.: Adversarial perturbation defense on deep neural networks. ACM Comput. Surv. (CSUR) **54**(8), 1–36 (2021)
40. Zheng, B., et al.: Black-box adversarial attacks on commercial speech platforms with minimal information. In: Proceedings of the 2021 ACM SIGSAC Conference on Computer and Communications Security, pp. 86–107 (2021)

An Empirical Study of Worldwide Plastic Waste Mitigation

Wang Zhonglin and Niu Guiqian(✉)

Ningbo University of Finance and Economics, Haishu District, Ningbo City, Zhejiang Province, China
279032562@qq.com

Abstract. In this paper, we refine the global target for the minimum achievable level of global single-use or disposable plastic product waste in 2030. Specifically, we first propose the model, MPMV, that estimates the Maximum Volume of single-use or disposable Plastic product waste that can safely be Mitigated without further environmental damage. Then, we design a three-level evaluation system for Plastic waste Mitigation Capacity, PMC, to investigate the minimal achievable level of global waste of single-use or disposable plastic products. Thereafter, we propose a target for the minimum achievable level of global waste of single-use or disposable plastic products in 2030 via perturbing the indicators in the PMC model, i.e., increasing the PMC curve to 0.6 by 2030. Finally, we put forward the SPMV (Suggested Plastics Mitigation Volume) model via combining MPMV and PMC models, to ensure the equity of task distribution of plastic waste reduction among countries. At last, we evaluate the performance of the proposed models via selecting thirteen countries with different levels of development, i.e., United States, Germany, India, Philippines, Vietnam, Canada, Yemen, Japan, Brazil, Chilie, Cuba, Singapore, and Italy.

Keywords: Plastic waste Waste mitigation · Environmental damage · Task distribution · Achievable level

1 Introduction

"I want to say one word to you. Just one word: Plastics." This occurs in Mike Nichols's 1967 film *The Graduate*. In the film, "plastics" is regarded as a cheap, sterile, ugly, and meaningless way of life [1,2,4,30–33]. While bringing convenience to life, single-use or disposable plastic products also pose a severe threat to the environment, like 83 trillion tons of plastic products are generated in the world by the 1950s, resulting in 63 trillion tons single-use or disposable plastic product waste [34–37]. According to the statement from the U.N. Environment

This work was supported in part by Natural Science Foundation of Ningbo (2021J233), in part by the 2022 Ningbo philosophy and Social Sciences Planning Project (G2022-2-76), in part by Zhejiang philosophy and Social Sciences Planning Project (23NDJC049Z).

Z. Xiao et al. (Eds.): ICECI 2022, LNICST 478, pp. 176–195, 2023.
https://doi.org/10.1007/978-3-031-28990-3_13

Programme (UNEP), 500 billion plastic bags are used worldwide every year, and at least 8 million tons of plastic product waste is injected into the ocean [3,5]. U.N. secretary-general Antonio Guterres claims that the amount of plastic product waste in the ocean will be much larger than the number of fishes by 2050 [6–8]. The large amount of single-use and disposable plastic products have severe environmental consequences. Furthermore, the time these products are useful is significantly shorter than the time it takes to decompose [44–49]. Therefore, it is desirable to improve the way we mitigate single-use or disposable plastic product waste and develop a plan to significantly reduce the amount of single-use or disposable plastic product waste in the world [38–43].

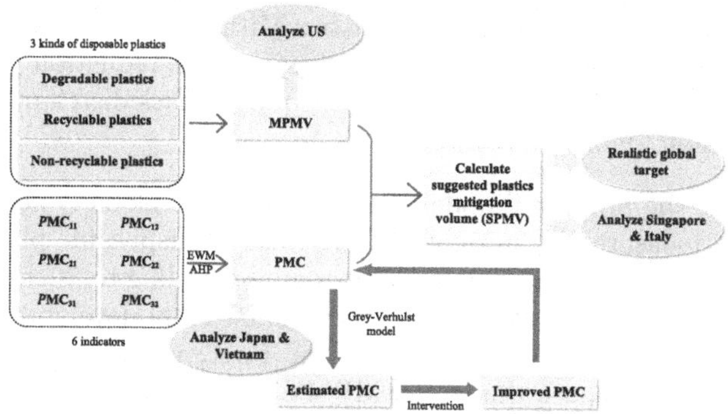

Fig. 1. The structure of our paper.

To this end, as shown in Fig. 1, we make the following main contributions:

- We first propose the model, MPMV, that estimates the Maximum Volume of single-use or disposable Plastic product waste that can safely be mitigated without further environmental damage. Specifically, we classify the single-use or disposable plastic product waste into degradable, recyclable, and non-recyclable plastic product waste. The former two kinds of plastic product waste can be wholly mitigated without further environmental pollution, and the latter are incinerated and may generate carbon dioxide and other toxic gases. So, we consider the amount of exhaust gas that the environment can withstand and the proportion of waste gas absorbed by incineration plants, and on this basis, we quantify the maximum levels of plastic product waste mitigated in an environmentally safe way.
- Then, we design a three-level evaluation system for Plastic waste Mitigation Capacity, PMC, to investigate the minimal achievable level of global waste of single-use or disposable plastic products. To concrete, based on Analytic Hierarchy Process (AHP) and Entropy Weight Method (EWM), we select six indicators indicating generating less and mitigating more single-use or disposable plastic product waste, and on this basis, construct the three-level evaluation system. To validate the generalization of the designed three-level

evaluation system, we apply it to Japan and Vietnam and compare the minimal achievable level of waste of single-use or disposable plastic products in Japan and Vietnam. On this basis, we highlight several suggestions for future mitigation of single-use or disposable plastic product waste.
- Thereafter, we propose a target for the minimum achievable level of global waste of single-use or disposable plastic products in 2030 via perturbing the indicators in the PMC model. To concrete, we use the Grey-Verhulst model to predict and compare the PMC curve and the perturbed PMC curve to evaluate the effectiveness of the perturbed PMC. Then, on this basis, we discuss the impacts of achieving such a level on laws and regulations, human life, ecological environment, and the multi-trillion-dollar plastic industry.
- Finally, we conduct the in-depth analysis of MPMV and PMC models, and put forward the SPMV (Suggested Plastics Mitigation Volume) model based on the careful consideration of national plastic waste reduction potential and development status, in order to ensure the equity of task distribution of plastic waste reduction among countries.

In summary, the proposed models formalize a fairer globally achievable goal and promotion measures for mitigating single-use or disposable plastic product waste. What's more, they can dynamically adapt according to, including but not limited to, the amount of plastic product waste, national development capacity.

The remainder of this paper is as follows. First, we introduce preliminary in Sect. 2, and then propose the model MPMV in Sect. 3. Thereafter, we design a three-level evaluation system for plastic waste reduction capability, PMC in Sect. 4. Then, we propose a target for the minimum achievable level of global waste of single-use or disposable plastic products in 2030 via perturbing the indicators in the PMC model in Sect. 5. We discuss the equity issues that might arise in allocating national responsibility for plastic waste mitigation in Sect. 6, followed by performance evaluation in Sect. 7. Finally, we conclude the whole paper in Sect. 8.

2 Preliminary

In this section, we in advance present the assumptions in this work as follows:

- We assume that the areas we study are concerned about plastic waste pollution.Plastic waste pollution is a global issue that concerns every region, so we expect the authorities to take a proactive approach to it.
- We assume that the region is the smallest unit of analysis.For the convenience of analysis, we do not consider the differences within the region, such as the different distribution of cities and forests.
- We assume that the data obtained are accurate and reliable.We get data from trusted websites and papers.

The symbols used in this paper are listed in Table 1.

Table 1. Symbol table.

Symbol	Definition
V_1	The volume of degradable plastics
V_2	The volume of recyclable plastics
PIV	Plastics Incineration Volume
$MPMV$	Maximum Plastics Mitigation Volume
PMC	Plastics Mitigation Capability
PMC_1	Ecological indicator
PMC_2	Economic indicator
PMC_3	Political indicator
PMC_{11}	Forest area per capita
PMC_{12}	Technical ability to decompose plastics
PMC_{21}	GDP per capita
PMC_{22}	Trade per capita
PMC_{31}	Enforcement of laws
PMC_{32}	Laws governing plastics
w_j	Weight of jth sub-indicator
$SPMV$	Suggested Plastics Mitigation Volume

3 Maximum Plastics Mitigation Volume (MPMV) Model

As shown in Fig. 2, disposable plastics can be classified into two categories: degradable plastics and non-degradable plastics. Degradable plastics are a new kind of environmentally friendly plastics that can degrade into harmless substances under certain conditions after use. Non-degradable plastics can be subdivided into recyclable and non-recyclable plastics. The American plastics industry association mandated recycling labeling for plastics in 1988 [9]. This set of signs uses plastic identification codes on containers or packages, from 1 to 7.

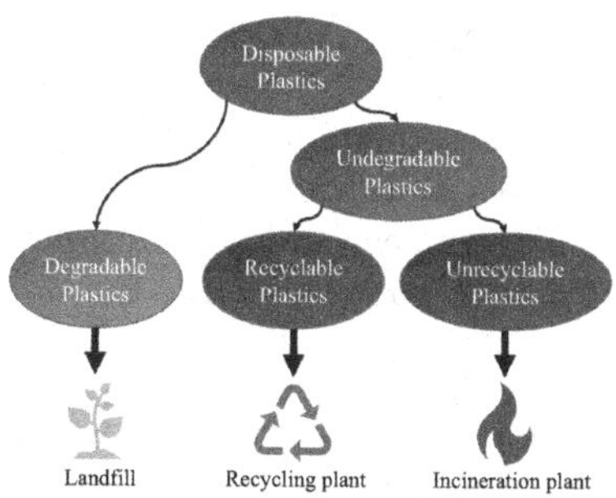

Fig. 2. Classification and treatment of disposable plastics.

Among them, #1-PET, #2-HDPE, and #5-PP are recyclable plastic materials, while other plastic materials are challenging to recycle.

In order to maximize the mitigation of plastic waste without imposing further damage to the environment, recyclable plastics are recycled as far as possible and continue to enter production activities. There are two main routes for the remaining non-recyclable plastics: landfill and incineration. Landfills are passive and straightforward, where plastics take thousands of years to break down and slowly release methane, a greenhouse gas 25 times more potent than carbon dioxide [10]. Therefore, incineration is one of the most innocuous ways of disposing of plastic waste in the mainstream of society; thus, it is the treatment method adopted in our model.

Inevitably, incinerating plastic does not entirely evade the risks of environmental pollution. The incineration of plastics produces carbon dioxide and a certain amount of toxic gases containing sulfur or nitrogen [11]. These gases need to be cleaned by the incinerator plant before they can be discharged. Nevertheless, we need to understand that an area has a limited capacity for toxic gases.

Therefore, to discuss the maximization of plastic waste mitigation, our model's core is to determine the maximum capacity of an area for the waste generated by incineration. Incineration in less than the limit can purify the environment; otherwise, the aggravate in air pollution will outweigh the reduction in plastic pollution. Note that the maximum volume for incineration in this area is not a threshold at which the environment is on the verge of collapse, but a state of equilibrium at which the environment is just capable of purifying itself.

To sum up, in our model, there are three ways to treat disposable garbage: natural degradation, recycling, and incineration. Degradable plastics degrade by themselves, and non-degradable but recyclable plastics can be recycled. For non-degradable and non-recyclable plastics, incineration is the only environmentally friendly treatment. Next, we focus on the *incineration of disposable plastic waste.*

Incineration of disposable waste produces CO_2 and other toxic gases. Therefore, evaluating the maximum level of plastic waste reduction is equivalent to evaluating the amount of plastic incineration when CO_2 and toxic gases reach the maximum environmental capacity.

CO_2 Constraint on Incineration Volume. First, we need to determine the amount of plastic incineration when CO_2 reaches the maximum capacity of the environment. We believe that the amount of plastic incineration when CO_2 emissions reach the maximum capacity of the environment is closely related to the planned CO_2 emissions in a given year and the carbon dioxide generated by the incineration of one ton of plastic, so we have Eq. 1:

$$PIV_{CO_2} = \frac{M_1 \times P_1}{M_2}, \tag{1}$$

where M_1 is planned CO_2 emissions, P_1 is the ratio of CO_2 emitted by an incinerator to total CO_2 emissions, and M_2 is the carbon dioxide generated by burning a ton of plastic.

Other Toxic Gases Constraint on Incineration Volume. Then we need to determine the amount of plastic incineration when the toxic gases reach its maximum environmental capacity. The toxic gases from burning plastic are equal to the total amount of toxic gases produced by incineration multiplied by the emission ratio. The maximum limit for incinerating plastic is the maximum amount of toxic gases emitted by burning plastic divided by the mass of toxic gases produced by burning a ton of plastic. We acquire Eq. 2:

$$PIV_{tox} = \frac{M_3}{(1 - P_2) \times M_4}, \tag{2}$$

where M_3 is maximum toxic gas emissions, P_2 is the proportion of toxic gases absorbed by incineration plants to the total amount of toxic gases generated, M_4 is the mass of toxic gases produced by burning a ton of plastic in an incineration plant.

When the amount of plastic incineration exceeds the maximum carrying capacity of the environment, it exceeds the maximum level at which disposable plastic waste can be safely reduced, causing further damage to the environment. The maximum capacity of the environment to bear the toxic gases released by the incineration of plastics is the minimum values of PIV_{CO_2} and PIV_{tox}.

$$PIV = Min(PIV_{CO_2}, PIV_{tox}). \tag{3}$$

Therefore, we can get the maximum plastics mitigation volume:

$$MPMV = V_1 + V_2 + PIV, \tag{4}$$

where V_1 is the volume of degradable plastics, V_2 is the volume of recyclable plastics.

4 Plastics Mitigation Capability Assessment Model

The above model discusses the maximum incineration limit of non-recyclable plastics in the optimal case, that is, all recyclable plastics are recycled, all degradable plastics are degraded, and all non-recyclable plastics are incinerated at the maximum. However, in reality, that is hard to achieve. In order to make countries or regions have a clear understanding and measurement of their own plastic waste mitigation capability, we combine the Analytic Hierarchy Process (AHP) with Entropy Weight Method (EWM) to establish a plastic waste mitigation capability evaluation system.

4.1 Indicator Selection

Every piece of plastic waste is first generated, then littered. Thus, to reduce plastic waste to a minimal level, we should consider both the capability to lessen plastic waste generation (hereinafter referred to as Cap1) and the capability to mitigate plastic without further environmental damage (hereinafter referred to as Cap2) . Therefore, the evaluation model we built will include the above two factors. However, while selecting indicators, we found that some of them can evaluate Cap1 and Cap2 simultaneously. Hence, for the sake of convenience, we need to find out more precise boundaries to classify various indicators.

Table 2. Introduction to indicators

Target Layer	Indicator layer	Sub-indicator layer	Direction	Belongs to
Plastics mitigation capability(PMC)	Ecological indicator (PMC_1)	Forest area per capita(PMC_{11})	+	Cap1, Cap2
		Technical ability to decompose plastics(PMC_{12})	+	Cap2
	Economic indicator (PMC_2)	GDP per capita(PMC_{21})	+	Cap1
		Trade per capita(PMC_{22})	+	Cap1
	Political indicator (PMC_3)	Government bribery rate(PMC_{31})	−	Cap1, Cap2
		Effectiveness of laws governing plastics(PMC_{32})	+	Cap1, Cap2

The evaluation system of plastic mitigation capability is divided into three layers: the target layer A, the indicator layer B and the sub-indicator layer C. Combined with the source of disposable plastic, the availability of plastic substitute, impact on residents' lives as well as the national policy , we selected the indicators which are not only convenient to obtain but also easy for the comparison in the study area to reflect a region's plastic mitigation capability from various angles. Finally, six indicators were put into three categories: ecological, economic, political, to construct a three-level evaluation system for plastics mitigation capability, as shown in Table 2.

Ecological indicator

- **Forest area per capita**: It refers to the average forest area owned by each person in the region, and it is a vital indicator to reflect the availability of forest resources and woodland in an area. Here is what it means: (1) Extensive forest cover could provide a significant number of alternatives to plastics, thereby reducing plastic production from the origin. (2) The large forest area per capita indicates that the area has a sizeable ecological environment capacity and a strong capability to deal with the waste gas generated by burning plastics.
- **Technical ability to decompose plastic**: It refers to the ability to use scientific and technological means to break down plastic waste. To quantify this, we introduced the human development index (HDI) for evaluation.

Economic Indicator

- **GDP per capita**: It is one of the most important macroeconomic indicators, reflecting the economic development of a region. If GDP per capita is high, then the region's economy is going well, and people are more likely to accept plastic items made from degradable materials at slightly higher prices.

- **Trade per capita**: It reflects both the prosperity of a region's foreign economic exchanges and the economic strength of the region. The more foreign trade per capita, the more likely it is to import materials that can replace plastic, such as bamboo and paper.

Political Indicator

- **Government bribery rate**: It reflects the transparency of a country's system of government. We use the country's corruption index to evaluate. The higher the level of corruption, the weaker the enforcement of environmental laws. It also indirectly hampers income growth.
- **Effectiveness of laws governing plastics**: It reflects the soundness of the relevant laws in a country. The stronger the regulations, the less disposable plastic is used and discarded by businesses and residents.

4.2 Data Normalization

The data used to evaluate the indicators comes from multiple databases, including WorldBank [16]. If data in a region is missing, we do not evaluate the region so that to get the most accurate results. We obtained data from 162 countries and regions for four separate years. Since the evaluation indicators contain both positive and negative ones and there exist dimensional differences among most indicators, we use range normalization to normalize data [17].

While analyzing all the indicators, we find that they can be divided into two types. Symbol + means that for the indicator, the higher, the better. Similarly, Symbol − means that the lower, the better. Therefore, for those indicators with symbol +, the equation should be

$$r_{ij} = \frac{x_{ij} - r_{min}}{r_{max} - r_{min}}.$$

As for those indicators with symbol −, the equation should be

$$r_{ij} = \frac{r_{min} - x_{ij}}{r_{max} - r_{min}},$$

where x_{ij} and r_{ij} represent the original value and standardized value of item j in the ith region, while r_{min} and r_{max} represent the minimum and maximum value of item j in all years.

4.3 Weight Determination

The determination of indicators' weight plays a crucial role and has a direct impact on the accuracy of evaluation results. Entropy weight method (EWM) is an objective weighting method; therefore we use it to determine the weight of the indicators [18].

First, we calculate the weight of the jth indicator in the ith country.

$$f_{ij} = \frac{r_{ij}}{\sum_{i=1}^{n} r_{ij}}.$$

According to the concept of self-information and entropy in information theory, the information entropy e_j of each evaluation indicator can be calculated, and thus

$$e_j = -ln(n)^{-1} \sum_{i=1}^{n} f_{ij} ln(f_{ij}).$$

Based on the information entropy, we will further calculate the weight of each evaluation indicator we defined before.

$$w_j = \frac{1 - e_j}{n - \sum_j e_j}, j = 1, 2, \cdots, n.$$

We also used AHP to cover the shortages that indicator weight under EWM vary with samples.

4.4 The Result

After determining the weight of each indicator, we weighted and summed each indicator to get PMC:

$$PMC_i = \sum_{j=1}^{n} r_{ij} w_j, \tag{5}$$

where PMC_i, w_j and r_{ij} represent the comprehensive indicator of the PMC for the ith country, the weight of item j and the normalized value of item j for the ith country respectively. Besides, PMC_i values range from 0 to 1, the larger the value, the higher the plastics mitigation capability.

5 Target for the Level of Plastic Waste

5.1 Outline

Based on our models and discussions, we can assess a country's capability to mitigate plastic waste. There is no doubt that the process of mitigating plastic waste is the process of getting plastic waste to a minimum level. Therefore, to set a target for the minimum level of plastic waste on a global scale which is to assess the global target capability to mitigate plastic waste. In other words, when $PMC = PMC_{target}$, the global level of plastic waste reaches the lowest.

5.2 The Process of Setting Targets

Current Situation. With an average of 162 regions, according to the world bank, we got a result for the six indicators of PMC. In 2018, the global forest area per capita indicator was 0.42, the HDI indicator was 0.65, the GDP per capita indicator was 0.49, trade per capita indicator was 0.54, the corruption indicator was 0.39, and the relevant policies and regulations indicator was 0.38. By multiplying the six indicators by the corresponding weight, we obtained the total global PMC of 0.4921 in 2018.

The Intervention Idea. In order to maximize the global capability to mitigate plastic waste, but also in line with the discipline of social development, we plan to intervene in several aspects. All the countries are working hard to develop their economies, which relate closely to the HDI, trade per capita and GDP per capita. Therefore, we assume that these three indicators will continue to grow at the current average rate. GDP per capita will continue to grow by 4.8%, the HDI index will grow by 0.72%, and trade per capita will grow by 1.56% annually. The level of forest area per capita has shown a negative growth trend in recent years, with an annual degradation rate of 0.125%. While we argued that this indicator would have a particular impact on the global capability to mitigate plastic waste. So we decided to intervene in this indicator and set it to increase by 0.6% in the future. The global corruption indicator scored lowly, indicating much room for improvement. However, due to the complexity of political issues and the low feasibility of the intervention, we assume that it will continue to grow at the current average rate of 0.4%. The related laws and regulations indicator was the lowest among the six indicators in 2018, and the plastic waste issue is now getting increasing global attention with the promotion of the United Nations, so we intervene and set it to grow at a rate of 3.59% in the future.

As shown in Fig. 3, with our intervention, the six global indicators will change 12 years later, in 2030, as follows: PMC_{11} will rise to 0.45, PMC_{12} to 0.7, PMC_{21} to 0.76, PMC_{22} to 0.65, PMC_{31} to 0.41, and PMC_{32} to 0.58. We ended up with a PMC of 0.6. Compared to 2018, the PMC has increased by 21.90%, which is our target, meaning that the global plastic waste can reach the lowest level.

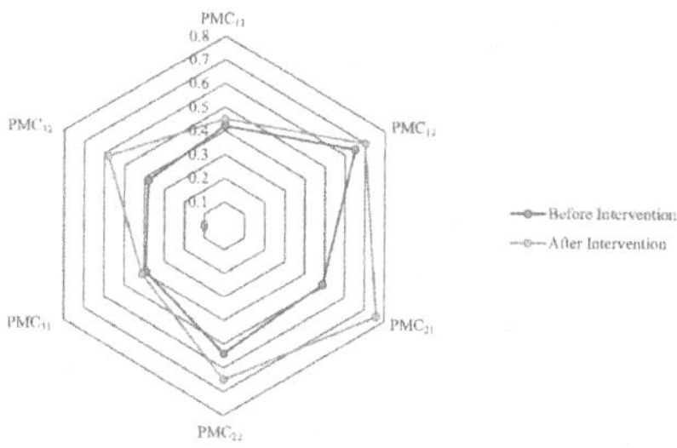

Fig. 3. Comparison of global PMC before and after intervention.

5.3 Impacts for Achieving Such Levels

In order to achieve the minimum level of the global plastic waste, we discussed the impact on laws and regulations, human life, ecological environment and the plastic industry.

Laws and Regulations. In 2019, at the Congress of the Basel Convention, 187 countries around the world revised the convention to include plastic waste as an import and export restriction object, deciding to include plastic waste pollution as one of the globally recognized environmental problems [24]. In March 2007, San Francisco became the first city in the U.S. to ban the use of non-biodegradable plastic bags, encouraging using recyclable and biodegradable plastic bags [25]. After that, although global countries started to implement 'plastic limit orders', proposing to restrict and ban the use of disposable plastic products, there were differences in the implementation effect between countries. Therefore, as a global target, governments should revise laws and regulations, extend the 'plastic limit orders' to all industries. Also, we should continue to increase investment in R&D and marketing of biodegradable plastics, providing tax incentives to encourage the production of biodegradable plastics. Last but not least, global countries have to speed up the construction of a more comprehensive marine plastic waste monitoring system, monitoring key areas in real time.

Human Life. According to the report by Medical University of Vienna and Austria's Federal Environment Agency, preliminary confirmation that plastic ends up in the human gut proves that the spread of plastic waste could have harmful effects on human health [26]. Therefore, the importance of harmless treatment of plastic waste is evidenced. However, the vast majority of the world's material cannot be recycled, especially plastic waste, only about 9% of which can be recycled [27]. The main reasons lie in the neglect of waste classification and the abuse of plastic products. In order to mitigate plastic waste to a great extent, people have to substitute eco-friendly materials for plastics gradually and do household waste sorting consciously.

Ecological Environment. The ways of dealing with plastic waste are accelerating the mitigation of plastic products and controlling the use of plastic products. Expanding the size of forests will help in both ways: it will increase the environment's capacity to withstand harmful emissions, and it will also provide the raw materials to make plastic substitutes. The governments need to ban deforestation and balance production with environmental protection. They should also formulate and implement ecological engineering projects which will help to reduce disasters.

Plastic Industry. When the idea of 'controlling plastics' emerges, the plastic industry has to reform. The traditional plastic industry would suffer if it did not actively seek change. Not only will these plastic manufacturer be pressured by policies and taxes from the top, but sales will suffer as demands fall. Therefore, the plastic industry must actively respond to the national call for plastic control and take the initiative to innovate plastic production technology.

In addition to plastic factories that need to change, plastic waste companies need to keep up. Incinerators do most of the work, but doubts remain about whether they can safely dispose of plastic without causing air pollution. Incineration plants need to continually improve their treatment to ensure that the waste gases can be purified to the maximum extent before discharge. Relevant authorities need to adequately evaluate the emission channels of incineration plants before deciding whether to approve them.

6 Equity Issues Model

6.1 Overview

When it comes to the apportionment of national responsibility for plastic waste, it is generally assumed that better-developed countries should shoulder more of the burden, as also demonstrated by the PMC score. However, the target set by the PMC model assumes the global capability to deal with plastic waste from six indicators at the aspects of Cap1 and Cap2, the volume of each country is not taken into account. For example, if country A has a shallow level of development, it gets a meagre PMC score. But it relies heavily on industrial development, such as incineration plants, and has a large population, so the country's theoretical MPMV is greater. The development level of country B is also very low, but the country as a whole is small, and the MPMV is small. If we allocate the responsibility for plastic waste to them equally, it raises the issue of unfairness. In fact, country A should bear more of the burden than country B. Therefore, we need to take equity into account and improve our approach.

6.2 An Improved Approach

Based on the discussion above, we decided to consider the maximum plastic mitigation volume and plastic mitigation capability when recommending the plastic waste mitigation volume of a country or a region. The equation is as follows:

$$SPMV = MPMV \times PMC. \tag{6}$$

Such consideration not only takes into account a country's industrial development background, national size, population, environmental carrying capacity and other factors but also takes into account the country's ability to reduce plastic waste. The SPMV thus generated can minimize the risk of a country taking on a mismatched task of reducing plastic waste.

7 Evaluation

7.1 Evaluation on MPMV Model

To illustrate our model more intuitively, we choose the United States in 2010 as a case. According to Hannah Ritchie and Max Roser's work on plastic pollution [12], the United States discarded 40,580,700 tons of plastic in 2010, including about 405,807 tons of biodegradable plastic. According to Rick Lingle's report on plastic recycling [13], the United States had 1,179,360 tons of recycled plastic in 2010. Also, the study shows that the United States plans to emit 5,702,880,000 tons of CO_2 in 2010 [14],the proportion of carbon dioxide emitted by incineration plants is about 0.506% [15]. Excluding power generation potential, the net carbon dioxide emissions would be 2.9 metric tons for every ton of plastic burned. We believe that the United States has one of the world's leading waste gas treatment capabilities and that the primary constraint on its environmental carrying capacity lies in CO_2 emissions. Based on the data above and Eqs. (1), (2), and (3), the amount of plastic incineration when CO_2 emission reaches the maximum capacity of the environment is

$$\frac{5702880000 \times 0.506\%}{2.9} = 9950542ton.$$

According to Eq. (4), the total amount of disposable plastic that can be safely reduced in the United States in 2010 is:

$$\begin{aligned} MPMV_{US} &= V_1 + V_2 + PIV \\ &= 405807 + 1179360 + 9950542 \\ &= 11535709ton. \end{aligned}$$

7.2 Evaluation on PMC Model

Table 3. The PMC and HDI values of 10 countries.

	Germany	India	Philippines	Vietnam	Canada	Yemen	Japan	Brazil	Chilie	Cuba
PMC	0.7653	0.3837	0.3445	0.4167	0.819	0.2739	0.7754	0.4784	0.5487	0.3731
HDI	0.939	0.647	0.712	0.693	0.922	0.463	0.915	0.761	0.847	0.778

We selected ten countries with different levels of development in 2018 for analysis. We assigned weights to each indicator based on the discussion of Sect. 4.3 and 4.4, and the weight results are as follows: Forest area per capita (0.1524), technical ability to decompose plastic (0.2530), GDP per capita (0.1734), trade per capita (0.1012), the degree of corruption (0.1833)and related laws and regulations (0.1316). As can be seen in Fig. 4 and Table 3, there was a strong correlation between the HDI and the PMC in these countries, indicating that technology plays a significant role in mitigating the level of single-use plastic waste. Germany, Canada, and Japan scored high on the PMC, which is reasonable for their high HDI levels as they are developed countries. Yemen, on the other hand, had a deficient HDI level, only half that of developed countries, which primarily affected its PMC. In India, the Philippines and Vietnam, where HDI levels were

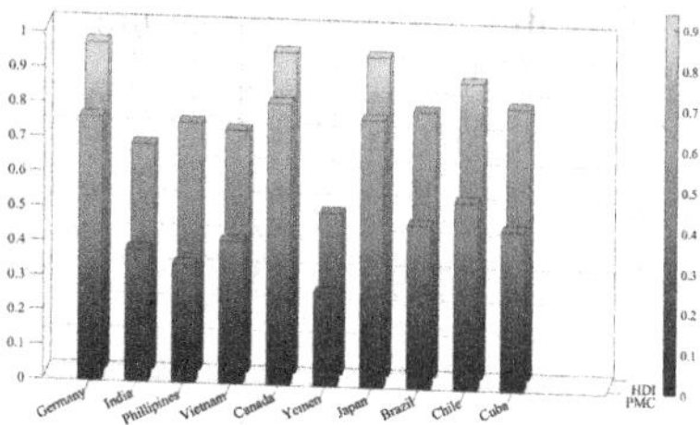

Fig. 4. Effect of HDI on PMC composite score.

not poor, the PMC remained at a low level, mainly because such indicators as the corruption indicator for developing countries had a more pronounced effect on PMC levels. In general, HDI played a decisive role in promoting PMC levels. In addition, to verify the applicability of the model, we applied two cases for analysis. Based on the six indicators, we collected and processed the raw data related to Japan and Vietnam in 2018. As a result, the PMC was 0.769571 for Japan and 0.405891 for Vietnam.

By investigating Fig. 5 and Table 4, we can intuitively analyze their capability to mitigate plastic waste. In terms of PMC_{12}, which contributes the most to PMC, Japan scores much higher than Vietnam, indicating that Japan has a higher technical ability to decompose plastic waste than Vietnam. Vietnam is also well behind Japan in the PMC's second-most-weighted indicator of corruption and has lost initiatives in mitigating plastic waste because of the inefficient political system. As a developed Asian country, Japan's GDP per capita is approximately six times that of Vietnam, which means the residents in Vietnam struggle financially to afford more expensive biodegradable plastics. Additionally, Vietnam only scored slightly higher than Japan in forest area per capita, which ranked fourth in PMC weighting. Obviously, Vietnam's lead in this aspect did not contribute enough to the comprehensive PMC. Therefore, our model has implications for the Vietnamese government to improve its plastic waste mitiga-

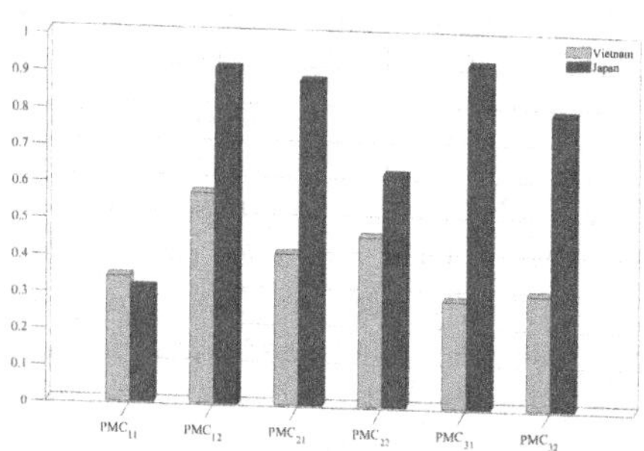

Fig. 5. Comparison of the PMC indicators between Vietnam and Japan.

Table 4. Indicator values of Japan and Vietnam.

	PMC_{11}	PMC_{12}	PMC_{21}	PMC_{12}	PMC_{31}	PMC_{32}	PMC
Vietnam	0.3449	0.5796	0.418	0.4614	0.2992	0.3142	0.4059
Japan	0.3155	0.9128	0.8896	0.6396	0.9397	0.8016	0.7696

tion capability. By collecting information on plastic waste in Vietnam, we learn that the country ranks third in Southeast Asia in terms of plastic waste per capita, and has increased more than tenfold in the last 30 years. According to a report by Ipsos Business Consulting, a global growth strategy consulting firm, Vietnam consumed 41.3 kg of plastic per capita in 2018 [19].

The reasons for the problematic situation are complicated. In addition to the low local recycling rate and a large number of landfills, the people's environmental awareness is not keen, and the national policy and regulatory system for plastics are not sound. Therefore, many countries take advantage of the policy gap to send plastic waste to Vietnam [20]. Applying our model to confirm it, we found that Vietnam has an inferior technical ability in decomposing plastic waste, which results in a low degradation rate of plastic waste. Thus the majority can merely be decomposed by such simple and negative methods as landfills. Vietnam's economic level is relatively backward. Since the economic level of a country has a fundamental impact on education. In weak areas, it is not very easy to require people to have a keen environmental awareness. Vietnam's low PMC score in political indicators is in line with the government's inadequate policies and legislations on plastics. Therefore, the Vietnamese government should continue to innovate and promote the environmentally friendly treatment of plastics. At the same time, it should vigorously develop the economy in a green way and avoid the route of 'pollution first, treatment later.' Last but not least, the governments should strengthen legislation to ban foreign shipments of plastic waste, support the production of biodegradable plastics, offer subsidies, and impose higher taxes on non-recyclable and non-biodegradable plastics.

Meanwhile, our model can also inspire the Japanese government. According to the information from the Asahi Shimbun and the United Nations [21], Japan is second only to the United States in single-use plastic consumption. Japan also produces more plastic per capita than China and the rest of Asia combined, at 106 kg, according to Statista, an online statistics website [22]. Moreover, according to a study by CarterJMRN in 2018, Japanese attitudes toward plastic products have reached 'fever levels', with Japanese consumers taking an average of 400 plastic shopping bags a year [23–28]. In 2018, Japan even refused to sign the G7 agreement to mitigate the use of single-use plastics and prevent plastic pollution. Japan's PMC score indicates that it has sound plastic waste mitigation capability [29–33]. In the long run, however, if Japan does not intervene in the abuse of plastic, the ecological consequences will be irreversible sooner or later. Therefore, from the perspective of sustainable development, Japan must change its attitude towards plastic at the cultural level and use as many recyclable and environmentally friendly materials as possible [34–38]. The government should also call for mitigation in the use of single-use plastics through policies and stricter legislation.

7.3 Advantage of Intervention in PMC Model

To show the change of PMC before and after the intervention, we used the Grey-Verhulst model to predict the PMC curve without intervention. Grey-Verhulst model can better reflect the saturation state of indicators than the commonly used grey GM(1,1). After calculation, the whitened differential equation is finally obtained:

$$\frac{dx^{(1)}}{dt} - 0.1838x^{(1)} = -0.3084\left(x^{1}\right)^{2}.$$

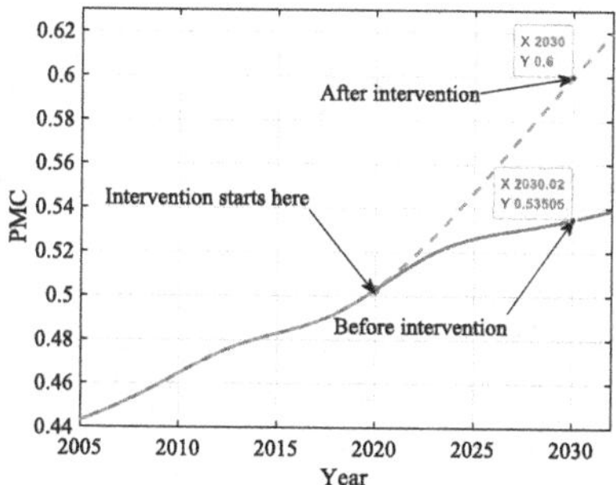

Fig. 6. Global PMC curves before and after intervention.

From Fig. 6, it can be seen that the PMC curve without intervention is relatively flat, reaching 0.535 in 2030, an increase of 8.7% from 0.4921 in 2018. After the human intervention, the PMC curve is steeper, and the PMC growth rate is faster, reaching 0.6 in 2030, an increase of 21.9% over 2018. By 2030, the PMC with the intervention is 1.12 times higher than the PMC without the intervention. This result suggests that the intervention we have developed will have a positive impact on global plastic waste mitigation capability and contribute to the goal of minimizing plastic waste in the world.

7.4 Evaluation on Equity Issues Model

To verify the validity of the model, we will analyze two examples. The results are listed in Table 5. In 2018, the PMC value of Singapore was 0.7052, while that of Italy was 0.7049, showing a small gap between the two countries. Both from a PMC perspective and from a common-sense perspective, one would argue that the two countries should undertake similar plastic waste reduction tasks. But in fact, because Singapore has a smaller land area than Italy and different geographical locations, it can carry different emissions, the calculated MPMV is quite different. The MPMV of the two is multiplied by the corresponding PMC to obtain the SPMV which is of referable significance to the relevant plans and measures of the two countries.

Table 5. Indicator values of Singapore and Italy.

	PMC_{11}	PMC_{12}	PMC_{21}	PMC_{22}	PMC_{31}	PMC_{32}	PMC	$MPMV$	$SPMV$
Singapore	0.06	0.9	0.93	0.9	0.87	0.43	0.7052	347945	245370.81
Italy	0.27	0.87	0.81	0.66	0.69	0.83	0.7049	967969	682321.35

8 Discussions

- Our PMC model inherits the advantages of AHP and EWM. Specifically, when weighing the indicators, we utilize weight average method combining the AHP with EWM. To some extent, this method not only provides a supplement of indicator's horizontal comparison with EWM but also covers the shortages that indicator weight under EWM vary with samples and is even overwhelmingly dependent on samples. Furthermore, this method reduces the subjectivity of AHP.
- Our model combines the potential and reality of each region. To concrete, in the construction of the SPMV model, we have included the maximum plastic mitigation volume and plastic mitigation capability of each region, taking full account of the development potential and reality. It is fairer and more comprehensive to use our model to distribute national responsibilities.
- The indicators selected by the PMC model cover a comprehensive range of fields.

In summary, we have studied the global target for the minimum achievable level of global single-use or disposable plastic product waste in 2030 via designing serval models, and we finally evaluate the performance of the proposed models via selecting thirteen countries with different levels of development.

Acknowledgement. This paper is was supported in part by 2022 Ningbo philosophy and Social Sciences Planning Project (G2022-2-76), in part by the Natural Science Foundation of Ningbo (2021J233), in part by the 2021 Zhejiang philosophy and Social Sciences Planning Project (21NDJC168YB).

References

1. Chaulya, S.K., et al.: Modelling for air quality estimation for a planned coal washery to control air pollution. Environ. Model. Assess. **25**(6), 775–791 (2020). https://doi.org/10.1007/s10666-020-09721-x
2. Costa, C., Domínguez, J., Autrán, B., Márquez, M.C.: Dynamic modeling of biological treatment of leachates from solid wastes. Environ. Model. Assess. **23**(2), 165–173 (2018). https://doi.org/10.1007/s10666-018-9592-8

3. Ozmen, M., Aydogan, E.K., et al.: Developing a decision-support system for waste management in aluminum production. Environ. Model. Assess. **21**, 803–817 (2016)
4. National Geographic, A whopping 91% of plastic isn't recycled (2020). https://www.nationalgeographic.com/news/2017/07/. plastic-produced-recycling-waste-ocean-trash-debris-environment. Accessed 25 June 2020
5. UNEP, This World Environment Day, it's time for a change (2020). https://www.unenvironment.org/interactive/beat-plastic-pollution/. Accessed 25 June 2020
6. United Nations, 'We face a global emergency' over oceans: UN chief sounds the alarm at G7 Summit event (2020). https://news.un.org/en/story/2018/06/1011811. Accessed 25 June 2020
7. COMAP, 2020 ICM Problem E (2020). https://www.comap.com/undergraduate/contests/mcm/contests/2020/problems. Accessed 25 June 2020
8. Galloway T.S., Micro- and nano-plastics and human health. Mar. Anthropogenic Litter (2015)
9. Wikipedia, Resin identification code (2020). https://en.wikipedia.org/wiki/Resin_identification_code. Accessed 25 June 2020
10. Royer, S.J., et al.: Production of methane and ethylene from plastic in the environment. Public Libr. Sci. **13**, 1–13 (2018)
11. Verma, R., Vinoda, K.S., et al.: Toxic pollutants from plastic waste- a review. Proc. Environ. Sci. **35**, 701–708 (2016)
12. Ritchie, H., et al.: Plastic Pollution, OurWorldInData.org (2020). https://ourworldindata.org/plastic-pollution. Accessed 25 June 2020
13. American Chemistry Council, Plastics and Sustainability: A Valuation of Environmental Benefits, Costs and Opportunities for Continuous Improvement (2020). https://plastics.americanchemistry.com/Plastics-and-Sustainability. Accessed 25 June 2020
14. WorldBank, CO2 emissions (kt) - United States (2020). https://data.worldbank.org/indicator/ EN.ATM.CO2E.KTlocations=US. Accessed 25 June 2020
15. GAIA, The Hidden Climate Polluter: Plastic Incineration (2020). https://www.no-burn.org/hiddenclimatepolluter/. Accessed 25 June 2020
16. Worldbank (2020). https://data.worldbank.org/. Accessed 25 June 2020
17. Codecademy, Normalization (2020). https://www.codecademy.com/articles/normalization. Accessed 25 June 2020
18. Wang, Y., et al.: Study of the comparison and selection method of the mining project investment based on entropy-weight method. Adv. Struct. Eng. **94**, 1752–1756 (2011)
19. Vnexpress, Vietnam plastic waste problem goes from bad to worse (2020). https://e.vnexpress.net/news/news/vietnam-plastic-waste-problem-goes-from-bad-to-worse-3978124.html. Accessed 25 June 2020
20. Reuters, Vietnam to limit waste imports as shipments build up at ports (2020). https://www.reuters.com/article/us-vietnam-waste/vietnam-to-limit-waste-imports-as-shipments-build-up-at-ports-idUSKBN1KG0KL. Accessed 25 June 2020
21. The Asahi Shimbun, EDITORIAL: Japan must get with program, stop incinerating plastic waste. https://www.asahi.com/ajw/articles/AJ201907310028.html. Accessed 25 June 2020
22. Statista, Disposal volume of plastic waste in Japan from 2006 to 2015. https://www.statista.com/statistics/695382/japan-plastic-waste-disposal-volume/. Accessed 25 June 2020

23. Carterjmrn, PLASTIC IS NO LONGER FANTASTIC CMARKET POTENTIAL FOR ALTERNATIVES IN JAPAN. https://www.carterjmrn.com/market-research-blog/plastic-is-no-longer-fantastic-market-potential-for-alternatives-in-japan.php. Accessed 25 June 2020
24. CNN, Over 180 countries - not including the US - agree to restrict global plastic waste trade. https://edition.cnn.com/2019/05/11/world/basel-convention-plastic-waste-trade-intl/index.html. Accessed 25 June 2020
25. The New York Times, San Francisco Board Votes to Ban Some Plastic Bags. https://www.nytimes.com/2007/03/28/us/28plastic.html. Accessed 25 June 2020
26. Medicalxpress, Microplastics discovered in human stools across the globe in 'first study of its kind' (2018). https://medicalxpress.com/news/2018-10-microplasticshuman-stools-globe-kind.html. Accessed 25 June 2020
27. Geyer, R., Jambeck, J.R., Law, K.L., et al.: Production, use, and fate of all plastics ever made. Sci. Adv. **3**(7), e1700782 (2017)
28. The Guardian, 'Plastic recycling is a myth': what really happens to your rubbish?. https://www.theguardian.com/environment/2019/aug/17/plastic-recycling-myth-what-really-happens-your-rubbish. Accessed 25 June 2020
29. Wang, Z., Dang, Y., et al.: Unbiased grey verhulst model and its application. Syst. Eng. Theory Pract. **29**, 138–144 (2009)
30. Jiang, H., et al.: An energy-efficient framework for internet of things underlaying heterogeneous small cell networks. IEEE Trans. Mob. Comput. **21**(1), 31–43 (2021)
31. Xiao, Z., et al.: TrajData: on vehicle trajectory collection with commodity plug-and-play obu devices. IEEE Internet Things J. **7**(9), 9066–9079 (2020)
32. Xiao, Z., et al.: Resource management in UAV-assisted MEC: state-of-the-art and open challenges. Wireless Netw. **28**, 3305–3322 (2022)
33. Li, J., et al.: Drive2friends: inferring social relationships from individual vehicle mobility data. IEEE Internet Things J. **7**(6), 5116–5127 (2020)
34. Ali, T.A.A., et al.: Optimal design of IIR wideband digital differentiators and integrators using salp swarm algorithm. Knowl. Based Syst. **182**, 104834 (2019)
35. Dai, X., et al.: Task co-offloading for D2D-assisted mobile edge computing in industrial internet of things. IEEE Trans. Ind. Inf. **19**, 480–490 (2022). https://doi.org/10.1109/TII.2022.3158974
36. Jiang, H., et al.: Joint task offloading and resource allocation for energy-constrained mobile edge computing. IEEE Trans. Mob. Comput. (2022). https://doi.org/10.1109/TMC.2022.3150432
37. Long, W., et al.: Unified spatial-temporal neighbor attention network for dynamic traffic prediction. IEEE Trans. Veh. Technol. **72**, 1515–1529 (2022). https://doi.org/10.1109/TVT.2022.3209242
38. Hu, Z., et al.: Computation efficiency maximization and QoE-provisioning in UAV-enabled MEC communication systems. IEEE Trans. Netw. Sci. Eng. **8**(2), 1630–1645 (2021)
39. Zeng, F., et al.: A price-based optimization strategy of power control and resource allocation in full-duplex heterogeneous macrocell-femtocell networks. IEEE Access **6**, 42004–42013 (2018)
40. Huang, Y., et al.: Road network construction with complex intersections based on sparsely-sampled private car trajectory data. ACM Trans. Knowl. Discov. Data **13**(3), 1–28 (2019)
41. Xiao, Z., et al.: A joint information and energy cooperation framework for CR-enabled macro-femto heterogeneous networks. IEEE Internet Things J. **7**(4), 2828–2839 (2020)

42. Zhang, W., et al.: WiFiMap+: high-level indoor semantic inference with WiFi human activity and environment. IEEE Trans. Veh. Technol. **68**(8), 7890–7903 (2019)
43. Zhao, P., et al.: Synthesizing privacy preserving traces: enhancing plausibility with social networks. IEEE/ACM Trans. Netw. **27**(6), 2391–2404 (2019)
44. Huang, Y., et al.: Exploring individual travel patterns across private car trajectory data. IEEE Trans. Intell. Transp. Syst. **21**(12), 5036–5050 (2019)
45. Jiang, H., et al.: RobloP: towards robust privacy preserving against location dependent at-tacks in continuous LBS queries. IEEE/ACM Trans. Networking **26**(2), 1018–1032 (2018)
46. Ma, X., et al.: Exploring sharing patterns for video recommendation on You Tube-like social media. Multimedia Syst. **20**(6), 675–691 (2014)
47. Jiang, H., et al.: Continuous multi-dimensional top-k query processing in sensor networks. In: 2011 Proceedings IEEE INFOCOM, pp. 793–801 (2011)
48. Wang, S. , Vasilakos, A. , et al.: Energy efficient broadcasting using network coding aware protocol in wireless ad hoc network. In: ICC, Kyoto, Japan (2011)
49. Jiang, H., et al.: Load balancing for SIP server clusters. In: IEEE INFOCOM, pp. 2286–2294 (2009)

Prediction for Surface Subsidence of Shield Construction in Water-Rich Sand Egg Stratum Based on Edge Intelligence

Yanxia Gao[1,2,3], Yiwen Liu[1,2,3](✉), Chunqiao Mi[1,2,3], Pengju Tang[1], and Yuanquan Shi[1,2,3]

[1] School of Computer and Artificial Intelligence, Huaihua University, Huaihua 418000, China
gyx@hhtc.edu.cn, 87134537@qq.com

[2] Key Laboratory of Wuling-Mountain Health Big Data Intelligent Processing and Application in Hunan Province Universities, Huaihua 418000, China

[3] Key Laboratory of Intelligent Control Technology for Wuling-Mountain Ecological Agriculture in Hunan Province, Huaihua 418000, China

Abstract. The refinement and intelligent control of shield tunneling is the development trend of modern tunnel construction technology. In order to better predict and control the surface subsidence caused by shield excavation, this paper takes the shield construction of Luoyang Metro Line 2 from Longmen Station to Longmen Avenue Station as the background, and proposes a method based on edge intelligence for shield construction in water-rich sand egg strata. Methods for predicting land subsidence. First, low latency and faster data processing are achieved by collecting a large amount of data containing dynamic information about geological conditions and surrounding environments during the shield tunneling process; then using the iFogSim simulator to create different configurations; second, establishing support A surface subsidence model based on vector regression was established, and the model was deployed on the edge equipment; finally, the model was evaluated using the monitoring data of surface subsidence of the water-rich sand egg formation in Luoyang area. The research results show that the edge computing-based system has lower latency and higher processing speed than only deploying cloud data centers. After Pearson-related parameter tuning and model comparison training with Linear as the kernel function, the mean square error of the predicted value and the collected value of the surface subsidence is better than the other two kernel functions. The method proposed in this paper can provide real-time prediction service for large-scale surface subsidence prediction caused by shield construction, and is more practical.

Keywords: Surface deformation · Upper soft and lower hard soil layer · Curved shield construction · Mindlin solution · Random medium theory

1 Introduction

In recent years, with the continuous acceleration of urban development and the continuous increase of population, the situation of ground traffic congestion is getting worse and

Z. Xiao et al. (Eds.): ICECI 2022, LNICST 478, pp. 196–212, 2023.
https://doi.org/10.1007/978-3-031-28990-3_14

worse. In order to solve this problem, my country has begun to focus on the development of underground railway transportation, and the subway has played an indispensable role in urban transportation. The construction methods of subway sections generally include open-cut method, cover-cut method, shield method, etc. Among them, shield method has become the most important construction method due to its advantages of safety, reliability and high efficiency, but it is still unavoidable in the construction process. It will affect the surface buildings and surrounding pipelines to a certain extent, causing large surface subsidence [1]. Therefore, the prediction and control of surface deformation is one of the important measures to ensure the safety of tunneling.

At present, many scholars at home and abroad have carried out research on the prediction of surface subsidence caused by shield construction, mainly including theoretical analysis method [2–4], model test method [5, 6], numerical simulation calculation method [7, 8] and other methods. With the advent of the era of "big data", the operation monitoring of shield machines is becoming more and more perfect, and the construction of shield tunnels presents the "three highs" requirements of high-capacity data storage capability, efficient real-time data processing capability and high-strength multi-source heterogeneous adaptability. The recorded measured data not only contains a large amount of information about the operation process of the shield machine, but also contains the interaction mechanism inside the shield machine and the external environment. Through machine learning and other methods to analyze and excavate the hidden between the construction monitoring data. It is of great significance for predicting surface subsidence. Ye et al. [9] used a time-series-based back-propagation neural network (TS-BPNN) to predict soil subsidence in the fast and slow subsidence stages, respectively. Li et al. [10] studied the influence of different machine learning algorithms and model parameter choices on the prediction of land subsidence. Hu et al. [11] established a surface subsidence prediction model based on rough set-support vector regression (RS-SVR) to predict the surface subsidence of the soft and hard uneven strata caused by shield construction. Wang et al. [12] propose a shield tunneling underneath railroad risk evaluation model based on set pair analysis, and the importance of each evaluation index in the model is optimized by rough set theory. The factors of surface settlement caused by shield construction are complex, and although the above methods of predicting settlement have achieved some success, there are still some shortcomings and limitations in practical engineering application.

With the advantages of ultra-high data rate, ultra-low latency and ultra-large-scale access, cloud computing and 5G technology provide solutions for the development of intelligent, safe and green underground space engineering construction combined with edge intelligence, which will effectively respond to the current industrial Many challenges faced by Internet development [13–26]. At present, edge intelligence research at home and abroad has penetrated into key industries and fields such as power, transportation, and mining. For example, Chen et al. [27] design a traffic control algorithm based on label-less learning on the edge cloud;Zhu et al. [28] design a method for vehicle safety control based on internet of vehicles;Hu, et al. [29] design and implement BlinkRadar using UWB Radar for Non-Intrusive Driver Eye-Blink Detection with; Jiang et al. [30] propose a novel user authentication system SmileAuth;Shao et al. [31] proposed A general three-step framework to reduce the inference latency than baseline methods;Zhang et al. [32] design a credit-differentiated edge transaction approval mechanism. Ma et al. [33] proposed a new method to apply edge intelligence to terminal-level identification and diagnosis of transmission line ice thickness. Xie et al. [34] proposed a partial offloading scheme of computing tasks based on the assistance of Reconfigurable Intelligent Surface. Zhang et al. [35] proposed an urban street garbage detection and cleanliness evaluation method based on mobile edge computing and deep learning. Qu et al. [36] combined edge computing technology, mine IoT environment perception technology and data transmission and other related technologies to establish a system architecture based on cloud, edge, and end three-level methane edge monitoring mode.

At present, cloud computing and the Internet of Things have insufficient technical integration in underground space engineering, and there are few successful cases of applying edge intelligence methods to surface prediction caused by shield construction. The edge intelligence method used for surface settlement prediction in shield construction has the following advantages:

(1) The cost is low, and the data of edge intelligence is mainly processed at the near end, so it is used in various links such as network transmission, central computing, central storage and backhaul., can save a lot of server, storage, switching, bandwidth, security, electricity and even physical space and many other costs, so as to achieve low cost.
(2) Low latency, edge intelligence processes data closer to the data source, reducing the bandwidth and delay of data uploading to the cloud platform, and can perform real-time calculation of surface settlement during construction and excavation. When the predicted settlement is too large. It can be remedied in time, but on-site monitoring takes a lot of time, and construction risks cannot be found in time.
(3) The density is high, and the monitoring sections for on-site monitoring often have a distance of 5–15 m. In order to facilitate the calculation and modeling of the numerical model, the side length of the soil unit is generally 2–5 m, and the model based on edge intelligence can be quickly and accurately constructed. The settlement value of any point can be obtained, and the calculated point density in the final output result is much larger than that of field monitoring and numerical model. Therefore, it is of great significance to apply edge intelligence to the surface prediction caused by shield construction.

Based on the shield construction of Luoyang Metro Line 2 from Longmen Station to Longmen Avenue Station as the background, this paper proposes a method for predicting the surface subsidence caused by shield construction of tunnels in water-rich sand egg strata based on edge intelligence. Firstly, by collecting a large amount of data including the dynamic change information of geological conditions and surrounding environment in the process of shield tunneling, and then establishing a surface subsidence model based on rough set-support vector regression, and deploying the model on edge equipment, Finally, the model is evaluated using the monitoring data of surface subsidence of the water-rich sand egg formation in Luoyang area.

There are three main contributions of this paper:

(1) Aiming at the problems of difficult acquisition and processing of surface subsidence data in harsh construction environments, poor prediction quality and high delay in shield construction, a surface subsidence prediction method based on edge intelligence is proposed.
(2) Aiming at the problems of "low value density" in industrial big data, the feature selection method is used to screen the key influencing factors of surface subsidence, and the Pearson correlation coefficient is used to obtain 7 optimal attribute sets.
(3) Comparing and analyzing the calculation results of the support vector machine model using different kernel functions, it is found that the RBF function as a kernel function has better fitting effect and prediction accuracy.

2 The Proposed Method

2.1 Edge Intelligent System Architecture Based on iFogSim

An edge intelligent system architecture based on iFogSim is proposed, as shown in Fig. 1. The surface subsidence data is transmitted to the side layer through the end layer sensor for prediction of the surface subsidence prediction model, and the abnormal situation is returned to the construction party. Subsequently, the edge layer transmits important data and analysis results through the network to the cloud layer server for archiving, storage and supervision, and the cloud layer summarizes and manages the analysis results.

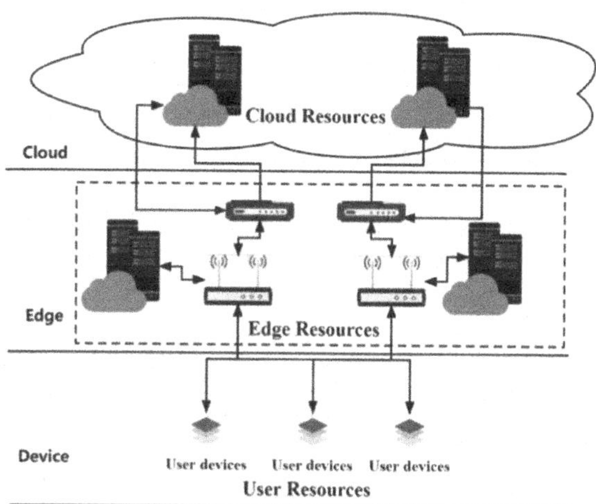

Fig. 1. The edge intelligent system architecture is designed according to the three layers of cloud-edge-device. The edge layer is mainly responsible for the analysis of surface subsidence data, model training and result transmission, and the device layer is mainly responsible for the collection and accumulation of surface subsidence data within the edge of the entire region.

2.2 Round-Trip Time

In computer networks, Round-Trip Time is an important performance indicator.The time required for the entire process from the sender sending data to the sender receiving the acknowledgment signal from the receiver [37], as shown in formula (1):

$$RT_{ij} = (S_i/b_i) + d_i + (k_i/n_j) + d_i \tag{1}$$

In the formula, S_i is the size of the task, b is the bandwidth, d is the delay, k_i is the number of instructions required to execute the task, and n_j is the number of instructions executed per second.

2.3 Total Execution Cost

The execution cost is also an important performance indicator of the network. The total cost required for task execution, including resource cost and execution cost [37], is shown in formula (2):

$$EC_{ij} = (l_i/n_j) * RC + (f_i/b_j) * C/b_j \tag{2}$$

$$\mathrm{RC} = \mathrm{R} * (\mathrm{C}/\mathrm{m}) + \mathrm{S} * \mathrm{C}/\mathrm{st}$$

where RC is the resource cost, f_i is the file size, C is the cost of executing the task, R is the RAM of the virtual machine, S is the size of the virtual machine, and st is the amount of storage.

2.4 Pearson Correlation Coefficient

In statistics, the Pearson correlation coefficient (PPMCC or PCCs) is widely used to measure the degree of closeness between two variables, and its value is between −1 and 1. Representation [38].

The Pearson correlation coefficient between two variables is defined as the quotient of the covariance between the two variables and the standard deviation of the two, as shown in Eq. (3):

$$\mathrm{r_{xy}} = \frac{\mathrm{cov(x, y)}}{\sigma \mathrm{x} * \sigma \mathrm{y}} = \frac{\sum_{\mathrm{i}=1}^{\mathrm{n}} (\mathrm{x_i} - \overline{\mathrm{x}})(\mathrm{y_i} - \overline{\mathrm{y}})}{\sqrt{\sum_{\mathrm{i}=1}^{\mathrm{n}} (\mathrm{x_i} - \overline{\mathrm{x}})^2} \sqrt{\sum_{\mathrm{i}=1}^{\mathrm{n}} (\mathrm{y_i} - \overline{\mathrm{y}})^2}} \tag{3}$$

where, x and y are two random variables, respectively, and n is the sample size. If $r = 0$, it means that the two variables are not correlated; if $r < 0$, it means that the two variables are negatively correlated; if $r > 0$, it means that there is a linear correlation between the two variables.

2.5 Support Vector Regression

Support vector regression method is a common machine learning modeling prediction method. Compared with neural networks, which need to train a large amount of sample data, support vector regression is mainly used for the learning of small sample problems, with fast calculation speed and strong prediction ability.

The basic idea is to use a nonlinear mapping function to map the input vector into a feature vector of a high-dimensional space, thereby simplifying the solution of the problem.

For a given training sample

$$D = \{(x_1, y_1), (x_2, y_2), \ldots, (x_n, y_n)\}, y_i \in R$$

where x_i, y_i are the input vector and output response, respectively, and n is the number of training samples.

The linear regression model we want to build in a high-dimensional space is

$$f(x) = \omega^T\#(x) + b \tag{4}$$

In the formula, ω and b are the model parameters, #(x) representing the feature vector to be mapped.

According to the support vector machine regression principle, the linear regression problem can be transformed into a constrained optimization problem:

$$\min_{\omega, b} \frac{1}{2}\|\omega\|^2 + C\sum\nolimits_{i=1}^{m} l_\varepsilon(f(x_i), y_i) \tag{5}$$

where C is the regularization constant and l_ε is the insensitive loss function.

$$l_\varepsilon(z) = \begin{cases} 0 \ \mathit{if} \ |z| \le \varepsilon \\ |z| - \varepsilon \ \mathit{otherwise} \end{cases} \tag{6}$$

Finally, as shown in formula (7), the support vector machine regression function is defined as:

$$f(x) = \sum\nolimits_{i=1}^{m} \left(\widehat{a_i} - a_i\right)k(x_i, x) + b \tag{7}$$

Among them, a_i and $\widehat{a_i}$ are the non-negative Lagrange multiplier; $k(x_i, x)$ is the kernel function.

The kernel functions used in this paper is shown in Table 1.

Table 1. Kernel functions involved in this paper

Kernel function	Expression	Remark
Linear kernel	$K(x_i, x_j) = {x_i}^T x_j$	
Polynomial kernel	$K(x_i, x_j) = {x_i}^T {x_j}^d$	$d \geq 1$ is the degree of polynomial
Rbf Kernel	$K(x_i, x_j) = \exp\left(\frac{\|x_i - x_j\|^2}{2\sigma^2}\right)$	$\sigma > 0$ is the bandwidth of the Gaussian kernel

2.6 Support Vector Machine Regression Prediction Model

The support vector machine regression prediction model is divided into four parts: data preprocessing, feature selection, model training and validation, evaluation and analysis, as shown in Fig. 2.

The basic principle is: firstly collect and analyze data such as tunnel geometry, shield construction parameters and stratum parameters, and preprocess the data, including: data cleaning, data integration, data transformation and data reduction. The correlation coefficient between the site construction data and the surface subsidence is analyzed by using the correlation coefficient, and the feature selection is carried out in combination with the correlation, and the attribute set is obtained. On this basis, the support vector machine regression model is used to perform regression prediction on the reduced data, and in order to compare the influence of different kernel functions on the PPMC-SVR model, the Linear kernel function, the Poly kernel function and the Rbf kernel function are selected respectively. Training set predictions. At the same time, the SVR model without feature selection is compared and analyzed, so as to analyze the influence of different features and kernel functions on the prediction structure.

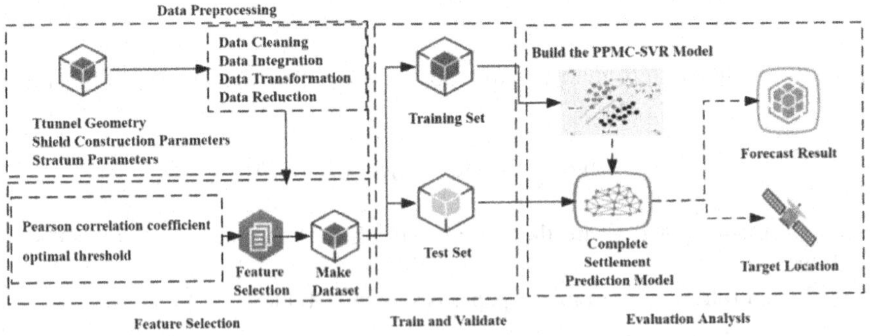

Fig. 2. Support vector machine regression prediction model include four stages: data preprocessing, feature selection, training and validate and evaluation and analysis.

3 Experiments

3.1 Engineering Background

Take the interval between Longmen Station and Longmen Avenue Station of Luoyang Metro Line 2 Project in Henan Province as an example. Starting from Luoyang Longmen Station, it goes down through Tongqu Road, Houzaimen Street, Yiluo Road and ends at Longmen Avenue Station. The interval is mainly located in the municipal Below the road and the planned road block, there are fewer buildings above the section. The total length of the tunnel is 1344.40 m, of which CK22 + 774.804 ~ CK23 + 821.163 is the shield method interval, the length of the shield section is 1046.359 m, the axis is 13.6–17.1 m from the ground, the outer diameter of the lining ring is 6.2 m, and the length of the ring piece is 1.5 m. The terrain of the tunnel excavation route is an alluvial-proluvial plain, and the site stratum is mainly mixed fill, loess-like silty clay, loess-like clayey silt, pebbles, and fine sand, with a thickness of 10–30 m. The groundwater is pore diving, buried at a depth of 10–20 m. The main physical and mechanical properties of each stratum are shown in Table 2.

Table 2. main physical and mechanical properties of each stratum

Soil layer	Thickness/m	Cohesion force/kPa	Internal friction angle/(°)	Poisson's ratio μ
Miscellaneous Fill	1.71	5	10	0.33
Silty clay	4.89	22	19	0.29
Sand and gravel layer	18.43	0	36	0.23

3.2 Data Source Description

On-site construction data is divided into three categories: tunnel geometry, shield construction parameters and stratum parameter data. The buried depth and radius of the tunnel are selected as geometrical factors. The main shield construction parameters include: total propulsion, soil bin pressure, cutter head torque, driving time, penetration, synchronous grouting amount, and slag output. The formation parameters include: cohesion, internal friction angle, and gravity γ. According to the needs of the project, combined with the method of sensor detection and manual collection, and all of them are transmitted remotely through the network. In this simulation experiment, we set up 1 cloud and 1 proxy-server in the cloud layer. In order to test the performance of ifogsim in different network topologies, the cloud system simulates and allocates 2, 3, 4, 4, 4, and 4 gateways, the corresponding sensors correspond to 4, 4, 4, 8, 12, and 16, respectively, named as config 1, config 2, config 3, config 4, config 5, and config 6, as shown in Table 3. In order to ensure the accuracy of the experiment, each group of experiments was performed 50 times, and the mean value was taken as the final value.

Table 3. Deployment configuration

User case	config 1	config 2	config 3	config 4	config 5	config 6
numbers of gateway	2	3	4	4	4	4
numbers of sensor	4	4	4	8	12	16

3.3 Test Method

(1) Simulation description

To realize the proposed edge intelligent computing architecture, we choose iFogSim simulation software. iFogSim is an improvement based on the cloud computing framework CloudSim. The physical components of iFogSim include Fog Device, Sensor, and Actuator, which can build multiple data centers, virtual machines, and effectively simulate actual scenarios [39–41].

In the experiment, we established the system architecture of the three-layer surface subsidence prediction model of cloud, edge and end, and designed two application module placement strategies: cloud-only placement strategy Cloud-only, edge placement strategy Edge-ward. Cloud-only placement strategy: All modules of the application are deployed in the data server, and users store and access information through the Internet; Edge placement strategy: The application modules are deployed near the edge of the network, and the processing is completed at the edge layer.

(2) Data preprocessing

The data preprocessing in this paper mainly includes two aspects: processing of outliers and data normalization.

Due to the poor observation conditions of shield construction, abnormal values of measurement data are often caused by factors such as abnormal environment, abnormal signals, and abnormal instruments. The surface subsidence data set contains some outliers, which need to be systematically analyzed and the errors should be eliminated. Because of the small amount of data in this dataset, this paper uses the boxplot method to determine outliers. The boxplot method is a method for finding outliers based on the interquartile range. The specific criterion is to calculate the minimum estimated value, maximum estimated value, first quartile, median and third quartile in the data. If the data exceeds the upper and lower limits, the boxplot will be automatically marked with circles. According to the principle of the boxplot method, this paper determines the outliers of the data set, and draws the boxplots of each parameter, taking the excavation time as the column, and it can be seen that the outliers are represented by red circles, as shown in Fig. 3. For outliers, the mean value is used instead, and the processed data set is combined into a new data set for subsequent modeling.

$$x = \frac{x_i - min(x_i)}{max(x_i) - min(x_i)} \tag{8}$$

Among them, x_i is the data to be normalized, $min(x_i)$ is the minimum value of the sample attribute, and $max(x_i)$ is the maximum value of the sample attribute.

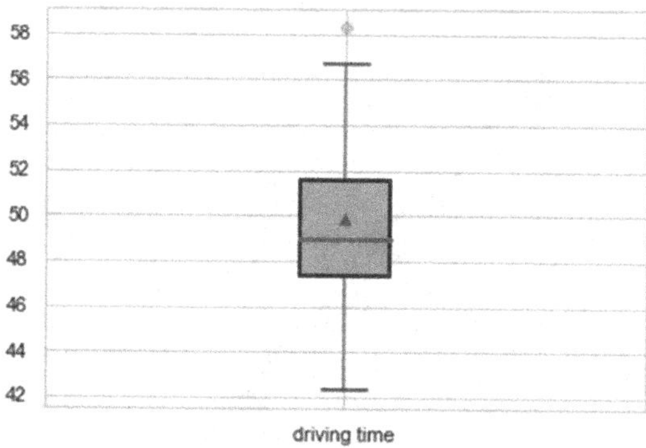

Fig. 3. Boxplot for driving time

In this paper, the characteristic parameters such as internal friction angle, severe γ, total thrust, soil bin pressure, cutter head torque, driving time, penetration, grouting amount, slag amount, settlement amount and other characteristic parameters are calculated by Pearson correlation coefficient. And draw the corresponding heat map to visualize the correlation between different factors, as shown in Fig. 4. Through this heat map, we can see that the settlement has a significant impact on the weight γ, total thrust, soil bin pressure, driving time, cutter head torque, grouting amount, and slag output. At the same time, settlement and penetration, The internal friction angle has a weak correlation. Similarly, we can see that the amount of grouting and the amount of slag are strongly correlated (two variables with a correlation of 0.84 in the figure), so we can only select the variable of grouting amount. The reason why we choose the feature of grouting amount is because The amount of grouting has a strong correlation with the amount of settlement. Similarly, we eliminated other features with little correlation, and finally selected the features for prediction as soil bin pressure, driving time, grouting amount, and settlement amount.

(3) Model training and testing

After correlation analysis, four items including soil bin pressure, excavation time, grouting amount, and settlement amount were selected as part of the input variables, and the corresponding normalized data were re-established as a sample set. The dataset was then divided by ten-fold cross-validation method. The Linear function, the Poly function, and the Rbf function are respectively selected as the kernel function for training to obtain the PPMC-SVR model. Also for comparison, the data set without feature selection is used for modeling, and comparative analysis and trial calculation are performed to analyze different features. And kernel function on the prediction structure.

4 Experimental Results

4.1 Round-Trip Time

Early detection of surface subsidence problems can effectively warn of major construction safety accidents, which requires sensor terminals that collect data, regional edge

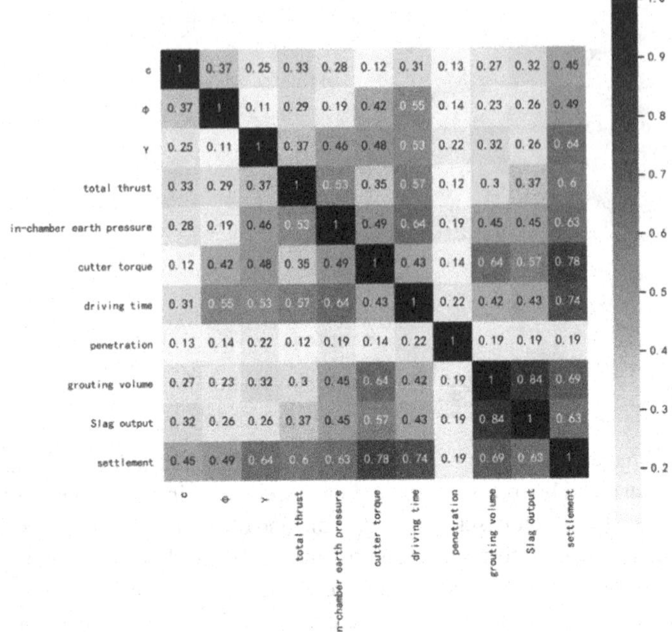

Fig. 4. Heat map for each feature

gateways that carry brain state classification, real-time communication modules between regional edge servers, and effective processing of prediction modules. The time lag in this cycle will seriously compromise the validity of surface subsidence predictions. In Fig. 5. It shows that the Round-Trip Time of the task scheduling algorithm using the Edge-ward placement strategy is significantly reduced compared to the cloud-only placement strategy environment.

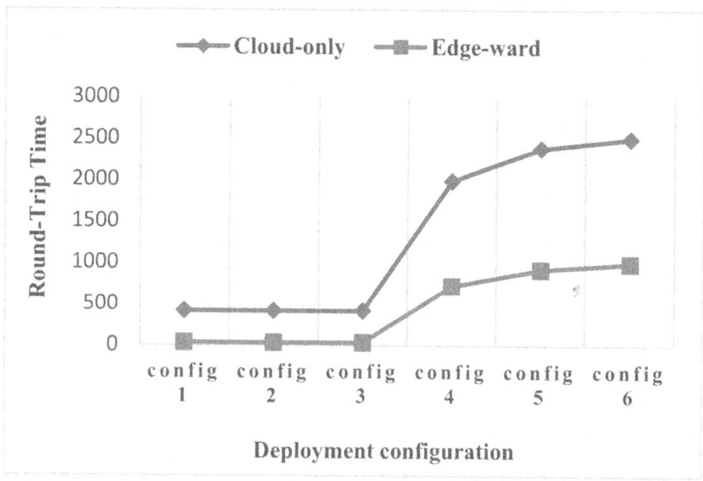

Fig. 5. Round-Trip Time

4.2 Total Execution Cost

As shown in Fig. 6, in the case of cloud-only placement strategy, as the number of sensors connected to the edge server increases, the execution cost of the network also increases significantly, resulting in further degradation of application performance. But if the edge-ward placement strategy is adopted, the network execution cost is greatly reduced.

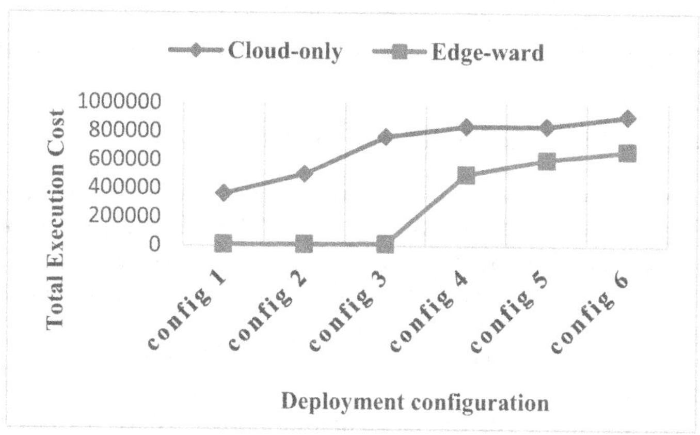

Fig. 6. Total Execution Cost

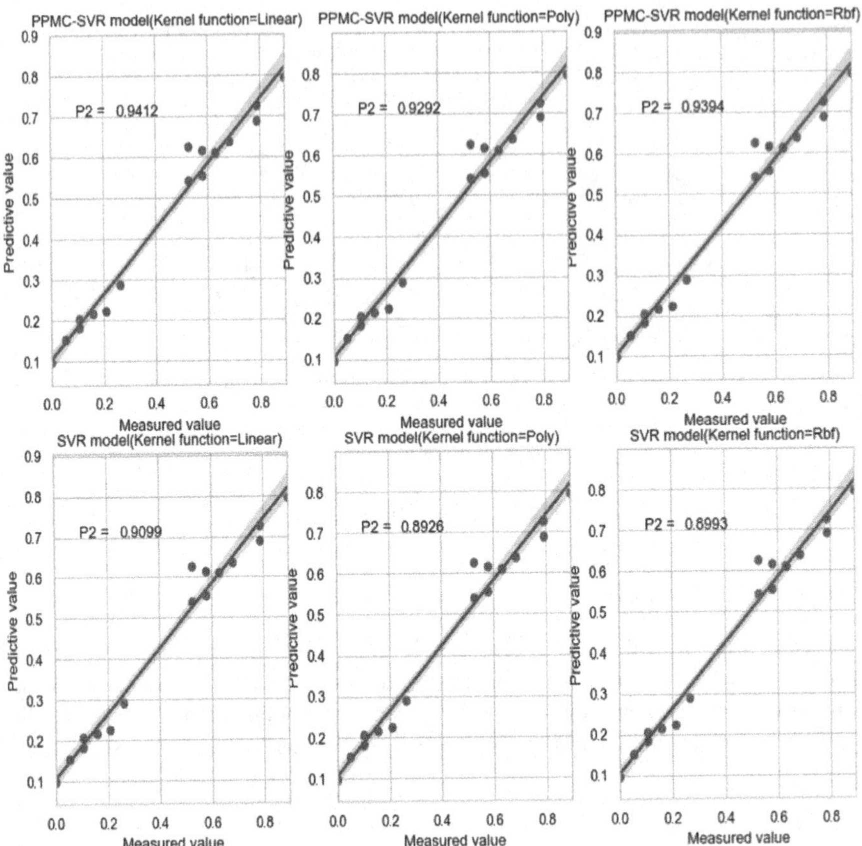

Fig. 7. Comparison of fitting effects of training samples with different kernel function

4.3 Comparison of Effects with Different Kernel Functions

In order to compare and analyze the performance of the PPMC-SVR model and the SVR model, this paper uses three kernel functions to model the PPMC-SVR model and the SVR model respectively, and compares the R2 of the training samples.

The results are shown in Fig. 7. From the fitting results of the training set, the horizontal comparison of similar models shows that the correlation between variables is higher and the error is smaller when Linear is selected as the kernel function. There is a better fitting effect.

It can be seen from Table 4 that the prediction errors of the PPMC-SVR model and the SVR model with Linear as the kernel function are 8.42% and 6.05%, respectively, which are smaller than the other two kernel functions; When comparing longitudinally with different kernel functions, the prediction errors of the PPMC-SVR model are smaller than those of the SVR model. In summary, the PPMC-SVR model with Linear as the kernel function is not only the fitting effect on the training samples, but also the generalization of the test samples. The ability is better than the other models.

Table 4. Prediction Error Comparison of Test Samples Using Different Kernel Functions

NO	model	Linear		Rbf		Poly	
		relative error	mean relative error	relative error	mean Relative error	relative error	mean relative error
1	PPMC-SVR	3.16	8.42	1.71	7.455	35.24	33.59
2		13.68		18.86		38.51	
3		13.18		−0.43		29.85	
4		3.66		− 8.82		30.77	
1	SVR	− 0.75	6.05	3.18	8.02	37.05	33.32
2		11.01		22.6		31.34	
3		12.22		0.41		40.36	
4		− 0.22		− 5.91		24.53	

5 Conclusions

"Safety first, prevention first" is the consistent policy of tunnel construction. Therefore, the timely and accurate prediction of surface subsidence has practical significance. In this paper, a surface subsidence prediction method based on edge intelligent environment is proposed, and various simulation results and performance indicators are evaluated through simulation experiments. The simulation results show that the method is feasible in the specific system framework of the three-layer surface subsidence prediction model of cloud, edge and end. Under the same kernel function, the performance of the PPMC-SVR model is better than that of the SVR model. The values are basically the same, the designed PPMC-SVR prediction model can accurately predict the surface subsidence, and the research results can provide reference for the prediction of the surface subsidence of the shield construction similar to the water-rich sand egg formation.

In future research, there is still much room for improvement, which can be summarized as follows:

(1) The problem of the experimental platform, the experiment in this paper is implemented on the iFogSim platform, and there is a certain error with the actual production environment.
(2) Dataset scenarios and quality issues. Data collection is not perfect, and there is a lack of post-consolidation and sub-consolidation settlement data, resulting in unpredictable long-term settlement.

Acknowledgment. This work was supported in part by the Scientific research projects funded by the Department of education of Hunan Province (No. 21C0628, No. 20C1472 and No. 22C0497), the Huaihua University Double First-Class initiative Applied Characteristic Discipline of Control Science and Engineering (No. ZNKZN2021–10), the National Natural Science Foundation of China (No. 62172182), the Hunan Provincial Natural Science Foundation of China (No. 2020JJ4490), the Project of Hunan Provincial Social Science Foundation (NO. 21JD046), the Huaihua University Project (No. HHUY2019–25), the Philosophy and Social Science Achievement Evaluation Committee of Huaihua (No. HSP2022YB40) and the Science and Technology Innovation 2030 Special Project Sub-Topics (No. 2018AAA0102100).

Data Availability. The data used to support the findings of this study are included within the article.

Conflicts of Interest. The authors declare that there are no conflicts of interest regarding the publication of this paper.

References

1. Jin, H., Yuan, D., Jin, D.L., et al.: Shield kinematics and its influence on ground settlement in ultra-soft soil: a case study in Suzhou. Can. Geotech. J. (2022). https://doi.org/10.1139/cgj-2021-0603
2. Kannangara, K.P.M., Zhou, W.H., Ding, Z., Hong, Z.H.: Investigation of feature contribution to shield tunneling-induced settlement using shapley additive explanations method. J. Rock Mech. Geotech. Eng. **14**(4), 1052–1063 (2022)
3. Nie, Q.K., Sun, G., Gao, S.Y., et al.: Disturbance process of sandy gravel stratum caused by shield tunneling and ground settlement analysis. Front. Earth Sci. **9**, 782927 (2021). https://doi.org/10.3389/feart.2021.782927
4. Deng, H.S., Fu, H.L., Yue, S., et al.: Ground loss model for analyzing shield tunneling-induced surface settlement along curve sections. Tunn. Undergr. Space Technol. **119**, 104250 (2022). https://doi.org/10.1016/j.tust.2021.104250
5. Zhang, J.S., Xu, M.Y., Cui, M.H., et al.: Prediction of ground subsidence caused by shield tunnel construction under hidden karst cave. Geotech. Geol. Eng. **40**, 3839–3850 (2022). https://doi.org/10.1007/s10706-022-02136-3
6. Xu, P., Xi, D.: Investigation on the surface settlement of curved shield construction in sandy stratum with laboratory model test. Geotech. Geol. Eng. **39**(8), 5493–5504 (2021). https://doi.org/10.1007/s10706-021-01840-w
7. Wang, R., Zhang, B., Wang, Y.: Analysis of settlement induced by shield construction of the metro passing under existing buildings based on the finite difference method. Geofluids **2022**, 1–15 (2022). https://doi.org/10.1155/2022/1206867
8. Wang, X.F., Liu, W., Yao, X.C., Yang, R.: Numerical simulation of pile settlement under large diameter submarine shield tunnel. In: Journal of Physics: Conference Series, vol. 2030, p. 012065 (2021). https://doi.org/10.1088/1742-6596/2030/1/012065
9. Ye, X.W., Tao, J., Chen, Y.M.: Machine learning-based forecasting of soil settlement induced by shield tunneling construction. Tunn. Undergr. Space Technol. **124**, 104452 (2022). https://doi.org/10.1016/j.tust.2022.104452
10. Li, C., Li, J.H., Shi, Z.Q., et al.: Prediction of surface settlement induced by large-diameter shield tunneling based on machine-learning algorithms. Geofluids 1–13 (2022)
11. Hu, M., Zhang, B., Lu, M.D.: Application of BP neural network in prediction of ground settlement in shield tunneling. In: IEEE, pp. 29–35 (2021)
12. Wang, H., Guan, Z., He, S.: Risk factor identification and evaluation on SPB shield underneath existing railroad settlement. Geotech. Geol. Eng. **39**(7), 5201–5212 (2021). https://doi.org/10.1007/s10706-021-01825-9

13. Zhang, B., Dong, K., Gao, D.B., Wu, H.: Development Trend Prediction of Patents Technology Thematic of Cloud Computing between China and the United States. World Sci-Tech R & D, 1–10 (2022)
14. Yu, J., Liu, D., Wang, X.C., Liu, G.: Explore the application scenarios of 5G technology in housing and urban and rural construction field. Urban Dev. Stud. **28**(04), 16–20 (2021)
15. Zeng, F., Li, Q., Zhu, X., Havyarimana, V., Bai, J.: A Price-based optimization strategy of power control and resource allocation in full-duplex heterogeneous macrocell-femtocell networks. IEEE Access **6**, 42004–42013 (2018)
16. Liu, D., Cao, Z., He, Y., Ji, X., Hou, M., Jiang, H.: Exploiting concurrency for opportunistic forwarding in duty-cycled IoT networks. ACM Trans. Sens. Netw. **15**(3), 31:1–31:33 (2019)
17. Liu, D., Wu, X., Cao, Z., Liu, M., Li, Y., Hou, M.: CD-MAC: a contention detectable MAC for low duty-cycled wireless sensor networks. In: SECON, pp. 37–45(2015)
18. Su, W., Liu, D., Zhang, T., Jiang, H.: Towards device independent eavesdropping on telephone conversations with built-in accelerometer. Proc. ACM Interact. Mob. Wearable Ubiquitous Technol. **5**(4), 177:1–177:29 (2021)
19. Liu, D., Cao, Z., Hou, M., Rong, H., Jiang, H.: Pushing the limits of transmission concurrency for low power wireless networks. ACM Trans. Sens. Netw. **16**(4), 40:1–40:29 (2020)
20. Qian, C., Liu, D., Jiang, H.: Harmonizing energy efficiency and QoE for brightness scaling-based mobile video streaming. In: IWQoS, pp. 1–10 (2022)
21. Zeng, F., et al.: Resource allocation and trajectory optimization for QoE provisioning in energy-efficient UAV-enabled wireless networks. IEEE Trans. Veh. Technol. **69**(7), 7634–7647 (2020)
22. Ali, T.A.A., Xiao, Z., Sun, J., Mirjalili, S., Havyarimana, V., Jiang, H.: Optimal Design of IIR Wideband Digital Differentiators and Integrators using Salp Swarm Algorithm. Knowl. Based Syst. **182**(15), 104834 (2019). https://doi.org/10.1016/j.knosys.2019.07.005
23. Jiang, H., Dai, X., Zhu, X., Arun, I.: Joint task offloading and resource allocation for energy-constrained mobile edge computing. IEEE Trans. Mob. Comput. (2022). https://doi.org/10.1109/TMC.2022.3150432
24. Jiang, H., Zhu, X., Li, Z., Xu, J., Zeng, F., Wang, D.: An energy-efficient framework for internet of things underlaying heterogeneous small cell networks. IEEE Trans. Mob. Comput. **21**(1), 31–43 (2022)
25. Liu, D., Hou, M., Cao, Z., He, Y., Ji, X., Zheng, X.: COF: Exploiting concurrency for low power opportunistic forwarding. In: ICNP, pp. 32–42(2015)
26. Hu, Z., Zeng, F., Zhu, X., Fu, B., Jiang, H., Chen, H.: Computation efficiency maximization and QoE-provisioning in UAV-enabled MEC communication systems. IEEE Trans. Netw. Sci. Eng. **8**(2), 1630–1645(2021). 23 March
27. Chen, M., Hao, Y., Lin, K., Yuan, Z., Hu, L.: Label-less learning for traffic control in an edge network. IEEE Netw. **32**, 8–14 (2018)
28. Zhu, X., et al.: Toward accurate vehicle state estimation under non-Gaussian noises. IEEE Internet Things J. **6**(6), 10652–10664 (2019)
29. Hu, J., et al.: BlinkRadar: non-intrusive driver eye-blink detection with UWB radar. In: Proceedings of IEEE ICDCS (2022)
30. Jiang, H., Cao, H., Liu, D., Xiong, J., Cao, Z.: SmileAuth: using dental edge biometrics for user authentication on smartphones. Proc. ACM Interact. Mob. Wearable Ubiquitous Technol. **4**(3), 84:1–84:24 (2020)
31. Shao, J., Zhang, J.: Communication-computation trade-off in resource-constrained edge inference. IEEE Commun. Mag. **58**, 20–26 (2020)
32. Zhang, K., Zhu, Y., Maharjan, S., Zhang, Y.: Edge intelligence and blockchain empowered 5G beyond for the industrial internet of things. IEEE Netw. **33**(5), 12–19 (2019)
33. Ma, F.Q., Wang, B., Dong, X.Z.: Receptive field vision edge intelligent recognition for ice thickness identification of transmission line. Power Syst. Technol. **45**(06), 2161–2169 (2021)

34. Xie, W.C., Li, B., Dai, Y.Y.: PPO based task offloading scheme in aerial reconfigurable intelligent surface-assisted edge computing. Comput. Sci. **49**(6), 3–11 (2022)
35. Zhang, P.C., Zhao, Q., Gao, Z.Y.: Urban street garbage detection and cleanliness assessment approach fusing mobile edge computing and deep learning. IEEE Access **40**(4), 901–907 (2019)
36. Qu, S.J., Wu, F.S.: Research on methane monitoring mode of coal mining face based on edge computing. Coal Sci Technol. **48**(12), 161–167 (2020)
37. Chen, Y., Jiang, Z.M., Zhang, Y.: Multi objective task scheduling algorithm based on improved SOS in cloud environment. Comput. Eng. Des. **43**(5), 1214–1312 (2022)
38. Van den Heuvel, E.R., Zhan, Z.: Myths about linear and monotonic associations: Pearson's r, Spearman's ρ, and Kendall's τ. Am. Stat. **76**(1), 44–52 (2021)
39. Gupta, H., et al.: iFogSim: A Toolkit for Modeling and Simulation of Resource Management Techniques in Internet of Things Edge and Fog Computing Environments (2016). http://cloudbus.org/tech_reports.html.
40. Yang, Z., Zhang, Y. Tian, J.: The effect of QoS and QoE requirements for designing task processing controller based on fuzzy logic on IoT environments. Cluster Comput. 1–17 (2022)
41. Bichi, B.Y., Islam, S.U., Kademi, A.M., et al.: An energy-aware application module for the fog-based internet of military things. Discover Internet Things **2**, 4 (2022)

Highly Accurate Dynamic Gesture Recognition Method Based on Edge Intelligence

Lu Changkai[1], Liu Yiwen[1,2,3], Gao Yanxia[1,2,3](✉), Shi Yuanquan[1,2,3], and Peng Xiaoning[1,2,3]

[1] School of Computer and Artificial Intelligence, Huaihua University, Huaihua 418000, China
3129437633@qq.com

[2] Key Laboratory of Wuling-Mountain Health Big Data Intelligent Processing and Application in Hunan Province Universities, Huaihua 418000, China

[3] Key Laboratory of Intelligent Control Technology for Wuling-Mountain Ecological Agriculture in Hunan Province, Huaihua 418000, China

Abstract. In recent years, gestures have been widely used in many fields. For example, human-computer interaction, virtual reality, gesture translation, etc. The reason for its rapid development is due to the emergence of deep learning and artificial intelligence under today's society. Due to dynamic gestural interactions, such large intelligent models are often characterized by many parameters, large sample size, frequent parameter updates, and high communication volume. Based on this feature, we propose a cloud-based edge design architecture approach for gesture recognition based on an improved YOLOv5 network model optimization by changing different gestures, background interference, which uses a 21-layer model for the neural network. With the use of edge intelligence, the computational accuracy can be improved by 10.6% over the traditional YOLOv5 with a MAP value of 93.3%. The final recall rate is also improved by 3.6%. The parameter model is only 43.6% of the original one. This shows the practicality and operability of using edge computing as a technique in gesture recognition, as well as the small improvement cost and obvious effect.

Keywords: Edge Intelligence · Gesture Recognition · Neural Networks · YOLOv5

1 Introduction

With the continuous development of the Internet, people's living standard has been improving. Gesture interaction [1–3] began to gradually enter our life. We began to have higher requirements for smart devices [4], from operating machines with remote controls; voice recognition [5]; playing games with gamepads. To now, through gestures can command the device to complete the functions we need to complete, by posing a variety of postures can make people have an immersive gaming experience.

At the same time, while the terminal device is greatly enhanced, it enables a large number of services and response requests to be residual at the terminal. This is really

Z. Xiao et al. (Eds.): ICECI 2022, LNICST 478, pp. 213–225, 2023.
https://doi.org/10.1007/978-3-031-28990-3_15

difficult to load for server cloud servers [6] and the cost is very huge. To make these new technologies a win-win in terms of cost and experience, we introduced the concept of edge intelligence, on top of which edge computing is added to solve this problem.

For different response requests generated by terminals, we propose a method to judge the direction of data processing, and propose a method to dynamically allocate and process data based on an initial judgment of the complexity of current data processing during a specific time period with a large number of users, many variables, complex network conditions, and low resolution efficiency. The simple and easy data are processed at the edge [7] and then returned directly to the terminal, which can save a lot of resources and bandwidth consumption in data processing and can lead to a good experience. To a certain extent, it can also ensure the user's privacy and improve the stability of the software without giving a bad experience or even unresponsive errors due to the high latency of the network or server. As application software becomes richer and more powerful, the amount of computing required is also increasing. If the traditional cloud computing method is used, it will lead to the need to constantly upgrade the server configuration, which is a considerable expense for enterprises. Therefore, it is crucial to use edge intelligence in this aspect of gesture recognition.

This study focuses on improving YOLOv5 by using this as the support model for this edge computing.

YOLOv5 [8–12], is a single-stage target detection algorithm that adds some new improvement ideas to YOLOv4 [13], which results in a great performance improvement in both speed and accuracy. The purpose of improving this model is to maximize the edge computing capability and provide applications with characteristic capabilities such as ultra-low latency, high bandwidth, and real-time access [14]; distributed clouds [15–20] mainly have the following capability features: distributed, low latency, high performance, safe and reliable, green and energy efficient, and open capabilities. Able to manage its cloud nodes independently, it can provide more business capabilities than a single location cloud service.

Edge intelligence [21–23] is defined as an open platform that combines network, compute, storage, and application core capabilities as a whole to provide services at the end close to the object or data source, with the goal of providing services on the side of the data input or endpoint. This is done so that the data is not affected by the latency issues of the application. In this way, an efficient and cost-saving approach can be achieved. As shown in Fig. 1, the basic data processing and analysis model for this project.

Edge computing for gestural interaction systems [24] has the following advantages. First, it reduces the cost of the server and reduces the bandwidth usage. The series of data generated during the recognition process will be partially computed at the edge, which will reduce the process of responding to server requests. Let most of its computation produce results on the user end device. Second, it is fast and reliable. The process of sending data waiting for the server response takes a long time and when the server is busy, there may also be a problem of request failure, which may cause a series of problems such as packet loss in a complex network environment. Finally, the stability of the system is enhanced. Malicious accesses are reduced, and the inclusion of edge computing can effectively reduce malicious attacks [25–29] and prevent most of the problems of wasted

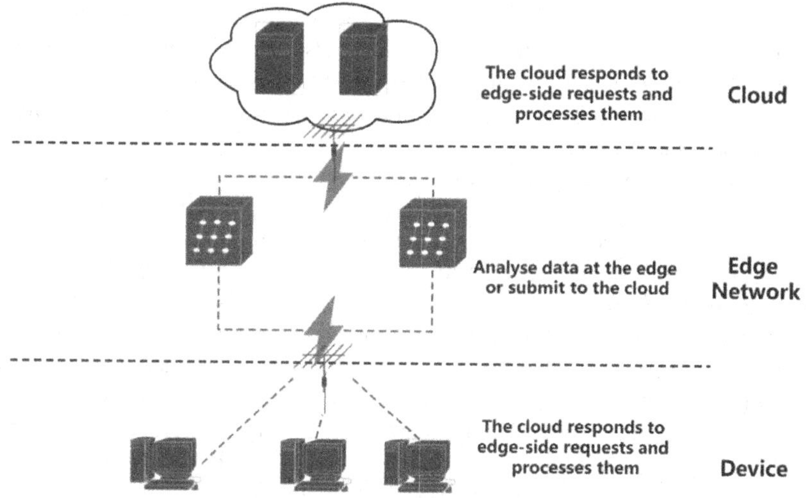

Fig. 1. Edge Intelligent Data Delivery Model

server resources. It also enhances confidentiality, and some confidential information can be processed at the edge without server processing, which effectively [30] improves the security of data.

2 Gesture Interaction Design

2.1 Holistic Approach

According to the requirements, the method design of the gesture recognition system based on edge computing is proposed, based on the architecture designed according to three layers: cloud - edge computing node - user terminal.

The server side is mainly responsible for user information management, big data analysis of recognition results and visual data display, model building, and response requests for special complex scenarios. The edge side is mainly responsible for collecting and analyzing the terminal data, and the preliminary analysis performed by the edge side can lead to the result or need to request the cloud side for further analysis and processing. And each time the recognition result log is transmitted back to the cloud. The cloud can analyze the data sent back by the edge layer so as to carry out the analysis of the recognition model, with the purpose that the recognition data provided to the edge layer next time can be more accurate, enhance the efficiency of recognition, and realize the process of continuous optimization of recognition.

2.2 Gesture Interaction Processing

Gesture interaction [31] requires large processor power [32] and storage space for images and videos, as well as high requirements for network stability. In gesture control, gesture-operated games, real-time machine translation, and in the interaction process, most human communication is not only delivered through language, voice, intonation, facial expressions, gestures, etc. This time delay often causes many problems, and if in for a simple gesture, it takes a lot of time to respond, then these applications will lose the value he originally should have. Resulting in a very poor user experience, or even the inability to use properly.

In this regard, it seems that interaction is often accompanied by complex computation as well as reasoning [33–36], and he is different from the previous recognition, which may be just a picture, and the picture is not like interaction, the picture needs to be collected and changed in real time. And once the lag occurs, then it will cause a lot of important information loss, incoherence and a series of problems. To solve these problems, it needs to have strong hardware and good algorithms as support.

In this problem, a set of cloud-based edge-end model is designed. First, the information collected in the terminal is first handed over to the edge end for judgment and processing, and when the edge end thinks that the task is within the processing capability of the edge equipment, then the request from the terminal is processed immediately and the processed information is transmitted back to the terminal in time. When the edge device checks that this recognition may require more computation or cannot be completed on the edge device, it forwards the request to the cloud for request response. This design makes it possible to make the valuable computing resources of the server, fully utilized.

Based on this design, more user requests will be completed at the edge for response, greatly improving efficiency. It also saves valuable bandwidth resources and reduces latency. There is also an improvement in security. These interactive devices, often collect a large amount of user information, and edge intelligence is deployed and trained on this side closer to the user, which can effectively reduce data hijacking [37, 38], tampering, and other problems caused by data during network transmission. The specific design is shown in Fig. 2.

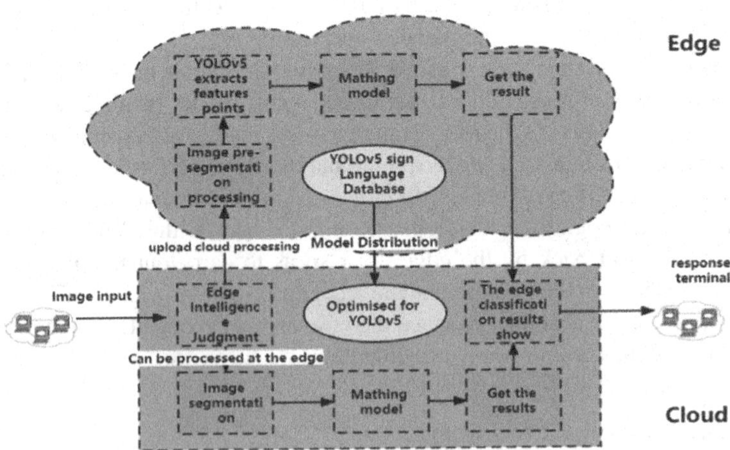

Fig. 2. Gesture recognition framework

The image is first input from the end device, uploaded to the edge device, and pre-analyzed on the edge device. If the initial analysis is relatively simple, it can be sent to the server at the edge for processing and response to execute the trained and optimized YOLOv5, and uploaded to the server when the analysis of that image may require a larger amount of operations or when the resources of the edge device cannot be satisfied. This is because the server [39] has a richer database and analysis model. Ultimately it is the edge server that responds to the data directly to the user. This design makes more rational use of valuable server resources, speeds up the response [40] time and requests of the whole system, and reduces to some extent the resource overhead of the server and the risk of server downtime caused by illegally conducted malicious attacks.

3 Intelligent Processing Solutions at the Edge

3.1 YOLOv5 Algorithm

In June 2020, the first version of the algorithm YOLOv5 was officially released, and its release has caused extensive research, discussion, and use in the field of computer vision. Unlike previous versions of the YOLO model, YOLOv5 is actually a model family containing four models (YOLOv5s, YOLOv5m, YOLOv5l, and YOLOv5x), including three main components, as shown in Fig. 3

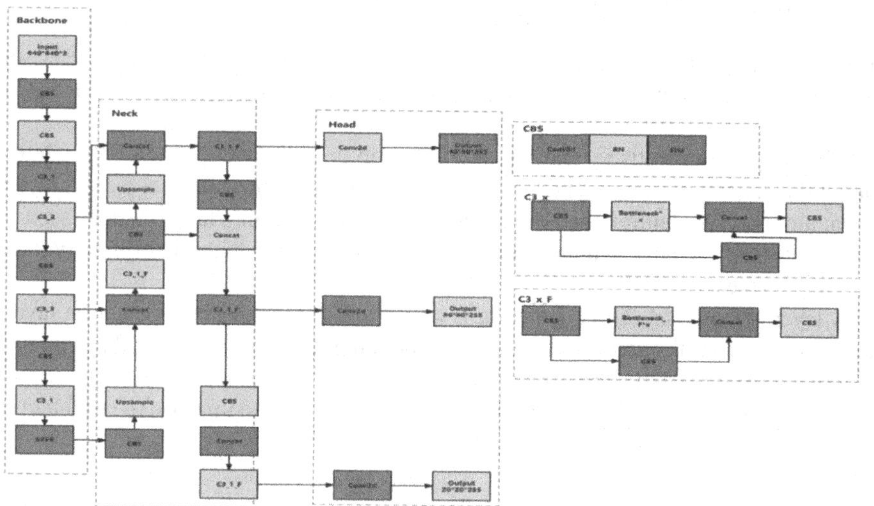

Fig. 3. Original YOLOv5 network structure

Backbone
The convolutional neural network that aggregates and extracts image features on different subcategories of images, including the Focus structure and the CSP structure.

Neck
Using the FPN + PAN structure, the network layer of blended image features is used to pass the feature images of relevant targets to the prediction layer.

Head
Has multiple prediction scales to perform target prediction on images, generate target bounding boxes and predict relevant classes. Among them, YOLOv5s is the smallest model in the YOLOv5 series, but it is still resource-consuming in some cases where the environment is complex and has more elements. For edge devices, the model size and computation are overwhelming, and in addition to that, memory reads and writes and loading large scale models will incur a huge additional overhead. This algorithm can be run on the server side with high performance. For edge-side devices with limited computing [41] power. Based on this algorithm, this paper proposes a faster detection algorithm based on a more lightweight approach to reduce resource overhead and improve efficiency [42] without sacrificing accuracy as much as possible. The efficiency of the model is better balanced with the availability.

3.2 Improved YOLOv5 Algorithm

In order to improve the accuracy as well as the performance of the gesture image detection algorithm for this situation. In this paper, the following improvements are made to YOLOv5.

Introduce a cooperative attention mechanism in the network. The reason for introducing this mechanism is to, divide the recognized images into different weight layers so that more useful features can be extracted and other distracting factors, such as extraneous factors of the environment, can reduce the interference with the originally main recognized objects.

A layer of complex target detection is added to the original three detection layers of different scales. It is dedicated to the corresponding recognition [43] of those images that are not recognized accurately.

At the output side, a boundary loss function is introduced to improve the problem of loss function in the original network [44].

3.3 Coordinate Attention

A Coordinate Attention block can all be considered as a computational unit with the purpose of enhancing feature representation in Mobile Network. He can take any intermediate feature tensor:

$$X = [x_1, x_2 \ldots, x_c] \in R^{c \times H \times w} \tag{1}$$

As input and by transforming the output with the same size as the tensor and with enhanced representation:

$$Y = [y_1, y_2 \ldots, y_c] \quad (2)$$

In order to describe CA attention more clearly, the SE block is discussed here first. Structurally, it is possible to divide the SE block into 2 steps Squeeze and Excitation, which are used for the input of global information and the adaptive Re-weight of the channel relationship, respectively. Conditional on the input X, the squeeze step of the cth channel can be expressed as:

$$z_c = \frac{1}{H * W} \sum_{i=1}^{H} \sum_{j=1}^{W} x_{c(i,j)} \quad (3)$$

where z_c is the output associated with the cth channel.

The input X comes from a convolutional layer with a fixed kernel size. The purpose of Excitation is to completely capture the dependencies between channels, which can be expressed as:

$$\widehat{X} = X \cdot \sigma(\hat{z}) \quad (4)$$

Coordinate Attention encodes channel relationships and long-term dependencies by precise location information, which is divided into two steps: Coordinate information embedding and Coordinate Attention generation, as shown in Fig. 4.

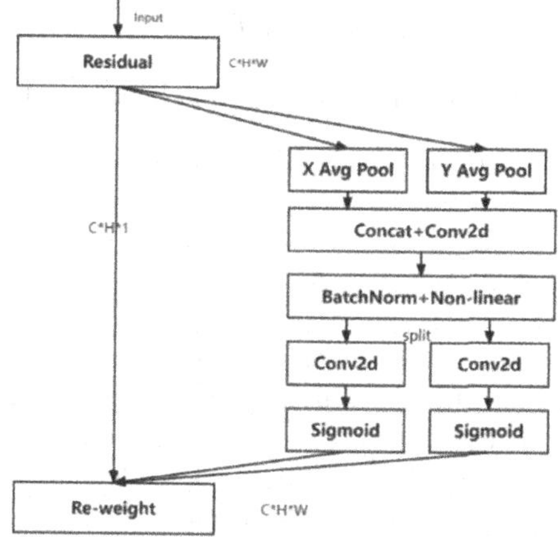

Fig. 4. Structure of the Coordinate Attention mechanism

Coordinate information embedding [6, 45], the global pooling approach is commonly used for global encoding of spatial information for channel attention encoding, but it makes it difficult to preserve location information because it compresses global spatial information into channel descriptors. To motivate the attention module to capture remote spatial interactions with precise location information, this paper decomposes the global pooling into a pair of one-dimensional feature encoding operations according to the following equation:

$$z_c = \frac{1}{H * W} \sum\nolimits_{i=1}^{H} \sum\nolimits_{j=1}^{W} x_{c(i,j)} \tag{5}$$

Specifically, given the input X, each channel is first encoded along the horizontal and vertical coordinates using a pooling kernel of size (H, 1) or (1, W), respectively. Thus, the output of the cth channel with height h can be expressed as:

$$Z_c^h(h) = \frac{1}{W} \sum\nolimits_{0 \le i < W} x_c(h, i) \tag{6}$$

Similarly, it can be shown that the output of channel c with width w can be written as:

$$Z_c^w(w) = \frac{1}{H} \sum\nolimits_{0 \le j < W} x_c(j, w) \tag{7}$$

The last is Coordinate Attention generation, after the transformations in the information embedding, this part performs the concatenate operation on the above transformations and then uses the convolutional transform function to transform them.

$$f = \delta(F_1(\left[z^h, z^w\right])) \tag{8}$$

$$g^h = \sigma(F_h(f^h)) \tag{9}$$

$$g^w = \sigma(F_w(f^w)) \tag{10}$$

Finally, the output Y of the Coordinate Attention Block can be written as:

$$y_c(i, j) = x_c(i, j) \times g_c^h(i) \times g_c^w(j) \tag{11}$$

3.4 Improved Overall Network Model

An improved overall network modelSeveral additional corresponding feature extraction layers are also added, that is, after the 17th layer of the network, continue to use the C3 model block and CONV module for feature extraction, and feature sampling in the 20th layer to further expand it. In the 21st layer, the sampled feature map of size 640*640 is fused with the feature map obtained from the second layer in the extraction network to obtain the detection of complex gestures.

4 Experimental Environment and Experimental Data

4.1 Training of Models

All experiments in this paper are executed under Windows 10 operating system, with AMD Ryzen 5 4600H processor; 16G memory and NVIDA GeForce GTX 1650 graphics card. This paper is based on the deep learning framework PyTorch1.10, and the built environment includes Anaconda3.0, python3.7, and CUDA11.1.1.

In this paper, precision, recall, and mean average precision metrics are used to synthesize the effect of improving the model, and the specific calculation methods of each metric are as follows.

$$Pre = \frac{TP}{TP + FP} \tag{12}$$

$$Re = \frac{TP}{TP + FN} \tag{13}$$

$$MAP = \frac{\sum_{i=1}^{k} AP_i}{k} \tag{14}$$

In the above equation, Pre denotes the precision of recognition [44], Re denotes the recall rate, and MAP denotes the mean average precision. In this experimental design, the average precision with a threshold of 0.5 is used as a measure, APi denotes the average precision of the ith category, TP denotes the number of positive samples predicted by positive samples, FP denotes the number of positive samples predicted by negative samples, FN denotes the number of positive samples predicted by negative samples, and k denotes the number of categories in the experiment. Comparing with the training data of the original YOLOv5 algorithm, we can see that the improved YOLOv5 algorithm has improved the MAP, precision, and recall in comparison with the original one. The MAP value is 93.3%, and the final recall rate is 87.3%, up from 83.7%, an improvement of 3.6%. The memory occupied by the model decreased from 7.8 MB to 3.4 MB. The experiment shows that all the metrics have improved and are better than the original YOLOv5's algorithm. And after 60 rounds, these metrics are basically converged, which proves the effectiveness of this algorithm. As shown in Figs. 5, 6 and 7.

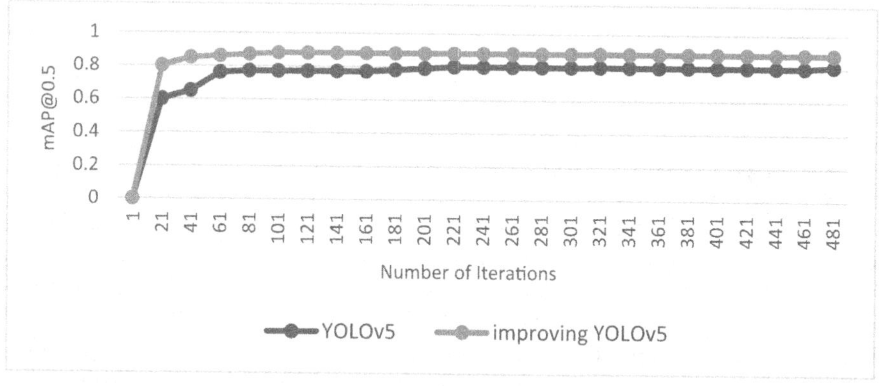

Fig. 5. MAP

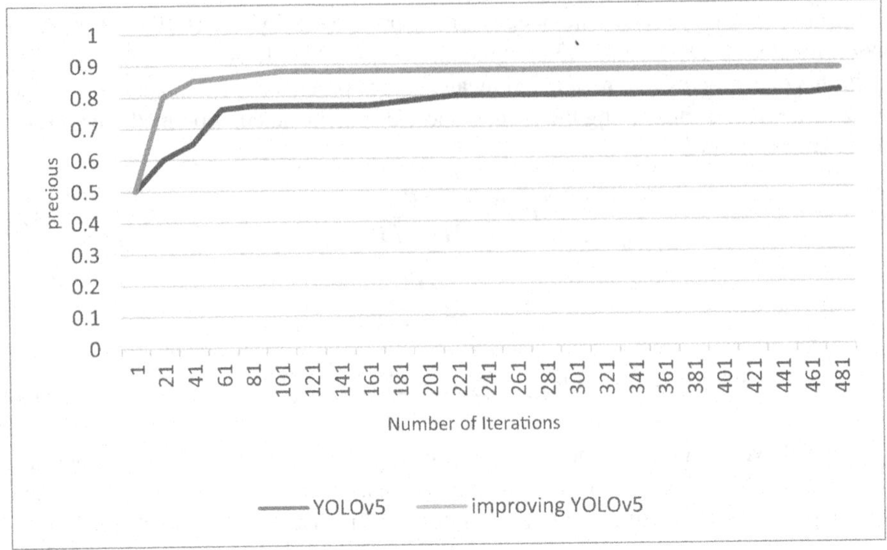

Fig. 6. Precious

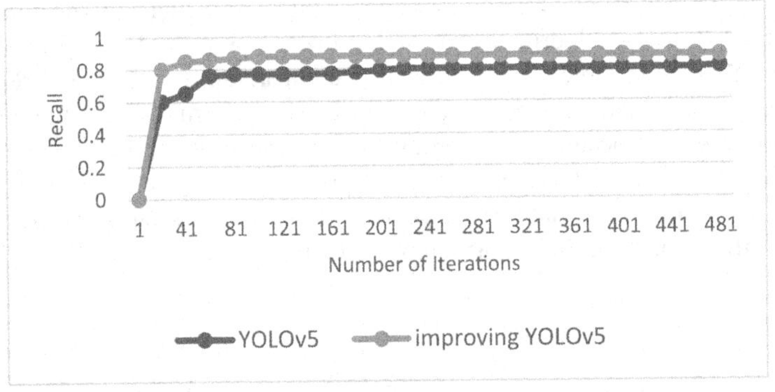

Fig.7. Recall

4.2 Comparison of Different Algorithms

In order to be able to show that the algorithm in this paper outperforms other algorithms, we use the same data set, on the same configuration of computers, with the same setup. They were trained with as few extraneous variables as possible to influence the environment, and the final results are shown in Fig. The control algorithm is YOLOv4 and SSD, which are commonly used for detection and target recognition. 4.8% accuracy improvement compared to the original YOLOv4, 83% of the original computation time, and only 5.1% of the original model size can be seen that the improved algorithm is still better than other [46] algorithms in general and has a better prospect for edge devices.

Table 1. Comparison of detection performance of each model

Algorithm	MAP	Recall/%	Times/s	Params/MB
SSD	86.3	77.9	0.0617	26.15
YOLOv4	88.2	81.6	0.01	61.58
Refine YOLOv5	92.5	87.9	0.00083	3.14

5 Conclusion

In this paper, we propose an improved YOLOv5 gesture recognition method for edge computing, which targets the problem of complex neural networks running on edge terminal devices with insufficient computing power. Improvements to YOLOv5 are made from the introduction of Coordinate Attention and the introduction of a feature detection layer. The feasibility is experimentally verified and the accuracy as well as efficiency is balanced to reduce the performance requirements, as well as the resource consumption.

In future practical engineering applications. The gesture recognition model should be dynamically adjusted to the actual scenario. When the gesture is not particularly complex and there is not much interference from external factors, the number of detection layers should be appropriately reduced to reduce the size of the model; or the number of detection layers can be appropriately increased to make the gesture recognition more accurate if the performance of the edge-end device is detected to be high.

This study is an experimental use case for gesture recognition, and the accuracy and effectiveness of the improved algorithm are verified. It also proposes a feasible research solution for the study of computer vision tasks under edge computing.

Acknowledgment. This work was supported in part by the Scientific research projects funded by the Department of education of Hunan Province (No. 21C0628, No. 20C1472 and No. 22C0668), the Huaihua University Double First-Class initiative Applied Characteristic Discipline of Control Science and Engineering(No. ZNKZN2021–10), the National Natural Science Foundation of China (No. 62172182), the Hunan Provincial Natural Science Foundation of China (No. 2020JJ4490), the Project of Hunan Provincial Social Science Foundation (NO. 21JD046), the Huaihua University Project (No. HHUY2019–25), the Philosophy and Social Science Achievement Evaluation Committee of Huaihua (No. HSP2022YB40) and the Science and Technology Innovation 2030 Special Project Sub-Topics(No. 2018AAA0102100). Hunan University Students' Innovation and Entrepreneurship Training Program (2021–3502).

References

1. Huiming, Z.: Design and implementation of a containerized edge computing platform for intelligent video surveillance scenarios. University of Electronic Science and Technology, MA thesis, pp.6–23 (2022)
2. Xiaoyue, M.: Research on the design of children's cognitive development and learning products based on gesture interaction: the example of Kids' Companion application. Electron. Compon. Inf. Technol. **6**(05), 83–87 (2022)

3. Lin, X.Y., et al.: Real-time interaction system for hovering true 3D display based on Leap Motion gesture recognition. Liq. Cryst. Display **37**(05), 654–659+546 (2022)
4. Zhang, W., et al.: A review of dynamic gesture understanding and interaction. J. Softw. **32**(10), 3051–3067 (2021)
5. Zeng, F., Li, Q., Xiao, Z., Havyarimana, V., Bai, J.: A price-based optimization strategy of power control and resource allocation in full-duplex heterogeneous macrocell-femtocell networks, IEEE Access, **6**, 42004–42013 (2018). -8
6. Jiang, H., Cao, H., Liu, D., Xiong, J., Cao, Z.: SmileAuth: using dental edge biometrics for user authentication on smartphones. Proc. ACM Interact. Mob. Wearable Ubiquitous Technol. **4**(3), 84:1–84:24 (2020)
7. Liu, D., Cao, Z., He, Y., Ji, X., Hou, M., Jiang, H.: Exploiting concurrency for opportunistic forwarding in duty-cycled IoT networks. ACM Trans. Sens. Netw. **15**(3), 31:1–31:33 (2019). -9
8. Lumeng, C., Yanyan, C., Min, H., Xinguang, X.: A flame detection method based on improved YOLOv5. Comput. Eng. 1–17(2022)
9. Wenbo, Z., et al.: An improved YOLOv5-based method for sugarcane stem node identification. J. Huazhong Agric. Univ. 1–9(2022)
10. Zhang, Z.M., Wu Z.: A dense pedestrian detection method based on improved YOLOv5. Appl. Sci. Technol. 1–7(2022)
11. Xu, H.-D., Ma, W., Yu, T., Xingxing, L., Zheng, Y.-J., Tian, Z.-W.: A YOLOv5 deep learning based method for tea shoot yield estimation. J. China Agric. Univ. **12**, 213–220 (2022)
12. Yang, G-L., Zhao, M., Huang, C., Huang, J-W.: Improvement of mask wearing detection algorithm by YOLOv5s. J. Heilongjiang Inst. Technol. (Compr. Ed.), **22**(10), 51–57 (2022)
13. Hao, S., Xingfa, D., Jun, W., Zhiyuan, C.: Improved YOLOv4-tiny-based lightweight on-campus pedestrian target detection algorithm. Comput. Eng. Appl. 1–12 (2022)
14. Yanhua, Z., et al.: MEC and blockchain empowered UAV-assisted IoT resource optimization. J. Beijing Univ. Technol. 1–909 (2022)
15. Liang, C., Kang, Y., Jianjun, Z.: Research on distributed cloud storage for electric safety apparatus management. Electr. Appl. **41**(02), 32–35 (2022)
16. Hao, C.: Research and application of online education system based on distributed cloud computing. East China Normal University, MA thesis, pp.10–27(2021)
17. Wang, X.: A distributed cloud-based approach to virtual machine template management. Metall. Autom. **45**, 169–176 (2021)
18. Shengli, G.: An analysis of distributed cloud data center solutions. China Financ. Comput. 96 (2022)
19. Xue, H.-M.: A distributed cloud computing data mining approach based on MapReduce. J. Anyang Normal Coll. **05**, 24–27 (2020)
20. Liu, Y, Zhang, N.: An integrated processing platform for urban and rural planning big data based on distributed cloud data center. J. Henan Urban Constr. Inst. **29**(03), 81–86+92 (2020)
21. Mao. J.: Deep reinforcement learning based collaborative caching for edge intelligence. East China Normal University, MA thesis, pp.63–70(2022)
22. Wenyong, D.: Exploring the application of integrated industrial Internet edge computing system based on edge intelligence plus network security. Autom. Expo **39**(01), 83–87 (2022)
23. Qiao, D.W., et al.: Edge intelligence: research advances and challenges. Radio Commun. Technol. **48**(01), 34–45 (2022)
24. Sowmya, M., et al.: SmartDefense: A distributed deep defense against DDoS attacks with edge computing. Comput. Netw. **209**, 108874 (2022). prepublish
25. Wei, Q., et al.: Research on face recognition method based on edge-cloud collaboration. Comput. Sci. **49**(05), 71–77 (2022)
26. Zifeng, W., et al.: Wider or deeper: revisiting the ResNet model for visual recognition. ArXiv abs/1611.10080 (2019)

27. Chengmin, L., et al.: Image recognition of peach tree pests based on multiscale attention residual network. J. Shandong Agric. Univ. (Nat. Sci. Ed.) **53**(02), 253–258 (2022)
28. Chen, Y., Dang, S.W., Nie, B.: A loopback detection algorithm based on ResNet model. Intell. Comput. Appl. **12**(08), 196–199 (2022)
29. Hu, Z., Zeng, F., Zhu, X., Fu, B., Jiang, H., Chen, H.: Computation efficiency maximization and QoE-provisioning in UAV-enabled MEC communication systems. IEEE Trans. Netw. Sci. Eng. **8**(2), 1630–1645 (2021)
30. Li, Z., et al.: A study on tree species identification based on improved ResNet34 network. Foreign Electron. Meas. Technol. **41**(07), 119–125 (2022)
31. Shuang, W.: Research and implementation of flower recognition algorithm based on machine learning. Chengdu: University of Electronic Science and Technology (2018)
32. Qian, C., Liu, D., Jiang, H.: Harmonizing energy efficiency and QoE for brightness scaling-based mobile video streaming. In: IWQoS, pp. 1–10 (2022)
33. Aifang, C.: Research on edge computing technology for optimization of target detection execution efficiency. Beijing Jiaotong Univ. 40–65 (2021)
34. Li, L.: Research on the theory and application of FDTD and its hybrid algorithm in microstrip antenna computing, Harbin Engineering University, PhD dissertation, pp.10–15(2015)
35. Liu, Y.: Research on coverage calculation and optimization methods for mobile communication networks. University of Science and Technology Beijing, PhD dissertation (2021)
36. Yang, Y.: Research on Internet inter-domain routing hijacking and its defense. Tsinghua University, PhD dissertation, pp.45–47 (2020)
37. Heng Li, L.-L., Yue, B.-S., Yung, S.-C.: Threat detection of hijacking attacks on vulnerable data under tenacious robust information. J. Xi'an Eng. Univ. **34**(06), 92–98 (2020)
38. Zhu, X., et al.: Toward accurate vehicle state estimation under non-Gaussian noises. IEEE Internet Things J. **6**(6), 10652–10664 (2019)
39. Liu, D., Hou, M., Cao, Z., He, Y., Ji, X., Zheng, X.: COF: exploiting concurrency for low power opportunistic forwarding. In: ICNP, pp. 32–42 (2015)
40. Jiang, H., Zhu, X., Li, Z., Xu, J., Zeng, F., Wang, D.: An energy-efficient framework for internet of things underlaying heterogeneous small cell networks. IEEE Trans. Mob. Comput. **21**(1), 31–43 (2022)
41. Liu, D., Wu, X., Cao, Z., Liu, M., Li, Y., Hou, M.: CD-MAC: a contention detectable MAC for low duty-cycled wireless sensor networks. In: SECON, pp. 37–45 (2015)
42. Hu, J., et al.: BlinkRadar: Non-intrusive driver eye-blink detection with UWB radar. In: Proceedings of IEEE ICDCS (2022)
43. Jiang, H., Dai, X., Xiao, Z., Iyengar, A.K.: Joint task offloading and resource allocation for energy-constrained mobile edge computing. IEEE Trans. Mob. Comput. (2022). https://doi.org/10.1109/TMC.2022.3150432
44. Ali, T.A.A., Xiao, Z., Sun, J., Mirjalili, S., Havyarimana, V., Jiang, H.: Optimal design of IIR wideband digital differentiators and integrators using salp swarm algorithm. Knowl Based Syst. **182**(15), 104834 (2019). https://doi.org/10.1016/j.knosys.2019.07.005
45. Zeng, Z., Li, Q., Xiao, Z., Havyarimana, V., Bai, J.: A Price-based optimization strategy of power control and resource allocation in full-duplex heterogeneous Macrocell-femtocell networks. IEEE Access **6**, 42004–42013 (2018)
46. Liu, D., Cao, Z., Hou, M., Rong, H., Jiang, H.: Pushing the limits of transmission concurrency for low power wireless networks. ACM Trans. Sens. Netw. **16**(4), 40:1–40:29 (2020)

Distributed Computing in IoT

Adversarial Example Attacks in Internet of Things (IoT)

Yuzhe Gu[1], Na Jiang[1], Yanjiao Chen[2], and Xueluan Gong[3(✉)]

[1] School of Cyber Science and Engineering, Wuhan University, Wuhan, China
{yuzhegu,na.jiang226}@whu.edu.cn

[2] College of Electrical Engineering, Zhejiang University, Hangzhou, China
chenyanjiao@zju.edu.cn

[3] School of Computer Science, Wuhan University, Wuhan, China
xueluangong@whu.edu.cn

Abstract. Recently, the Internet of Things (IoT) technology has made tremendous progress, and it is beginning to enter many areas of social life, such as autonomous driving, medical care, etc. Due to the massive data in IoT, deep neural networks (DNN) are often involved in helping process and analyzing data, but DNNs still face many security threats. Adversarial example attack is a common attack against DNN models, which interferes with model decisions through processed samples. It will undoubtedly threaten DNN-based IoT systems. This paper presents the possible attack scenarios of adversarial example attacks in IoT systems and extensively studies the defense methods of adversarial example attacks in IoT systems.

Keywords: Adversarial Example Attacks · IoT · Deep Learning

1 Introduction

In the past few years, the field of IoT is developing well, and the number of IoT devices has also exploded. According to statistics, by 2025, the number of IoT devices connected to the global network will increase to more than 7.544 billion units [6,46]. At the same time, the IoT is gradually covering all areas of social life, such as automation, health, transportation, energy, manufacturing, and other industries [9,10,22,24,25,29,42–44]. It also has produced practical applications such as autonomous driving and smart cities [41]. Obviously, for the IoT, which is already closely related to life, it is very important to ensure its security. However, the current IoT system still faces many security threats. Among them, the security threat caused by the vulnerability of deep neural networks is an important part that needs to be solved urgently.

In recent years, deep learning has played an important role in multiple fields, including pattern recognition [13], face recognition [36], speech recognition [2], and autonomous driving [21,32]. Of course, because of its ability to analyze a

Z. Xiao et al. (Eds.): ICECI 2022, LNICST 478, pp. 229–235, 2023.
https://doi.org/10.1007/978-3-031-28990-3_16

large amount of data, it is also used in IoT field, where abundant data is generated every day. Nevertheless, many works have verified the vulnerability of DNN in handling adversarial operations [7,11,15–19,30,31,33,38], for example, adversarial examples have the ability to confuse DNN models by slightly changing the network input data [38]. Therefore, the DNN in the current IoT scenario urgently needs high robustness to efficiently and accurately process IoT data of different accuracy [8].

In this paper, we describe the attack scenarios of adversarial example attacks in IoT. And we study the current representative works on improving the reliability of DNN to adversarial example attacks. Those works can well handle adversarial example attacks in IoT scenarios.

2 Background

2.1 Internet of Things (IoT)

IoT is a network infrastructure consisting of various sensing, communication, networking, and information processing devices [39]. Its main structure consists of infrared sensors, radio frequency identifiers, laser scanners, GPS, and other information equipment. Nowadays, IoT is widely used in smart cities, autonomous driving, health care, and other fields [1,23,28,35,37].

In the IoT system, all kinds of devices can access the IoT according to the protocols and standards formulated by the industry and realize the exchange and communication of information in the network system. Because the system is too large, a lot of data is generated and waiting to be processed every day, so DNN is often incorporated into IoT decision-making, which also gives attackers opportunities. The entire IoT roughly consists of three parts: a perception layer such as receiving data, a network layer that exchanges data, and an application layer that processes data. The adversarial example attack discussed in this paper mainly uses carefully designed sample input from the perception layer to achieve the effect of misjudging the DNN at the application layer.

2.2 Adversarial Example

The adversarial example is the original sample with invisible perturbation added, which misleads the deep neural network model to make a wrong judgment [38]. In the experiments of [20], for the original sample of the panda, after adding the adversarial perturbation, the judgment of the model changed from a high confidence "panda" to a "gibbon".

The high complexity of DNN models has resulted in a variety of different hypotheses for adversarial examples at present. [20] argues that the high-dimensional linearity of neural networks is the leading cause of adversarial examples and that the small changes in the input data can lead to decision errors after being amplified by multiple layers of the network; [34] argues that there exists a low-dimensional subspace containing a large number of normal vectors at the decision boundary, and perturbations within this subspace have an important impact on the model decisions. Multiple hypotheses have their focus, advantages, and disadvantages, which provide room for adversarial example attacks.

Recently, adversarial sample attacks have been successful in scopes such as CV and NLP [4,20,45]. Meanwhile, more attack scenarios have emerged in the real world [26]. In the era of IoT, a large number of perceptrons are collecting and generating data involving various domains daily. The involvement of DNN can help analyze and process a large amount of data in the IoT domain, but this also brings security analysis that may be subject to adversarial sample attacks.

3 Adversarial Example Attacks Scenario in IoT

In IoT system, DNNs use data gathered from IoT devices (perception layer), trained in a supervised or unsupervised manner, and apply the results to specific applications (application layer) to guide their decision-making behaviors [5]. However, in real-world scenarios, IoT devices may be attacked, destroyed, and tampered with, which in turn affects the data they collect and generate. As described in Sect. 2, adversarial example attacks fool the DNN model by modifying the input data to make wrong judgments, which will greatly affect the reliability of the DNN model. In some IoT application scenarios, there are extremely high requirements for the reliability of DNN models, such as pedestrian detection in autonomous driving [12], diagnostic opinion judgment of medical auxiliary detection equipment, process control in industrial production, etc. Adversarial example attacks will pose a great threat to these IoT application scenarios.

4 Adversarial Example Attack Countermeasures

In this section, we discuss some state-of-the-art studies which focus on improving the reliability of DNN-based IoT systems. For the convenience of introduction, the following discussion will not overemphasize the specific deployment and use of these methods in IoT systems but will focus on improving the robustness of the DNN model.

4.1 Learning with Reject Option

Learning with reject option (LRO) [3] is a special training method that can make the reliability of DNN achieve a better effect when the performance of standard models cannot be guaranteed. Different from the traditional optimization method that optimizes the general accuracy of all examples, LRO selects the subset with better performance from the example set and leaves the rest to judgments such as manual processing to make the average prediction accuracy high enough. For example, for a medical detection system whose prediction accuracy is not high enough, only the items it is good at will be detected, and other items will be handled by doctors, which can effectively improve the reliability and robustness of the system. The most important step in this is to determine which samples in the test data set are selected, n other words, to determine a reliable sample region.

Gao et al. [14] proposed generative adversarial learning with variance expansion (GALVE), in which the sample generator is obtained through a generative adversarial network (GAN), and in the discriminator part of the GAN, high-variance adversarial samples are used for fine-tuning to ensure the performance of the discriminator.

4.2 Model Understanding Through Subspace Explanation

As mentioned in [20], the reason why adversarial sample attacks are valid and difficult to defend is because of the high-dimensional linearity of neural networks, which causes small perturbations to be amplified and behaviors that are often difficult to explain. If a method can be found that allows we to understand the learning process of neural networks and can understand the behavior of the model within different feature subspaces, we can know when to trust a DNN model based on observations. This has important implications for defending against adversarial attacks and improving the reliability of the model.

Lakkaraju et al. [27] proposed a method for model interpretation through subspaces (MUSE). This interpretation framework quantifies the authenticity, reliability, and interpretability of the model. In MUSE, a new objective function will be constructed to explain the original model, which will be helpful in improving the robustness of the model.

4.3 Software Testing

To improve the interpretability of the model, in addition to observing the various behaviors and characteristics of the model during the training process, the method of sotfware testing can also be used.

Tian et al. [40] proposed a software testing method named DeepTest, an automatic testing tool that can automatically detect the wrong behavior of DNN. By generating test inputs that maximize the number of activated neurons, DeepTest can maximize the understanding of different logics in various parts of the DNN.

The tool can find various model decision errors in different real-world conditions, which will be of great help to the IoT system defense against adversarial example attacks. More importantly, the authors conducted this study in the context of autonomous vehicles using DNN decision-making, which fully demonstrates the feasibility of the method in the IoT system.

5 Conclusion

We believe that the use of deep neural networks in IoT systems may be subject to adversarial example attacks, which will pose security risks in many application scenarios. In this paper, not only do we introduce adversarial example attack scenarios in IoT, but we also summarize the state-of-the-art works to improve the reliability of DNN in IoT systems. In general, adversarial example attacks in IoT scenarios are still a promising research direction. More aggressive attack schemes can be further proposed to find potential security risks in IoT systems and to design more powerful defense methods to ensure the reliability of IoT services.

References

1. Ali, T.A.A., Xiao, Z., Sun, J., Mirjalili, S., Havyarimana, V., Jiang, H.: Optimal design of IIR wideband digital differentiators and integrators using salp swarm algorithm. Knowl.-Based Syst. **182**, 104834 (2019)
2. Amodei, D., et al.: Deep speech 2: End-to-end speech recognition in English and mandarin. In: International Conference on Machine Learning, pp. 173–182. PMLR (2016)
3. Bartlett, P.L., Wegkamp, M.H.: Classification with a reject option using a hinge loss. J. Mach. Learn. Res. **9**(8), 1–18 (2008)
4. Chakraborty, A., Alam, M., Dey, V., Chattopadhyay, A., Mukhopadhyay, D.: Adversarial attacks and defences: a survey. arXiv preprint arXiv:1810.00069 (2018)
5. Chen, M., Hao, Y.: Label-less learning for emotion cognition. IEEE Trans. Neural Netw. Learn. Syst. **31**(7), 2430–2440 (2019)
6. Chen, Y., Gong, X., Ou, R., Duan, L., Zhang, Q.: Crowdcaching: incentivizing D2D-enabled caching via coalitional game for IoT. IEEE Internet Things J. **7**(6), 5599–5612 (2020)
7. Chen, Y., Gong, X., Wang, Q., Di, X., Huang, H.: Backdoor attacks and defenses for deep neural networks in outsourced cloud environments. IEEE Netw. **34**(5), 141–147 (2020)
8. Chen, Y., Ran, Y., Zhou, J., Zhang, J., Gong, X.: MPCN-RP: a routing protocol for blockchain-based multi-charge payment channel networks. IEEE Trans. Netw. Serv. Manage. **19**, 1229–1242 (2021)
9. Cheng, L., et al.: SCTSC: a semicentralized traffic signal control mode with attribute-based blockchain in IoVs. IEEE Trans. Comput. Soc. Syst. **6**(6), 1373–1385 (2019)
10. Dai, X., et al.: Task co-offloading for D2D-assisted mobile edge computing in industrial internet of things. IEEE Trans. Ind. Inform. **19**, 480–490 (2022)
11. Dong, J., Gong, X., Xue, M.: Adversarial examples in wireless networks: a comprehensive survey. In: Wu, K., Wang, L., Chen, Y. (eds.) Edge Computing and IoT: Systems, Management and Security, ICECI 2021. Lecture Notes of the Institute for Computer Sciences, Social Informatics and Telecommunications Engineering, vol. 437, pp. 92–97. Springer, Cham (2022). https://doi.org/10.1007/978-3-031-04231-7_8
12. Duchesne, L., Karangelos, E., Wehenkel, L.: Recent developments in machine learning for energy systems reliability management. Proc. IEEE **108**(9), 1656–1676 (2020)
13. Feichtenhofer, C., Pinz, A., Zisserman, A.: Convolutional two-stream network fusion for video action recognition. In: Proceedings of the IEEE Conference on Computer Vision and Pattern Recognition, pp. 1933–1941 (2016)

14. Gao, J., Yao, J., Shao, Y.: Towards reliable learning for high stakes applications. In: Proceedings of the AAAI Conference on Artificial Intelligence, vol. 33, pp. 3614–3621 (2019)
15. Gong, X., Chen, Y., Huang, H., Liao, Y., Wang, S., Wang, Q.: Coordinated backdoor attacks against federated learning with model-dependent triggers. IEEE Netw. **36**(1), 84–90 (2022)
16. Gong, X., et al.: Defense-resistant backdoor attacks against deep neural networks in outsourced cloud environment. IEEE J. Sel. Areas Commun. **39**(8), 2617–2631 (2021)
17. Gong, X., Chen, Y., Wang, Q., Kong, W.: Backdoor attacks and defenses in federated learning: state-of-the-art, taxonomy, and future directions. IEEE Wirel. Commun. (2022)
18. Gong, X., Chen, Y., Wang, Q., Wang, M., Li, S.: Private data inference attacks against cloud: model, technologies, and research directions. IEEE Commun. Mag. **60**, 46–52 (2022)
19. Gong, X., Chen, Y., Yang, W., Mei, G., Wang, Q.: InverseNet: augmenting model extraction attacks with training data inversion. In: IJCAI, pp. 2439–2447 (2021)
20. Goodfellow, I.J., Shlens, J., Szegedy, C.: Explaining and harnessing adversarial examples. arXiv preprint arXiv:1412.6572 (2014)
21. Gupta, A., Anpalagan, A., Guan, L., Khwaja, A.S.: Deep learning for object detection and scene perception in self-driving cars: survey, challenges, and open issues. Array **10**, 100057 (2021)
22. Hu, Z., Zeng, F., Xiao, Z., Fu, B., Jiang, H., Chen, H.: Computation efficiency maximization and QoE-provisioning in UAV-enabled MEC communication systems. IEEE Trans. Netw. Sci. Eng. **8**(2), 1630–1645 (2021)
23. Jiang, H., Dai, X., Xiao, Z., Iyengar, A.K.: Joint task offloading and resource allocation for energy-constrained mobile edge computing. IEEE Trans. Mob. Comput. (2022)
24. Jiang, H., Xiao, Z., Li, Z., Xu, J., Zeng, F., Wang, D.: An energy-efficient framework for internet of things underlaying heterogeneous small cell networks. IEEE Trans. Mob. Comput. **21**(1), 31–43 (2020)
25. Jiao, L., Wu, Y., Dong, J., Jiang, Z.: Toward optimal resource scheduling for internet of things under imperfect CSI. IEEE Internet Things J. **7**(3), 1572–1581 (2019)
26. Kurakin, A., Goodfellow, I.J., Bengio, S.: Adversarial examples in the physical world. In: Artificial Intelligence Safety and Security, pp. 99–112. Chapman and Hall/CRC (2018)
27. Lakkaraju, H., Kamar, E., Caruana, R., Leskovec, J.: Faithful and customizable explanations of black box models. In: Proceedings of the 2019 AAAI/ACM Conference on AI, Ethics, and Society, pp. 131–138 (2019)
28. Li, J., et al.: Drive2friends: inferring social relationships from individual vehicle mobility data. IEEE Internet Things J. **7**(6), 5116–5127 (2020)
29. Li, S., Da Xu, L., Zhao, S.: 5g internet of things: a survey. J. Ind. Inf. Integr. **10**, 1–9 (2018)
30. Li, W., et al.: Hu-Fu: Hardware and software collaborative attack framework against neural networks. In: 2018 IEEE Computer Society Annual Symposium on VLSI (ISVLSI), pp. 482–487. IEEE (2018)
31. Liu, Y., Xie, Y., Srivastava, A.: Neural trojans. In: 2017 IEEE International Conference on Computer Design (ICCD), pp. 45–48. IEEE (2017)
32. Long, W., et al.: Unified spatial-temporal neighbor attention network for dynamic traffic prediction. IEEE Trans. Veh. Technol. **72**, 1515–1529 (2022)

33. Luo, X., Qin, Q., Gong, X., Xue, M.: A survey of adversarial attacks on wireless communications. In: Wu, K., Wang, L., Chen, Y. (eds.) ICECI 2021. Lecture Notes of the Institute for Computer Sciences, Social Informatics and Telecommunications Engineering, vol. 437, pp. 83–91. Springer, Cham (2022). https://doi.org/10.1007/978-3-031-04231-7_7
34. Moosavi-Dezfooli, S.M., Fawzi, A., Fawzi, O., Frossard, P.: Universal adversarial perturbations. In: Proceedings of the IEEE Conference on Computer Vision and Pattern Recognition, pp. 1765–1773 (2017)
35. Moustafa, N., Keshk, M., Choo, K.K.R., Lynar, T., Camtepe, S., Whitty, M.: Dad: a distributed anomaly detection system using ensemble one-class statistical learning in edge networks. Futur. Gener. Comput. Syst. **118**, 240–251 (2021)
36. Schroff, F., Kalenichenko, D., Philbin, J.: FaceNet: a unified embedding for face recognition and clustering. In: Proceedings of the IEEE Conference on Computer Vision and Pattern Recognition, pp. 815–823 (2015)
37. Setiaji, T., Budiyanto, C., Yuana, R.: The contribution of the internet of things and smart systems to agricultural practices: a survey. In: IOP Conference Series: Materials Science and Engineering. vol. 1098, p. 052100. IOP Publishing (2021)
38. Szegedy, C., et al.: Intriguing properties of neural networks. arXiv preprint arXiv:1312.6199 (2013)
39. Tan, L., Wang, N.: Future internet: the internet of things. In: 2010 3rd International Conference on Advanced Computer Theory and Engineering (ICACTE), vol. 5, pp. V5–376. IEEE (2010)
40. Tian, Y., Pei, K., Jana, S., Ray, B.: DeepTest: automated testing of deep-neural-network-driven autonomous cars. In: Proceedings of the 40th International Conference on Software Engineering, pp. 303–314 (2018)
41. Wu, J., Luo, S., Wang, S., Wang, H.: NLES: a novel lifetime extension scheme for safety-critical cyber-physical systems using SDN and NFV. IEEE Internet Things J. **6**(2), 2463–2475 (2018)
42. Xiao, Z., et al.: Resource management in UAV-assisted MEC: state-of-the-art and open challenges. Wireless Netw. **28**(7), 3305–3322 (2022)
43. Xiao, Z., et al.: TrajData: on vehicle trajectory collection with commodity plug-and-play OBU devices. IEEE Internet Things J. **7**(9), 9066–9079 (2020)
44. Yin, B., Wu, Y., Hu, T., Dong, J., Jiang, Z.: An efficient collaboration and incentive mechanism for internet of vehicles (IoV) with secured information exchange based on blockchains. IEEE Internet Things J. **7**(3), 1582–1593 (2019)
45. Zhang, J., Li, C.: Adversarial examples: opportunities and challenges. IEEE Trans. Neural Netw. Learn. Syst. **31**(7), 2578–2593 (2019)
46. Zhou, W., Jia, Y., Peng, A., Zhang, Y., Liu, P.: The effect of IoT new features on security and privacy: new threats, existing solutions, and challenges yet to be solved. IEEE Internet Things J. **6**(2), 1606–1616 (2018)

Training Node Screening in Decentralized Trusted Federated Learning

Hao Wang[1], Jiahua Yu[2], Shichang Xuan[1](✉), and Xin Li[1]

[1] Harbin Engineering University, Harbin 150001, China
xuanshichang@hrbeu.edu.cn
[2] Heilongjiang Branch of CNCERT/CC, Harbin 150023, China

Abstract. The emergence of federated learning has to some extent solved the current problems of privacy protection of terminal data and the processing technology of massive data. However, its centralized architecture still has problems such as limited access and high establishment cost, so the trend of decentralization is inevitable. Although decentralized federated learning architecture circumvents the drawbacks of centralized structure, it also loses the convenience of third-party supervision. Therefore, to address the problem of missing supervision mechanisms for worker node training behavior in decentralized federated learning architecture, this paper proposes a backdoor-based supervision mechanism for arithmetic node training behavior. The mechanism can be applied to general classification tasks. Experiments revealed that this mechanism can accurately assess the training behavior of worker nodes while maintaining the accuracy of the original task. In addition, this paper proposes a rotation scheme for the watermarked datasets involved and gives a corresponding replacement prediction method, which further ensures that the training behavior of arithmetic nodes can be quantified completely by predicting and replacing the watermarked datasets, aiding the arithmetic party training operation of the behavior monitoring mechanism.

Keywords: Federated Learning · Digital Watermark · Training Behavior Supervision

1 Introduction

In recent years, with the rapid development of IoT [1, 2], Internet of Vehicles [3, 4], edge computing [5, 6], and unmanned aerial vehicles [6, 7], more and more intelligent terminal devices are connected to the Internet, which generates a huge amount of terminal data. This is certainly a valuable asset in the field of artificial intelligence [8]. However, while massive data provides a solid foundation for the development of artificial intelligence technology, it also makes the privacy protection and processing technology of smart terminals for massive data face more serious threats and challenges [9, 10]. Although federated learning provides a feasible solution to these problems through its unique advantage of "data does not move, model moves" [11–13]. However, most of the current federated learning applications are established by business or equipment

Z. Xiao et al. (Eds.): ICECI 2022, LNICST 478, pp. 236–261, 2023.
https://doi.org/10.1007/978-3-031-28990-3_17

owners, which have problems of limited access scale, difficulty in data expansion, and high system construction cost, resulting in a large number of data demanders and data owners not being able to effectively interface with each other and limiting the value of data. Therefore, a decentralized federated learning system structure has emerged. In this structure system, data demanders and data owners form a 1-to-N or N-to-N relationship, so that the docking between demanders and owners is no longer restricted by the platform.

As the executor of the training behavior in the decentralized federated learning architecture, the stable operation of the architecture must keep its behavior honest, and any bad behavior in the model training will limit the development of the architecture. Dishonest worker nodes may falsify training data and thus claim rewards without performing the actual training behavior, affecting the fairness of the system. Therefore, it is necessary to monitor the training behavior of worker nodes. Dishonest training behavior not only affects the stability of the entire architecture but also has a more direct impact on the training results of the model, i.e., the task publisher needs to pay more to get the expected results. Therefore, introducing data and training behavior trustworthy detection mechanism before model aggregation helps to screen out malicious nodes before model aggregation, prevent performance degradation or even failure of aggregated models, and improve model accuracy.

To address the above problems, this paper proposes a digital watermarking-based training behavior supervision mechanism for worker nodes to falsify training results and affect the overall accuracy of model training to obtain unreal gains in the decentralized federated learning architecture, which can quantify and visualize the training behavior of each worker node by expanding the application scenarios of digital watermarking, to reach the goal of promoting worker nodes to remain honest in their training behavior and provide credible arithmetic support for the decentralized federated learning system.

The main contributions of this paper are as follows.

- A digital watermarking-based training behavior supervision mechanism is proposed for the screening of trusted training nodes for the worker node training behavior supervision scenario in the decentralized federated learning scenario.
- Quantifying the training behavior of worker nodes and reducing the computational and communication redundancy in existing mechanisms by migrating the digital watermarking technique to a decentralized federated learning environment with the help of the digital watermarking construction process.

The remainder of this paper is organized as follows: the second part introduces the work related to training behavior supervision as well as digital watermarking; the third part describes the architecture of decentralized federated learning; the fourth part introduces the digital watermarking-based training behavior supervision mechanism; the fifth and sixth parts provide theoretical analysis and experimental validation of the feasibility of the mechanism, respectively; and finally, the conclusion.

2 Related Work

There is very little work on the authenticity of worker node training behavior alone as a supervised object in current research for federated learning, but it is possible to borrow from some other fields. The solution given by Nishant et al. [14] is to make multiple replications of a subset of the data and then compare the models on the replicated subset for consistency, where, to ensure the non-repudiation of the behavior of COs blockchain is introduced as a way to record the behavior of COs model release. Another solution for the supervision of the training behavior of worker nodes is the evaluation of their model quality. A method for evaluating model quality is proposed by Lu et al. [15]. It uses prediction accuracy to quantify the quality of the trained local model and completes the assessment of the model quality by measuring the accuracy through the mean absolute error (MAE) metric. The lower the MAE value of the model, the higher its accuracy. In addition to MAE, Kang et al. [16], used an ONLAD model to calculate the prediction error by establishing a representative subset of normal data as a validation standard set for each parameter model received.

The current supervision of the authenticity of the training behavior of worker nodes either has a large amount of redundant computation and communication or is assessed by the quality of the local model, but the quality of the local model is not only determined by the training behavior, so this approach is not comprehensive. Even if the model upload behavior of worker nodes is recorded through the blockchain, the parameters uploaded by worker nodes still have the possibility of forgery. Therefore, a more in-depth study on the mechanism of supervising the authenticity of the training behavior of training nodes is needed from a fresh perspective.

Digital watermarking as additional information embedded in the model [17–19], the completeness of the watermark embedding is gradually increased with the training process. Therefore, the technique is naturally suitable for evaluating the training behavior of workers. Since there is no prior work on this topic, the current state of research when digital watermarking works for the original model protection purpose is given below.

A white-box solution to the DNN model intellectual property attribution problem was first proposed by Uchida et al. [20]. White-box watermarking requires prior knowledge of the model at the time of watermark embedding and embedding the watermark information into the static content of the model through the knowledge of the model information so that the tokens are also extracted from the verification model. Rouhani et al. [21] provide a way to embed watermark information into the dynamic content of a DNN model. Unlike white-box watermarking, black-box watermarking requires no prior knowledge of any model when embedding the watermark. Adi et al. [22] were the first to apply backdoor techniques to the work on watermark embedding in black-box scenarios. In this work, backdoor embedding occurs during the training of the model or fine-tuning, and is done by adding backdoor samples to the training set, which need to have a different distribution than the training samples. In addition to the above methods, other studies include adding the author's signature to the watermark [23], constructing watermarking models [24], expanding the representation of watermarking samples [25], introducing one-way hash functions to form a one-way chain pattern of trigger samples [26], and blind (blind) watermarking [27].

In terms of the protection of federated learning models, Buse et al. [28] proposed WAFFLE, a watermark embedding method for federated learning. by introducing a retraining process after model aggregation, the watermark can be embedded without accessing the training data and without affecting the accuracy of the normal task. Li et al. [29] proposed a watermarking protocol for protecting models in a fuzzy logic environment that satisfies the need to verify model ownership in FL scenarios by combining state-of-the-art watermarking schemes and cryptographic primitives.

In summary, the application of digital watermarking technology in federated learning is still in the early stage of development [30–32], and the existing schemes are not perfect either in theory or in the process of practical application, but digital watermarking can play a role in model protection, and its application in the scenario of training behavior authenticity supervision is feasible and has great research space.

3 Decentralized Federated Learning Architecture

The architecture of decentralized federated learning is shown in Fig. 1. The architecture contains two behavioral entities, the task publisher and the executor of training, i.e., the worker node. The main actions of the task publisher in different phases of the whole decentralized federated learning system are: in the initialization phase, model initialization, validation dataset (containing watermarked dataset and standard data validation set) preparation, and initial worker selection; in the training phase, model training using the validation set in parallel with the worker nodes; in the aggregation phase, data quality evaluation and training behavior evaluation, model aggregation and worker re-selection. The worker nodes, on the other hand, perform two main actions, i.e., data preparation and local training. The local data quality of a worker node and its training behavior jointly determine the quality of the local model trained by the worker node. On the one hand, a worker node may have several local datasets, which can correspond to different training tasks, but the quality of the datasets may be uneven, and having one high-quality dataset does not mean that all the datasets of the worker node reach the high-quality standard; in addition, different models have different functions and require different data characteristics, so the quality of the data is not constant but varies dynamically depending on the model requirements. On the other hand, even if a worker node has data that fits well with the training task of a certain model, but the worker node does not perform the actual training behavior or falsifies the training data due to factors such as malicious purposes or lazy behavior, then the contribution of the worker node to the task is insufficient or even negative. The above-mentioned problems of low data quality and falsified training behaviors will eventually affect the quality of the local model trained by the worker node and the stability and trustworthiness of the whole architecture.

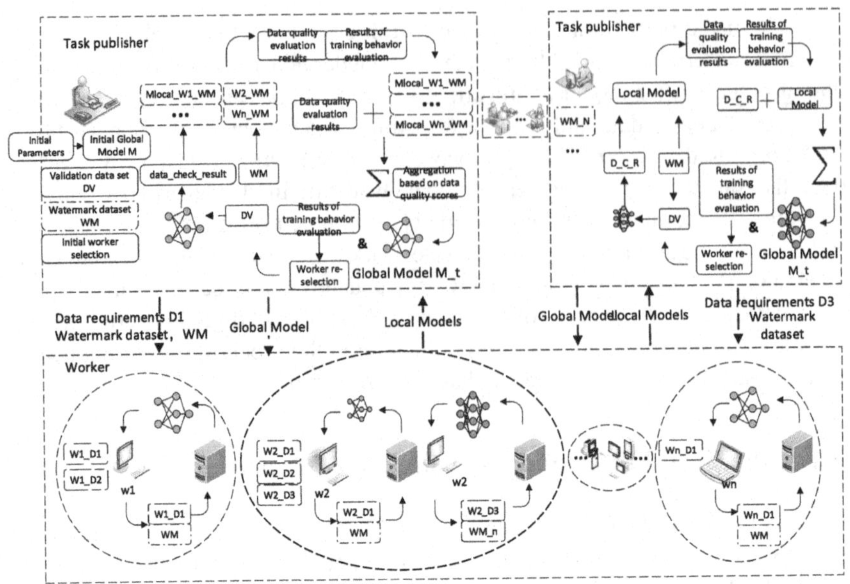

Fig. 1. Architecture of the decentralized federated learning system

The description of the entities in this architecture and the interaction process between the entities are as follows.

1. System initialization process: this process mainly consists of the initial preparation of both parties for the respective upcoming federated learning process.

   a. Task publisher. The task publisher, as the party that proposes the training requirements, first needs to initialize the required model to obtain the initial model $M^{\theta}_{G(0)}$, and construct the corresponding standard validation dataset D_v, watermark dataset D_{wm}, where the standard validation dataset D_v is mainly used to assist in evaluating the data quality of worker nodes, and the watermark dataset D_{wm} is mainly used for worker authenticity evaluation of node training behavior; after that, the task publisher will select the appropriate set of worker nodes S for training. And sends the initial model $M^{\theta}_{G(0)}$, data requirements, and the watermark dataset D_{wm} together to all selected worker nodes.
   b. Worker nodes: After receiving the requirements from the task publisher, the selected worker nodes first need to prepare their own local datasets D_k, k $\in$ S according to the data requirements of the task publisher, and after processing their own local datasets, they will be trained locally according to the training requirements of the task publisher.

2. Training phase: the training phase is jointly participated by both parties.

a. Task publisher. The initial model will be trained locally using the standard validation dataset D_v and the obtained results will be used for the evaluation of data quality.
b. Worker Node. Start the local training process and send the resulting local model $M^{\theta}_{W_k(t)}$ back to the task publisher after the training is completed, waiting for it to aggregate the local models of all worker nodes and to downlink the new global model. If no new global model is sent down, the training task will be ended.

3. Aggregation phase. Done by the task publisher. In this phase, the task publisher needs to inspect the local model sent by the worker node to complete data quality evaluation and authenticity detection of the worker's training behavior, and then finish the aggregation process of the local model according to the corresponding aggregation algorithm to get the new global model $M^{\theta}_{G(t+1)}$, and finally check its performance, and send it to the worker node if it does not meet the requirements The training continues and the worker nodes continue the training phase; if the model meets the requirements then the current training task is ended.

In this architecture, the data quality evaluation of the task publisher and the training behavior check correspond to the quality detection of the local dataset and the supervision of the training behavior of the worker node, respectively. These two supervision mechanisms are important to ensure that worker nodes upload high quality local models. The results of data quality evaluation will be applied on top of the federated aggregation algorithm.

4 Supervisory Mechanism for Training Behavior of Worker Nodes Based on Digital Watermarking

4.1 Overall Architecture

In decentralized federated learning scenarios, worker nodes may have malicious or lazy behaviors, thus not performing training or faking the training process. Therefore, a digital watermarking-based mechanism for monitoring the authenticity of training behavior (WM-TBM) is proposed to ensure that worker nodes perform the training behavior honestly. Firstly, the overall framework of the mechanism is introduced, and the role roles of each participant and the overall interaction process are introduced, followed by a detailed description of the mechanism, specifically, the watermarking dataset construction process, the digital watermark embedding process, the worker node training behavior checking process, and the watermarking dataset replacement process.

Federated learning is an iterative process, so WM-TBM will run through the whole interaction process between task publisher and worker nodes. WM-TBM consists of three parts, where the execution of the task, i.e., the training process of the federated learning task, is done by the worker nodes and the rest is done by the task publisher. Its overall framework is shown in Fig. 2.

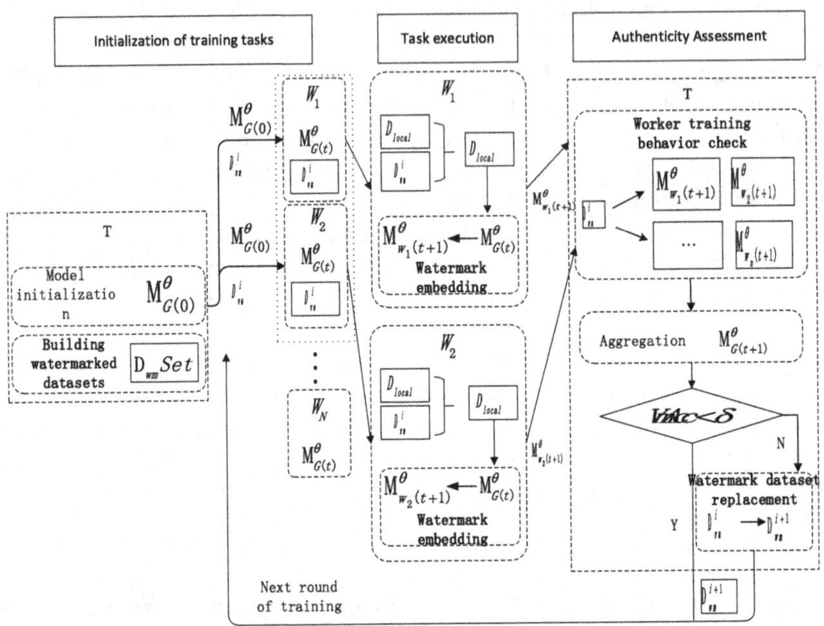

Fig. 2. Overall framework of the WM-TBM mechanism

Initialization of the Training Task. In the initialization phase, the task publisher needs to initialize the local model to get the global model $M_{G(0)}$ and prepare n watermarked datasets $D_{wm}Set\{D^1_{wm}, D^2_{wm}, \cdots D^n_{wm}\}$ for detecting the training behavior of worker nodes. The initial global model $M_{G(0)}$ and one of the watermarked datasets D^i_{wm} are sent to the selected worker nodes after the above preparatory work is prepared.

Task Execution. In this phase, the worker node uses the global model issued by the task publisher instead of the local model and receives the watermark dataset D^i_{wm}. After merging the local dataset D_{local} with D^i_{wm} into the new local dataset D_{local}, the worker node starts the local training process and gives the training results back to the task publisher in a timely manner.

Specifically, at a specific round t, the task publisher will send the current global model $M_{G(t)}$ to N workers, and the selected worker $s \in S$ will perform the training task $t_i(w)$ locally using its own local dataset D_{local} and learning rate l_r, and after the local E rounds of training, get a new local model $M^{wm}_{s(t)}$, and returns that model to the task publisher.

This training process can be summarized as finite-times aggregation optimization by.

$$min_{w \in R^d}\left[T(w) := \frac{1}{N}\sum\nolimits_{i=1}^{N} t_i(w)\right] \tag{1}$$

where N worker nodes use the local privacy dataset $D_{local} = \{x_j^i, y_j^i\}$ for the local training task $t_i(w)$, and $\{x_j^i, y_j^i\}$ represents the data samples and the labels of the samples; the training task performed locally by the workers can be described as $t_i(\mathrm{w}_i) = l(\{x_j^i, y_j^i\}_{j \in D_i}, w_i)$, l being the loss resulting from the prediction using the local weights. The worker nodes will complete the embedding process of the watermark while performing the local task.

Authenticity Assessment. This phase will involve three main assessments, namely, worker training behavior authenticity assessment, model accuracy assessment on the primary task, and watermarking task assessment.

The worker training behavior authenticity assessment will use the digital watermark dataset D_{wm}^i issued by the task publisher to check all local models and test the accuracy of the local model on D_{wm}^i, specifically two dimensions will be checked, and the results of this phase will be used as the main basis for the worker training behavior evaluation, which will be used by the task publisher to make a decision on whether to continue to select the worker for subsequent training tasks.

The accuracy evaluation of the watermarking task will be performed using the watermarked dataset on the aggregated new global model, which is mainly used to determine whether watermarked model replacement is required. Performing watermarked dataset replacement when necessary ensures that the training behavior of worker nodes is quantified completely and consistently.

The accuracy evaluation of the model on the primary task occurs after the training behavior of the workers is evaluated. The task publisher aggregates the training results returned by the workers according to Eq. (4–2) to obtain a new global model $\mathrm{M}_{G(t+1)}$.

$$\mathrm{M}_{G(t+1)} = \mathrm{M}_{G(t)} + \frac{\eta}{n}\sum\nolimits_{s=1}^{s}\left(M_{s(t)}^{wm} - \mathrm{M}_{G(t)}\right) \tag{2}$$

After completing the aggregation process of the global model, the task publisher needs to validate the performance of the new global model using the validation set of the main task, determine whether it meets the requirements for use, and make a decision on whether to continue with the next round of the training process of federated learning.

The specific process is shown in Algorithm 4.1:

Algorithm 4.1: WM-TBM

Input: D_{local}: Training set; D_{test}: Test set; $M_{G(0)}$: Initial Model;
S: Selected set of workers; T: Global Training Round;
$D_{wm}Set\{D_{wm}^{1}, D_{wm}^{2}, \cdots D_{wm}^{n}\}$: Collection of watermarked data sets;
η: Global model learning rate; η_s: Local learning rate of worker s;
E: Local training rounds
Onput: $M_{G(T)}$ Global Model
// **Task publisher execution:**
TaskInit():
  $M_{G(0)} \leftarrow M_{G(0)} - \eta \nabla l(M_{G(0)})$
  $W_{G(0)} \leftarrow (parameters\ of\ M_{G(0)})$
TaskEvaluation():
  for each epoch t from 1 to T **do**
    WorkerEval()
    $W_{G(t+1)} \leftarrow \sum_{s=1}^{S} \frac{1}{m} W_{s(t)}$
    $M_{G(t+1)} \leftarrow W_{G(t+1)}$
    $Acc_{test}^{global} \leftarrow M_{G(t+1)} + D_{test}$
  end for
  return $W_{G(t+1)}$
WorkerEval():
  for each s ∈ S **do**
    $VmAcc_{test}^{s} \leftarrow M_{s(t)}^{wm} + D_{wm}$
    if $VmAcc_{test}^{s}$ *is not available*
      exchange D_{wm}^{i} *to* D_{wm}^{i+1}
      send D_{wm}^{i+1} to each s ∈ S
    end if
  end for
// **Worker execution:**
TaskExec(W):
  receive $W_{s(t)}$ *and* , D_{wm}^{i} *from task publisher*
  $M_{s(t)} \leftarrow$ (*replace the parameters of* $M_{G(t-1)}$ *with* $W_{s(t)}$)
  $\boldsymbol{D_{local}} \leftarrow \boldsymbol{dataset\_patch(D_{local}, D_{wm})}$
  for each epoch t from 1 to E **do**
    for batch b ∈ D_{local} **do**
      $M_{s(t+1)}^{wm} \leftarrow M_{s(t)}^{wm} - \eta \nabla l(M_{s(t)}^{wm}, b)$
      $W_{s(t+1)} \leftarrow (parameters\ of\ M_{s(t+1)}^{wm})$
    end for
  end for
  end for
  return $W_{s(t+1)}$

4.2 Watermarking Dataset Construction

One of the necessary requirements for watermarking data is that it should not interfere with the execution of the main task in federated learning, so the watermarked data should be independent of the training data, and the watermarked data chosen to be independent of the training data outperforms the pre-specified Gaussian noise patterns in terms of performance [14]. Therefore, a new idea is provided for the construction of the watermarked dataset based on the previous studies, which is to embed a fixed pattern in the images that are independent of the training set. The pattern will act as a trigger for the watermarked backdoor and is used to detect the completion of this backdoor, which identifies whether the worker has performed the training process honestly or not.

Specifically, the images that are not related to the main task are first selected as watermarks, and then corresponding patterns are embedded for each image, which are different in terms of color, category, position and orientation, and are given a random label from the actual task category. Thus, for the specified pattern, the model with an accompanying watermark backdoor will output its assigned label.

The advantages of using this approach to construct the watermarked dataset are that (1) using a watermarked dataset that is independent of the main task and adding different patterns to it ensures that the watermarked set is independent of the other training sets, greatly improving the generalizability of the watermarked dataset so that it can act on multiple federated learning tasks; (2) the randomly generated embedding patterns for each category of the main task further ensures that each sample noise is unique; (3) since each image can correspond to a different pattern, the same set of watermarked data can be reused, reducing the difficulty of data preparation. Figure 3 gives the style of a partial watermarking dataset, and the text in the figure indicates the assigned label to which the image is assigned, and the source of the label is the Cifar10 dataset.

Fig. 3. Partial watermarking dataset

4.3 Watermark Embedding

After generating the watermark data, the next step is to embed the watermark into the target DNN, which can be done with the help of deep neural network due to its strong intrinsic learning ability. The embedding algorithm SF-WE is shown as follows.

Algorithm 4.2: SF-WE

```
Input: D^i_{non-wm} = {X_i, Y_i}^C_{c=1}: Prepared watermark dataset;
       σ = {Y_o, Y_n}(o ≠ n): Mapping of the original label Y_o to the new label Y_n
Output: M^{wm}_{s(t)} Partial model with watermark; D^i_{wm}: Watermark dataset
// Task publisher execution:
watermarkingEmbedding():
    D^i_{wm} ← ∅
    D^i_{temp} ← sample(D^i_{non-wm}, Y_o, percentage)
    for each d ∈ D^i_{temp} do
        x_{wm} = embedding_pattern(d[x], pattern), y_{wm} = y_n
        D^i_{wm} = D^i_{wm} ∪ {x_{wm}, y_{wm}}
    end for
// Worker node execution:
M^{wm}_{s(t)} = TaskExec(M_{s(t)}, D^i_{wm})
return M^{wm}_{s(t)}
```

The algorithm SF-WE takes as input the original watermark dataset D^i_{non-wm} and the label mapping relation $\sigma = \{Y_o, Y_n\}(o \neq n)$ and outputs the watermark dataset D^i_{wm}, which in turn outputs the local model $M^{wm}_{s(t)}$ with the watermark after the worker nodes are trained. The label mapping relationship will be defined by the task publisher indicating how the watermark will be labeled. Y_o is the true label of the original data and Y_n is the pre-defined watermark label that will include the fingerprint used for training behavior verification. Next, the algorithm's watermarkingEmbedding() function will draw all the labels labeled with Y_o from the trained dataset, on which the corresponding patterns are generated and re-labeled with Y_n, which will generate both the patterns and the carefully prepared labels. After receiving the complete watermarked dataset D^i_{wm}, the worker node will use this D^i_{wm} dataset and the local dataset D_{local} for local training, during which the DNN will automatically learn the patterns of these watermarked data, so that the watermark specified by the task publisher is embedded in the local model of this worker node. The completion of the digital watermark will gradually increase with the number of local training rounds of the worker node. The completion of the digital watermark will be used as one of the main metrics for subsequent checks of the training behavior of the worker nodes.

4.4 Worker Training Behavior Check

When the task publisher receives the local model M_(s(t))^wm from the worker node, the complete degree of the watermark will be checked, and this result will further identify whether the worker node has performed the training process truthfully. To ensure the objectivity of the evaluation, the training honesty of the worker node will be checked from two perspectives separately, and the final score of the authenticity of the training behavior of this worker will be obtained. The specific checking process is shown in Algorithm 4.3.

Algorithm 4.3 Checking Process

Input: $D_{wm}Set\{D_{wm}^1, D_{wm}^2, \cdots D_{wm}^n\}$: Watermark dataset collection;
$M_{s(t)}^{wm}(s \in S)$: Local model of worker nodes
Onput: $\{\xi_{s_1}^t, \xi_{s_2}^t \cdots \xi_{s_m}^t\}$: Training authenticity score set for workers selected in that round
// **Task publisher execution:**
WorkerEval():
  $D_{wm}^i \leftarrow D_{wm}Set\{D_{wm}^1, D_{wm}^2, \cdots D_{wm}^n\}$
  for each $M_{s(t)}^{wm}$ **do**
    $acc_{s_i}^t \leftarrow Acc(M_{s(t)}^{wm}, D_{wm}^i)$
  end for
  $acc_{avg}^t \leftarrow \frac{1}{m}\sum_{i=1}^{m} acc_{s_i}^t$
  if $acc_{s_i}^t > Acc(M_{s(t-1)}^{wm}, D_{wm}^i)$ and $acc_{s_i}^t \geq acc_{avg}^t$
    $\xi_{s_i}^t \leftarrow acc_{s_i}^t$
  end if
  return $\{\xi_{s_1}^t, \xi_{s_2}^t \cdots \xi_{s_m}^t\}$

After receiving the local models $M_{s(t)}^{wm}$ for all worker nodes, the task publisher first needs to determine the watermark dataset D_{wm}^i used for the current training in the watermark dataset set $D_{wm}Set\{D_{wm}^1, D_{wm}^2, \cdots D_{wm}^n\}$, and after that use this dataset D_{wm}^i to detect all local models and the The accuracy of all worker nodes is averaged as one of the comparison metrics. After the above steps, the following checks are performed on the local models of each worker node.

- Compare horizontally the accuracy of all selected workers and the average accuracy to ensure that they did not undergo falsification training.
- Check the test accuracy of the local model submitted by the workers for D_{wm}^i to ensure that it is higher than the accuracy of the global model in the previous round, and ensure that the complicity can be detected in the case that the vast majority of workers perform falsification training that makes the average accuracy rate decrease and leads to the failure of this evaluation metric.

After the checks have been performed, the accuracy $acc_{s_i}^t$ of the local model of the worker node for the current round on the watermarked dataset is recorded as the training score $\xi^t_{s_i}$ of that node, which is used as the basis for the selection of worker nodes performing subsequent training tasks.

4.5 Watermark Dataset Replacement

Throughout the training process of federated learning, the task publisher and worker nodes will communicate several times, and to ensure the observability of the watermark completion, the watermark dataset needs to be rotated when it reaches the unavailable state. Specifically, the rotation of the watermark dataset to enable another watermark task and the natural extinction of the current watermark task ensures that the watermark task can continuously and completely quantify the training behavior of the worker nodes. The watermark dataset replacement process is shown in Algorithm 4.4.

Algorithm 4.4 Watermarked Dataset Replacement

Input: $D_{wm}Set\{D^1_{wm}, D^2_{wm}, \cdots D^n_{wm}\}$: Watermark dataset collection;
$M^{wm}_{s(t)}(s \in S)$: Local model of worker nodes
// **Task publisher execution:**
$\boldsymbol{WMDataSetExchange}()$:
  for each $t \in T$ **do**
    $M^{wm}_{G(t+1)} = M_{G(t)} + \frac{\eta}{n}\sum_{s=1}^{S}(M^{wm}_{s(t)} - M_{G(t)})$
    $VmAcc^{test}_{s(t)} \leftarrow M^{wm}_{G(t+1)} + D^i_{wm}$
    if $(VmAcc^{test}_{s(t)} - VmAcc^{test}_{s(t-1)} > \Delta\delta)$ $and(Cnt_{useless} > \vartheta)$
      exchange D^i_{wm} *to* D^{i+1}_{wm}
      send D^{i+1}_{wm} to each $s \in S$
    end if
  end for

Define the observable coefficient as δ. When the difference between the accuracy $VmAcc^{test}_{s(t)}$ of the global model $M^{wm}_{G(t+1)}$ on the watermarked dataset D^i_{wm} and the accuracy $VmAcc^{test}_{s(t-1)}$ of the previous round t is less than the observable coefficient, it means that the watermarked dataset has reached the unavailable state ΔF. To make this criterion have some fault tolerance, the tolerance factor $Cnt_{useless}$ is defined as the number of times that the unavailable state can be tolerated, and the watermarked dataset is considered to be always in the available state until this number is satisfied. When the performance of the watermarked dataset on the global model satisfies the above conditions at the same time, the replacement of the watermarked dataset $\{D^i_{wm} \rightarrow D^{i+1}_{wm}\}$ is performed, the reinforcement of the watermarking task T_x corresponding to the watermarked dataset D^i_{wm} is canceled, and the watermarking task T_y corresponding to the watermarked dataset D^{i+1}_{wm} is enabled.

As the training rounds proceed, the performance of task T_x on the main task T will gradually decline and the watermarking task will gradually die out, and after the performance of T_x on the main task T declines to a certain degree, T_x will return from the unavailable state to the available state and can participate in the next watermarking rotation, i.e., the above watermarking rotation process can be expressed as follows.

$$\forall \text{i} < \text{E}, \text{if } S_i^{T_x} \xrightarrow{e_f} S_{false}, \text{exchange } T_x \text{ } to \text{ } T_y$$
$$where \text{ } S_{false} \text{ } is \left(Acc_{e_f} - Acc_{e_f - 1}\right) < \Delta\delta \tag{3}$$

where e_f is the number of rounds elapsed when the task reaches the unavailable state, and $S_i^{T_x}$ denotes the state exhibited by task T_x at the ith round.

Since the speed of watermark extinction is smaller than the speed of watermark creation, two watermark tasks T_1 and T_2 corresponding to two watermark datasets of the same size are taken as an example, assuming that task T_1 rotates with task T_2 after reaching the unavailable state, and task T_2 needs to rotate when it reaches the unavailable state, task T_1, with which it should rotate, does not completely extinguish, thus will continue to watermark tasks from the partially extinguished state, and this time the number of turns required to reach the unavailable state will be lower than the number of turns required to reach the unavailable state in the previous time, that is, after k times of the above repeated exchanges, the initial state of both tasks will become unavailable and the subsequent tasks cannot be completed. The number of rounds required for both tasks to reach the unavailable state is

$$e_f^{T_1} + e_f^{T_2} + \sum_{i=1}^{k} (e_{dis_i}^{T_1} + e_{dis_i}^{T_2}) \tag{4}$$

where $e_{dis_i}^{T_1}$ denotes the number of rounds elapsed when task T_1 reaches the unavailable state again at the i-th extinction. Therefore, with the same size of watermarking dataset, the number of datasets required to complete the entire federated learning training can be determined by determining the creation rate and extinction rate of watermarking tasks.

To ensure observability of watermark completion, i.e., to be able to completely quantify the training behavior of worker nodes, the watermark data needs to have different patterns. In theory, when the given watermarking dataset is large enough, the state of that watermarking task may not reach the unavailable state during the whole execution of the training task. This reduces the complexity of watermark rotation to a certain extent, but also lengthens the time required for the entire training task, and may even appear that the time spent on the watermarking task far exceeds the time spent on the main task, which is undoubtedly more than worth the loss. Instead, consider another scenario: prepare a number of small-scale watermarking data for constant rotation. This approach reduces the time taken by the watermarking task, but it injects a large number of backdoors into the model, which has a significant impact on the security of the model. In addition, there is a potential pitfall of small-scale datasets, namely, the accuracy of backdoor watermarking can no longer accurately quantify the training behavior of workers before all rounds of training tasks are completed, and frequent replacement of watermarked datasets will increase the communication overhead of worker nodes in terms of data acquisition.

Communication bottleneck has been one of the important problems facing federated learning. During the whole training process of federated learning, the communication between task publisher and worker nodes is focused on exchanging model data and replacing watermark datasets. Since the volume of model data is significantly smaller than that of watermarked datasets, the main communication overhead mainly comes from the transfer of watermarked datasets. Although the addition of watermarked datasets increases the communication overhead of federated learning, this part of consumption can be minimized by a reasonable dataset size design.

5 Feasibility Analysis of Training Behavior Monitoring Mechanism

The feasibility analysis of the training behavior supervision mechanism includes the analysis of the inherent characteristics of digital watermarking, the analysis of the data independence of worker nodes, and the analysis of the additional computational cost introduced. The training behavior supervision in federated learning uses digital watermarking technology, and although it is different from the traditional model protection application scenario, the inherent characteristics of digital watermarking technology should be retained intact, i.e., the original functionality of the model and the security of the watermark should not be destroyed; secondly, the inclusion of the watermarked dataset should not have an impact on the independence of the local data of the worker nodes; finally, for the additional watermarking verification process introduced, a comparison with DDSM for a comparative analysis on computational and communication redundancy.

- The original functionality of the model is not destroyed

That is, the watermarking task cannot have an impact on the main task, both tasks need to be performed independently and both perform well on the relevant targeted tests. Therefore, the model obtained by noting the participation in the watermarking task is M′, and M′ should satisfy the following conditions.

$$\underset{x \in D/T}{Pr}[f(d) \neq Classify(M', d)] \leq \varepsilon$$
$$and \underset{x \in T}{Pr}[T_L(d) \neq Classify(M', d)] \leq \varepsilon \tag{5}$$

The total error rate of M′ is at most $\varepsilon' = \varepsilon + n/|D|$, since D is much larger than n, ε' will be infinitely close to ε. In summary, the watermarking task can be performed simultaneously with the main task while ensuring that the main task is not disturbed.

- Security

Security refers to the fact that the watermark itself is not easy to forge. The guarantee of watermark security mainly comes from two aspects: first, in the construction of the watermark dataset, the choice of using the insertion of specific patterns on irrelevant data, the size and color of the patterns are specified by the task publisher, which creates difficulties for the forgery of the dataset; second, forging the watermark dataset does not bring expected or additional benefits to the worker nodes, and the bad behavior they show in the training behavior will probably lead to their disqualification from participating in the next round of training.

For the watermarked dataset $\mathrm{T} = \{t^{(1)}, \ldots, t^{(1)}\}$ and the watermarked dataset label $T_L = \{T_L^{(1)}, \ldots, T_L^{(n)}\}$, the task publisher has absolute control as well as the right to know. Even if a worker forges the backdoor watermark dataset T_{false} and submits the model $M_{local}^{T_{false}}$, it will still be checked out at the WorkerEval() step as follows.

$$VmAcc_{test}^{c} \leftarrow M_{local}^{T_{false}} + T < VmAcc_{test}^{c} \leftarrow \mathrm{M}_{local}^{c} + T \tag{6}$$

- Data independence of worker nodes

The task publisher does not need to know any prior knowledge of the training data during the whole federated learning process, and the task publisher does not need the training data of worker nodes to generate its own watermark sequence, and the data of worker nodes will be saved locally independently to meet the requirements of federated learning.

- Computational cost analysis

The computational cost includes computational resources and communication volume. In the work of Somy et al. [33] (DDSM), DOs need to sign offline agreements with a certain number of COs and securely send subsets of data to selected COs, and to ensure data privacy, DOs need to partition the entire dataset such that each CO has a range of all classes and values for which the subset does not contain data, and the subset cannot contain a single class from most of the data. The solution to the problem of false training by COs is to perform replication of data subsets among multiple COs, as shown in Fig. 4. During federated learning training, model training is performed by all m*n COs holding subsets of the dataset, so that when a dishonest CO reports false information about training behavior, it can be compared with other COs of the same replicated subset, as long as the dishonest CO node is less than one-half of the total number of COs, the dishonest behavior of that CO can be identified.

Assume that there are m copies of data involved in training in each round, i.e., m DOs in DDSM, m × n COs in training, and m worker nodes in WM-TBM in training. Let the GPU computational resources required for training a data of size S be c.

The computational resources required for training and the computational resources required for validation in the DDSM are

$$C_{Train} = m \times n \times c \tag{7}$$

$$C_{Verify} = m \times n \times (m \times n - 1) \tag{8}$$

Therefore, the total computational resource consumption of DDSM is

$$C_{Total} = C_{Train} + C_{Verify} = m \times n \times c + m \times n \times (m \times n - 1) \tag{9}$$

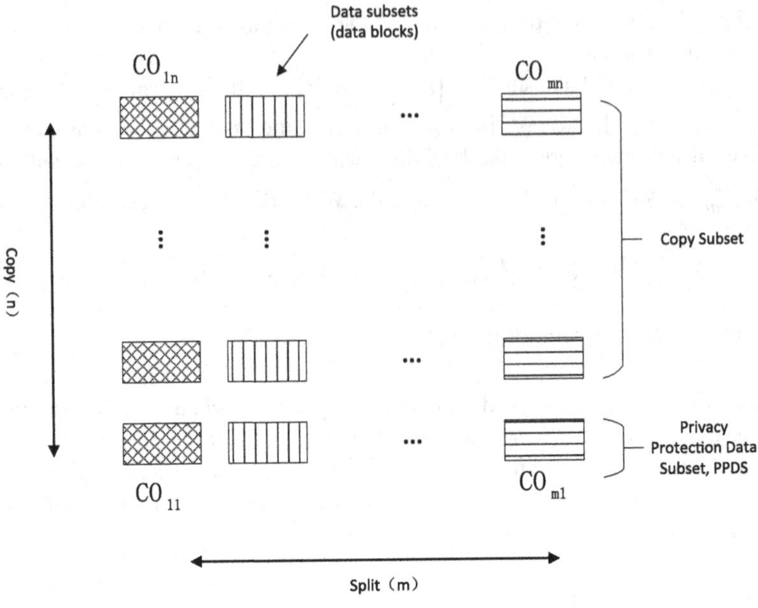

Fig. 4. DDSM Solutions

In WM-TBM, the size of the watermarked dataset received by the worker nodes is W, so the computational resources required for each round of training and the computational resources required for validation are:

$$C_{W-Train} = m \times c \tag{10}$$

$$C_{W-Verify} = m \times c \times \frac{W}{S} \tag{11}$$

Therefore, the total computational resource consumption of WM-TBM is

$$C_{W-Total} = C_{W-Train} + C_{W-Verify} = m \times c + m \times c \times \frac{W}{S} \tag{12}$$

Define the savings index C_{Save} as the ratio of the computational resources required by DDSM to those required by WM-TBM, so that when the value of C_{Save} is greater than 1, it indicates that WM-TBM performs better.

$$C_{Save} = \frac{C_{Total}}{C_{W-Total}} = \frac{S}{S+W}(n + m \times n^2 \times \frac{1}{c} - \frac{n}{c}) \tag{13}$$

The analysis of the values of C_{Save} using modeling is distinguished from centralized training in that the number of worker nodes required for federated learning is at least 2, i.e., $m \geq 2$; in addition, DDSM requires segmentation and replication of the dataset, i.e., $n \geq 2$. Consider two configurations of watermarked dataset sizes, one for the normal training case where the watermarked dataset is much smaller than the training dataset,

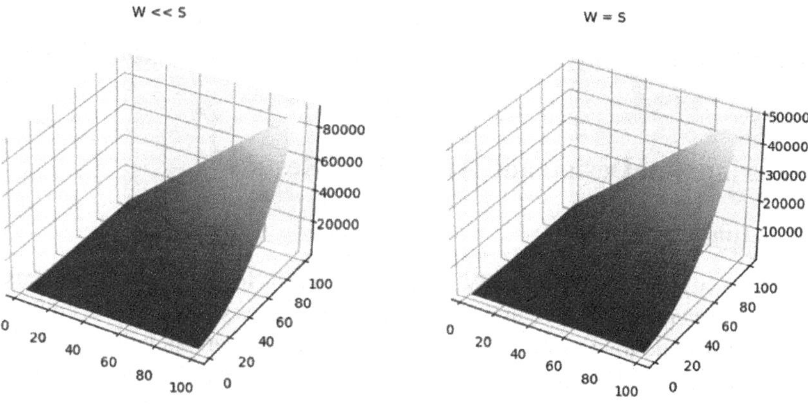

Fig. 5. Comparison results of computing resources

and the second for the extreme case where the watermarked dataset is the same size as the training set, and the results obtained are shown in Fig. 5.

The minimum values obtained for the two configuration cases are 2.834 as well as 5.152, which are in accordance with the expected logic. In summary, WM-TBM can save more computational resources than DDSM when the federated learning condition is satisfied, and the improvement of this saving index is more obvious as the scale of federated learning increases.

In terms of communication volume, assuming that the communication volume required to transmit a data set of size S is t_1 and the communication volume required to transmit model parameters is t_2, the transmission of model parameters is mainly divided into two transmission processes, namely, transmission from CO to blockchain and downloading parameters from blockchain by MO, so the communication volume required by DDSM is

$$T_{Total} = T_{dataset} + T_{model} = m \times t_1 + m \times n \times t_2 \times 2 \tag{14}$$

The amount of communication required by the WM-TBM is:

$$T_{W-Total} = T_{W-dataset} + T_{W-model} = m \times t_1 \times \frac{W}{S} + m \times t_2 \tag{15}$$

Define T_{Save} as the difference between the amount of communication required by the DDSM and the amount of communication required by the WM-TBM. Similarly, a value of T_{Save} greater than 0 indicates that the WM-TBM performs better:

$$T_{Save} = T_{Total} - T_{W-Total} = m \times t_1 \times (1 - \frac{W}{S}) + m \times t_2(2 \times n - 1) \tag{16}$$

The size of the validation dataset W is much smaller than the size of the training dataset S. Therefore, $T_{Save} > 0$ holds for both DDSM and WM-TBM configurations, so the amount of communication required by WM-TBM is always smaller than that of DDSM.

In summary, WM-TBM has a very obvious advantage over DDSM in terms of computation and communication volume, especially when the scale of federated learning is large.

6 Experimental Design and Analysis of Results

6.1 Experimental Design

In order to verify the feasibility of WM-TBM, a total of five sets of experiments are designed for watermarking task impact validation, watermarking dataset usability validation, worker node training behavior authenticity assessment validation, watermarking task periodicity validation, and watermarking dataset rotation validation from the perspective of watermarking task itself and watermarking dataset replacement.

The experiments use the Cifar10 dataset, and the watermark dataset is a small-scale dataset constructed according to the above watermark dataset construction method.

6.2 Analysis of Experimental Results

Experiment 1: Impact Validation of the Watermarking Task. The Cifar10 dataset is used for the classification task in a federated environment, the aggregation algorithm uses the federated average algorithm, and the dataset is subjected to non-IID processing. The results obtained by running 1000 rounds each without and with the watermarking task, where the size of the watermarked data for the watermarking task is 1000, the number of locally set workers is 4, and the number of local rounds for training each worker locally is 5, are shown in Fig. 6.

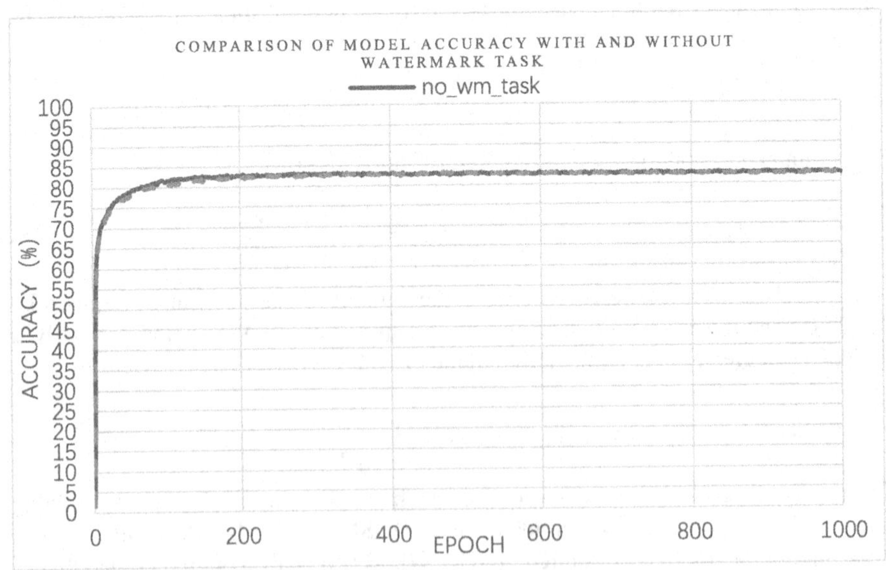

Fig. 6. Comparison of model accuracy with and without watermarking task

From the experimental results, it can be seen that the convergence trend of the accuracy of the resulting model on the main task is smooth with or without the watermarking task involved, and eventually converges to about 82%, which shows that the watermarking task does not have an impact on the main task.

Experiment 2: Watermarking Dataset Availability Validation. The size of the watermarked dataset was experimented from 100–1000 in units of 100 to obtain the number of rounds required for its creation and extinction, respectively, and the experimental results are shown in Fig. 7.

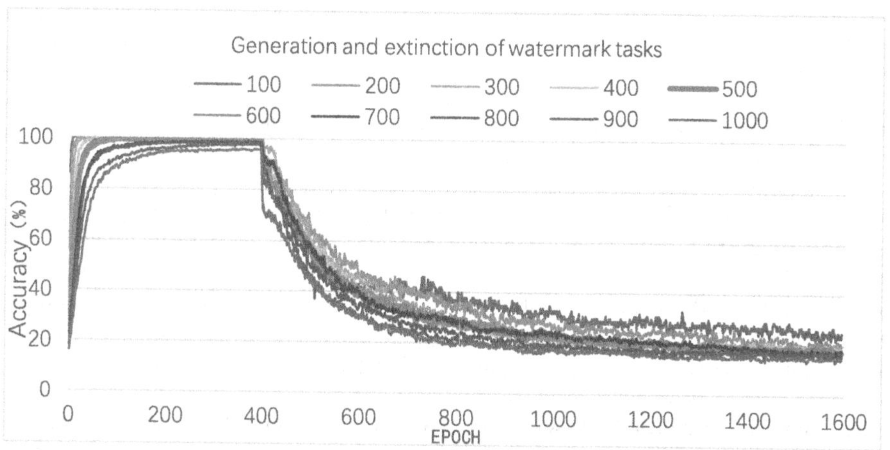

Fig. 7. The generation and extinction cycle of watermarking

As can be seen from the experimental results, the extinction of the watermark task will remain at a uniform level for a long time after maintaining it for a period of time, so it is unwise to wait for its accuracy rate to extinguish to zero before rotation, and the rotation operation can be performed when the extinction rate of the watermark task is reduced to a point where the floating change is not significant.

In order to determine the unavailability status of the watermark, the data of the first 100 rounds of the task are organized separately as follows (Fig. 8).

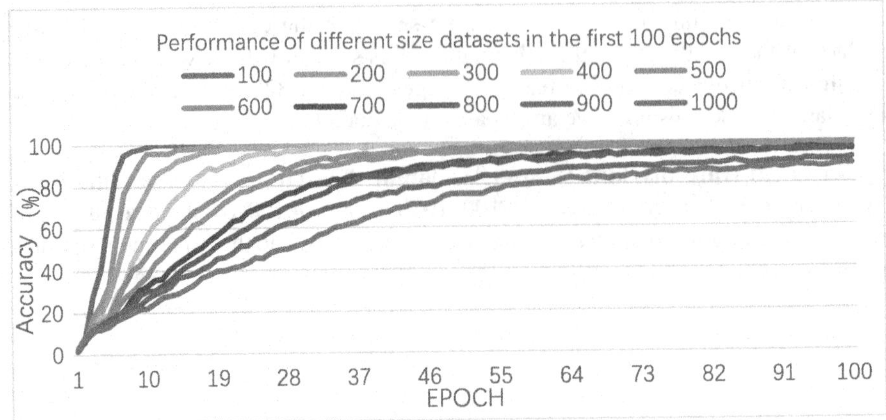

Fig. 8. Performance of different dataset sizes in the first 100 rounds

From the above experimental results, it is clear that watermarked datasets of different sizes have roughly the same trend in convergence; however, the dataset with a data size of 1000, for example, has a relatively flat convergence rate, and the difference in accuracy from round to round is not very helpful in determining the training behavior. Therefore, in subsequent experiments, a dataset of size 800 that can be maintained for as many rounds as possible while observing significant changes was chosen.

Experiment 3: Authenticity Assessment of Workers Training Behavior Validation. In the following experiments, one worker among all four workers will be randomly selected for spurious training, and the local model submitted by the worker will be examined for the watermarking task before aggregation, and it will be determined whether the worker has been trained or not. The results of the experiments are shown in Fig. 9.

From the experimental results, it is clear that the inspection before aggregation can accurately quantify the training behavior of workers. The local models submitted by workers with dishonest training behavior have a large gap in testing accuracy on the watermarking dataset with the local models submitted by worker nodes that honestly perform training, and therefore, dishonest workers can be identified.

Experiment 4: Periodic Validation of the Watermarking Task. Define the observable coefficient as 2 and the tolerable coefficient as 3. When the current watermarking data task reaches the unavailable state, the execution of the watermarking task is canceled, and the above task is continued after the extinction rate of the watermarking task is stabilized. The experimental results are shown in Fig. 10.

Worker 1 does not participate in training

Worker 1 Worker 2 Worker 3 Worker 4

All workers participate in training

Worker 1 Worker 2 Worker 3 Worker 4

Worker 4 does not participate in training

Worker 1 Worker 2 Worker 3 Worker 4

All workers participate in training

Worker 1 Worker 2 Worker 3 Worker 4

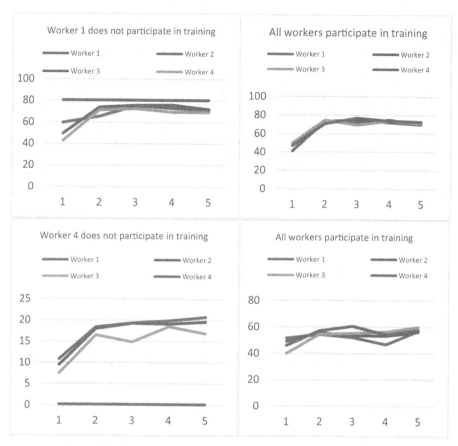

Fig. 9. Comparison of the training behavior of workers

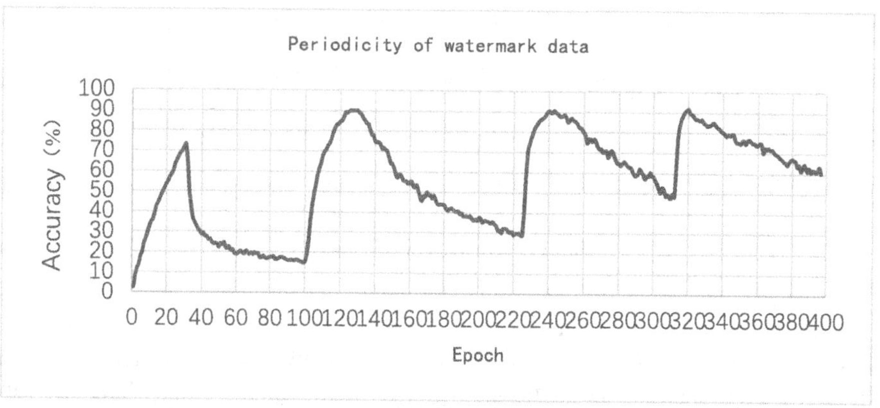

Fig. 10. Periodicity of watermarked data

From the experimental results, it can be seen that the watermarking task is cyclical in nature. And in each cycle of watermarking, its extinction rate is much smaller than the generation rate, and the watermarked dataset of size 800 has reached the unusable state after only 9 rounds at the fourth cycle.

Experiment 5: Watermarking Data Set Rotation Verification. Two watermark datasets of size 800, D_1 and D_2, are added to the training process, and when D_1 reaches the unusable state, the D_2 dataset is used for rotation, and the two datasets are worked on alternately. Before performing the dataset replacement, it is necessary to know the performance of both datasets on the model when they are not involved in the watermarking task, and experiments are conducted on both datasets to obtain the following results (Table 1).

Table 1. Performance of the watermarked dataset on the model when the watermarking task is not joined

Dataset	Major Task Test Set	Watermark dataset
D_1	82.60	9.875
D_2	82.64	9.625

With both watermarked datasets participating in the rotation, the experimental results are shown in Fig. 11.

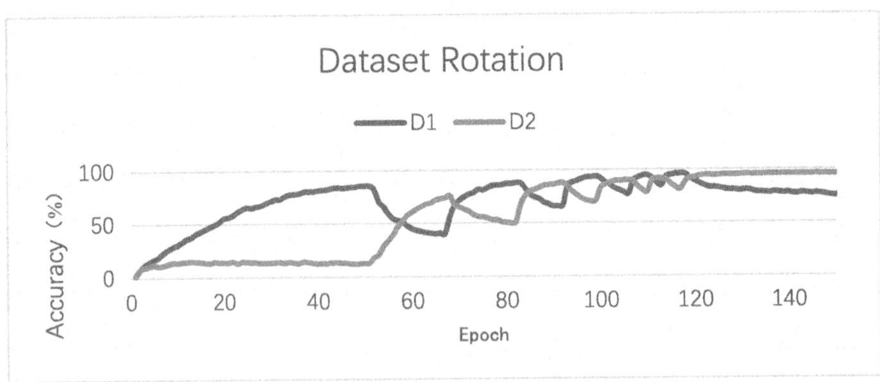

Fig. 11. Rotation of the dataset

From the experimental results, it can be seen that the rotation of watermarking datasets is feasible. Although the availability of the two watermarking datasets is in a gradually decreasing trend during the crossover for training, the watermarking task can be made complete by configuring a suitable number of replacement datasets to cover the whole federated learning process and to quantify the training behavior of the worker nodes completely.

7 Summary

In this paper, we propose a new digital watermarking-based training behavior authenticity supervision mechanism WM-TBM for decentralized federated learning, which motivates worker nodes to remain honest when participating in federated learning by supervising the authenticity of their training behavior. Specifically, the quantification of the authenticity of worker nodes' training behavior is accomplished by transposing the usage scenario of digital watermarking technology to decentralized federated learning worker node training behavior supervision. Theoretical analysis demonstrates that WM-TBM can save significant computational and communication resources compared to the existing scheme DDSM. The effectiveness of WM-TBM and the practicability of dataset replacement theory are then further verified through experiments, which effectively solve the problems in the current research on worker node training behavior supervision mechanism in decentralized federated learning oriented.

Acknowledgments. This work was supported by the National Natural Science Foundation of China (grant numbers U2003206 and U20B2048), the Defense Industrial Technology Development Program (grant number 2020604B004), and the Heilongjiang Provincial Natural Science Foundation of China (grant number LH2021F016).

References

1. Jiang, H., et al.: An energy-efficient framework for internet of things underlaying heterogeneous small cell networks. IEEE Trans. Mob. Comput. **21**(1), 31–43 (2020)
2. Dai, X., et al.: Task co-offloading for D2D-assisted mobile edge computing in industrial internet of things. IEEE Trans. Industr. Inform. (2022)
3. Xiao, Z., et al.: TrajData: on vehicle trajectory collection with commodity plug-and-play OBU devices. IEEE Internet Things J. **7**(9), 9066–9079 (2020)
4. Long, W., et al.: Unified spatial-temporal neighbor attention network for dynamic traffic prediction. IEEE Trans. Veh. Technol. (2022)
5. Jiang, H., et al.: Joint task offloading and resource allocation for energy-constrained mobile edge computing. IEEE Trans. Mob. Comput. (2022)
6. Xiao, Z., et al.: Resource management in UAV-assisted MEC: state-of-the-art and open challenges. Wireless Netw. **28**(7), 3305–3322 (2022)
7. Wang, L., et al.: Multiple access mmWave design for UAV-aided 5G communications. IEEE Wirel. Commun. **26**(1), 64–71 (2019)
8. Chen, H., Chen, J., Ding, J.: Data evaluation and enhancement for quality improvement of machine learning. IEEE Trans. Reliab. **70**(2), 831–847 (2021)
9. Konen, J., Mcmahan, H.B., Ramage, D., et al.: Federated optimization: distributed machine learning for on-device intelligence. arXiv:1610.02527 [cs] (2016)
10. Wang, L., Wu, K., Hamdi, M.: Combating hidden and exposed terminal problems in wireless networks. IEEE Trans. Wireless Commun. **11**(11), 4204–4213 (2012)
11. Mcmahan, H.B., Moore, E., Ramage, D., et al.: Communication-efficient learning of deep networks from decentralized data. arXiv:1602.05629 [cs] (2016)
12. Mcmahan, H.B., Moore, E., Ramage, D., et al.: Federated learning of deep networks using model averaging. arXiv:1602.05629 (2016)

13. Yang, Q., Liu, Y., Chen, T., et al.: Federated machine learning: concept and applications. ACM Trans. Intell. Syst. Technol. **10**(2), 1–19 (2019)
14. Nishant, B.S., Kalapriya, K., Vijay, A., et al.: Ownership preserving AI Market Places using Blockchain. In: 2019 IEEE International Conference on Blockchain (Blockchain), pp. 156–165. IEEE, Atlanta (2020)
15. Lu, Y.-L., Huang, X.-H., Dai, Y.-Y., et al.: Blockchain and federated learning for privacy-preserved data sharing in industrial IoT. IEEE Trans. Industr. Inf. **16**(6), 4177–4186 (2019)
16. Kang, J.-W., Xiong, Z.-H., Niyato, D., et al.: Incentive mechanism for reliable federated learning: a joint optimization approach to combining reputation and contract theory. IEEE Internet Things J. **6**(6), 10700–10714 (2019)
17. Weng, J.-S., Weng, J., Zhang, J., et al.: DeepChain: auditable and privacy-preserving deep learning with blockchain-based incentive. IEEE Trans. Dependable Secure Comput. **18**(5), 2438–2455 (2021)
18. Wang, H., Sreenivasan, K., Rajput, S., et al.: Attack of the tails: yes, you really can backdoor federated learning. In: Advances in Neural Information Processing Systems. (2020)
19. Schyndel, R., Tirkel, A.Z., Osborne, C.F.: A digital watermark. In: 1st International Conference on Image Processing, pp. 86–90. IEEE, Austin (1994)
20. Uchida, Y., Nagai, Y., Sakazawa, S., et al.: Embedding watermarks into deep neural networks. In: 2017 ACM on International Conference on Multimedia Retrieval, pp. 269–277. ACM, New York (2017)
21. Rouhani, B.D., Chen, H., Koushanfar, F.: DeepSigns: an end-to-end watermarking framework for ownership protection of deep neural networks. In: Twenty-Fourth International Conference on Architectural Support for Programming Languages and Operating Systems(ASPLOS), pp. 485–497. ACM, Providence (2019)
22. Adi, Y., Baum, C., Cisse, M., et al.: Turning your weakness into a strength: watermarking deep neural networks by backdooring. In: 27th USENIX Security Symposium, pp. 1615–1631. USENIX, Baltimore (2018)
23. Guo, J., Potkonjak, M.: Watermarking deep neural networks for embedded systems. In: 2018 IEEE/ACM International Conference on Computer-Aided Design (ICCAD), pp. 1–8. IEEE, San Diego (2018)
24. Jebreel, N.M., Domingo-Ferrer, J., Sánchez, D., et al.: KeyNet: an asymmetric key-style framework for watermarking deep learning models. Appl. Sci. **11**(3), 999–1021 (2021)
25. Zhang, J.-L., Gu, Z.-S., Jang, J.-Y., et al.: Protecting intellectual property of deep neural networks with watermarking. In: 2018 on Asia Conference on Computer and Communications Security, pp. 159–172. ACM, Incheon (2018)
26. Zhu, R., Zhang, X., Shi, M., et al.: Secure neural network watermarking protocol against forging attack. EURASIP J. Image Video Process. **37**(2020) (2020)
27. Li, Z., Hu, C.-Y., Zhang, Y., et al.: How to prove your model belongs to you: a blind-watermark based framework to protect intellectual property of DNN. In: The 35th Annual Computer Security Applications Conference, pp. 126–137. ACM, San Juan (2019)
28. Atli, B.G., Xia, Y.-X., Marchal, S., et al.: WAFFLE: watermarking in federated learning. arXiv:2008.07298 [cs] (2020)
29. Li, F.-Q., Wang, S.-L.: Towards practical watermark for deep neural networks in federated learning. arXiv:2105.03167 [cs] (2021)
30. Chen, M., Niu, X., Yang, Y.: The reach developments and applications of digital watermarking. J. Commun. **22**(5), 71–79 (2001)
31. Boenisch, F.: A systematic review on model watermarking for neural networks. Front Big Data **4**, 1–16 (2021)

32. Wang, T., Kerschbaum, F.: Robust and undetectable white-box watermarks for deep neural networks. arXiv:1910.14268 [cs] (2019)
33. Somy, N.B., et al.: Ownership preserving AI market places using blockchain. In: 2019 IEEE International Conference on Blockchain (Blockchain). IEEE (2019)

Exploration and Practice of Course Homework Metaverse Based on Extended Reality Under Edge Computing

Jinrong Fu[1], Yiwen Liu[1,2,3](✉), Haobo Yan[1], Yanxia Gao[1,2,3], and Jianhua Xiao[1,2,3]

[1] School of Computer and Artificial Intelligence, Huaihua University, Huaihua 418000, China
87134537@qq.com

[2] Key Laboratory of Wuling-Mountain Health Big Data Intelligent Processing and Application in Hunan Province Universities, Huaihua 418000, China

[3] Key Laboratory of Intelligent Control Technology for Wuling-Mountain Ecological Agriculture in Hunan Province, Huaihua 418000, China

Abstract. The metaverse originated from science fiction at first, but it gradually came into reality with the continuous power of technology. Aiming at the problems of course work in Chinese universities, such as its function is weakened or suppressed, its form is too abstract, and it lacks elaborate design, this paper proposes a design method of course work meta-universe based on extended reality under edge computing. XR technology is used to realize the interactive immersion of the coursework meta-universe, in order to improve students' learning enthusiasm and ability to solve abstract problems. Based on the international perspective, this paper systematically combs and analyzes the integration architecture, application scenarios and future trends of the meta-universe education application based on Edge computing (MEC). Four key processes are described: teacher-student interaction, data collection, data feedback and comprehensive evaluation. In order to promote the application of the metaverse in the field of education to provide mirror. The validity of the method is illustrated by the data.

Keywords: Extended Reality · Edge Computing · Metaverse · Multi person collaboration

1 Introduction

In recent years, the concept of the metaverse has already set off a great stir in the current science and technology world, which has become one of the biggest points in the century of technological changes.

Jeremy, Virtual Human-Computer Interaction Laboratory, Stanford University Professor Bailenson points out that education is one of the "killer" application scenarios in the metaverse [1]. Professor FrankPiller of RWTH Aachen University is convinced that metaverse teaching is closer to the learning experience of classroom teaching than network teaching [2]. Professor Stylianos Mystakidis of the University of Patras points out

Z. Xiao et al. (Eds.): ICECI 2022, LNICST 478, pp. 262–276, 2023.
https://doi.org/10.1007/978-3-031-28990-3_18

that the metauniverse will become an important factor in promoting the democratization of education, enabling global learners to participate and learn together on an equal basis [3].

However, the current exploration of the educational application of the Metaverse is still in its infancy, lacking mature theoretical achievements and clear ideas for the construction and application [4].

Moreover, the Metaverse is a virtual digital world, and to be highly synchronized with the real society, the scenes in the real world must be materialized into the virtual world, such as in the form of data [5, 6]. Therefore, the first thing to be solved is the problem of data transmission.

However, the original cloud computing method will lead to many problems such as high delay, high cost, low experience and low data processing capacity in the Metaverse and extended reality interaction, which makes the Metaverse education and extended reality technology unable to be really applied. In addition, deploying XR devices equipped with Mobile Edge Computing (MEC) [7] servers to provide computing services at the edge of the network has also become an emerging approach to Metaverse education.

In view of this, based on the international perspective, this study will systematically sort out and analyze the fusion architecture, application scenarios and future trends of the Metaverse education application based on Edge computing (MEC) [8], in order to provide a mirror for promoting the application of Metaverse in the education field, and propose a distributed security architecture based on master-slave multi chain, breaking through the traditional single chain performance bottleneck. Table 1 below shows the concepts and technologies that are characteristic of the Metaverse.

Table 1. Related concepts and technologies with characteristics of the metaverse.

Time	Name	Technology	Important changes
In 1992	Snow Crash	concept	The concept of "Metaverse" was put forward for the first time
In 2003	Second Life	Internet	The most popular virtual world game in the world
Since 2006	Roblox	Metaverse and VR	It is the first public offering with the concept of metaverse, allowing users to construct 3D and VR, and design their own interactive activities to achieve their own content creation
In 2009	Open Simulator	Multiple clients	The world's first open source multi-client, multi-protocol access 3D virtual world server, it provides a distributed configuration solution for the construction of the metaverse
Since 2018	Ready Player One	Virtual World	Breaking down the boundary between reality and games, bringing the "Metaverse" to the masses

2 Related Work

2.1 Overview and Research Status of Extended Reality (XR)

Extended reality (XR), as the development trend of virtual technology in the future, is actually a general term, which includes VR, MR and AR, namely virtual reality (VR), mixed reality (MR), augmented reality (AR) and everything in between [9]. The following table (Table 2) shows the differences between VR, MR and AR.

However, with the continuous update of technology, the concepts of the three are often confused. XR is now commonly used to refer to this type of highly interactive "Virtual World" created using computers.

Table 2. Comparison Among VR/MR/AR

Comparison Item	Virtual Reality	Mixed Reality	Augmented Reality
Common display devices	VR glasses ,HMD helmet	MR glasses, Holographic projection	Phone,Projector
Common auxiliary interactive equipment	Handle, eye tracker, motion capture equipment	Hand capture	Not necessarily required
Current limitations	Fixed display space layout and positioning equipment are required	The software needs to be installed in the user's mobile phone in advance	The sense of immersion is weak, the motion capture is unstable.
Main advantages at present	Widely used and mature technology	It has broad development prospects, is not limited by space, and has a better user experience	It is not limited by space, portable, low cost and easy to promote

Since Ivan Sutherland, the father of computer graphics, designed the first head mounted AR and VR combined display (HMD: Head Mounted Display) in 1968, it has always been human's dream to recreate a world.

Although the concept of XR was put forward many years ago, it has been limited by computer software and hardware, and XR technology has not been well developed and applied. Nowadays, the development of digital twins, computer graphics, human-computer interaction and other technologies have paved the way for the advent of the virtual world.

XR technology has gradually entered the public's vision and has been applied into various fields. Based on the increasing popularity of Virtual Reality (VR) and Augmented Reality (AR) applications, on March 7th, 2022, Professor Georgios Minopoulos and Professor Konstantinos E. Psannis revealed the necessity of implementing Extended Reality (XR) to users and proposed a simplified Tangible XR system to solve Opportunities and Challenges of Tangible XR Applications for 5G Networks and Beyond.

On February 10th, 2022, Professor BaoTrinh and Professor Gabriel-Miro Muntean proposed a resource management scheme for SDN-MEC supporting XR application, based on deep reinforcement learning.

2.2 Bloom Model

B.J.Bloom, an American educational psychologist, divides educational goals into three fields [10]: cognitive field, emotional field and operational field, which constitute the educational goal system.

In the field of cognitive learning, the teaching objectives are divided into eight levels which include memorization, understanding, application, analysis, synthesis, evaluation, design and innovation from the lowest to the highest.

Although the traditional course homework also adopts a similar model, Bloom model pays more attention to the role and relationship of these eight levels, which is more in line with the blended teaching structure once required by the "Golden class [11]".

Under the background of "Internet + Education", scholars at home and abroad have focused on blended teaching, and the course assignments realized by expanding reality and blended teaching based on Bloom theoretical model will become a new trend of contemporary education development in the future.

3 Metaverse and Edge Computing Fusion Architecture

3.1 Overall Architecture Design

With the advent of the 5G era, the 5G cloud network fusion service gateway for the educational metauniverse is deployed by combining the 5G network, the double gigabit education private network and the 5G base station, which supports routing, bridging, bypass and other modes.

Flexible deployment is made according to the equipment of the metauniverse immersion, making it possible to interact with the multi-user metauniverse network. Compared with the previous network environment, 5G environment can realize real-time XR image transmission, natural image and voice transmission, seamless cross-ground interaction, real-time sharing of big data, and smooth metaverse application transmission.

There are new developments in network slicing technology. This technology can through virtualization technology will calculation, storage and network resources and dedicated hardware decoupling, form a unified resource pool, according to a certain operation rules for different requirements of applications, meet different demand for resources, make the best use of existing hardware resources [12, 13] form a reliable virtual network environment. This environment can serve as the basis for the implementation of an edge computing system architecture. The overall architecture is shown in Fig. 1 below.

However, at this stage, VR/AR/MR There are problems such as high investment cost of computer teaching and lack of unified operation and management mechanism. The development of the meta universe also has problems such as industrial support, difference in ideas, and imperfect governance system of the meta universe.

In the course of multi person collaboration, the meta universe proposed by me decreases the throughput of the network due to the increase of network data volume. There are problems such as insufficient processing capacity of huge data, extended transmission time, and information loss. In order to meet the needs of delay sensitive businesses, and solve the problems of Internet device security authentication, limited

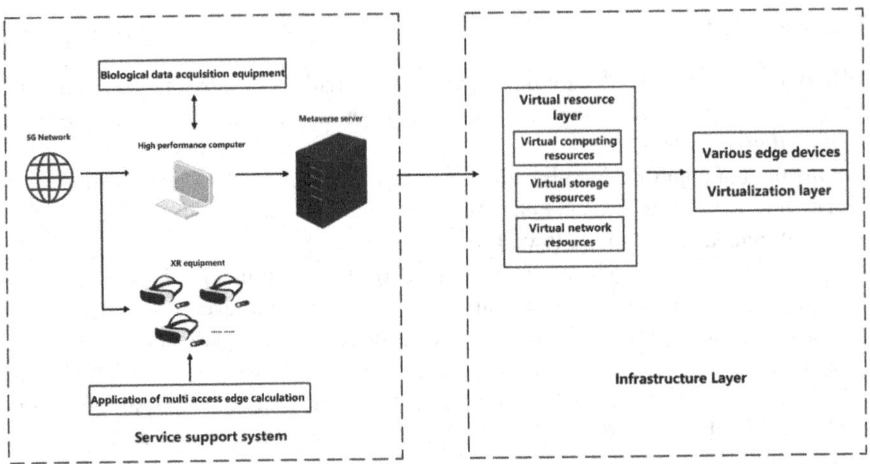

Fig. 1. Overall architecture diagram.

edge server resources, etc., time delay and security are taken as optimization goals, The improved deep reinforcement learning algorithm is used to allocate the resources of the meta universe scene.

To solve the optimization problem of network congestion control, the original edge computing architecture is not suitable for the course assignment universe I designed, and its edge nodes have poor security and high latency.

In order to solve the problems of data security, privacy protection and high latency caused by the original edge computing mode, this paper proposes a distributed secure trusted authentication model based on edge computing. Based on the traditional single chain, a master-slave multi chain structure is designed, and a three-tier architecture is deployed by integrating edge computing; It is predicted that this model is safe and reliable.

Compared with the single chain architecture of traditional deployment mode, the storage overhead is reduced by 50% on average, and the delay will also be significantly reduced. Compared with the existing schemes, the scheme in this paper has greater advantages in throughput.

The ratio of transmission rate to throughput will reach 1:1, which can meet the practical application requirements of large-scale meta universe, with high scalability and high security It makes the network load more balanced and avoids network congestion, providing a basis for design and testing.

3.2 Service Support System

To build an educational metaverse, hardware should be configured in the 5G network coverage environment, the central server of the metaverse should be deployed, and each learner should be equipped with a set of virtual reality equipment.

Second, it should be configured with a high performance computer in the meta-universe environment, the operating system must be Windows10 or above version, the processor is intelcorei5-4590 with the same performance and above, and the graphics card is NVIDIA GeForce GTX970 with the same performance and above. It should also be configured with gigabit wired network port and 5G router.

Network port, router and computer network cable require six types of cable and above specifications. For users, multiple access devices can be configured, such as smart phones, tablets and other wireless devices to directly access the server, high performance computers can also be used to access the web, or directly with the server for wired streaming connection to access the meta-universe content.

At the same time, the bioelectrical analysis of learners should also be equipped with physiological analysis equipment, mainly including ECG, EEG, skin and other biological collection equipment, which is used to detect the changes of immersion, concentration, flow experience and other conditions of learners when they are immersed in the metaverse environment. In order not to affect the immersion of learners, the bioelectricity collection equipment does not choose professional medical psychological analysis equipment, but simple equipment such as hand bracelet, maker brain wave kit, maker skin electric kit and so on.

3.3 Infrastructure Layer

The infrastructure layer is the lowest layer of the entire network architecture, including the hardware resource layer, virtualization layer and virtual resource layer.

The hardware resource layer consists of a large number of geographically dispersed edge devices of different types and models, which can provide computing, storage, and network resources for the network system.

However, since many edge devices are simple iot sensors, etc., with limited computing, storage and networking capabilities, lightweight virtualization technologies are needed to make full use of them [14]. The virtualization layer uses lightweight virtualization technology to achieve strong isolation of each virtual machine.

The micro operating system oriented to micro service or container runs in the virtual machine, which can simplify a lot of useless functions and realize the transformation of embedded device-level hardware resources into virtual resources [15]. In the virtual resource layer, hardware resources are virtualized into virtual computing, storage, and network resources, facilitating unified management and control.

4 Metaverse Data Analysis

It is difficult to use a consistent standard to judge the collected multi-dimensional user data due to its different dimensions, so entropy method is used for mining and analysis. The entropy method regards the object as a system, according to the probability Pi (I = 1, 2, …, m) to determine the entropy value E of the system, see Eq. (1). The smaller the entropy, the higher the stability.

$$\mathrm{e} = \sum\nolimits_{i=1}^{m} P_i \times lnP_i \tag{1}$$

At the same time, the combination of atomic economy algorithm and Cosine algorithm can calculate the similarity of the learner's behavior, see formula (2) and formula (3). In formula (2), AE is the atomic economic value, MW is the MolecularWeight, and AE is the percentage of the ratio between the molecular mass of educational output MW and the original educational input ΣMW. In Formula (3), (X1, X2) is the first kind of atomic economic value vector AE1, and (Y1, Y2) is the second kind of atomic economic value vector AE2. The cosine of the included Angle represents the similarity of learner behavior data. The closer the value is to 1, the more similar the two kinds of learning behaviors are.

$$\mathrm{AE} = \frac{\mathrm{MW}}{\Sigma MW} \times 100\% \tag{2}$$

$$\cos\theta = \frac{x_1x_2 + y_1y_2}{\sqrt{x_1^2 + y_1^2} + \sqrt{x_2^2 + y_2^2}} \tag{3}$$

5 Research Design

5.1 Extended Reality Based Metaverse of Course Homework

Taking *Principle of Computer Composition* as an example, the main teaching contents are decomposed based on Bloom model. There are some problems in traditional course homework, such as too abstract concept, repeated and rigid content, single evaluation method and so on. Here, we divide the Bloom model into four layers [16]. The first layer is to remember and understand; Application and analysis of the second layer; The third level is comprehensive evaluation; The fourth layer is design and innovation.

Comprehensive extension reality XR technology characteristics of the interaction of the different aspects of computer constitute principle design method, this article in view of the course content and extension reality (XR) technical characteristics of yuan respectively designed the universe VR, MR different application scenarios and AR, explore the three show effect in course feedback, interaction, and the difference between the usage scenario [17, 18]. The specific frame design is shown in Fig. 2 [18].

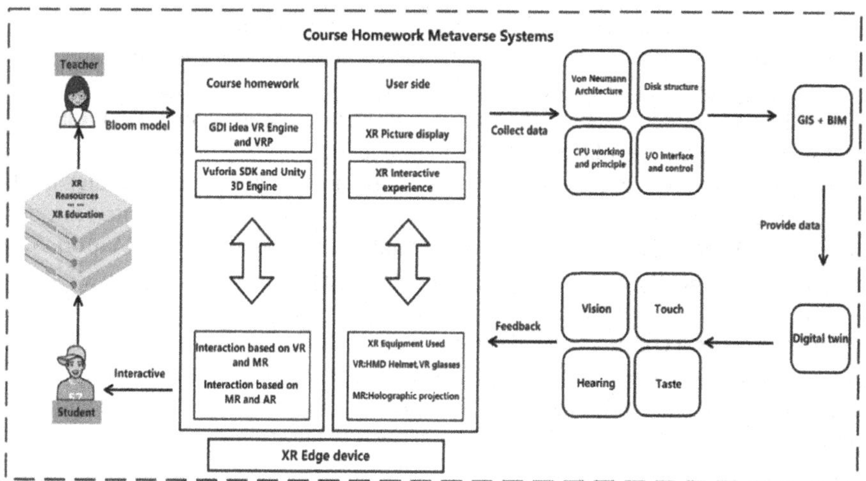

Fig. 2. A metaverse framework for course homework

5.2 Interaction Derived from VR and MR

XR technology as the core to establish teaching practice course assignments Metaverse, "expanding the real leading" hybrid teaching mode, will Bloom model with BOPPS mode structure of the hybrid teaching fusion, in combination with the practical situation of students in the learning process and the content of the course of computer constitute principle, design meet the requirements of the "Gold" gender once course assignments.

Based on BOPPPS teaching mode will "online and offline" organic integration of teaching, the autonomous learning before and after class and class feedback teaching, the combination of class assignments, students through XR platform into yuan universe on autonomous learning before class, by extending the reality (XR) technology design display of abstract concepts, build a model of the course assignments independently. For example, the 3D simulation based on the 3D engine Unity3D shows the abstract concept, and the ideaVR engine and VRP are added to the immersive VR and MR interactive system, so as to break the inherent abstract concept and enable students to immersive learning and achieve the first level of memorization and understanding.

5.3 Scenes Presented in AR and MR

The Metaverse of coursework designed in this paper enables students to master basic knowledge points by extending immersive online learning with realistic technology. Traditional teaching listens to students' expressions and communicates with students in class according to the feedback of offline learning effects and after the teacher's checking and making up for gaps and key breakthroughs. However, XR-based course work is highly interactive and expressive. Its core is supported by digital twin technology, which restores the teaching model one-to-one and collects students' learning data.

With the MR device, students can see the real image through the semi-permeable membrane lens, and the semi-permeable membrane can reflect the projection to superimpose the computer-rendered image onto the real image. MR devices can also draw images based on realistic scenes and allow users to see three-dimensional images through left-right eye disparity. Students can control the computer through gestures and voice. In the teaching activities of participatory learning, timely and targeted examination of students' learning effects, and guide students to draw inferences by analogy through AR model scenes, etc., to consolidate what they have learned.

The AR technology used starts with the course information and computer model data, and uses the graphics and modeling software to process the data into text, two-dimensional image, three-dimensional model and video. Combined with VuforiaSDK and Unity3D engine, the design and development of online computer hardware model interactive teaching system based on AR technology is realized. After class, homework should be adjusted according to the different learning effects of each student, and online and offline learning content and teaching methods should be adjusted according to the learning results of students to maximize the learning effect. In line with the second layer of application, analysis and the fourth layer of design, innovation.

5.4 Master Slave Multi Chain Design

In order to break through the bottleneck of traditional single chain performance, a master-slave multi chain structure is designed, as shown in Fig. 3 [20].

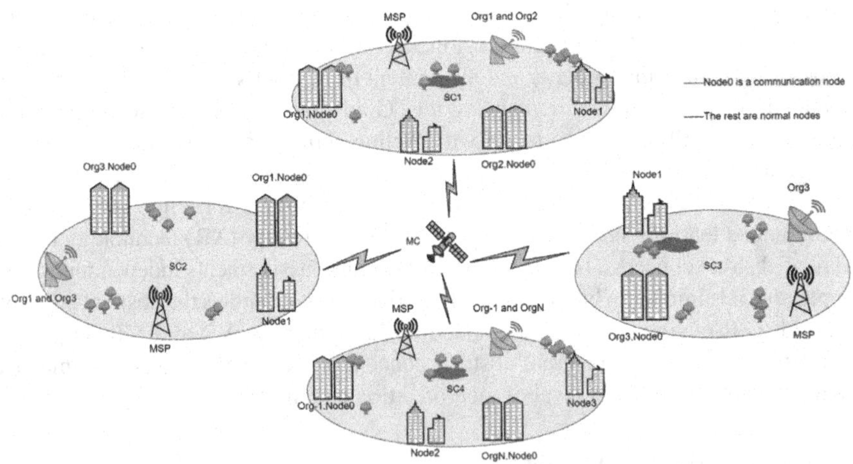

Fig. 3. Master-slave multi-chain structure

The master-slave multi chain structure includes a main chain (MC) and multiple slave chains (SC). As a trusted platform in the domain, the SC manages access operations in the domain, and defines common nodes and communication nodes.

Common nodes are responsible for data storage, communication nodes are the hub of network interaction, and connecting to MC. MC is the bridge of interaction between slave chains, which is used to resolve cross chain requests, Realize trusted identity authentication. MC defines communication nodes and cache nodes [21].

Communication nodes interact with SC networks to achieve interconnection and interworking between chains. Cache nodes cache cross domain data through CouchDB state database. Communication nodes form the index of MC and SC, connecting multiple SCs to form an infinitely expanded master-slave multi chain, It has good flexibility and scalability.

The membership service provider (MSP) is a certificate management server that participates in the maintenance of the local blockchain ledger, and conducts identity audit and certificate issuance for the nodes joining the blockchain.

The advantage of master-slave chain structure lies in its strong scalability. The slave chain can be dynamically expanded, so that the performance of the entire system will not be limited to a certain chain, breaking its scalability bottleneck.

As a trusted authentication platform, the main chain stores the hash time lock of its transactions, maintaining the atomicity of transactions between secondary chains.

5.5 Distributed Security Architecture Based on Master-Slave Multi Chain

Integrated edge computing under master slave multi chain, a three-layer distributed security architecture is designed, as shown in Fig. 4, including the device layer, slave chain network and master chain network, and three-layer bottom-up services.

The device layer provides trusted computing services for the upper layer. After the identity registration process, the edge devices in this layer access the slave chain network to form the "miner" of the slave chain network - the edge node (En).

En stores the data in the SC node after preprocessing, and the SC provides a secure data storage environment and access control within the domain for the devices in the current domain [22]; The communication nodes in SC and MC jointly maintain reliable communication and provide services for cross domain access control. The main chain network supports access across different SC domains.

The three-tier architecture covers the core functions of blockchain and edge computing, and provides distributed security services from different levels of storage, network and computing.

The slave chain and edge nodes in the architecture can be developed according to needs, and it is an unlimited expansion alliance.

(1) The lower layer is the device layer, which has two functional modules: the perception module and the device management module. The device management module has designed a secure access process based on cryptography, and the device can become a legitimate En only after being verified by this process.
(2) The middle layer is a slave link network, which includes two functional modules: data processing and intra domain access control.

    In the data processing module, En preprocesses the data collected by the device layer, packs them into blocks in a unified format, and stores them in the SC ledger; The intra domain access control module is the core function module of the middle layer, which realizes the intra domain access management of the Internet of Things.
(3) The upper layer is the main chain network. As a trusted sharing platform between domains, this layer is the controller for cross domain management of data.

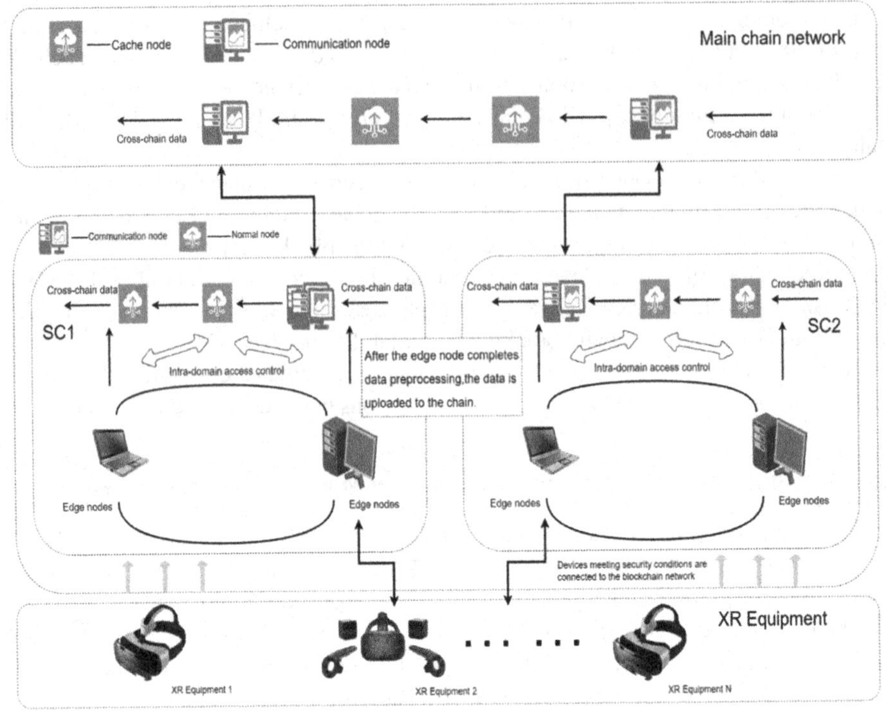

Fig. 4. Distributed Security Architecture

This layer is equipped with a cache module and an inter domain access control module. The inter domain access control module jointly manages cross domain access behavior with SC, and the cache module caches cross domain data and related information.

5.6 Metaverse Comprehensive Evaluation System

The Course homework Metaverse records the course work progress and standards achieved by each learning module. While paying attention to the learning process of students, the process evaluation of students is carried out, the behavior of students in the meta-universe is assessed, and the learning effect of students is evaluated through exams and tests. Course assignments with different difficult exercises and test, in view of teaching difficult point to incorporate knowledge in each layer of computer constitute principle, make learning content modular, convenient students according to their own needs in the yuan universe for selective learning, abstract concept abstract content by XR technology in coursework yuan show in the universe, enhance students' acceptance, deepen knowledge understanding. In teaching design, from the perspective of students, embodies the student-centered teaching idea, and designs meta-universe content in line with students' cognitive laws.

During teaching, students should pay close attention to students' feedback through interactive communication design, adjust teaching content and teaching strategies in time, and guide students to get timely answers to questions through active and active thinking and creative exploration activities. Teachers summarize and analyze the problems left by students in the meta-universe of course work before class, and explain these problems in simple and profound ways in class. After class, teachers assign homework of different difficulty to facilitate students of different levels to review, consolidate and apply the knowledge points, timely grasp the completion of students' homework, reasonably design the subsequent teaching content and teaching methods, and help each student to maximize the learning effect from the perspective of individualized teaching. In terms of the assessment content, the students' mastery of curriculum knowledge, emotional attitude and comprehensive ability are evaluated. The evaluation index system of the effect of students' learning advanced mathematics course and the teaching process of teachers is established based on the high order, innovation and challenge standards of "gold course".

5.7 Application Scenarios of the Coursework Metaverse

John Smart, the project leader of the American metaverse roadmap, proposed a very pioneering and inclusive metaverse application scenario classification framework [23], which was widely recognized because it reflected the consistency of cognition, body and environment, and had rich cognitive embodied thoughts and educational implications [24]. Contemporary embodied cognitive theory reexamines the relationship between body, cognition and the world, and proposes that "body is the core of cognitive process" and "cognition is generated in the interaction between body and environment" [25].

The accompanying embodied learning encourages and supports learners' embodied interaction and perceptual experience, aiming to realize the close coupling and dynamic evolution of learners, learning environment, learning resources and other elements. Embodied cognition theory provides a new perspective for understanding the educational application scenarios of the metaverse.

The learning process in the metaverse is embodied in the practice of the learner's body, that is, the interaction and interweaving between the body and the learning environment. Thus, the practice in the metaverse can be understood as Dewey's "learning by doing" [26].

6 Practical Challenges for Metaverse Educational Applications

Compared with foreign countries, Chinese researchers keep up with the frontiers of international metaverse research and have made preliminary achievements, but the depth of research and the breadth of practice need to be improved. At present, the metaverse has been widely concerned by the society, and the majority of educators have fully realized that the metaverse has important value in promoting education intelligence, realizing education scale and individuation. However, the current industrial layout of the metaverse has not yet been formed and is still in the initial exploration stage.

Since 2022, the governments of Wuxi, Beijing, Shanghai, Xiamen and many other places have stepped up the layout of the metaverse industry and issued intensive policies related to the development of the metaverse. However, few policies and technology enterprises have laid out the application of the metaverse education. How to fully implement the metacosmic educational application and how to form a scalable mature application mode is still a big problem in our educational circles.

Therefore, it is suggested that top-level design and scientific layout should be carried out at the national level, and development suggestions and construction guidelines for the application of metaverse education should be issued. To organize universities and scientific research institutions to set up specialized metaverse education and research institutions to carry out prospective research and solve difficult problems in the application of metaverse education; Combined with the strategic needs of the digital transformation of education, some typical and valuable metaverse education application models and cases are extracted and summarized, and first tried in the smart education demonstration zone to lead the educational innovation and application of the Metaverse.

7 Future Trends in Metaverse Educational Applications

The Metaverse is a new direction of online education [27], which is helpful to meet the growing lifelong learning needs of human beings and adapt to the needs of learners in school, family and society, and is of great significance for the construction of a learning society in which "everyone can learn, everywhere can learn, and can learn all the time".

With the development of Web3.0, XR, artificial intelligence, 5G and other technologies, the integration of virtual world and physical world will accelerate, and the metauniverse education application and market scale may show the following development trends [28]. Forecast of development trend is shown in Fig. 5 below.

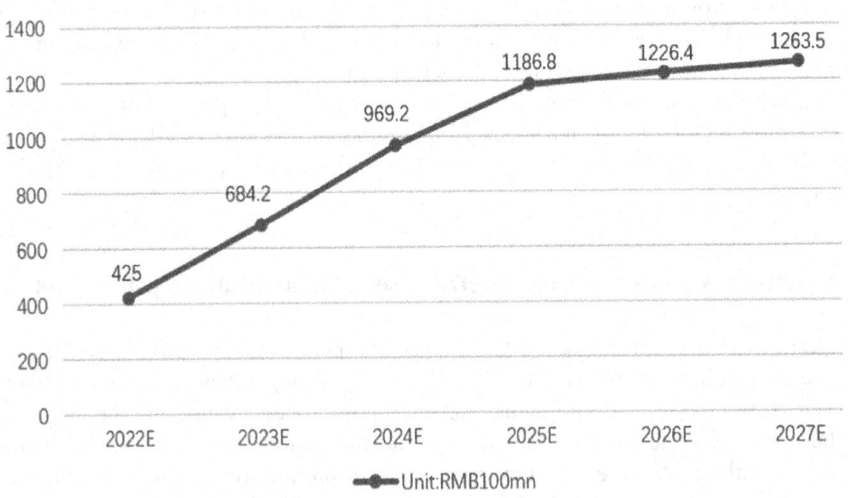

Fig. 5. Forecast of development trend

At present, VR/AR/MR has some problems, such as high investment cost and lack of unified operation and management mechanism. The development of the metaverse also has some problems, such as industrial support, concept differences, and imperfect governance system of the metaverse [29].

Looking into the future, in the era of 5G and 6G, the arrival of XR technology and the rise of the metauniverse will subvert the teaching method of computer teaching, reduce and reduce the cost of user terminals, unify the content of teaching resources, and greatly improve the quality of talent training.

The super-high-speed network experience will bring a qualitative and quantitative leap to computer teaching.

Especially with the popularity of 5G communication technology, the reduction of data delay and the increase of bandwidth, as well as the research and development of high-performance graphics processors, XR technology hardware can enter the mass production stage like smart phones, into thousands of households; With the support of new technology and metaverse, computer science will usher in a new era [30].

Acknowledgment. This work was supported in part by the Scientific research projects funded by the Department of education of Hunan Province (No. 22C0497), the Huaihua University Double First-Class initiative Applied Characteristic Discipline of Control Science and Engineering (No. ZNKZN2021-10), the National Natural Science Foundation of China (No. 62172182), the Hunan Provincial Natural Science Foundation of China (No. 2020JJ4490), the Project of Hunan Provincial Social Science Foundation (NO. 21JD046), the Huaihua University Project (No. HHUY2019-25), the Philosophy and Social Science Achievement Evaluation Committee of Huaihua (No. HSP2022YB40) and the Science and Technology Innovation 2030 Special Project Sub-Topics (No. 2018AAA0102100).

References

1. Nover, S.: The Metaverse Will mostly be for Work [EB/OL] (2021). https://qz.com/2083099/the-metaverse-will-mostly-be-for-work/. Accessed 17 Apr 2022
2. Almirall, E.: Teaching in the Metaverse Is much Closer to Being in the Classroom than in an Online Session [EB/OL] (2022). https://dobetter.esade.edu/en/technology-virtual-reality-education. Accessed 21 Apr 2022. Author, F.: Article title. Journal 2(5), 99–110 (2016)
3. Mystakidis, S.: Metaverse. Encyclopedia **2**(1), 486–497 (2022)
4. Liu, D., Cao, Z., He, Y., Ji, X., Hou, M., Jiang, H.: Exploiting concurrency for opportunistic forwarding in duty-cycled IoT networks. ACM Trans. Sens. Netw. 15(3), 31:1–31:33 (2019)
5. Digital Intelligent Human: a fundamental unit in the meta-universe, and a new manifestation of service intelligence, [EB/OL] (2022–03–19). https://www.shangyexinzhi.com/article/4684994.html. Accessed 14 June 2022
6. Zhao, X., Lu, Q.W.: Governance of the metaverse: a vision for agile governance in the future data intelligence world. J. Libr. Sci. China **48**(1), 52–61 (2022)
7. Hu, Z., Zeng, F., Xiao, Z., Fu, B., Jiang, H., Chen, H.: Computation efficiency maximization and QoE-provisioning in UAV-enabled MEC communication systems. IEEE Trans. Netw. Sci. Eng. **8**(2), 1630–1645 (2021)
8. Kimkylin. What is edge computing and what is the difference between it and cloud Calculation. https://m.elecfans.com/article/1684192.html
9. Lee, M.J, Georgieva, M.,Alexander, B., et al.: The State of XR and Immersive Learning Outlook Report (2020). https://immersivelrn.org/ilrn2020/

10. Bloom, B.S., Englehart, M.D., et al.: Taxonomy of Educational Objectives: the Classification of Educational Goals,Handbook 1. Cognitive domain. Longmans Green, NY (1956)
11. Wu, Y.: Building China's 'golden course.' China Univ. Teach. **12**, 4–9 (2018)
12. Samdanis, K., Wright, S., Banchs, A., et al.: 5G network slicing: part 1-concepts, principles, and architectures. IEEE Commun. Mag. **55**(5), 70–71 (2017)
13. Ordonez-Lucena, J., Ameigeiras, P., Lopez, D., et al.: Network slicing for 5G with SDN/NFV: concepts, architectures, and challenges. IEEE Commun. Mag. **55**(5), 80–87 (2017)
14. Jiang, H., Dai, X., Xiao, Z., Iyengar, A.: Joint task offloading and resource allocation for energy-constrained mobile edge computing. IEEE Trans. Mob. Comput. **1**(3), 733–747 (2022). https://doi.org/10.1109/TMC.2022.3150432
15. Tiburski, R.T., Moratelli, C.R., Johann, S.F., et al.: A lightweight virtualization model to enable edge computing in deeply embedded systems. Softw. Pract. Experience **51**(9), 1964–1981 (2021)
16. Samsung. The Next Hyper--Connected Experience for All. https://chinaflashmarket.com/Uploads/Report/20200714145321809946.pdf
17. Myrden, A., Chau, T.: Effects of user mental state on EEG-BCI performance. Front. Hum. Neurosci. **9**, 308 (2015). https://doi.org/10.3389/fnhum.2015.00308
18. Rashkov, G., Bobe, A., Fastovets, D., Komarova, M.: Natural image reconstruction from brain waves: a novel visual BCI system with native feedback. bioRxiv (2019)
19. El Meouche, R., Rezong, M., Hijazi, I.: Integrating and managing BIM in GIS, software review. ISPRS-Int. Arch. Photogrammetry Remote Sens. Spat. Inf. Sci. **1**(2), 31–34 (2013)
20. Minmin, H., Lingyun, Y., Xue, P.: Secure and trusted authentication model under edge computing and multi-block chain [J/OL]. Mod. Distance Educ. Res. (2022)
21. Jiang, H., Xiao, Z., Li, Z., Xu, J., Zeng, F., Wang, D.: An energy-efficient framework for internet of things underlaying heterogeneous small cell networks. IEEE Trans. Mob. Comput. **21**(1), 31–43 (2022)
22. Su, W., Liu, D., Zhang, T., Jiang, H.: Towards device independent eavesdropping on telephone conversations with built-in accelerometer. Proc. ACM Interact. Mob. Wearable Ubiquitous Technol. **5**(4), 177:1–177:29 (2021)
23. Smart, J., Cascio, J., Paffendorf, J.: A Metaverse Roadmap: Pathways to the 3D Web [EB/OL] (2007). http://www.metaverseroadmap.org/MetaverseRoadmapOverview.pdf. Accessed 22 Apr 2022
24. Kye, B., Han, N., Kim, E., et al.: Educational applications of metaverse: possibilities and limitations. J. Educ. Eval. Health Prof. **18**, 1–13 (2021)
25. Chen, X., Wang, G.: The research process, theoretical development and technological turn of international embodied learning. Mod. Distance Educ. Res. **31**(6), 78–88,111 (2019)
26. Yarchi, M., Baden, C., Kligler-Vilenchik, N.: Political polarization on the digital sphere: a cross-platform, over-time analysis of interactional, positional, and affective polarization on social media. Polit. Commun. **1**, 1–42 (2020)
27. Liu, G., Wang, X., Gao, N.: Metaverse exploration based on extended reality under edge computing. Res. Mod. Distance Educ **33**(6), 12–22 (2021)
28. China Commerce Industry Research Institute. Forecast and analysis of China's metaverse market size and future development trend in (2022). http://wap.seccw.com/Document/detail/id/12637.html
29. Xu, Z.: Introduction and enlightenment of computer programming courses in American colleges and universities. Comput. Edu. **12**, 169–172 (2019)
30. Zhao, Q., et al.: A brief survey on virtual reality technology. Sci. Technol. Rev. **34**(14), 71–75 (2016)

Federated Learning Based User Scheduling for Real-Time Multimedia Tasks in Edge Devices

Wenkan Wen[1], Yiwen Liu[1,2,3](✉), Yanxia Gao[1,2,3], Zhirong Zhu[1], Yuanquan Shi[1,2,3], and Xiaoning Peng[1,2,3]

[1] School of Computer and Artificial Intelligence, Huaihua University, Huaihua 418000, China
lyw@hhtc.edu.cn

[2] Key Laboratory of Wuling-Mountain Health Big Data Intelligent Processing and Application in Hunan Province Universities, Huaihua 418000, Hunan, People's Republic of China

[3] Key Laboratory of Intelligent Control Technology for Wuling-Mountain Ecological Agriculture in Hunan Province, Huaihua 418000, Hunan, People's Republic of China

Abstract. Edge networks are highly volatile and the quality of device communication and computational resources change not only over time but also according to the movement of users. Current federation learning suffers from poor device network state and failure of devices to upload models in a timely manner. To address these problems, an intelligent scheduling mechanism that uses the predicted device state based on device information to select the appropriate device for federated learning is proposed in this paper. By focusing on information such as communication quality, computational resources, and location information, the information of edge devices is collected to analyze and predict the device network and computing resources to further analyze the state of devices in depth. Experiments are conducted on real datasets, and the experimental results show that the proposed scheduling method can make the global model fit faster than without the algorithm, which significantly improves the training efficiency of federated learning.

Keywords: Federated Learning · User Scheduling · Mobile Computing · Machine learning

1 Introduction

1.1 Background

With the development of technology and the increasing improvement of people's living standard, electronic products such as mobile communication devices and wearable devices are becoming more and more popular, and a large amount of data is generated in the use of these devices by users. At the same time, artificial intelligence is also developing rapidly and a dilemma has arisen: on the one hand, most of the application models of artificial intelligence technology need a large number of rich sources of real user data as the basis for training. On the other hand, the importance of user privacy and data

Z. Xiao et al. (Eds.): ICECI 2022, LNICST 478, pp. 277–290, 2023.
https://doi.org/10.1007/978-3-031-28990-3_19

security has been increasing in recent years [1]. In addition, the lack of an effective interoperability and collaboration among commercial companies applying AI technologies has resulted in the potential data value not being fully exploited and applied. Federated Learning (FL) [2] can be a good solution to the above dilemma as a technical solution that enables multiple devices distributed in multiple regions to collaboratively train AI models using local data while ensuring privacy. Specifically, federal learning differs from the traditional learning model in that the server does not need direct access to the user's local data, but rather allows the device to train its own data locally. In each round of training, the local client can download the current global model from the server, update the model by training on local data, and upload the updated model to the server. Then, the server will integrate all the uploaded models with the updated global model through the algorithm. In this way, local data from different clients do not exchange with each other, and the transmission information of model updates can be further protected by encryption algorithms [3]. For example, an approach based on model summation averaging enables Google's G Board input method to effectively predict the next character the user wishes to type [4].

Google proposed a scalable federation learning system based on mobile devices in 2019 and defined three phases of federation learning. First is the Device Selection Phase, which requires the central Parameter Server (PS) of federation learning to select a set of devices. Clients, for model training. Next is the Local-training Phase, which requires the devices selected in the previous phase to be trained locally. Finally, the Model Synchronization Phase, also known as the Reporting Phase, requires the devices that have completed local training to upload the updated local models or gradients to the parameter server, and the parameter server completes the global model aggregation. After the above three phases are completed, the next device selection phase is entered again, and the cycle is repeated until the model performance meets the expected requirements.

1.2 Challenge

One of the keys to the quality of federation learning training for edge networks lies in the devices involved in model training and synchronization, and there are two main factors in edge networks that can greatly affect the final global model merit.

(1) Mobile devices may fluctuate in network communication quality due to their irregular locations and frequent movements. This will easily make it difficult for the device to communicate with the base station or the parameter server, thus affecting the effectiveness of federal learning.
(2) The computing power of the device is influenced by the tasks performed by the device itself, so the computing power of the device is a dynamic situation, and the high or low computing power of the device will directly affect the overall federal learning training efficiency and the final recognition ability of the model.

The instability of mobile devices is high, and the network communication of devices in edge networks is always in constant change. Therefore, a good device scheduling method can steadily and effectively improve the training efficiency and model stability of federation learning [5–9]. In this paper, we propose an intelligent scheduling mechanism that uses mobile device state information to predict the device state and then selects the device with better performance for federation learning. The network and computing resources of the predicted devices are analyzed by collecting information from edge devices to further analyze the state of the devices. A machine learning approach is used to model the real mobile devices based on their state data, and the information provided by the current devices such as computational performance, network state, and location information is used to make a comprehensive decision to ensure that the most stable device is selected in each round of federal learning device selection.

2 Related Review

Distributed machine learning has received a great deal of scholarly attention and has yielded numerous results [10, 11], and a number of large-scale cloud-based distributed systems have been put into use. Many systems support multiple data processing schemes, including model parallelism and data parallelism [12]. Distributed edge intelligence is a disruptive area of research that enables machine learning and deep learning (ML/DL) algorithms to be executed where the data is generated. Machine learning and deep learning (ML/DL) algorithms are executed close to where the data is generated [13]. Current distributed learning considers devices with high storage and computational power and stable network connections, such as computers, micro servers, etc. Not much attention has been paid to devices with weaker performance and susceptible to fluctuations such as cell phones, wearable devices, etc.

Federated Learning, first proposed by Google, aims to enable multiple parties to work together on machine learning tasks while protecting data privacy. With the enactment of the European Union's General Data Protection Regulation (GDPR), large Internet companies are no longer free to collect user data for machine learning. As a result, Google proposed in 2016 a new policy to protect user data. Therefore, Google proposed a federal learning approach for Android phone users in 2016, which can train a federated model while ensuring that user data does not leave the local device. The literature [14] extends Google's federated learning concept with a more general definition and classifies federated learning into horizontal federated learning, vertical federated learning and federated migration learning for different ways of slicing data [15]. In either scenario, there are several common challenges [14].

In the case of two datasets with more repetition of user's feature dimensions and less overlap of users, we slice the dataset horizontally and take out the data with the same but not identical features for training. Longitudinal federation learning refers to the case where the users overlap more and their feature dimensions overlap less in the two datasets, the dataset is cut vertically and the data with the same but not all the same features are taken out from the two datasets for training. Federal transfer learning [16] refers to the case where there is little overlap in both user dimensions and user feature dimensions in both datasets. In this case migration learning techniques are used to overcome the problem of data and label imbalance.

L. U. Khan [17] considered the need for a new protocol to select a set of local devices with sufficient resources to provide the standard. The selection criteria for the devices must include persistent backup power, sufficient memory, accurate data and high processing power [18–22]. The article [23] argues that in federated learning, the participating users are heterogeneous in terms of their computational power and willingness to participate; communication cost is one of the bottlenecks in federated learning, and it is very natural and reasonable to introduce mobile edge computing into federated learning to leverage communication and computational costs. When using mobile edge computing in federation learning, the latency from the client to the edge server is considered lower than the link between the client and the cloud, so the edge server is introduced for local parameter aggregation, and considering the heterogeneity of the clients, various resources should be carefully allocated to improve the training efficiency, such as client grouping, joint radio and computational resource management, and adaptive aggregation. The paper [24] proposes a dynamic sampling strategy that first uses a higher sampling rate for dynamic sampling and then decreases the sampling rate at each communication. First to speed up the beginning phase of convergence, so by involving more users in the model training. When training reaches a certain level, the number of users involved in training is dynamically reduced to save communication costs. The initial cost of federal learning is high, but after a few rounds of training, the number of users selected for model training decreases rapidly. The rate of reduction can be freely chosen to suit the situation in different environments. The article [25] shows that different users have different network speeds and communication methods. And the distribution of the data owned by the clients is unbalanced during the training process. If all users are allowed to participate in the training process of joint learning, then there will be participants who are behind in the iterations. If some users do not respond for a long time, the whole system may not be able to complete the joint training. Therefore, considering how to select the right devices to participate in federated learning is also a major urgent problem.

The above research results show that federated learning for edge computing has certain requirements on the computational power, network stability, and available memory of the devices. Therefore, it is important to collect the information of edge devices and consider the device performance to select the appropriate devices for federated learning.

3 Data and Algorithm

The experimental environment is a mobile edge communication (MEC) environment consisting of a cloud server, several groups of base stations (including macro and micro base stations) and several mobile candidates, represented by the set of N = {1, 2, 3,..., N}. Each device has a certain amount of available CPU and memory resources, as well as a network connection with a certain bandwidth already, which are set to be determined by the available computing power and the upload/download rate of the device, respectively. A candidate device's available CPU resources and memory size represent its currently available computational resources, while its network connectivity determines whether it can download a global model or upload a locally trained model at a reasonable time.

As shown in Fig. 1, the learning process consists of collaboration between the cloud server, macro base stations, micro base stations and mobile terminals to collaborate on model training. The cloud server broadcasts the global model to the macro base station, which in turn broadcasts it to all micro base stations, which in turn forwards the received global model to the edge devices. After training, the edge devices upload

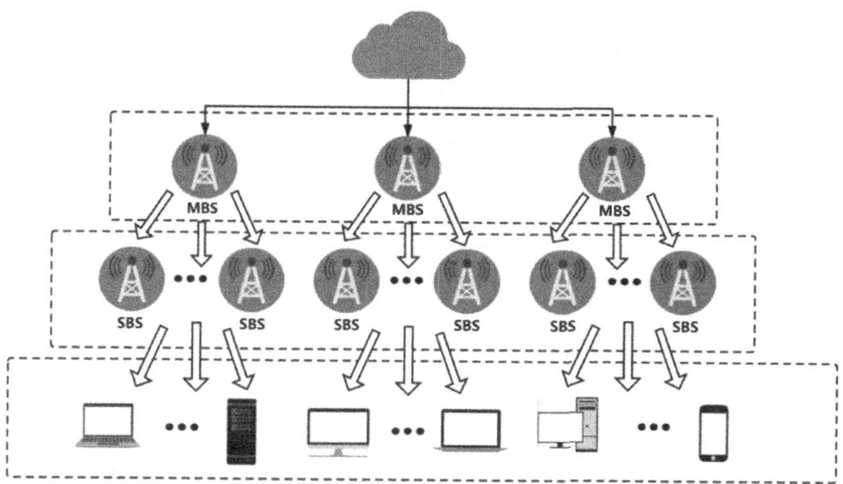

Fig. 1. An edge federation learning environment consists of four components: cloud servers, macro base stations, micro base stations, and edge device.

the generated local models to the associated micro-base stations. The micro-base station receives all the updated local models, performs a weighted average of the local models, and then sends the results to the macro-base station. Finally, the macro base station then pushes the models to the cloud server. Considering the large number of edge devices, the performance and communication capability are inconsistent. Each micro-base station has an uncertain update time for each round, so an asynchronous update strategy will be used between the macro-base station and the micro-base station (Table 1).

Table 1. Notations and their description in this paper

Symbols	Description
N	Number of mobile devices
S	Number of base stations
n	Mobile Devices
s	Micro Base Station
B_e	Device remaining battery
D_n	Dataset to be processed
P_n	Calculated power consumption
L_n	Device training rounds

(*continued*)

Table 1. (*continued*)

Symbols	Description
B_c	Power required for training
A_n	Device Performance
T_t	Training time
N_u	Network upload rate
N_d	Network download rate
N_n	Network Quality

3.1 Data

The dataset in this paper is from the article [26], the device generates a large amount of data during operation, by collecting this information the following dimensional information can be obtained: Latitude, Longitude, Date and Time, Available Memory, Upload Rate, Download Rate, Battery Whether the device is able to pass the completed training parameters to the base station at a reasonable time will be used as a label for the suitability of the device (Table 2).

Table 2. Dataset information table

Num	Item	Description
1	Latitude	Device current latitude coordinates
2	Longitude	Device current longitude coordinates
3	Date and Time	Current date and time
4	Available Memory	Device available memory
5	Upload Rate	Network upload rate
6	Download Rate	Network download rate
7	Battery Remain	Device remaining battery
8	Max CPU Frequency	CPU Max Frequency
9	Min CPU Frequency	CPU Min Frequency
10	Current CPU Frequency	CPU Current Frequency

3.2 Algorithm

In edge computing environments, where performance varies greatly between devices, many factors can affect the quality of the final model of federation learning. The power of the device, network status, and location are all information to focus on.

(1) **Device residual power constraint**

The power of the device is affected by the power consumption of the device, the size of the data set to be processed and the number of training rounds required. In order to ensure that the device can have enough power to complete the training and parameter transfer, the selected device needs to be constrained. The formula is shown below:

$$\mathrm{B_c} = \mathrm{D_n} * \mathrm{P_n} * \mathrm{L_n} \tag{1}$$

$$|\mathrm{B_e} - \mathrm{B_c}| > \lambda \mathrm{B_c} \tag{2}$$

Formula (1) can calculate the approximate power demand for this round of training, formula (2) is to determine the difference between the remaining power of the device and the power required for training needs to ensure that it is at least twice as large as the power required for training before it can be selected as a training device, otherwise the device will not be selected as a training device.

(2) **Device network state constraints**

In real scenarios the network bandwidth of mobile devices may be affected by users resulting in slow or even failed transmission. And the bandwidth that the edge devices can provide is small [27], so if the parameters are disconnected during the transmission process, it will affect the performance of the federation learning global model, so the selected devices need to be constrained. The formula is shown as follows:

$$N_n = \frac{U_n}{\sum_{i=1}^{N} \frac{U_i}{N}} + \frac{D_n}{\sum_{i=1}^{N} \frac{D_i}{N}} \tag{3}$$

$\sum_{i=1}^{N} \frac{U_i}{N}$ and $\sum_{i=1}^{N} \frac{D_i}{N}$ is the average of the current network upload and download rates of all candidate devices, The sum of the network upload rate U_n of the currently selected device and the network download rate D_n of the currently selected device and the corresponding ratio of all candidate devices is the current device network quality N_n. The device network quality N_n is a greater than zero constant, the larger the value the worse the quality of the currently selected device network and vice versa.

(3) **Device Computational Performance Constraints**

The processing performance of mobile devices and the time required for transmission in real-world scenarios are the key concerns. Edge devices are usually weak in computation, and if the training time is long, it will affect the performance of the federated learning global model, so constraints need to be placed on the selected devices. The formula is shown as follows:

$$A_n = \frac{(P_{cur} + P_{\max})}{P_{\max}} \times P_{\min} \tag{4}$$

$$\mathrm{T_t} = \frac{\mathrm{D_n}}{\mathrm{A_n}} * \mathrm{L_n} \tag{5}$$

The relative performance of the mobile device can be calculated by formula (4), and the actual computing performance of the device can be judged by the relative performance. Combined with Eq. (5) will calculate the approximate training time, the smaller the training time the better the performance will be, the higher the probability of being selected, and vice versa.

(4) **Device position offset constraint**

Mobile devices usually do not stay fixed in one location and may continuously switch sites [28], in which process it can cause the base station assigned to the mobile device task to have difficulty receiving mobile device information or the mobile device is out of the signal range of the base station. So it is necessary to make restrictions on the mobile information of the device.

$$\text{haversin}(\frac{d}{R}) = \text{haversin}(\varphi_2 - \varphi_1) + \cos(\varphi_1)\cos(\varphi_2)\text{haversin}(\Delta\lambda) \tag{6}$$

$$\text{haversin}(\theta) = \sin^2(\theta/2) = (1 - \cos(\theta))/2 \tag{7}$$

$$D_m = \text{haversin}(|L_{\tilde{x}} - L_x|) + \cos(L_x)\cos(L_{\tilde{x}})\text{haversin}(\left|L_{\tilde{y}} - L_y\right|) \tag{8}$$

$$O(S_a, D_m) = \begin{cases} 1 \; |S_a - D_m| < 0 \\ 0 \; 0 \leq |S_a - D_m| \end{cases} \tag{9}$$

$$O_c = \sum_{i=1}^{t} O(S_a, D_m) \tag{10}$$

The device latitude and longitude information is obtained and the Haversine algorithm [29] (Formula (6), (7), and (8)) is used to calculate the distance between the previous moment and the current moment of the device movement. After that, formula (9) is used to determine whether the device exceeds the coverage range of the base station, and the departure from the coverage range of the base station will cause the device communication to be affected. Formula (10) records the number of times the device switches base stations to determine whether the device is stable or not. The lower the number of times the device switches base stations, the higher the quality of the device, and vice versa (Fig. 2).

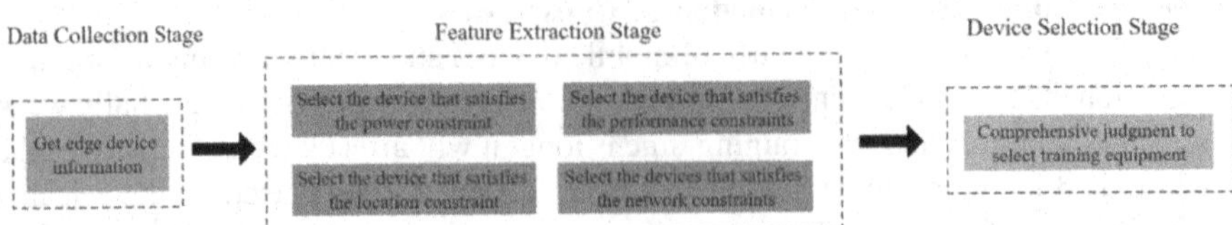

Fig. 2. The scheduling process can be divided into three stages: data collection stage, feature extraction stage, and device selection stage

4 Experiments

This experiment will use several machine learning models for comparative validation experiments to better verify the performance of the intelligent scheduling algorithm in different models.

Native Bayesian classification is an NB algorithm proposed by Maron and Kuhns based on Bayesian theory for classification based on probabilistic principles. The Native Bayesian algorithm is a classification method based on probabilistic statistics and is often used as an evaluation criterion for text classification. After obtaining the prior probability and conditional probability of the sample data, the algorithm can find the posterior probability according to the Bayesian formula, the probability that the sample corresponds to different categories, and the category with the largest posterior probability is the predicted category of the sample corresponding to the algorithm [30].

Support vector machines, as a powerful classification and regression method, have achieved very remarkable research results and are widely used in many fields. Support vector machines are based on the statistical principle of structural risk minimization and obtain the optimal division hyperplane between positive and negative classes by maximizing the soft interval [31].

Decision tree (DT) algorithms can be used in classification and regression problems and have been widely used in knowledge discovery, pattern recognition, and other fields. Compared with other machine learning models, decision trees have the advantages of high generalization ability, fast construction, few parameters, and easy understanding. To this day, decision trees are still one of the research hotspots in the field of machine learning, with specific research focusing on tree construction methods, node partitioning methods and partitioning criteria decision tree integration models, combinations with other classifiers, and other directions [32].

The random forest (RF) algorithm is concerned with integrated learning of decision trees and was proposed by Breiman in 2001. This algorithm requires simulation and iteration and is classified as a method in machine learning. Later, some scholars borrowed the proposed random decision forests approach to combine classification trees into random forests, i.e., to randomize the use of variables (columns) and data (rows) to generate many classification trees, and then aggregate the results of classification trees. Later Breiman published the algorithm of random forest designed by him and Cutler in the Journal of Machine Learning, and this article was cited extensively and became a milestone in the field of machine learning [33].

4.1 Evaluation Metric

The experimental procedure will use accuracy (Precision, P) (as in Eq. 10), recall (Recall, R) (as in Eq. 11), the overall evaluation metric (F1-score) (as in Eq. 12), and the ROC curve to evaluate the performance of the classifier algorithm (TP: correct rate; FP: false alarm rate; FN: missed alarm rate). F1-score is widely used in information retrieval, machine learning, sentiment analysis, and other fields involving binary classification.

The ROC curve provides a global assessment of the classifier's accuracy, and it contains all possible decision thresholds without a specific decision threshold. In addition, ROC curves do not depend on the scale of the test results, i.e., monotonic transformations of the classification results can maintain invariance, thus, in most practical problems, the problem of uneven sample distribution and inconsistent cost of misclassification may affect the evaluation results, and ROC curves are a good solution to this challenge. In terms of performance diagnosis, ROC curves are free distribution assumptions in the full sense of the word, without the need to use the parametric form of the assumed class distribution, thus ensuring the wide applicability of ROC curves [34].

$$Precision = \frac{TP}{TP + FP} \tag{11}$$

$$Recall = \frac{TP}{TP + FN} \tag{12}$$

$$F_1 = 2 \times \frac{Precision \times Recall}{Precision + Recall} \tag{13}$$

4.2 Result

Precision (P), which is specific to our prediction results, indicates how many of the positive predictions are actually positive in the original sample. Recall (R), which is specific to our original sample, indicates how many of the positive cases in the original sample were predicted correctly, the percentage of true and accurate positive predictions among the positive cases in the original sample. F1-score is a composite precision and recall metric, and F1 value is the summed mean of precision and recall. According to the above Eqs. (11), (12) and (13), the P-value, R-value and F1-score before and after comparing q using the scheduling algorithm are shown in Table 3.

Table 3. Model Performance Table

Model	Accuracy	Precision	Recall	F1-score
Native Bayesian	78.89%	0.72	0.74	0.73
SVM	83.73%	0.79	0.77	0.78
Decision Tree	91.78%	0.88	0.90	0.89
Random Forest	92.31%	0.89	0.91	0.90

As seen in Table 3, the models all achieved good results, with Random Forest achieving the highest F1-score score, Decision Tree also achieving better prediction results, SVM the next best, and Native Bayes the worst. Among them, random forest obtained 92.31% accuracy, which shows that the selected features can effectively represent the state of the device and can effectively and stably predict the state of the device selected with better performance to participate in the federal learning.

Figure 3 shows that the model still has good performance in predicting the suitable candidate devices even at 0.1. It can be shown that the selected features can achieve a

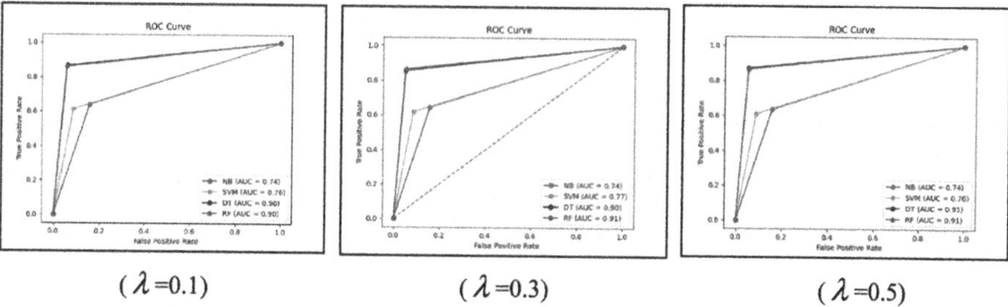

Fig. 3. It can be found that the model still predicts the device that should be selected well for different λ values, indicating that the features extracted by the algorithm are effective.

more satisfactory accuracy rate, which lays the foundation for the subsequent experiments and analysis. Afterwards, the RESNET50 model will be tested using the classical MNIST dataset to verify the effectiveness of the intelligent scheduling algorithm in federal learning by comparing the convergence speed of the global model before and after 1000 rounds of federal learning training using the intelligent scheduling algorithm.

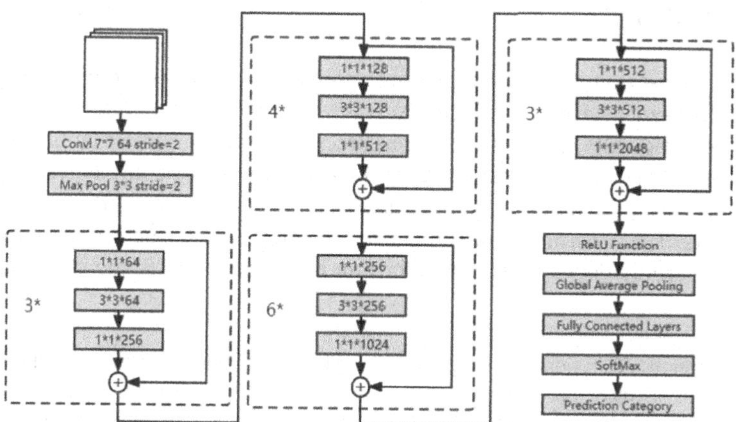

Fig. 4. This is a diagram of a classic Resnet50 network structure with 49 convolutional layers and one fully connected layer

Figure 4 shows the network structure of Resnet50 used for the experiments by combining the data set mobile device information with a randomly generated unique ID to derive the data set. We randomly select 1000 devices for the simulation, and each device randomly selects a default base station to communicate with. Afterwards, 80% of the data from MNIST is used as the training set for federal learning, and the remaining 20% is used as the test set to verify the performance of the trained global model.

A comparison of the convergence performance using the smart scheduling algorithm with and without is shown in Fig. 5. It is clearly observed from the figure that the model using the smart scheduling method has a faster convergence rate and obtains high accuracy compared to the model without smart scheduling. This is a good indication of the

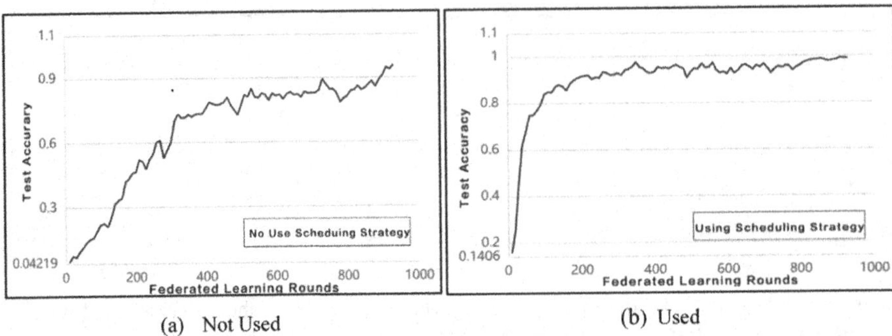

(a) Not Used (b) Used

Fig. 5. It is obvious that the model converges significantly faster with the scheduling algorithm than without it

advantage of the smart scheduling algorithm with more stable convergence. Therefore, it is a feasible and effective solution to collect and analyze the device information for intelligent scheduling to select the appropriate devices for federal learning.

5 Conclusion

This paper focuses on a federated learning approach to device scheduling, and judges the capabilities of devices comprehensively by focusing on three important features: communication quality, computational resources, and location information. And considering that edge networks have a large turbulence, the device communication quality and computational resources not only change over time but also according to the movement of users. The experiments are conducted by invoking the machine learning model for federal learning device selection and using Resnet50 to verify the effectiveness of the algorithm.

Acknowledgment. This work was supported in part by the Scientific research projects funded by the Department of education of Hunan Province (No. 22C0497), the Huaihua University Double First-Class initiative Applied Characteristic Discipline of Control Science and Engineering (No. ZNKZN2021-10), the National Natural Science Foundation of China (No. 62172182), the Hunan Provincial Natural Science Foundation of China (No. 2020JJ4490), the Project of Hunan Provincial Social Science Foundation (No. 21JD046), the Huaihua University Project (No. HHUY2019-25), the Philosophy and Social Science Achievement Evaluation Committee of Huaihua (No. HSP2022YB40) and the Science and Technology Innovation 2030 Special Project Sub-Topics (No. 2018AAA0102100).

References

1. Su, W., Liu, D., Zhang, T., Jiang, H.: Towards device independent eavesdropping on telephone conversations with built-in accelerometer. Proc. ACM Interact. Mob. Wearable Ubiquitous Technol. **5**(4), 1–29 (2021)

2. Bonawitz, K., et al.: Towards federated learning at scale: system design. Proc. Mach. Learn. Syst. **1**, 374–388 (2019)
3. Aono, Y., Hayashi, T., Wang, L., Moriai, S.: Privacy-preserving deep learning via additively homomorphic encryption. IEEE Trans. Inf. Forensics Secur. **13**(5), 1333–1345 (2017). https://doi.org/10.1109/TIFS.2017.2787987
4. Hard, A., et al.: Federated learning for mobile keyboard prediction. arXiv preprint arXiv:1811.03604 (2018)
5. Zeng, F., Li, Q., Xiao, Z., Havyarimana, V., Bai, J.: A price-based optimization strategy of power control and resource allocation in full-duplex heterogeneous macrocell-femtocell networks. IEEE Access **6**, 42004–42013 (2018)
6. Zeng, F., et al.: Resource allocation and trajectory optimization for QoE provisioning in energy-efficient UAV-enabled wireless networks. IEEE Trans. Veh. Technol. **69**(7), 7634–7647 (2020)
7. Ali, T.A.A., Xiao, Z., Sun, J., Mirjalili, S., Havyarimana, V., Jiang, H.: Optimal design of IIR wideband digital differentiators and integrators using salp swarm algorithm. Knowl.-Based Syst. **182**, 104834 (2019)
8. Jiang, H., Cao, H., Liu, D., Xiong, J., Cao, Z.: SmileAuth: using dental edge biometrics for user authentication on smartphones. Proc. ACM Interact. Mob. Wearable Ubiquitous Technol. **4**(3), 1–24 (2020)
9. Liu, D., Cao, Z., Hou, M., Rong, H., Jiang, H.: Pushing the limits of transmission concurrency for low power wireless networks. ACM Trans. Sens. Netw. **16**(4), 1–29 (2020)
10. Xiao, Z., et al.: Toward accurate vehicle state estimation under non-Gaussian noises. IEEE Internet Things J. **6**(6), 10652–10664 (2019)
11. Hu, J., et al.: BlinkRadar: non-intrusive driver eye-blink detection with UWB radar. In: 2022 IEEE 42nd International Conference on Distributed Computing Systems (ICDCS), pp. 1040–1050. IEEE (2022)
12. Lu, X., Liao, Y., Lio, P., Pan, H.: An asynchronous federated learning mechanism for edge network computing. J. Comput. Res. Dev. **57**(12), 2571–2582 (2020)
13. Filho, C.P., et al.: A systematic literature review on distributed machine learning in edge computing. Sensors **22**(7), 2665 (2022). https://doi.org/10.3390/s22072665
14. Yang, Q., Liu, Y., Chen, T., Tong, Y.: Federated machine learning: concept and applications. ACM Trans. Intell. Syst. Technol. **10**(2), 1–19 (2019). https://doi.org/10.1145/3298981
15. Zhang, P.-C., Wei, X.-M., Jin, H.-Y.: Dynamic QoS optimization method based on federal learning in mobile edge computing. Chin. J. Comput. **44**(12), 2431–2446 (2021)
16. Liu, Y., Kang, Y., Xing, C., Chen, T., Yang, Q.: A secure federated transfer learning framework. IEEE Intell. Syst. **35**(4), 70–82 (2020). https://doi.org/10.1109/MIS.2020.2988525
17. Khan, L.U., et al.: Federated learning for edge networks: resource optimization and incentive mechanism. IEEE Commun. Mag. **58**(10), 88–93 (2020). https://doi.org/10.1109/MCOM.001.1900649
18. Liu, D., Cao, Z., He, Y., Ji, X., Hou, M., Jiang, H.: Exploiting concurrency for opportunistic forwarding in duty-cycled IoT networks. ACM Trans. Sens. Netw. **15**(3), 1–33 (2019)
19. Hu, Z., Zeng, F., Xiao, Z., Fu, B., Jiang, H., Chen, H.: Computation efficiency maximization and QoE-provisioning in UAV-enabled MEC communication systems. IEEE Trans. Netw. Sci. Eng. **8**(2), 1630–1645 (2021)
20. Jiang, H., Dai, X., Xiao, Z., Iyengar, A.K.: Joint task offloading and resource allocation for energy-constrained mobile edge computing. IEEE Trans. Mob. Comput. (2022). https://doi.org/10.1109/TMC.2022.3150432
21. Jiang, H., Xiao, Z., Li, Z., Xu, J., Zeng, F., Wang, D.: An energy-efficient framework for internet of things underlaying heterogeneous small cell networks. IEEE Trans. Mob. Comput. **21**(1), 31–43 (2020)

22. Liu, D., Hou, M., Cao, Z., He, Y., Ji, X., Zheng, X.: COF: exploiting concurrency for low power opportunistic forwarding. In: 2015 IEEE 23rd International Conference on Network Protocols (ICNP), pp. 32–42. IEEE (2015)
23. Qin, Z., Li, G.Y., Ye, H.: Federated learning and wireless communications. IEEE Wireless Commun. **28**(5), 134–140 (2021). https://doi.org/10.1109/MWC.011.2000501
24. Ji, S., Jiang, W., Walid, A., Li, X.: Dynamic sampling and selective masking for communication-efficient federated learning. IEEE Intell. Syst. **37**(2), 27–34 (2022). https://doi.org/10.1109/MIS.2021.3114610
25. Alferaidi, A., Yadav, K., Alharbi, Y., Viriyasitavat, W., Kautish, S., Dhiman, G.: Federated learning algorithms to optimize the client and cost selections. Math. Probl. Eng. **2022**, 8514562 (2022). https://doi.org/10.1155/2022/8514562
26. Huang, H., Li, R., Liu, J., Zhou, S., Lin, K., Zheng, Z.: ContextFL: context-aware federated learning by estimating the training and reporting phases of mobile clients. In: 2022 IEEE 42nd International Conference on Distributed Computing Systems (ICDCS), pp. 570–580. IEEE (2022)
27. Liu, D., Wu, X., Cao, Z., Liu, M., Li, Y., Hou, M.: CD-MAC: a contention detectable MAC for low duty-cycled wireless sensor networks. In: 2015 12th Annual IEEE International Conference on Sensing, Communication, and Networking (SECON), pp. 37–45. IEEE (2015)
28. Qian, C., Liu, D., Jiang, H.: Harmonizing energy efficiency and QoE for brightness scaling-based mobile video streaming. In: 2022 IEEE/ACM 30th International Symposium on Quality of Service (IWQoS), pp. 1–10. IEEE (2022)
29. Inman, J.: Navigation and Nautical Astronomy: For the Use of British Seamen 3. In: Woodward, W.C., Rivington, J. (eds.) London, UK 1835 (1821)
30. Li, X., Yang, Z., Ren, J.: Improved naive bayes algorithm based on dual feature selection of mutual information and hierarchical clustering measurement & control technology **41**(02), 36–40+69 (2022). https://doi.org/10.19708/j.ckjs.2022.02.005
31. Wang, X., Dong, Y., Yu, Q., Geng, N.: Review of structural support vector machines. Comput. Eng. Appl. **56**(17), 24–32 (2020). (in Chinese)
32. Liu, Z., Chu, N.: A weighted clustering splitting decision tree algorithm. Telecommun. Eng. **60**(11), 1354–1360 (2020)
33. Li, X.: Using "random forest" for classification and regression. Chin. J. Appl. Entomol. **50**(4), 1190–1197 (2013)
34. Wang, Y., Zhu, H., Xu, W.: A review on ROC curve and analysis. J. Guangdong Univ. Technol. **38**(01), 46–53 (2021)

A Co-caching Strategy for Edges Based on Federated Learning and Regional Prevalence

Zhirong Zhu[1], Yiwen Liu[1,2,3](✉), Yanxia Gao[1,2,3], Wenkan Wen[1], Yuanquan Shi[1,2,3], and Xiaoning Peng[1,2,3]

[1] School of Computer and Artificial Intelligence, Huaihua University, Huaihua 418000, Hunan, People's Republic of China
lyw@hhtc.edu.cn

[2] Key Laboratory of Wuling-Mountain Health Big Data Intelligent Processing and Application in Hunan Province Universities, Huaihua 418000, Hunan, People's Republic of China

[3] Key Laboratory of Intelligent Control Technology for Wuling-Mountain Ecological Agriculture in Hunan Province, Huaihua 418000, Hunan, People's Republic of China

Abstract. With the rise of data storage computing and IoT technology. The increase in data volume and user demand, the accurate delivery of data and low latency during transmission become important factors that affect the end-user experience. To address this issue, previous authors have proposed the concept of edge computings. In the general environment of edge computing, reasonable scheduling of edge caches can largely achieve low latency and high efficiency, thus improving user experience. In this paper, based on existing research, we propose a combination of a joint learning framework for cache prediction based on region popularity and an edge collaborative cache value optimization method to further improve cache hit rate and cache utilization efficiency. The method obtains excellent expected results through simulation experiments.

Keyword: Data Storage Computing · IoT Technology · Edge Computing · Cache Hit Rate

1 Introduction

With the advent of wireless network services and the era of Big Data Internet. Tens of thousands of users have chosen to access the Internet. And with the popularity of network technology, the corresponding data volume is increasing and the data type is complicated. And because of the previous cloud storage computing using a single form of storage distribution. This makes the server load too large, resulting in long latency and poor user experience. In order to solve this problem, the concept of edge computing has emerged in recent years to address this status quo [1].

Edge computing is a computing facility where data resources are deployed in the data center department and close to the user, and through this facility, a series of network devices link the edge computing devices to the user or process. This is how the Internet of

Z. Xiao et al. (Eds.): ICECI 2022, LNICST 478, pp. 291–307, 2023.
https://doi.org/10.1007/978-3-031-28990-3_20

Things and Smart Networks are born. [2]. The previous edge computing model and due to the open nature of edge computing, data privacy security is also a major challenge that we need to address. It also affects the efficiency of data transfer in the face of too large amount of data. Both are caused by the improper allocation of edge cache. And according to related studies [3, 4] in the Internet in the same type or region of the population will have roughly similar search content and browsing trends. Then this means that we can cache the data that users search frequently and may be hotly searched in advance in the user's edge device by using edge caching wisely. The content that may not be of interest to the user will be reduced or stopped. Thus, we can solve the large data traffic congestion to a certain extent and thus reduce the latency.

Under this hypothesis. In this paper, we categorize the population of possible viewers [5] with the same attributes based on machine learning and try to segment the regions according to the browsing popularity. The segmentation signal is transmitted to the corresponding edge cache controller. It then filters and distributes the content to be cached. And to ensure further improvement in accuracy and optimization of performance. In this paper, we use federation learning for data localization training, and the training process is shown in Fig. 1. The trained primitive models localized by each edge device are uploaded to an aggregation center consisting of collection base stations and aggregators. The aggregation center aggregates the sub-models to form a combined model. The combined model is then distributed by the collection base station to each edge device for the next round of training tests. The aggregation cycle results in a more accurate prediction model that fits the user's needs. Only parameters are transmitted between the base station and the edge devices. Thus, the amount of data transmission is reduced. And to a certain extent, the privacy and security of the data are guaranteed and the overall performance is optimized. And the strategy designed in this paper is experimentally verified to obtain better optimization results than the comparison model. The feasibility of the design is proved.

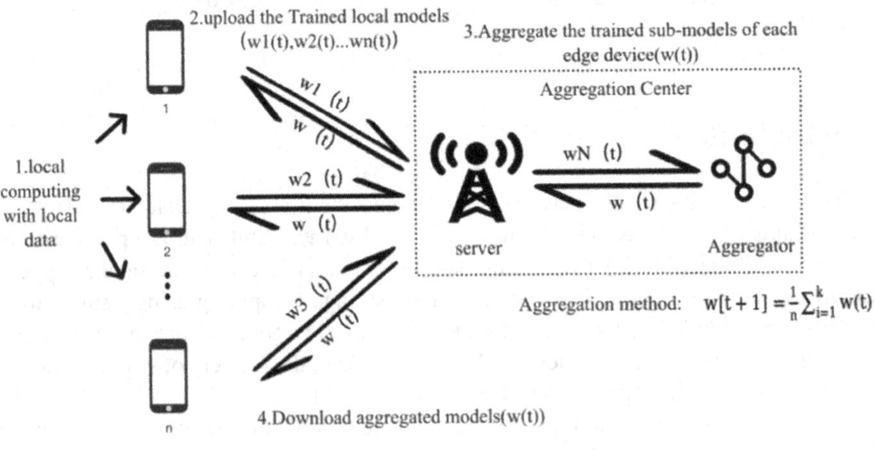

Fig. 1. Federal learning model training method under edge-based computing model

2 Relevant Domestic and International Studies

In the literature [2] the authors categorize and study the breakthroughs in edge computing technologies in recent years. And the study of edge caching technology becomes the most important and at the same time the most critical part of the optimized edge computing model.

A task scheduling based cache placement user approach is proposed in the literature [6] by starting from the cache scheduling mechanism. In contrast, the literature [7] builds a user-object-aware network. The user's perception of the network information is analyzed to filter the cache content, thus reducing information congestion. In contrast, the literature [8–10] preempts data with high cache demand into the edge cache pool by building a new secure resource allocation algorithm. And the data with small cache demand is stored in the data center. This can reduce the data congestion caused when the data volume is too large to some extent. At the same time, the security lock and key encryption are combined to ensure the security of data privacy.

In recent years, with the development of machine learning, deep learning and other content mining. It has led to a new foothold in the optimization of edge cache. For example, the literature [11] combines machine learning with statistical methods to derive a reference popularity scheme for cache storage. In contrast, the literature [12, 13] uses a fusion of machine learning and reinforcement learning to derive an optimal solution to the cache allocation scheme. Thus, it is demonstrated that artificial intelligence enables edge computing technology to step into a new level.

And if the cache hit rate is to be as high as possible. Then from the experience point of view. Then the preference data classes of edge end-users need to be taken into account. The literature [14] combines user and user data and analyzes its correlation to derive the differences in browsing data between users. This allows the edge cache to be able to store the desired data in a targeted manner, greatly improving the hit rate. In contrast, the literature [3, 4] analyzes from user behavior. The users with the same browsing class are clustered. So that the edge caching mechanism can be processed. The literature [5] uses user portraits to predict the click likelihood of different types of ads. And good experimental results were achieved.

In this paper, we further optimize the edge caching mechanism based on machine learning. And for the computational power reduction and possible security problems in processing data caused by large amount of data buffer processing in traditional edge computing. We use federation learning [15, 16] to ensure the processing performance of the policy and the security privacy of the data.

3 Caching Strategy Design

3.1 Regional Prevalence Prediction

Before making an edge cache resource allocation, we need to consider how to rationalize the limited resources in the best possible way. But it is not difficult to find out. There is a strong and weak relationship chain between users and users in terms of different demand information. Then we can assume. The more the requirement information between different users fits together, the stronger the relationship property between them. Then the more likely this group of information will be selected as cache data. And as the demand of a certain group of information increases, all user-related edge devices associated with it will form a regional network.

3.1.1 Content Popularity

In this paper, by examining the Movielens dataset we can assume that the more the number of views, the higher the popularity of that data. The literature [14] through user relationship perception can conclude that the number of visits in the dataset for video data information is in accordance with Ziff's law. Which Combined with the Salp Swarm algorithm [17] and Then it means that close to 70%–80% of the requested information topics originate from 20% of the content among all the users requesting to view. Then, we cite the literature [11, 14] for the calculation of regional prevalence. Let the total number of video data in the dataset be F. The popularity of the content ranked as j in the video dataset is

$$\overline{p_j^{pop}} = \frac{j^{-1}}{\sum_{c=1}^{|F|} c^{-l}}, 1 \leq j \leq |F| \tag{1}$$

where: l is the offset index that follows Ziff's law. The higher the offset index is, the higher we can conclude that the video is in demand index.

3.1.2 User Favorability

In general, the content that users choose to browse is not limited to popular content, but depends in large part on the users' own preferences for different content. Then, we can consider the user's preference for a certain type of data information as.

$$PR_{pop} = \frac{t_{total}}{w_{total}} \tag{2}$$

Among them. PR_{pop}: The goodness of a certain type of information.
t_{total}: The total time the user spent viewing the message.
w_{total}: Total user browsing time.

The user's favorability can, to some extent, determine the probability that the user will view such information. The higher the favorability, the higher the probability that the user will choose the information in the next random selection.

3.1.3 Prediction Model Selection

In the model selection part of data prediction, this paper decided to use XGBoost model for user requested content prediction after cross-validation of multiple literature queries [18–20]. And in order to fit the data, content popularity and user favorability will be added to the predictor as important weights for weighting. in order to get good prediction results. The validation results are shown in Fig. 2.

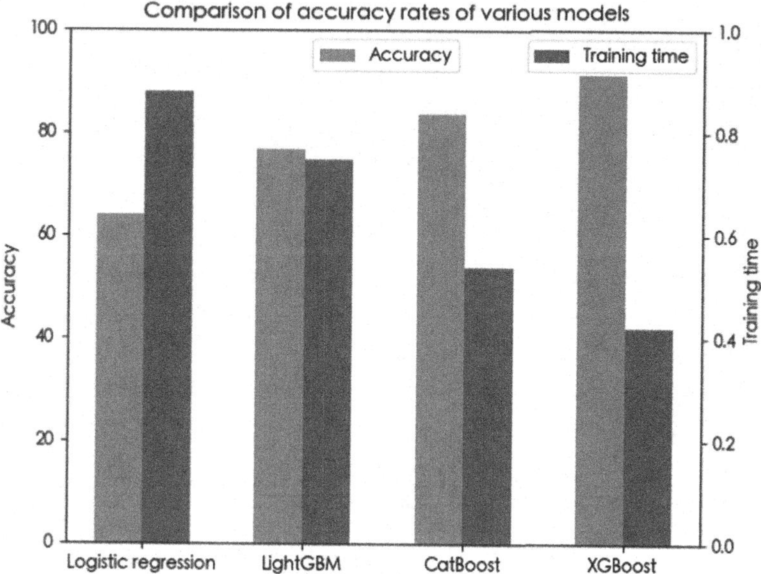

Fig. 2. Based on the single-model prediction results and training speed of Movielens dataset, it is not difficult to find that XGboost has the best actual results.

3.1.4 Regional Relationship Perception

According to studies [21, 22], there is a close relationship between the social relationships between users and their data needs on edge devices. The stronger the social relationship between users, the more similar their data needs are to each other, so we can establish their social relationship by calculating the similarity of needs between users. Then the users with strong social relationships are grouped into a regional network. The social relationships within the same region are stronger than those within different regions. Then the data requests within the same region can be considered to be roughly similar. Edge caching then allows for direct localization model training and cache allocation on a region-by-region basis. This reduces the pressure on caching and funding compared to one-to-one data training allocation. Increased efficiency of cache usage leads to improved architectural performance. And a significant reduction in resource overhead (Fig. 3).

where we can derive a request probability of user m for all types of data and integrate it into the vector formulation.

$$P_m^{re} = \left(P_{m,1}^{re} P_{m,2}^{re} \cdots P_{m,F}^{re}\right) \tag{3}$$

$\mathrm{P}_{\mathrm{m}}^{\mathrm{re}}$ can represent user m as a demand degree for all types of data. Then, we can map the social relationship between users and users by the similarity degree of demand degree between users. For example, the strength of the social relationship between users n1, n2

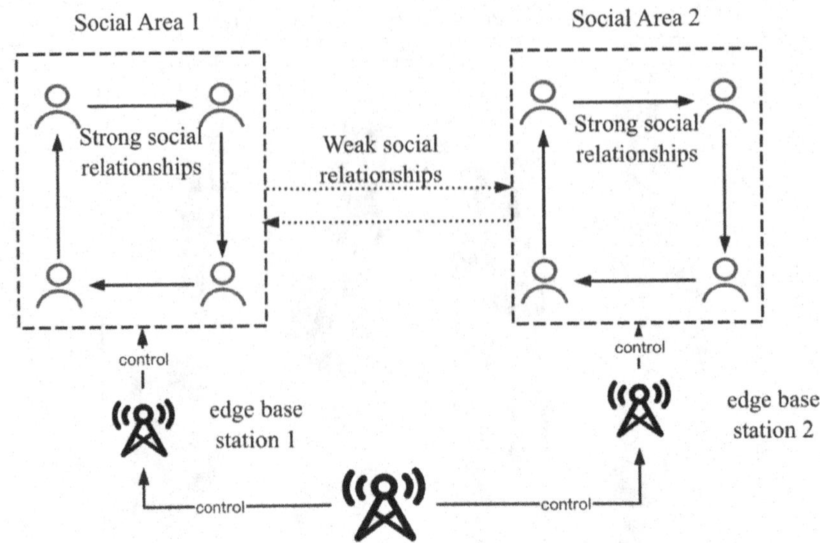

Fig. 3. Regional social relationship networks, where members in the same social area have strong social relationships with each other, while members in different areas have weak social relationships with each other, and each area has a sub-base station for independent control.

can be expressed as Eq. (4).

$$S_{n1,n2} = \frac{\left[P_{n1}^{re}\right] \bullet \left[P_{n2}^{re}\right]^T}{P_{n1}^{re} \times P_{n2}^{re}} = \frac{\sum_j^{|F|}\left(P_{n1,j}^{re} \times P_{n2,j}^{re}\right)}{\sqrt{\sum_j^{|F|}\left(P_{n1,j}^{re}\right)^2} \times \sqrt{\sum_j^{|F|}\left(P_{n2,j}^{re}\right)^2}} \tag{4}$$

Similarly, we can propose to impute all users based on the strength of the social relationship between two U_S ($n1, n2 \in U_S$) between the social relationship strength relationship matrix expressed as Eq. (5).

$$A = \begin{pmatrix} a_{1,1} & \cdots & a_{1,n} \\ \vdots & \ddots & \vdots \\ a_{U_s,1} & \cdots & a_{U_s,n} \end{pmatrix} \tag{5}$$

Then, the social intensity relationship of edge users in the same social area can be derived by combining Eqs. (4), (5) expressed as Eq. (6).

$$S_{area} = \frac{\left(\sum_{i=1}^{n} S_{ni,n(i-1)}\right) + S_{ni,n1}}{n} \tag{6}$$

Then, we can use Eqs. (4), (5), (6) to carry out the regional division of edge user devices, and divide the people with strong social relationship together. And the data popularity in the region is counted by Eq. (1) to get the data category with high popularity in the region.

Then the training parameters are pushed to the aggregation center after localization training by the machine learning model, and the model is distributed to regional base stations after aggregation by the aggregation center. The regional base stations use the models to make data predictions. The prediction results are pushed to the cache control center nearest to the requesting region to cache the most valuable cache content for that region, thus reducing edge requests and transmission latency.

3.2 Cache Optimization and Collaborative Model

Previous models of edge computing are based on a single base station [23] model network extended by the network. It provides services to all users within its coverage area. Suppose a user requests content data from a repository containing N different files, and for the purpose of edge caching, the cache space of the base station is assumed to cache up to n contents, where n < N. We assume that the user requests are generated sequentially one after another and the popularity of the requested content is not known. Suppose a user sends a request and the delivery flow after requesting content is shown in Fig. 4. When receiving a user's request, the base station first checks whether the requested content is in its cache. If it is, the base station delivers the content directly to the requesting user, a process called "cache hit". If the requested content is not in the cache, the base station requests the content from the data center first. Then it is forwarded to the requesting user, which is called a "cache miss" and takes much more time in the cache miss state than in the cache hit state.

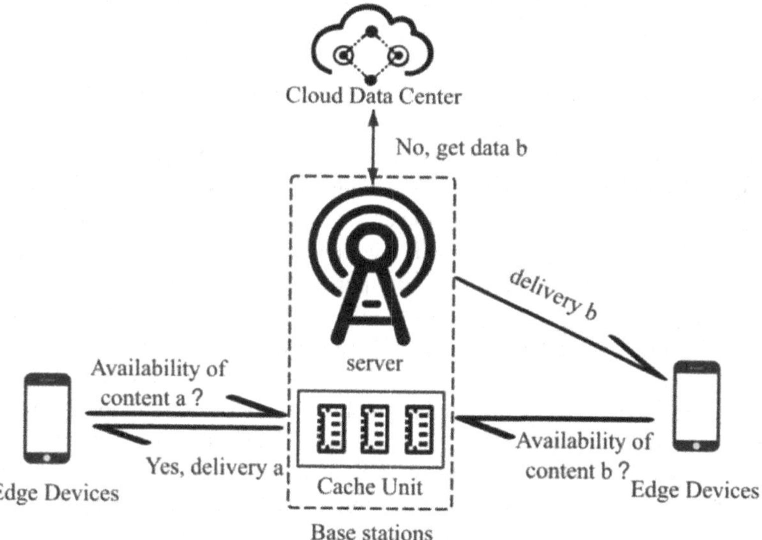

Fig. 4. Single base station based edge network request process, sending data directly to the terminal when the requested data is available in the cache, or fetching and sending from the data center if not

With the gradual normalization of the use of single base station mode, the problems brought about by it also come one after another. One is that the user needs to set up the local reference station by himself under the conventional situation of single base station mode. And there are errors when setting up the base station. It requires a lot of money and labor to set up and adjust. The most important problem is that the traditional network model does not have the ability of autonomous learning. Then it means that it cannot determine which resources are worth caching and which are not necessary. Therefore, conventional benchmarking strategies generally use random caching [24, 25]. When the cache space is already full, in each update, the total base station randomly selects the content in the cache to be replaced. And the cache hit rate of this caching method will generally be low. In most cases, there is no useful data stored in the cache, so the system can only go back to the cache one by one when the edge devices need data that is not in the cache and then distribute it to users. Both although with the advent of 5G era, ultra-dense networking, large-scale antenna technology, and millimeter wave technology [23] have alleviated the error latency problem to some extent. However, in terms of data updates, as each request and update must go through the cache control center, data center, and then return to the user. This request method will certainly bring about the problem of high latency, and this problem will become more obvious with the increase of data requests.

To address this pain, we design an autonomous edge cache request and update policy based on federated learning. Its update methods are divided into two types: passive and automatic updates.

Passive update: Assume that the cache has already stored the set of resources M predicted by the model. Edge users request resource d upward, at this time, the cache will automatically search whether there is resource d in M. If there is, the cache directly sends down the resource. If not, the cache center sends a request to the data center, which will obtain resource d to be dispatched to the corresponding edge device. At the same time, the aggregation center will send the most recently completed model of aggregation to the regional base station where the request is located for localization update training. After the training is completed, the trained update model is re-uploaded to the aggregation center for aggregation to complete the model update. The new model is also used to update the resources in the cache library to ensure high cache hit rate.

Automatic update: Considering the limited cache space of a single base station and the possible time-varying nature of content popularity, base stations deployed in each spatial region periodically update their cache contents to satisfy as many user requests locally as possible. Specifically, i.e., every N requests collected by the base station are recorded as a time series node t, where $t = \{1, 2 \ldots T\}$, and at each time node the base station starts to automatically update the prediction model with the cache content. Overall, the model update is divided into two processes: regional base station model update training and model reaggregation.The update of the cache is shown in Fig. 5: it consists of two actions: one is to select K new contents from the data center and put them into the cache, and the other is to remove K original contents from the cache space, where K indicates the number of contents to be replaced in each update. ($K \leq N$).

Another more direct reason for using Federated Learning is due to the fact that combining Federated Learning with spatial region technology allows for one-to-many request mapping. That is, regions are managed in a uniform manner. When there is a

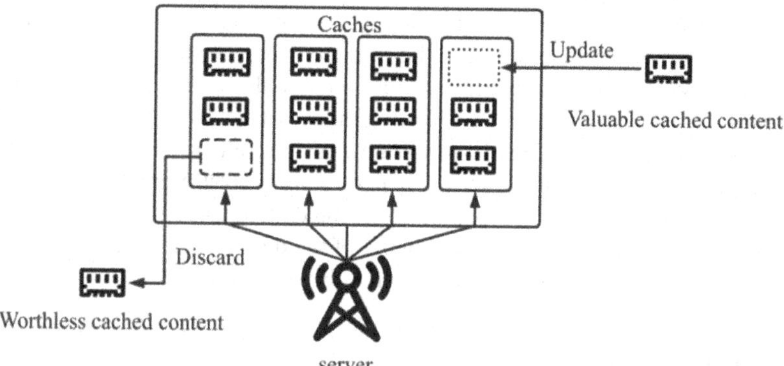

Fig. 5. The cache update process searches the cache for existing resources, and if there is data that has lost its value the cache controller will simply clear it and bring in valuable data from the data center to deposit it.

data update in a region, only the model needs to be trained for that region, and then the parent model and the corresponding cache center of that region can be updated. It avoids the traditional model of targetless.

The high latency and high resource consumption caused by cache updates. The specific control model is constructed as shown in Fig. 6.

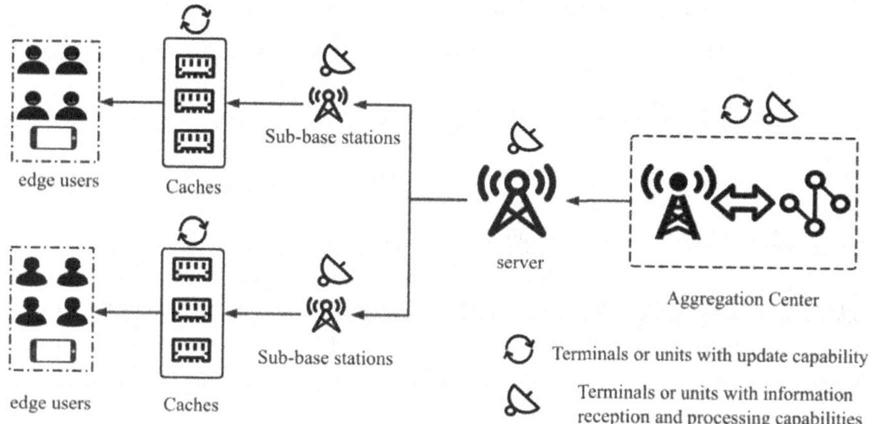

Fig. 6. Edge cache control process built based on federated learning, with the aggregation center distributing models to the corresponding sub-base stations in each region and indirectly controlling the corresponding cache controllers to store content

3.3 Co-caching Data Block Value Optimization

Edge co-caching [26] is an essential part of edge computing applications. Its as one of the prominent technologies to provide computing and communication capabilities as well as network caching capabilities, where the edge server is located at the same location as the regional base station and the content is closer to the user, which not only relieves the pressure during network transmission, but also avoids network congestion caused by repeated transmission of the same content and achieves low latency response of data. For edge caching, the main issue is how to choose the right cache content and the allocation of cache resources. In this paper, the optimization of data blocks in the cache is quantified in terms of the popularity of the data blocks and the real-time value of the data blocks to establish the value model of the data blocks. The cache resources are updated in a timely manner to ensure high utilization of the cache.

3.3.1 Data Block Prevalence

Data block popularity has similarities with content popularity. Both are related to the number of visits, frequency of visits, etc. We can derive the access frequency f of a data block t in the cache based on the content popularity as Eq. (7).

$$f_t^{re} = \frac{W_t}{T_t^{latest} - T_t^{Initial}} \tag{7}$$

where W_t: denotes the sum of the number of times data block t was accessed between the current time and the time it was first accessed.

T_t^{latest} : Indicates the time of the last access to data block t

$T_t^{Initial}$ Indicates when the data block t was first accessed

From this, we can obtain the prevalence of data block tP_{pop}^t as Eq. (8):

$$P_{pop}^t = \frac{f_t^{re} * \frac{1}{f_{te}}}{\frac{1}{T_t^{ratest} - T_t^{Intitial}}} = \frac{f_t^{re} * \frac{1}{T_t^{latest} - T_t^{Initial}}}{\frac{1}{f_t^{re}}} \tag{8}$$

3.3.2 Residual Value of Data Blocks

The residual value of a data block represents the residual value of the data in that data block for the entire system, as well as for the architecture and the users in many ways.

Then it can be deduced that the proportion of residual value of data block tRe_t as Eq. (9).

$$Re_t = \frac{T_t^{\exp} - T_t^{now}}{T_t^{\exp} - T_t^{store}} \tag{9}$$

where T_t^{exp} denotes the expiration time of data block i.

T_t^{now} indicates the current time of the data block.

T_t^{store} Indicates the time when the data block is stored in the cache.

Therefore, the residual value of data block t can be deduced by combining Eqs. (8), (9) as Eq. (10).

$$Value = P_{pop}^t * Re_t \tag{10}$$

Then, based on the residual value of the data block, this paper adds an elimination mechanism for data block updates in the cache: if there exists an updated data block with a residual value greater than the residual value of the data block in the internal cache. Then the new data block is replaced with the data block with the lowest value in the cache. Otherwise, it is not replaced. This ensures that the data in the data cache is updated in real time. It also further improves the cache hit rate and achieves full utilization of resources. The data block update mechanism is shown in Fig. 7.

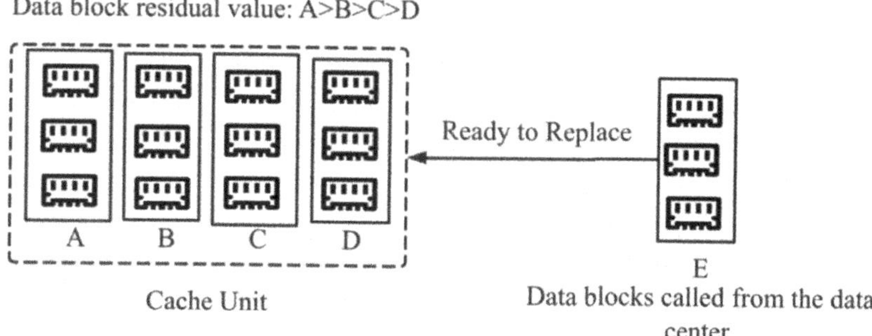
Data block residual value: A>B>C>D
Ready to Replace
A
B
C
D
E
Cache Unit
Data blocks called from the data center
*Example: If the remaining value of data block E is greater than the lowest remaining value of data block D in the cache, then replace E with D, otherwise no replacement

Fig. 7. Data block update elimination mechanism

4 Experiment and Analysis

To perform a validation analysis of the design strategy in this paper, we perform simulation experiments using pycharm in a python based environment. The dataset uses the publicly available dataset movielens to simulate the content of requests sent from edge endpoints to higher levels. The dataset has 18 hierarchies. Each sub-level contains more than 10,000 ratings from multiple users for various movies. The dataset is pre-processed with pycharm and datagrip to ensure that the results are not biased by human factors such as missing datasets.

Also, for statistical purposes, we consider each rating as a number of views. (i.e., each view is considered as a rating for each view). We will compare all aspects of this paper's strategy with the literature [14], literature [11], and literature [13] for effectiveness and draw final conclusions.

As can be seen from Fig. 8, the system cache capacity has a significant impact on the cache hit rate of all four policies in the experiments of this paper, and the cache hit rate of all three policies increases slowly as the system cache capacity increases. However, the federated learning and regional popularity-based edge collaborative caching strategy proposed in this chapter fully considers the data requests of different users in different regional environments, combines data popularity and regional users' own interests, reduces the redundancy of system cache contents, and improves the cache hit rate compared with the other three compared schemes. On the one hand, increasing the total cache space of the system reduces the redundancy of the system cache content, and on the other hand, considering the variability of regional users further improves the overall cache hit ratio [27].

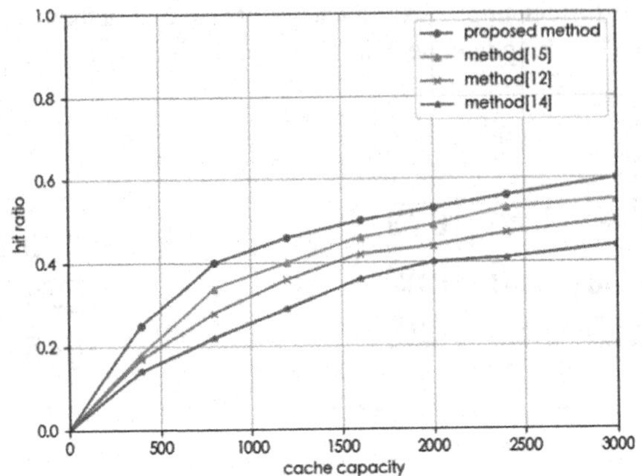

Fig. 8. Comparison of cache capacity-cache hit rate by policy

In addition, this paper also verifies the effect of cache size on the average download latency [28–31], and it is easy to see that the strategy with autonomous learning prediction clearly has a greater improvement than the traditional system strategy, while the strategy in this paper is more likely to get a lower latency in the comparison strategy. As shown in Fig. 9.

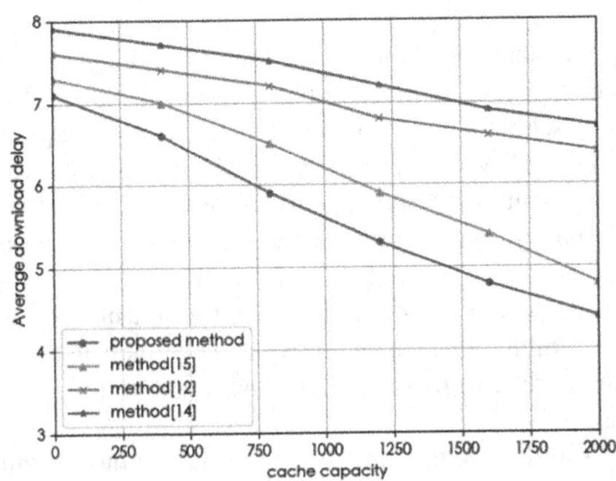

Fig. 9. Comparison of cache size - average download latency by policy

Also, considering the stability of the caching policy from the other side, we only consider the cache space of users. It can be concluded that the total number of users also has an impact on the cache hit rate. This is shown in Fig. 10.

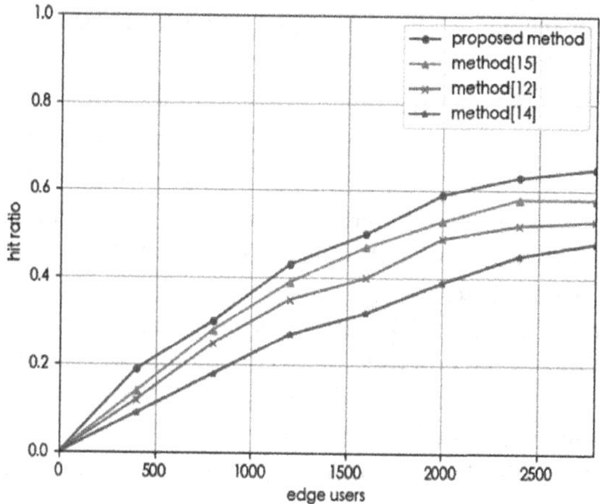

Fig. 10. Number of users at the edge of each policy - cache hit ratio comparison

Finally, from the economic efficiency consideration, this paper proposes the strategy with linear regression cache, literature [14], literature [11], literature [13] for the comparison of the number of edge users-energy savings as shown in Fig. 11.

(*Energy saving ratio [32] was derived from a comprehensive analysis of the number of devices, the time required for learning training of the devices, and the energy consumption for running the devices).

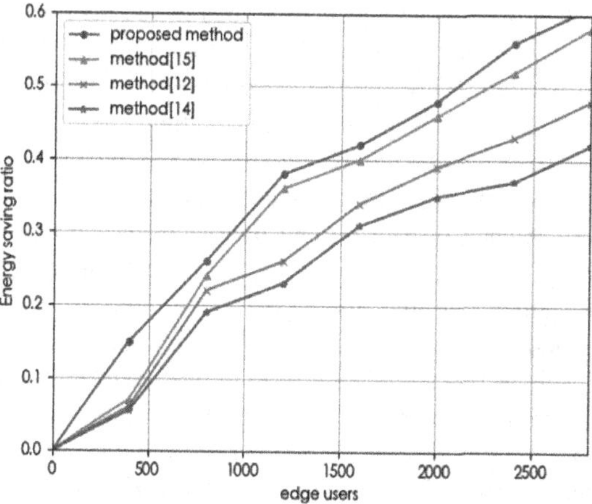

Fig. 11. Comparison of the number of users at the edge of each policy - energy savings ratio

这 From the above experiments, it is easy to see that the edge cache management policy with autonomous learning will be continuously updated with the increase of the user base and the prediction allocation accuracy will increase, which brings much higher positive benefits than the traditional allocation model. The policy proposed in this paper has better experimental results compared with the traditional autonomous learning policy.

5 Conclusion

In today's Internet era. Both mobile terminals and user data volume are exploding. In such a big data context. Edge computing has become the obvious choice to solve this dilemma, and as it is widely used. The drawbacks also come one after another. Cache clogging, low security, etc. become the problems we need to solve urgently. In this paper, based on this background, the proposed innovation points are as follows.

Firstly. The popularity prediction model proposed in this paper is able to have a better cache hit rate than the comparative classical model, and also has a stronger learning classification capability. At the same time, the prediction model will also be updated according to the micro-migration of user preferences. The popularity updateability of the data is guaranteed.

Secondly. For the resource allocation problem of the cache module, we refer to and optimize the cache block utility model [6] based on the cached data blocks, determine the comprehensive benefits of the data blocks through model construction so as to perform reasonable allocation scheduling, and introduce an elimination mechanism to ensure the update of the data blocks. So as to maximize the utilization of cache and also reduce the unnecessary system overhead to some extent than the classical strategy.

Finally. Due to the previous machine learning caching strategy. All the data needs to be put into a cloud learner for centralized training. And this will significantly reduce the processing efficiency in the face of a large number of data processing [33]. And there are inevitable data privacy and security issues in the data transmission of highly dense spatial data. So we adopt the form of federation learning. Its core idea is that in the presence of multiple data sources jointly participating in model training, the model is jointly trained only by interacting model intermediate parameters without the need for raw data flow, and the raw data can be kept out of the local terminal. This approach not only reduces the amount of data computation in the cloud, but also achieves a balance between data privacy protection and data sharing and analysis, which is also called "transparent model". It greatly increases the security of data. Moreover, through federal learning + machine learning, the model can be updated in time to achieve the optimal predictive scheduling effect when deviations in data browsing hobbies occur in some regional edge devices [34, 35]. The overall policy performance is improved. In the future, we may also optimize the real-time interaction of some edge devices based on this architecture. For example, precise recognition of vehicles, pattern estimation, state detection [36–38], or the analysis and optimization of privacy and security during the interaction [39, 40]. This is still an important direction to be developed in the field of edge computing and IoT.

Acknowledgment. This work was supported in part by the Scientific research projects funded by the Department of education of Hunan Province (No. 22C0497), the Huaihua University Double First-Class initiative Applied Characteristic Discipline of Control Science and Engineering(No. ZNKZN2021-10), the National Natural Science Foundation of China (No. 62172182), the Hunan Provincial Natural Science Foundation of China (No. 2020JJ4490), the Project of Hunan Provincial

Social Science Foundation (No. 21JD046), the Huaihua University Project (No. HHUY2019-25), the Philosophy and Social Science Achievement Evaluation Committee of Huaihua (No. HSP2022YB40) and the Science and Technology Innovation 2030 Special Project Sub-Topics (No. 2018AAA0102100).

Hunan University Students' Innovation and Entrepreneurship Training Program (202210548064).

References

1. Zhao, M.: A review of edge computing technologies and applications. Comput. Sci. **47**(S1), 268–272+282 (2020)
2. Zhou, J.: A review of edge computing technology research at home and abroad. Comput. Age **08**, 8–11 (2021). https://doi.org/10.16644/j.cnki.cn33-1094/tp.2021.08.002
3. He, Z.Y., Dong, X.C., Zhu, Q.H.: Research on the classification of Baidu encyclopedia entries based on the perspective of users' usage behavior. Data Anal. Knowl. Discov. **3**(06), 117–122 (2019)
4. Zhang, L.-B., Guo, Q., Wu, X.-B., Liang, Y.-Z., Liu, J.-G.: Research on user clustering method based on multidimensional behavior analysis. J. Univ. Electron. Sci. Technol. **49**(02), 315–320 (2020)
5. Zhou, K., Wu, Y.C., Wu, J.K.: Research on the prediction model of Internet advertising click rate based on user portrait. Software **42**(02), 171–174 (2021)
6. Chen, N.N.: Research on integrated utility-based cache placement and task scheduling optimization methods in edge computing environment. Zhengzhou University of Light Industry (2022). https://doi.org/10.27469/d.cnki.gzzqc.2022.000027
7. Jiang, H., Dai, X., Xiao, Z., Iyengar, A.: Joint task offloading and resource allocation for energy-constrained mobile edge computing. IEEE Trans. Mob. Comput. (2022). https://doi.org/10.1109/TMC.2022.3150432
8. Zhou, J., Shen, H.J., Lin, C.Y., Cao, Z.F., Dong, X.R.L.: Advances in privacy-preserving research on edge computing. Comput. Res. Dev. **57**(10), 2027–2051 (2020)
9. Wang, Q.: Research on security and privacy protection technologies in edge computing. J. Jinling Inst. Sci. Technol. **36**(04), 11–17 (2020). https://doi.org/10.16515/j.cnki.32-1722/n.2020.04.003
10. Fei, L.: Research on computational offloading and resource allocation strategies in edge computing. University of Electronic Science and Technology (2022). https://doi.org/10.27005/d.cnki.gdzku.2022.003502
11. Liu, H.-Y., Wang, G., Yang, W.-C., Wang, J.-L., Xu, Y., Zhao, D.-L.: Popularity edge caching strategy based on random geometry theory. J. Electron. Inform. **43**(12), 3427–3433 (2021)
12. Wu, R.: Research on efficient edge caching strategy based on machine learning. Huazhong University of Science and Technology (2021). https://doi.org/10.27157/d.cnki.ghzku.2021.001857
13. Kai, J.: Research on computational offloading and content caching based on reinforcement learning in mobile edge computing. Three Gorges University (2021). https://doi.org/10.27270/d.cnki.gsxau.2021.000193
14. Liu, M.: Research on edge caching strategy based on spatio-temporal correlation analysis of user experience. Nanjing University of Posts and Telecommunications (2021). https://doi.org/10.27251/d.cnki.gnjdc.2021.000586
15. Yan, M., Lin, Y., Nie, Z.S., Cao, Y.F., Pi, H., Zhang, L.: A training method to improve the robustness of federated learning models. Comput. Sci. **49**(S1), 496–501 (2022)

16. Yin, C., Qu, R.: Federated learning algorithms based on personalized differential privacy. Comput. Appl. 1–9 (2022)
17. Ali, T.A.A., Xiao, Z., Sun, J., Mirjalili, S., Havyarimana, V., Jiang, H.: Optimal Design of IIR wideband digital differentiators and integrators using salp swarm algorithm. Knowl.-Based Syst. **182** (2019)
18. Wu, X., Li, J., Mao, W., Wu, Y.H., Zheng, L.Y.: Prediction of e-commerce users' purchase behavior based on GA-XGBoost. J. Zhejiang Wanli Coll. **35**(04), 86–92 (2022). https://doi.org/10.13777/j.cnki.issn1671-2250.2022.04.011
19. Xu, D., Xiao, Y.: Website user behavior prediction based on machine learning technology. Mod. Electron. Technol. **42**(04), 94–96+100 (2019). https://doi.org/10.16652/j.issn.1004-373x.2019.04.022
20. Zhang, S.: Research on user purchase behavior prediction based on machine learning. Chang'an University (2020). https://doi.org/10.26976/d.cnki.gchau.2020.000772
21. Xiao, L.: Analysis of user behavior in social networks. Small and medium-sized enterprise management and technology. Zhongjian J. (08), 115–116 (2019)
22. Zeng, F., Li, Q., Xiao, Z., Havyarimana, V., Bai, J.: A Price-based optimization strategy of power control and resource allocation in full-duplex heterogeneous macrocell-femtocell networks. IEEE Access **6**, 42004–42013 (2018)
23. Fu, J.: Research on angular time delay estimation and single base station localization algorithm based on 5G large-scale antenna. Beijing University of Posts and Telecommunications (2021). https://doi.org/10.26969/d.cnki.gbydu.2021.000248
24. Hu, Q., Wu, M., Guo, S., Peng, L.: A cache random placement policy for content-centric networks. J. Xi'an Univ. Electron. Sci. Technol. **41**(06), 131–136+187 (2014)
25. Lv, H., He, Y.X., Huang, C.H.: Randomized caching reliable multicast algorithm. J. Wuhan Univ. Technol. **31**(18), 24–27+75 (2009)
26. Dynasty, Gao, L., Gao Full Force: Collaborative caching strategy for data hierarchy in edge computing. J. Basic Sci. Text. Univ. **33**(03), 106–112 (2020). https://doi.org/10.13338/j.issn.1006-8341.2020.03.017
27. Zeng, F., et al.: Resource allocation and trajectory optimization for QoE provisioning in energy-efficient UAV-enabled wireless networks. IEEE Trans. Veh. Technol. **69**(7), 7634–7647 (2020)
28. Zhou, T.Q., Wu, W.J., Li, H.L., Dong, J.Y., Gao, J.J.: Analysis of uplink transmission performance and design of base station configuration for ultra-dense networks enhanced by mobile edge computing. High. Tech. Commun. **31**(09), 942–952 (2021)
29. Wu, Z.: Research on dynamic resource allocation delay optimization scheme for edge computing. Civil Aviation Flight Academy of China (2022). https://doi.org/10.27222/d.cnki,gzgmh.2022.000050
30. Hu, Z., Zeng, F., Xiao, Z., Fu, B., Jiang, H., Chen, H.: Computation efficiency maximization and QoE-provisioning in UAV-enabled MEC communication systems. IEEE Trans. Netw. Sci. Eng. **8**(2), 1630–1645 (2021)
31. Liu, D., Cao, Z., Hou, M., Rong, H., Jiang, H.: Pushing the limits of transmission concurrency for low power wireless networks. ACM Trans. Sens. Networks **16**(4), 40:1–40:29 (2020)
32. Li, R..: Design and implementation of accurate sub-circuit metering of electricity consumption at base stations based on edge computing. Tianjin Normal University (2022). https://doi.org/10.27363/d.cnki.gtsfu.2022.000905
33. Qian, C., Liu, D., Jiang, H.: Harmonizing energy efficiency and QoE for brightness scaling-based mobile video streaming. In: IWQoS 2022, p. 1 (2022)
34. Liu, D., Cao, Z., He, Y., Ji, X., Hou, M., Jiang, H.: Exploiting concurrency for opportunistic forwarding in duty-cycled IoT networks. ACM Trans. Sens. Networks **15**(3), 31:1–31:33 (2019)

35. Liu, D., Hou, M., Cao, Z., He, Y., Ji, X., Zheng, X.: COF: exploiting concurrency for low power opportunistic forwarding. In: ICNP 2015, pp. 32–42 (2015)
36. Xiao, Z., et al.: Toward accurate vehicle state estimation under non-Gaussian noises. IEEE Internet Things J. **6**(6), 10652–10664 (2019)
37. Hu, J., et al.: BlinkRadar: non-intrusive driver eye-blink detection with UWB radar. In: Proceedings of IEEE ICDCS 2022 (2022)
38. Jiang, H., Xiao, Z., Li, Z., Xu, J., Zeng, F., Wang, D.: An energy-efficient framework for internet of things underlaying heterogeneous small cell networks. IEEE Trans. Mob. Comput. **21**(1), 31–43 (2022)
39. Liu, D., Wu, X., Cao, Z., Liu, M., Li, Y., Hou, M.: CD-MAC: a contention detectable MAC for low duty-cycled wireless sensor networks. In: SECON 2015, pp. 37–45 (2015)
40. Su, W., Liu, D., Zhang, T., Jiang, H.: Towards device independent eavesdropping on telephone conversations with built-in accelerometer. Proc. ACM Interact. Mob. Wearable Ubiquit. Technol. **5**(4), 177:1–177:29 (2021)

LSTM-DAM: Malicious Network Traffic Prediction for Cloud Manufacturing System

Longbo Zhao[1](✉), Bohu Li[1], and Mu Gu[2]

[1] School of Automation Science and Electrical Engineering, Beihang University, Beijing, China
zlbbuaa@126.com

[2] Beijing Aerospace Smart Manufacturing Technology Development Co., Ltd., Beijing, China

Abstract. With the rapid development of Internet of Things (IoT), the applications of cloud manufacturing system are growing dramatically, resulting in increasing network heterogeneity and complexity. Network traffic prediction plays an important role in the stable operation of cloud manufacturing systems and the optimal configuration of network systems. However, existing works perform poorly confronting the data which has long time series properties and complex temporal features. To address this problem, we construct a malicious network traffic prediction model based on long and short-term memory (LSTM) neural network and dual attention mechanism. Integrated with the dual attention units of feature space and time sequence, our LSTM model can realize the dynamic correlation between malicious traffic and features series. We first obtain the weight parameters of the input data based on feature attention mechanism, and then leverage LSTM model with the attention mechanism to form a temporal attention module. These two modules strengthen the influence of key historical information. Finally, the malicious traffic prediction result of cloud manufacturing systems can be obtained from our model. The experimental results on real industrial dataset show that the prediction effect of LSTM-DAM model is better than LSTM and CNN-LSTM. Based on CIC-IDS-2017 dataset, the method also performs well in Internet malicious traffic prediction, representing great generalization ability.

Keywords: Long and short-term memory neural networks · attention mechanism · malicious traffic prediction · deep learning · cloud manufacturing system

1 Introduction

In 2009, Academician Li Bohu and other scholars and their research teams proposed the notion of "cloud manufacturing" for the first time in the world, and explained systematically the connotation system and the theoretical system and technical framework of cloud manufacturing [1]. The cloud manufacturing system has developed from the phase in which its main characteristics are networked and servitization to the current cloud manufacturing 3.0 phase with more attention to intelligence and security [2]. Due to the highly centralized management of equipment and information in the mode of cloud

Z. Xiao et al. (Eds.): ICECI 2022, LNICST 478, pp. 308–320, 2023.
https://doi.org/10.1007/978-3-031-28990-3_21

manufacturing, the security risks of system continue to rise. As the core support of the cloud manufacturing system, the intelligent cloud platform provides a full-level security protection system as an important guarantee. The research of security technology plays an important role in preventing security risks and security threats, which can effectively reduce the occurrence of security incidents such as data breaches and data corruptions of the smart manufacturing cloud platform, and provide effective security for all kinds of users of the platform while using the service.

Cloud manufacturing system relies on the network and the cloud manufacturing service platform, and invoke the manufacturing resources (manufacturing cloud) according to the customer's needs, including resource access, perception, service-oriented and other levels, highly openness. With the rapid expansion of the Internet of Things (IoT) [3–5], the industrial Internet and cloud manufacturing system technology is accelerating. The Industrial Internet promotes intelligent production and realizes inter-industry communication and resource sharing [6, 7]. The cloud manufacturing system is a service-oriented digital, networked, and intelligent organization. This design integrates advanced information and communication technologies and manufacturing science such as IoT, high-performance cloud computing [8–10] and heterogeneous network resources [10, 11]. In this mode, the system utilizes virtualizing, resource pooling and other techniques to convert manufacturing products, resources and capabilities into manufacturing cloud services. The purpose of the construction is to provide users with various intelligent services on demand through centralized management and operation of cloud manufacturing services.

However, due to the growth of the Industrial Internet community, the scale of network traffic and the complexity of network have continued to increase. The network attacks against the cloud manufacturing field have become frequent and intensive. Therefore, it is necessary to take appropriate measures to predict malicious traffic to improve the security and attack resistance of the production system. Predicting malicious traffic can avoid problems that are easy to occur on the cloud manufacturing system. It can effectively optimize and adjust network resources, and further ensure network connections of important nodes. In addition, if the malicious traffic change can be accurately predicted, then it can reduce network congestion in advance which will help system enhance network performance and block network intrusion.

In the field of cloud manufacturing, the randomness of network attack behavior is high, and the impact of the input characteristics of malicious traffic on the prediction results is constantly changing over time. Therefore, the temporal correlation of the input data will also have an impact on the prediction results. Aiming at the characteristics of cloud manufacturing system malicious traffic and the problems in existing work, we propose a long and short-term memory (LSTM) neural network based on dual attention mechanism to improve the accuracy of malicious traffic prediction. With the attention mechanism, our method can learn the malicious traffic sequence of the Industrial Internet and assign greater parameter weights to key information. The design not only can fully exploit the connection before and after the malicious traffic time series, but also completely learn the overall characteristics of the malicious traffic. It can also avoid the defect that the weight of key features with a high impact factor on the accuracy of the results is diluted during the training iteration.

The remainder of this paper is organized as follows. Section 2 reviews methods and analyzes their differences in the application. Section 3 proposes an improvement of LSTM network integrated with dual attention mechanism. Section 4 describes the simulation setup and experiment results. The final section gives the conclusion of the whole paper.

2 Related Work

Network traffic prediction is a significant subfield of network traffic monitoring and analysis which is mainly focused on predicting the future of network load and its behavior [12, 13]. Network traffic prediction has become an important work in current network security research, which can support the effective defense of industrial IoT computer systems against various types of network attacks [14–16].

Traditional methods of network traffic prediction are currently divided into two main categories, linear prediction methods and nonlinear prediction methods. Linear prediction methods include the use of Markov models [17–19] and exponential smoothing [20, 21], etc. Linear methods can only be trained for network traffic features in a single dimension. Nonlinear prediction methods mainly include machine learning [22–25] and deep learning [26–29]. Particularly, deep learning has been increasingly studied on the field of time series prediction. [26] proposed a spatio-temporal convolutional network (LA-ResNet) which uses an attention mechanism to solve spatio-temporal modeling and predict wireless network traffic. [27] proposed a new network traffic prediction method based on ESN with adaptive reservoir (ESN-AR), ESN has strong nonlinear processing capability and short-term memory, which can achieve good performance in predicting nonlinear time series. [28] investigated a transfer learning strategy based on graph convolution neural network to achieve the task of large-scale traffic prediction. [29] proposed a new method using an enhanced deep reinforcement learning (EDRL) algorithm to enable intelligence-based network traffic prediction and solve network management problems.

LSTM with improved structure by Recurrent Neural Network (RNN) [30] is suitable for network traffic prediction with time-series features. [31] proposed a double LSTM structure, one of which acts as the main flow predictor, another as the detector of the time the burst flow starts at. The two LSTM units can exchange information about their internal states. [32] proposed a neural network model based on LSTM and transfer learning which can address the problem of small sample size in network traffic prediction. [33] investigated a radial kernelized LSTM-based connectionist Tversky multilayer deep structure learning (RKLSTM-CTMDSL) model to solve network traffic prediction. [34] proposed a novel hybrid prediction method ST-LSTM for such network traffic prediction, which synergistically combines the power of the Savitzky–Golay (SG) filter, the TCN and LSTM.

The above works are all traffic prediction researches in a general Internet environment. However, when the input data has long time series properties and the data characteristics are more complex, none of the existing methods can make accurate prediction. For cloud manufacturing systems [35] integrating cloud computing, IoT, virtualization and intelligent science, higher requirements are put forward for network security. Therefore, a more accurate prediction of malicious traffic in cloud manufacturing platform is eagerly needed to maintain stable operation of the system.

3 Model Design

For the malicious traffic prediction problem of the cloud manufacturing system, we propose the LSTM-DAM (Long Short-Term Memory network based on Dual Attention Mechanism) prediction model which contain the feature attention and the temporal attention modules.

3.1 Feature Attention Mechanism

The input of the feature attention mechanism is a single-step vector containing M features $x_t = [x_{1,t}, x_{2,t}, \cdots, x_{M,t}]$, the attention weight vector e_t is calculated using a single-layer neural network as:

$$e_t = \sigma\left(W_e x_t + b_e\right) \tag{1}$$

where $e_t = [e_{1,t}, e_{2,t}, \cdots, e_{M,t}]$ is the attention weights corresponding to the M input features, W_e is the weight matrix, b_e is the bias vector, and $\sigma(\cdot)$ is the Sigmoid activation function. The feature attention weights $\omega_t = [\omega_{1,t}, \omega_{2,t}, \cdots, \omega_{M,t}]$ are obtained by using the Softmax function, the subitem of ω_t is:

$$\omega_{m,t} = \frac{\exp(e_{m,t})}{\sum\limits_{i=1}^{M} e_{i,t}} \tag{2}$$

After the attention parameter weights are acquired, they are associated with each input feature and finally input to the LSTM network for learning training.

$$x'_{m,t} = x_{m,t}\omega_{m,t} \tag{3}$$

Figure 1 shows the feature attention mechanism model. The parameter weights of traditional LSTM models are shared among different features, and the output results are influenced by each feature to the same extent. However, most of the input features in practical scenarios have multi-level and multi-dimensional characteristics, and each feature has different degrees of influence on the output results. These existence will finally cause inefficient LSTM performance. Therefore, we use the feature attention mechanism to screen out the redundant information of feature sequences and thus focus on the important features.

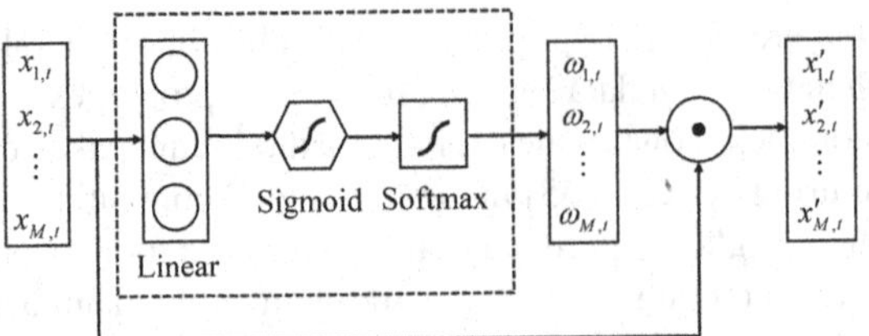

Fig. 1. Feature attention mechanism

3.2 Temporal Attention Mechanism

The input of the temporal attention mechanism is the hidden layer state $h_t = [h_{1,t}, h_{2,t}, \cdots, h_{K,t}]$ of the LSTM network at moment t. K is the length of the time of the input sequence. Define the historical temporal attention weights as:

$$s_t = ReLU(W_d h_t + b_d) \tag{4}$$

where $s_t = [s_{1,t}, s_{2,t}, \cdots, s_{K,t}]$, W_d is the weight matrix, b_d is the bias vector, and $RELU(\cdot)$ is the activation function to increase the feature difference. The temporal attention weight is $\mu_t = [\mu_{1,t}, \mu_{2,t}, \cdots, \mu_{K,t}]$, the subitem of μ_t is:

$$\mu_{k,t} = \frac{\exp(s_{k,t})}{\sum_{i=1}^{K} s_{i,t}} \tag{5}$$

We can obtain the integrated timing state h'_t as:

$$h'_t = \mu_t \otimes h_t = \sum_{k=1}^{K} \mu_{k,t} h_{k,t} \tag{6}$$

Figure 2 shows the temporal attention mechanism model. The feature attention mechanism only correlates the input features of the LSTM network before training with the target features, so the input features have the same weight at any moment. However in actual system, the correlation between cloud manufacturing system malicious traffic and feature sequences tends to change dynamically in real-time. Therefore, we introduce the temporal attention mechanism that can automatically extract the sequence data between each historical moment to further improve the information representation at important moments.

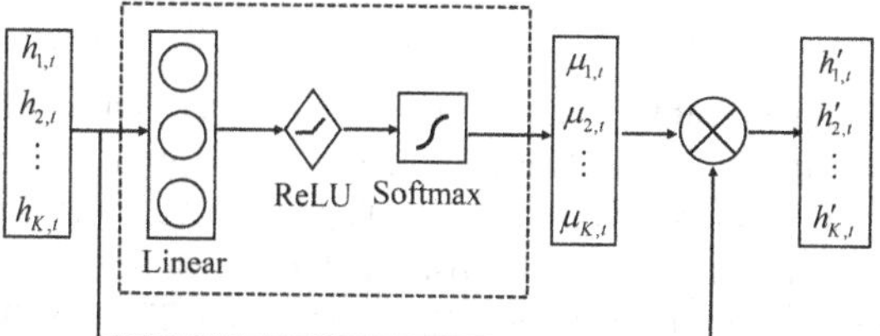

Fig. 2. Temporal attention mechanism

3.3 LSTM-DAM Model

The proposed LSTM-DAM model includes an input layer, a feature attention layer, an LSTM layer, a temporal attention layer, and a fully connected layer. Figure 3 shows the complete structure of the LSTM-DAM model.

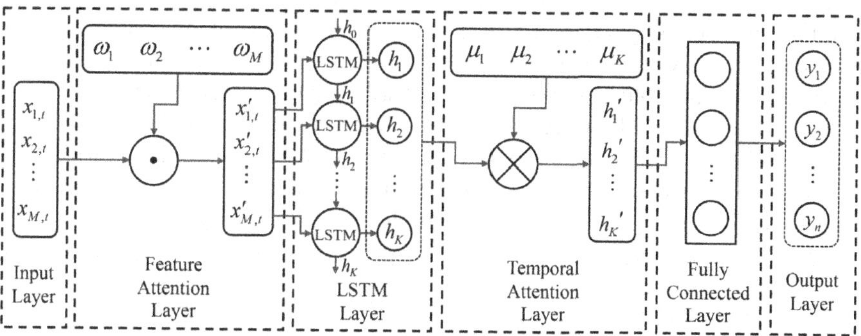

Fig. 3. LSTM-DAM Model Structure

The LSTM-DAM input layer sends the processed network traffic data history sequences combined with the feature sequences to the feature attention layer. Then the model uses the feature attention mechanism to perform dynamic weight assignment for the features to achieve the focus of key features. The LSTM layer performs learning calculations on the input sequences, which can obtain the hidden layer state h. After that, the temporal attention layer performs the periodic trend feature of the feature sequences learning to realize the weight assignment of temporal attention, thus improving the network expression capability. Finally, the temporal attention module inputs the global hidden layer state to the fully connected layer to complete the final malicious traffic prediction work.

4 Experiments Evaluation

In this section, we use recent datasets to evaluate our LSTM-DAM model. Firstly, we describe the detail of the datasets and the pre-processing method. Secondly, we show the metrics to evaluate our method's performance. Afterward, we demonstrate the key experiment setup. Finally, we justify our method in predicting malicious traffic with superior performance over other comparative methods.

4.1 Datasets

Cloud Manufacturing System. The source of the dataset is a real Industrial Internet and cloud manufacturing platform. Data collection is performed at the sampling point every minute from 0:00 on April 5, 2022 to 24:00 on April 23. Then, the private dataset with multiple labels including timestamp, historical traffic value and historical malicious traffic value is formed. After data cleaning, the dataset has 27342 valid samples.

CIC-IDS-2017. The CIC-IDS-2017 dataset is often used by researchers as experimental data for network intrusion detection, which contains both benign Internet data and common abnormal data. Similar to real-world data (PCAPs). The dataset contains various attack types such as brute force FTP, brute force SSH, DoS, Heartbleed, penetration, botnet and DDoS. We utilize four labels to clean the dataset: timestamp, flow duration, flow bytes/s and label. Finally, 1966 valid data are obtained.

Datasets preprocessing includes two phases: division and converting: firstly, the datasets are randomly divided into training data and test data in a ratio of 9:1. Then, we convert the time series data into sequence data containing pairs of input and output. For a given data, the converting method is as follows. We copy the data column and move the replicated data of the column forward or backward by N times. The data gaps generated after the movement will be filled with NaN. After the above steps, the lag value data column is completed, and a data format with supervised learning attributes is obtained. The purpose of converting data is to transform the problem into a supervised learning problem. The processing process is shown in Fig. 4.

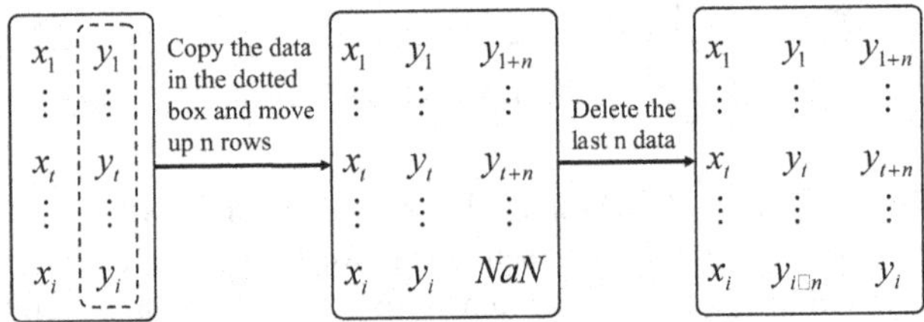

Fig. 4. Dataset processing

4.2 Metrics

Concerning malicious traffic prediction tasks in cloud manufacturing system, the results can be correct or incorrect. Therefore, the evaluation of the performance of LSTM-DAM is grounded on the accuracy of the prediction results. Related study generally uses the error-index to verify the performance of the model. The larger the error value, the lower the prediction accuracy, which also means the worse the performance of the experimental model. All results correspond to the following three outcomes:

1) Mean Absolute Error (MAE): It is the average value of absolute error. The index value can intuitively reflect the prediction error. The value range of MAE is [0, +

∞], 0 means the predicted value is consistent with the actual value. The larger the error, the larger MAE.

$$MAE = \frac{1}{K}\sum_{i=1}^{k}\left|x_i - x_i'\right|^2 \tag{7}$$

2) Root Mean Square Error (RMSE): It is also known as standard error, its range is [0, $+\infty$], the same as MAE, 0 means that there is no error in the model result. The larger the error, the larger RMSE.

$$RMSE = \sqrt{\frac{1}{K}\sum_{i=1}^{k}\left|x_i - x_i'\right|^2} \tag{8}$$

3) R-squared: It is the accuracy to convert the prediction result into a standard, and its value is [0, 1]. It can be used to determine which type of prediction problem the model is more suitable for. The larger the value of R^2, the better performance of the proposed model to fit the real value, when $R^2 = 1$, it is a perfect model.

$$R^2 = 1 - \frac{\sum_{i=1}^{k}(x_i - x_i')^2}{\sum_{i=1}^{k}(x_i - \overline{x_i})^2} \tag{9}$$

4.3 Experiment Setup

The LSTM-DAM model uses the Adam algorithm to adjust parameters for units, epochs, and batch size. Units represent the output dimension, which is the number of hidden neurons in the feedforward neural network in the LSTM neural network. Epochs represent the total number of rounds of training. We introduce the early stop mechanism to effectively avoid the result overfitting and long training time caused by manually inputting the epochs value. Batch size indicates the number of samples used in each batch for gradient descent in model training. The gradient descent is calculated to optimize the objective function when each batch sample is trained. After multiple rounds of testing, the parameters are set that the units value is 32, the stop training condition is 20 rounds and the batch size value is 32.

Under the situation of the above parameter values, set the time step parameter N in the interval [2, 7]. The prediction results with different values of N on the cloud manufacturing system dataset are shown in Table 1. Note that in the conducted experiments, when the time step N is 5, the MAE and RMSE results achieve the best 0.872 and 1.685 respectively. Therefore, the step parameter N is set to be 5.

Table 1. Time-step Tuning Result.

Time step	MAE	RMSE
n = 2	0.862	1.731
n = 3	0.853	1.725
n = 4	0.846	1.694
n = 5	0.827	1.685
n = 6	0.881	1.752
n = 7	0.832	1.690

4.4 Result Evaluation

To verify the performance improvement of the LSTM-DAM model, we use the traditional LSTM model and the CNN-LSTM model as the experimental comparison model. The prediction results on the cloud manufacturing system dataset in the proposed method and related research works are represented in Figs. 5, 6 and 7.

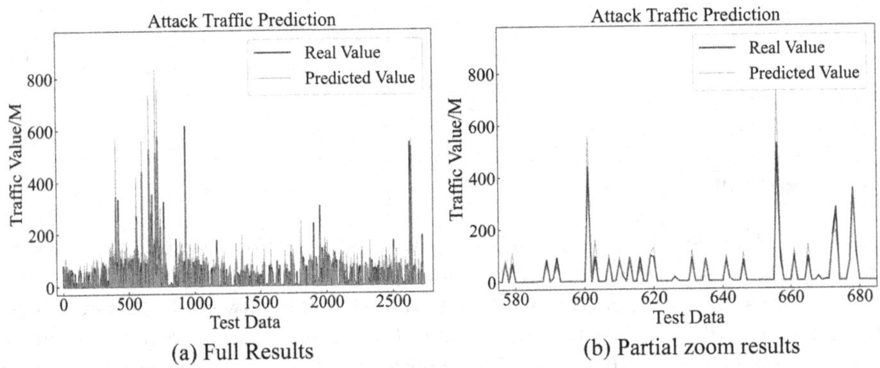

(a) Full Results (b) Partial zoom results

Fig. 5. LSTM model results for Cloud manufacturing system dataset

The results show that the LSTM-DAM model after the introduction of the dual attention mechanism has higher prediction accuracy than the traditional LSTM model. Although The trend of the prediction curve of the CNN-LSTM model is consistent with the actual value curve, the error of the prediction result is large, especially at the peak. Therefore, the performance of the prediction model is not ideal, and the overall accuracy of the prediction value is poorer than the LSTM-DAM model. In terms of the results, it shows that the accuracy and stability of the proposed LSTM-DAM model has been significantly improved. Moreover, the prediction results at the peak of the curve are more outstanding than the CNN-LSTM model.

To further demonstrate the outperformance of the LSTM-DAM model, we calculate the metrics of different models. The results are shown in Table 2. We can observe that the LSTM-DAM model has the highest prediction accuracy. Specifically, the CNN-LSTM

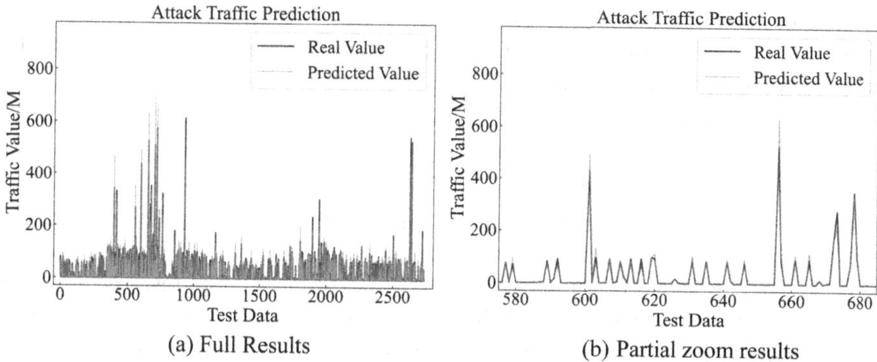

(a) Full Results (b) Partial zoom results

Fig. 6. CNN-LSTM model results for Cloud manufacturing system dataset

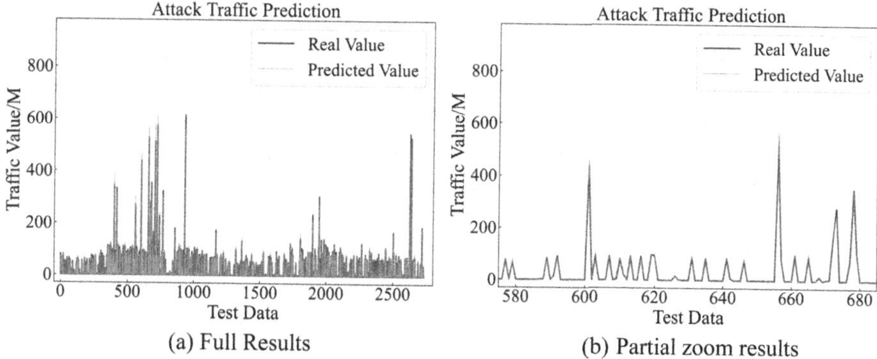

(a) Full Results (b) Partial zoom results

Fig. 7. LSTM-DAM model results for Cloud manufacturing system dataset

model extracts the input feature weights through the CNN network, and then combines them with LSTM to predict the Industrial Internet malicious traffic. The results show that the prediction accuracy is significantly higher than the traditional LSTM model after the feature attention layer is introduced. Compared with LSTM, the error of the LSTM-DAM model proposed in this paper is greatly reduced. The MAE and RMSE are decreased by 0.749 and 10.429 respectively, and the R-squared is 8.2% higher than that of LSTM. Compared with CNN-LSTM, LSTM-DAM model improves by 4% on R-squared, respectively drops 0.445 and 10.241 on MAE and RMSE.

Table 2. Result Comparison.

Prediction Model	R-Squared	MAE	RMSE
LSTM	90.4%	1.576	12.114
CNN-LSTM	94.6%	1.272	11.926
LSTM-DAM	98.6%	0.827	1.685

In terms of prediction performance, LSTM-DAM has high accuracy. The prediction results are significantly better than LSTM and CNN-LSTM models. The proposed model can achieve tremendous capability in the field of Industrial Internet malicious traffic prediction.

4.5 Generalization Analysis

Concerning the Internet malicious traffic has high similarity to the malicious traffic in cloud manufacturing system, we consider using the CIC-IDS-2017 dataset to verify the generalization ability of the proposed LSTM-DAM model. The results are shown in Fig. 8. The predicted value of the LSTM-DAM model is consistent with the actual value. Meanwhile, the predicted curve is stable without large fluctuations and the error value is small at the peak value.

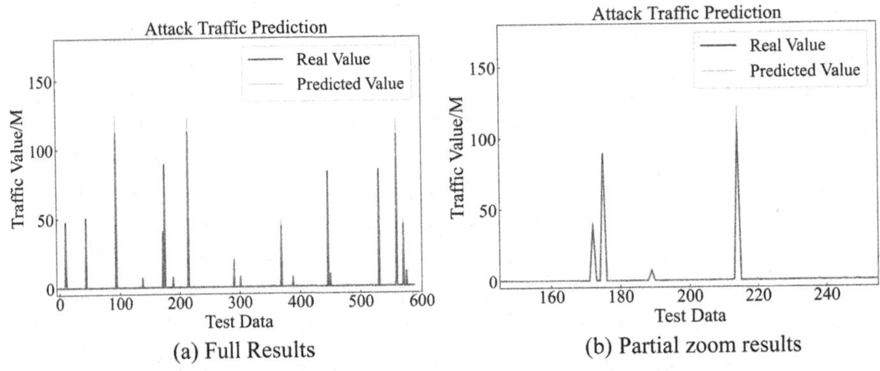

Fig. 8. LSTM-DAM model results for CIC-IDS-2017 dataset

Table 3 illustrates the result of CIC-IDS-2017 dataset. R-squared of the LSTM-DAM model is 98.5%, showing a high fitness. MAE and RMSE are 0.13 and 0.26, which represent the overall error is small and stable. The experimental results justify that our method is capable of predicting malicious network traffic in a different network environment.

Table 3. Prediction Result.

Prediction Model	R-Squared	MAE	RMSE
LSTM-DAM	98.5%	0.13	0.26

5 Conclusion

Security is the life of cloud manufacturing, and it is also the basic needs of every provider, users (including both manufacturing enterprise and manufacturing product) and operators of cloud manufacturing service. The real-time security status' monitoring and prediction of cloud manufacturing systems in the network environment has important practical significance. For industrial network malicious traffic mostly concentrated in the field of detection, there is a shortage of research for the prediction of malicious traffic values. We propose a LSTM network malicious traffic prediction model based on dual attention mechanism for the problem that existing methods cannot handle complex data features under long time sequences in the cloud manufacturing system. The experimental results show that the R-squared, MAE and RMSE performance indexes are significantly improved when compared with LSTM and CNN-LSTM models. Our method can fit the relationship between historical data and network malicious traffic well, which can improve the prediction accuracy of future malicious traffic. The generalization ability of the model is also verified using two different data sets, which further proves the effectiveness and superiority of this paper's model of predicting malicious traffic in cloud manufacturing system.

References

1. Li, B., Zhang, L., Wang, S., et al.: Cloud manufacturing: a new service-oriented networked manufacturing model. Comput. Integr. Manuf. Syst. **16**(01), 1–7+16 (2010)
2. Li, B., Chai, X., Hou, B., et al.: Cloud manufacturing system 3.0——new intelligent manufacturing system in era of intelligence +. Comput. Integr. Manuf. Syst. **25**(12), 2997–3012 (2019)
3. Jiang, H., Xiao, Z., Li, Z., et al.: An energy-efficient framework for internet of things underlaying heterogeneous small cell networks. IEEE Trans. Mob. Comput. **21**(1), 31–43 (2022)
4. Dai, X., Xiao, Z., Jiang, H., et al.: Task co-offloading for D2D-assisted mobile edge computing in industrial internet of things. IEEE Trans. Ind. Inform. 1 (2022)
5. Jiang, H., Dai, X., Xiao, Z., et al.: Joint task offloading and resource allocation for energy-constrained mobile edge computing. IEEE Trans. Mob. Comput. 1 (2022)
6. Hu, Z., Zeng, F., Xiao, Z., et al.: Computation efficiency maximization and QoE-provisioning in UAV-enabled MEC communication systems. IEEE Trans. Netw. Sci. Eng. **8**(2), 1630–1645 (2021)
7. Zhang, W., Zhou, S., Yang, L., et al.: WiFiMap+: high-level indoor semantic inference with WiFi human activity and environment. IEEE Trans. Veh. Technol. **68**(8), 7890–7903 (2019)
8. Xiao, Z., Chen, Y., Jiang, H., et al.: Resource management in UAV-assisted MEC: state-of-the-art and open challenges. Wirel. Netw. **28**(7), 3305–3322 (2022)
9. Ali, T.A.A., Xiao, Z., Sun, J., et al.: Optimal design of IIR wideband digital differentiators and integrators using salp swarm algorithm. Knowl. Based Syst. **182**, 104834 (2019)
10. Xiao, Z., Li, F., Jiang, H., et al.: A joint information and energy cooperation framework for CR-enabled macro–femto heterogeneous networks. IEEE Internet Things J. **7**(4), 2828–2839 (2020)
11. Zeng, F., Li, Q., Xiao, Z., et al.: A price-based optimization strategy of power control and resource allocation in full-duplex heterogeneous macrocell-femtocell networks. IEEE Access **6**, 42004–42013 (2018)
12. Lohrasbinasab, I., Shahraki, A., Taherkordi, A., et al.: From statistical- to machine learning-based network traffic prediction. Trans. Emerg. Telecommun. Technol. **33**(4) (2022)
13. Long, W., Xiao, Z., Wang, D., et al.: Unified spatial-temporal neighbor attention network for dynamic traffic prediction. IEEE Trans. Veh. Technol. 1–15 (2022)

14. Mohammadi, M., Al-Fuqaha, A., Sorour, S., et al.: Deep learning for IoT big data and streaming analytics: a survey. IEEE Commun. Surv. Tutor. **20**(4), 2923–2960 (2018)
15. Zhang, X.Y., Wu, Z.J., Zhang, J.W., et al.: An adaptive network traffic prediction approach for LDoS attacks detection. Int. J. Commun. Syst. **31**(5) (2018)
16. Zhao, P., Jiang, H., Li, J., et al.: Synthesizing privacy preserving traces: enhancing plausibility with social networks. IEEE/ACM Trans. Netw. **27**(6), 2391–2404 (2019)
17. Chen, Z.T., Wen, J.Y., Geng, Y.H.: Predicting future traffic using hidden markov models. In: 2016 IEEE 24th International Conference on Network Protocols (ICNP) (2016)
18. Tian, Z.D.: Network traffic prediction method based on wavelet transform and multiple models fusion. Int. J. Commun. Syst. **33**(11) (2020)
19. Guarino, I., Nascita, A., Aceto, G., et al.: Mobile network traffic prediction using high order Markov chains trained at multiple granularity, pp. 394–399 (2021)
20. Tran, Q.T., Hao, L., Trinh, Q.K.: Cellular network traffic prediction using exponential smoothing methods. J. Inf. Commun. Technol. Malays. **18**(1), 1–18 (2019)
21. Andrysiak, T., Saganowski, L., Kiedrowski, P.: Predictive Abuse Detection for a PLC Smart Lighting Network Based on Automatically Created Models of Exponential Smoothing. Security and Communication Networks (2017)
22. Wang, Q.-M., Fan, A., Shi, H.: Network traffic prediction based on improved support vector machine. Int. J. Syst. Assur. Eng. Manag. **8**(3s), 1976–1980 (2017)
23. Wang, Y., Nakachi, T.: Prediction of network traffic through light-weight machine learning. IEEE Open J. Commun. Soc. **1**, 1919–1933 (2020)
24. Szostak, D.: Machine learning ensemble methods for optical network traffic prediction, pp. 105–115 (2021)
25. Ke, G., Chen, R.-S., Ji, S., et al.: Network traffic prediction based on least squares support vector machine with simple estimation of Gaussian kernel width. Int. J. Inf. Comput. Secur. **18**(1/2), 1–11 (2022)
26. Li, M., Wang, Y., Wang, Z., et al.: A deep learning method based on an attention mechanism for wireless network traffic prediction. Ad Hoc Netw. **107**, 102258 (2020)
27. Zhou, J., Wang, H., Xiao, F., et al.: Network traffic prediction method based on echo state network with adaptive reservoir. Softw. Pract. Exp. **51**(11), 2238–2251 (2021)
28. Zhou, X., Zhang, Y., Li, Z., et al.: Large-scale cellular traffic prediction based on graph convolutional networks with transfer learning. Neural Comput. Appl. **34**(7), 5549–5559 (2022)
29. Balamurugan, N.M., Adimoolam, M., Alsharif, M.H., et al.: A novel method for improved network traffic prediction using enhanced deep reinforcement learning algorithm. Sensors **22**(13), 5006 (2022)
30. Hochreiter, S., Schmidhuber, J.: Long short-term memory. Neural Comput. **9**(8), 1735–1780 (1997)
31. Huang, L., Wang, D., Liu, X., et al.: Double LSTM structure for network traffic flow prediction, pp. 380–388 (2020)
32. Wan, X., Liu, H., Xu, H., et al.: Network traffic prediction based on LSTM and transfer learning. IEEE Access **10**, 86181–86190 (2022)
33. Govindarajan, M., Chandrasekaran, V., Anitha, S.: Network traffic prediction using radial kernelized-tversky indexes-based multilayer classifier. Comput. Syst. Sci. Eng. **40**(3), 851–863 (2022)
34. Bi, J., Zhang, X., Yuan, H.T., et al.: A hybrid prediction method for realistic network traffic with temporal convolutional network and LSTM. IEEE Trans. Autom. Sci. Eng. **19**(3), 1869–1879 (2022)
35. Liao, Y.X., Panetto, H., Stadzisz, P.C., et al., A notification-oriented solution for data-intensive enterprise information systems - a cloud manufacturing case. Enterp. Inf. Syst. **12**(8–9), 942–959 (2018)

Author Index

Z. Xiao et al. (Eds.): ICECI 2022, LNICST 478, pp. 321–322, 2023.
https://doi.org/10.1007/978-3-031-28990-3

Printed in the United States
by Baker & Taylor Publisher Services